D1808682

Prospects of the Ten Kingdoms of the Roman Empire Considered: Being the Third Series of Aids to Prophetic Enquiry

Benjamin Willis Newton

Nabu Public Domain Reprints:

You are holding a reproduction of an original work published before 1923 that is in the public domain in the United States of America, and possibly other countries. You may freely copy and distribute this work as no entity (individual or corporate) has a copyright on the body of the work. This book may contain prior copyright references, and library stamps (as most of these works were scanned from library copies). These have been scanned and retained as part of the historical artifact.

This book may have occasional imperfections such as missing or blurred pages, poor pictures, errant marks, etc. that were either part of the original artifact, or were introduced by the scanning process. We believe this work is culturally important, and despite the imperfections, have elected to bring it back into print as part of our continuing commitment to the preservation of printed works worldwide. We appreciate your understanding of the imperfections in the preservation process, and hope you enjoy this valuable book.

PROSPECTS

OF

THE TEN KINGDOMS

OF

The Roman Empire,

BEING

THE THIRD SERIES OF AIDS TO PROPHETIC ENQUIRY.

BY

BENJAMIN WILLS NEWTON.

———◆———

Second Edition, Revised.

———◆———

LONDON:

HOULSTON AND SONS,

9, PATERNOSTER BUILDINGS.

——

1873.

BS649
.R7 N4

62335

LONDON:
PRINTED BY WERTHEIMER, LEA AND CO.,
CIRCUS PLACE, FINSBURY.

Preface to Second Edition.

———

THE first edition of this work was published in the year 1849. The present edition has been prepared by me, at intervals, during a protracted and severe illness. Its revision, consequently, has not been so complete as I could have desired. It has, however, been revised, and some additions have been made.

The strength of my early convictions as to the truth of the opinions advanced, and as to the infinite importance of that truth, has been, each year, intensified, not enfeebled. Some remarks on the events of the last twenty-five years, and on the present condition of our own once favoured land, will be found in the concluding chapter. (See page 412.) I trust that these remarks may receive from some, candid and prayerful consideration. They may seem severe, perhaps, but there are occasions when severity, and severity only, is kindness.

It is distressing to observe that, whilst the principles and arrangements of the nations are every year approximating more and more nearly to that specific form which the Scripture says they will assume at the time of the end, men, instead of recognising this marked verification of God's Word, continue to mistrust, if not to revile that Word, more and more. Satan ever seeks to blind men to that which is the record of their own doom.

It is scarcely less painful to observe the attempts of many to serve God apart from the guidance of His Word. "We want," say they, "Christ, not doctrine;" as if Christ could be separated from His doctrine. We do not read of being sanctified apart from Truth. "Sanctify them by Thy Truth. Thy Word is Truth." We do not read of growth apart from the reception of "the unadulterated milk of the Word." We do not read of abiding in Christ, apart from abiding in the doctrine of Christ. He "that abideth not in the doctrine of Christ, hath not God." (2 John 9.)

God's Truth is very holy; yet we have often handled it with careless and irreverent hand. If it has not prospered, one great cause is our own failure in walking circumspectly. We need, as to this, humiliation and confession, and a turning unto Him whose mercies fail not. "Who is a God like unto Thee, that pardoneth iniquity, and passeth by the transgression of the remnant of His heritage? He retaineth not His anger for ever, because He delighteth in mercy." (Micah vii. 18.)

There can be no true practical unity—no holy co-operation, apart from the knowledge of God's holy Word. May He grant us grace to recognise, and welcome, and follow, that light which He hath graciously sent forth; and may we find practically that it guides us through paths of holy calmness, and peace, and certainty, on to His holy hill, and to His tabernacles. As evil increases around us (and it surely will), may we seek more earnestly than ever to be separate *from* the evil, and to be separate *unto* God according to His written Word.

December, 1873.

Table of Contents.

———

INTRODUCTION.

If there be any lesson which we learn as we advance in experimental acquaintance with realities around us, it is this—the necessity that God should effectuate, by His own power, His own designs of blessing. "Of him, and through him, and unto him are all things." *That* only prospers which is originated, executed, and completed by Him.

There are certain spheres in which it is easy to recognise the necessity of His agency, because they are spheres in which no one *can* act excepting God. No other can create : no other uphold by the word of His power that which hath been created. No one but God can reign over the inhabitants of Heaven : and Heaven is blessed, because all things emanate *from* Him, and all things are immediately regulated *by* Him. And as regards this earth, none but sceptics doubt that the unseen agency of God ultimately orders all things. Secretly, He sets bounds to the energies of evil which they cannot pass ; and all the activities of men and of Satan ultimately bend to His control so as to subserve the purposes of His holy and blessed will.

Yet, even where all this has been recognised, there has been strange incredulity as to any further

B

and more direct exercise of God's governmental power being intended for this earth. Delegated power has so long been committed by God to men, and they have so long, by means thereof, fashioned both national and individual life, that even the Church has well nigh forgotten that anything else is practicable. Men seem to think that they are quite competent to regulate for themselves the things of earth, and pretend that it would be derogatory to the dignity of God and of Christ to suppose that they could ever directly concern themselves with the minute arrangement of human things here. It is not believed that He who is now glorified above the heavens, will ever undertake the immediate government of Israel and of the nations.

Yet surely, when we reflect on the grace of Him who humbled Himself so as to wash the feet of His servants, and then submitted to the death of the Cross—One also who has ever cared for the sparrows, and counted the hairs of the head of His people—it would not seem unlikely that He should be willing to undertake anything that would subserve the happiness of men, especially if that which is essential to such happiness, can be effected by Himself alone.

We scarcely need ask the question, whether right and wise legislation be necessary for the purposes of human happiness here? Is there anything after which the wisdom of ages has laboured more than to discover some means of legislating rightly for the nations and families of earth? But even when men have hoped that the secret of good has been discovered, they have lacked the power to execute. Their resources have failed, or else the resistance of adversaries has prevailed, or there has been no sufficient wisdom to devise means to reach the intended end; and thus the general confession is that, although there is much to be desired, little has been attained; and men are obliged to own that the right regulation of human things is something without which human happiness cannot be, but that wisdom and power are alike wanting to accomplish that which is required. What country, what nation is satisfied with its condition?

Why, then, should it be deemed unlikely that God should withdraw from the hands of men the authority which He has so long delegated, and entrust it to One who *has* wisdom, and who *has* power to subject evil, and to establish good? It is not necessary for Christ to quit the sphere of heavenly being, because it may please Him to administer the government of earth. The angels, who even now secretly minister to the heirs of salvation, do not cease to have their home in heaven; and surely it is not less easy for the Son of God to retain the heavenly character of His glory, and yet to order the affairs of earth, and to visit it with His presence.

Nor will it be altogether a new thing for God to legislate and govern in the earth. The circumstances, indeed, in which He formerly acted as the Head of Israel, when He legislated for them in the

wilderness, were very different from those in which
He will again connect Himself with them as their
King. But still, it is a fact that God *did* descend
upon Sinai—that He *did* legislate for Israel—that
He *did* abide amongst them in the cloudy pillar;
and yet He ceased not to be what He ever had
been, and ever shall be, in the heaven of heavens.
It is, therefore, neither improbable, nor contrary to
experience, that God should undertake the governmental arrangement of earth.

But we are not, in determining this, left to conjecture, or to the calculation of antecedent proba-
bilities. If there be anything which the Old and
New Testaments reveal with concurrent clearness of
testimony, it is that the present agencies which
form the manners of the earth are to be set aside,
and that the Son of God is Himself to become the
Governor of the nations. "The seventh angel
sounded, and there were great voices in heaven,
saying, The sovereignty of the world* hath become
the sovereignty of our Lord, and of his Christ; and
he shall reign for ever and ever." And again:
" We give thee thanks, O Lord, the God Almighty,
the One who is and who was; because thou hast
taken to thee thy great power and reigned." Rev. xi.
17. The book of Psalms also abounds with songs
of thanksgiving appropriated to that hour. " O sing
unto the Lord a new song: sing unto the Lord, all

* 'Η βασιλεία τοῦ κόσμου. See Greek New Testament as
edited from ancient authorities by Dr. Tregelles. Bagster
and Sons.

the earth. . . . . Say among the Gentiles that
the Lord reigneth : the world also shall be established that it shall not be moved : he shall judge
the peoples righteously. Let the heavens rejoice,
and let the earth be glad ; let the sea roar, and the
fulness thereof. Let the field be joyful, and all
that is therein : then shall all the trees of the wood
rejoice before the Lord : for he cometh, for he cometh
to judge the earth : he shall judge the world with
righteousness, and the peoples with his truth."
Ps. xcvi. How strange that such words as these
should ever have been interpreted of a period respecting which the Scripture itself testifies, that
" creation groaneth in the bondage of corruption "
—" that darkness covereth the earth, and gross
darkness the peoples "—" that the foundations of all
things are out of course."

The universal joy of creation and its release from
its present groan, is continually mentioned in the
Scriptures as constituting one feature in the coming
scene of blessing. But how could this be, *apart*
from the reign of the Lord ? Such a rest of creation would ill consort with a condition in which the
governmental power of earth remained in the hands
of fallen man. And then, as to the spread and
maintenance of truth, it is not easy to see *how* it
could be maintained among the nations, unless the
Head of the Church and the Governor of the nations
were *one*. Accordingly, one of the chief objects of
His rule will be to sustain by His power the ministration of His truth. There will be still the same

message of reconciliation through faith in His blood;
the same indwelling of the Holy Spirit; the same
union between believers and a risen Lord; the same
great High Priest; the same intercession. Whether
now, or in the coming dispensation, flesh, wherever
found, is flesh, and needs the same mercies of the
same " *everlasting* gospel." The eternal verities of
God can never change; and to maintain them will
be one of the specific objects of the millennial reign.

But Christ will not undertake the government of
earth apart from His chosen City and His chosen
nation. He will give to Jerusalem and to Israel supremacy in the earth, and will govern instrumentally
through *them*. Thus, when the judgments by which
He will finally crush the present proud power of the
Gentiles shall be inflicted, Israel will be used as His
instrument. "When I have bent Judah for me,
filled the bow with Ephraim, and raised up thy
sons, O Zion, against thy sons, O Greece, and made
thee as the sword of a mighty man. And the Lord
shall be seen over them, and his arrow shall go
forth as the lightning: and the Lord God shall
blow the trumpet, and shall go with whirlwinds of
the south." Zech. ix. 13, 14. And when the hour
of judgment shall be succeeded by the peaceful
regulations of mercy, Israel will still be the channe
through which the appointments of His goodness
shall reach the nations. "The remnant of Jacob
shall be in the midst of many peoples as a dew from
the Lord, as the showers upon the grass, that tar-
rieth not for man, nor waiteth for the sons of men.'

Micah v. 7. "Many peoples shall go and say, Come ye, and let us go up to the mountain of the Lord, to the house of the God of Jacob; and he will teach us of his ways, and we will walk in his paths: for out of Zion shall go forth the law, and the word of the Lord from Jerusalem." Is. ii. 3.

The servants of God of old, such as Daniel, were not strangers to such expectations. Many things now clearly revealed to us, were to them unknown. But they *did* understand that Israel, and the God of Israel, should at last govern in the earth. They knew, also, that there were blessings long promised which could be received neither by creation, nor by the nations, until *that* government should have come.

Hence the bitter sorrow of spirit with which they beheld Israel (who for a time had been set in supremacy under Solomon) displaced from that position. The glory of the reign of Solomon quickly faded away; iniquity continued to increase, until at last the long-threatened blow fell upon Jerusalem, and the throne of David in God's chosen city sank before the power of Nebuchadnezzar of Babylon. This was the moment at which Daniel lived. The commencing words of his prophecy are the record of this fall of Jerusalem: "In the third year of the reign of Jehoiakim king of Judah came Nebuchadnezzar king of Babylon unto Jerusalem, and besieged it. And the Lord gave Jehoiakim king of Judah into his hand, with part of the vessels of the house of God: which he carried into the land of Shinar to the house of his god; and he brought the vessels into the treasure house of his god." Dan. i. 1, 2.

Daniel was not exempted from the general calamity. It fell heavily on him; for he was carried captive to Babylon. But it was there that he was called to be numbered among the prophets of God. Prophecy has always been connected with the place of suffering and reproach. Enoch, the *first* who prophesied, prophesied among the corruptions which brought on the judgment of the flood: and Samuel was not raised up until judgment was about to fall upon the priestly house in Israel. The disciples were prophetically instructed whilst they stood on the Mount of Olives around their *rejected* Lord: and John was an exile in Patmos when he received the Revelation. The hearts, therefore, of such were likely to be chastened and prepared to understand the history of present evil, whilst they waited for the future and long-delayed blessing. Among these Daniel was numbered. He had kept himself from the defilements of the hour. His heart was tender. It had learned to mourn over the evil of his people, as well as over their chastisements. He sought to humble himself before God, and to wait on Him. He was the man " greatly beloved," and to him were committed fresh testimonies from God—testimonies which through him have been transmitted to us. In the light of these testimonies many will walk, even in the midst of the deepest darkness of the latter day, prove the value of their guidance, and bless Him who gave them, for ever and ever.

The subject of the prophecy of Daniel is the history of those Gentile nations who have been appointed to hold supreme power in the earth throughout the period of Jerusalem's punishment. It is not the history of *all* Gentile nations. It is the history only of those Empires who were appointed, after trampling down Jerusalem, to rule successively in her stead; and they are but four —the empires of Chaldea, of Persia, of Greece, and of Rome. Nor is the history even of these Empires given in its completeness, or in much detail. Jerusalem is the centre of the prophecy; and the events among the Gentiles are only recorded because of their relation to that city. Accordingly, when Jerusalem ceased nationally to exist, *detailed* history in Daniel is suspended. The long period, already exceeding eighteen hundred years, which has elapsed since Israel ceased to exist nationally in Jerusalem, is passed over almost in silence. No dates, localities, or personages are, during this interval, mentioned, nor will the thread of prophetic history be resumed until Israel shall again assume a national position in Jerusalem, and again become a centre of Gentile energy, and Gentile iniquity.

Thus the prophecy of Daniel becomes available for purposes of instruction to the Church generally. If, in order to understand it, we were obliged to toil through the history of nearly two thousand years, who, whether learned or unlearned, could be expected to attend? But when, instead of this, the burden of the prophecy rests upon a brief and yet future time; and all *necessary* acquaintance with past history is limited to that which Scripture itself supplies, who is there that may not listen and learn?

A very slight acquaintance with that which is now passing around us is sufficient to show, that the ancient dominance of ecclesiastical systems is giving place to the superior strength of the secular powers. The corruptions and discords of ecclesiastical systems make men despair of obtaining from them any beneficial influence, and drive many to look to the secular systems as their hope. There is also in connection with this an increasing desire to substitute mere human brotherhood, for brotherhood in Christ. The sin of *past* ages has been, the assigning to men who were brought only *nominally* into the Church, the privileges and the duties of Christians. The sin *now* appearing is even worse than this. It is the rejection of all brotherhood, save human brotherhood. An attempt is being made to apply to men as men, principles and precepts which God restricts to those who are *really* brought into His Church by *faith*. This is a condition well adapted to secure the reign of the secular systems. They, of course, would naturally be regarded as the proper heads of a system of human fraternisation. Few things, therefore, can be more important than to see, in the light of Scripture, the real character of these secular systems; and this it is the especial object of the prophecy of Daniel to unfold. The object of his prophecy is not to treat of the *ecclesiastical* corruptions of Christendom, but to teach respecting the character of the *secular* power in the ruling Gentile Empires—whether those Empires do, or do not, profess the name of Christ.

When we consider how false and evil the relations, even of real Christianity, to the secular power have often been, and that those relations would probably never have been held, if the prophecies of Daniel had been understood; when we remember, too, that his prophecy utterly dissipates the delusions of false and unscriptural philanthropy, and of that deistic eclecticism which is now ensnaring so many, it will not surprise us to find that every attempt to revive the testimonies of this Book should be sternly resisted.

Accordingly, in one of the most popular books of the day, the inspiration of this holy Book is denied, and it is cast back among the fables of the Apocrypha.* It would seem as if the writer intuitively

---

* *See* "Dr. Arnold's Life," p. 195. Dr. Arnold ventures to say, " There can be no reasonable spiritual meaning made out of the kings of the north and south. I have long thought that the greater part of the Book of Daniel is most certainly a very late work, of the time of the Maccabees; and the pretended prophecy about the kings of Græcia and Persia, and of the north and south, is mere history, like the poetical prophecies in Virgil and elsewhere." Dr. Arnold then intimates that, as a whole, the Book of Daniel should be classed with the stories of the Apocrypha, though that there *may* be genuine fragments in it is very *likely*. The italics are

felt, that either *his* thoughts about man and man's amelioration must be sacrificed, or else the prophecy of this Book: and he sacrificed the latter. Yet it seems wonderful that it should never have occurred to this writer, that in assailing the authority of Daniel, he assailed a greater than he; for did the Lord Jesus deceive? And would it not be deception for the Lord Jesus solemnly to refer us to the words of "Daniel *the Prophet*" (Mark xiii. 14) if He knew that Daniel was not a prophet, and that his writings ought to be classed with Bel and the Dragon, and other similar tales in the Apocrypha?

It is a fearful thing to attack the authority of Scripture. We might almost say that it would be more easy to think with the infidel, that God had never given a revelation of His will, than to suppose that, after having given it, He had failed to watch over it by His providence, and had allowed it to descend to us falsified and untrue. Surely, if we can

---

mine. There is a temerity in these statements that almost makes one tremble, and at the same time a surprising want of calm reflection. The *most* important parts that have yet been accomplished in the prophecies of Daniel, have been accomplished since the date at which Dr. Arnold supposes it to have been written: the cutting off of the Messiah, and the desolation of Jerusalem by the Romans, are examples. It would be very strange that predictions, accompanied, be it observed, by dates, should be so marvellously fulfilled in a book which on Dr. Arnold's hypothesis must be full not merely of fables, but of deliberate lies; for almost every vision in Daniel marks its own chronology: therefore, if the chronology be false, the whole book is false.

can confide in God respecting any thing, we can confide in Him for the preservation of His own Scriptures—Scriptures which He Himself has termed "THE Scriptures of truth." This thought should be sufficient to silence every doubt. But in addition to this, each Book of the Holy Scriptures has an internal evidence of its own, which strengthens in proportion as we addict ourselves to the study and use of the Word of God. This is especially the case with the Book of Daniel. The more minutely we examine each individual *word*, the more shall we be struck with the consistency of the prophecy, not only with itself, but with the rest of Scripture. Indeed, it may be said to be necessary to the harmony of Scripture. It abundantly confirms Isaiah; and the prophecies of the New Testament, especially the Book of Revelation, stand or fall with it. Besides which, there is no past event that has come within the scope of its predictions which has not verified it; and every rising event is adding fresh corroboration. Without it, the rest of prophetic Scripture would be obscured; nor could we speak with certainty or precision of the prospects of any thing that is transpiring amongst the nations around us.

We cannot wonder, therefore, that such a Book should be vehemently assailed, especially by those who are ridiculing "Bibliolatry" (as they are pleased to term it), and are industriously seeking to substitute their own baseless and sceptical speculations for the sure record of the written Word. If it be "Bibliolatry" to believe that every word in the

Holy Scripture has been written under the direct and immediate suggestion of the Holy Ghost, and therefore, that we are to reverence the Scripture as being the testimony of the Holy Ghost, and that, consequently, the authority of the Scripture and the authority of the Holy Ghost are co-equal,* then

* The Scriptures ever speak of themselves as being the testimony of the Holy Ghost. Thus, in Hebrews x., speaking of the full and lasting acceptance *of the believer* by the offering of the holy body of the Lord Jesus on the cross, (an offering once and for ever made,) the Apostle goes on to say that the very fact of the expiation having been complete, and having effected the purgation of sins, renders it impossible that there should be a repetition of offering in any sense whatsoever. Where remission of sins is, there can be no more offering for them; for if further offering were required, then the sins could not have been remitted. The Apostle then adds, that the Holy Ghost also bears witness to this, in that He has said in *the Book of Jeremiah*, "their sins and iniquities will I remember no more." Thus, then a passage in Jeremiah is quoted by the Apostle as being the direct testimony of the Holy Ghost. "The Holy Ghost spake by the Prophets." *They* were the instruments, *He* the speaker. *See* Matt. ii. 15, τὸ ῥηθὲν ὑπὸ κυρίου διὰ τοῦ προφήτου.

We are also told, in the Epistle of Peter, that prophetic Scripture is not of "private interpretation," but set forth on the authority of the Holy Ghost. The word translated "interpretation" (ἐπιλύσις) is derived from a verb signifying *to explain, expound,* or *unravel,* and would be applied to the *solution* of an enigma. Thus it is said of the Lord Jesus that "when they were alone, he *expounded* (ἐπέλυε) all things unto his disciples." It is similarly used in Genesis xli. 12, of the interpretation or explanation of a dream. *See* LXX., and in Acts xix. 39, of the legal exposition of an involved or diffi-

may such "Bibliolatry" abound in the Church for ever. The conviction that such "Bibliolatry" will be promoted by increased enquiry into Prophetic Scripture, is one of my chief encouragements in writing these pages.

---

cult question in a judicial assembly. When it is said, therefore, that no prophecy of Scripture is of private "exposition" (ἰδίας ἐπιλύσεως), it means, that it is not an explanation put forth on the authority of private unauthorised individuals, but of holy men of God, publicly and duly accredited, and who spake as they were moved by the Holy Ghost.

Thus, also, prophecy is regarded not as an enigma, but as "*the solution*," not as the difficulty, but "*the explanation*" of the difficulty. The "*secret* things belong unto the Lord our God, but *the things that are revealed* belong unto us and to our children." Deut. xxix. 29. *See* further remarks on this subject in "*Occasional Papers*," No. 1. p. 115.

CHAPTER I.

ERROR OF MODERN INTERPRETATION AS TO THE SCOPE OF THE ROMAN EMPIRE.

It seems needful, before we enter upon the consideration of the first vision of the Book of Daniel, to notice an error of interpretation that has long and extensively prevailed—an error fatal to all right exposition of the prophecy, because it affects the *subject* about which the prophecy is. If the subject of a prediction be not ascertained, we shall certainly not understand that which is predicted concerning it.

In this first vision an Image was seen, composed of various metals. Its head was of fine gold; its breast and its arms of silver; its belly and its sides* of brass; its legs of iron.

---

* "*Sides*" is a rendering placed in the margin of our English version, and has been adopted by several translators. It can scarcely be regarded as a *strictly* accurate rendering, but it is certainly preferable to "thighs."

The Chaldee word is peculiar. It is not dual or plural, but singular, יַרְכָתֵהּ the *thigh-part* that is, that part of the human trunk whence the thighs issue. Thus, in several

As regards the four metals which compose this Image, almost all expositors agree that they represent the successive empires of Chaldæa, Persia, Greece, and Rome—an interpretation, indeed, that may well be given; for few things are more capable of being demonstrated both from Scripture and from fact. "That the Roman Empire," says Mede, "was the fourth kingdom of Daniel, was believed by the Church of Israel both before and in our Saviour's time, received by the disciples of the Apostles, and the whole Christian Church for the first 300 years, without any known contradiction; and I confess, having so good ground in Scripture, it is with me 'tantum non articulus fidei,' little less than an article of faith."

French versions it is rendered *les hanches*. In ordinary language, when a statue or a man is spoken of, the word "legs" is understood to include "the thighs," and certainly a word in the singular number would not have been used if the two thighs were to be denoted. Venema renders it "sides" in the following passage :—" Caput erat aureum : pectus et brachia ex argento ; venter et latera æs." Some translate it by "ilia." The lateral part of the lower belly is indicated and called "the thigh part," because the thighs issue thence. This, doubtless, is the true meaning. Geier seems to adopt it. מְעוֹהִי Intestina ejus (ab Hebræo מֵעַיִם viscera, intestina) ponitur hic pro continente, hoc est pro בֶּטֶן venter. Deinde יַרְכָּתֵה latera ejus (ab Ebræo latus, femur) facile intelliguntur hic posita pro partibus illis ventris, quæ sunt ex ejus ambobus lateribus, hoc est pro *ilibus*, sicuti duo brachia sunt ex latere pectoris, quibus lateribus seu femori annecti solebat gladius.—*Geier on Daniel.*

c

If, then, the iron legs of the Image denote the *whole* Roman empire, why do expositors, after admitting this, suddenly forget their admission when they begin to treat of the ten divided parts, and write as if *half* only of the Roman empire were indicated? If a *whole* is to be divided, we must divide that *whole*. Nothing but error can ensue, if we divide only *half*. Yet this is the mistake that has been committed. The *Greek* or *Eastern* half of the Roman empire has been forgotten, and the *Latin* or *Western* half only considered. Expositors have written as if the ten toes of the Image were all found on *one* of its feet; and have persisted in seeking the ten kingdoms which those toes represent, *in one part only* of the Roman empire. That *modern* expositors (for it was not the case in the more early ages*) should have committed so fatal a mistake, appears truly unaccountable. But it is sufficient to prevent any right result being attained, and accounts for the perplexity which many have imagined to be hopelessly connected with prophetic enquiry. And the error is the worse, because the eastern part of the Roman empire—that part which expositors have forgotten, has, even in secular history, as well as in Scripture,

* See evidence of this at the end of this volume.

See also a very interesting and conclusive paper giving the Scripture evidence as to the succession of these four empires, in a work entitled "Remarks on the prophetic visions in the Book of Daniel," by Dr. S. P. Tregelles. I would earnestly recommend the perusal of this work to all who are interested in prophetic inquiry.

a claim to be regarded as the more important division of the two.*

* As regards its secular history, the mere fact of the seat of the empire having been removed from Rome and planted at Constantinople, was sufficient to give a pre-eminence to the East. Constantinople was considered to be, and was, the seat of Roman power. Constantinople remodelled secularly and religiously the whole empire. So long did the Emperors at Constantinople claim supremacy over the western branch of the empire, that even after the barbarians had conquered Rome, Ricimer, the German Master of Rome, acquiesced in the claim of the Emperor of the East to nominate the Emperor of the West.

This was in A.D. 467. "The patrician Anthemius," says Heeren, "then at Constantinople, *(where they never gave up their pretentions to the right of naming or confirming the Sovereigns of the West,)* was, though with the consent of the mighty Ricimer, named Emperor of the West, April 12th, A.D. 467, by the Emperor Leo." Again after this, in A.D. 472, Julius Nepos Augustus was nominated at Constantinople. (*See* Heeren, "Manual of Ancient History," p. 469.) I need not say how long the Empire of the East survived the fall of its sister in the West. *See* also letter of the Senate to Zeno, Emperor of the East, when Augustulus, the last Western Emperor of the Roman lineage, was deposed. They disclaim the wish of continuing any longer the Imperial succession in Italy, and state their opinion that one Monarch is sufficient for East and West. In their own name, and the name of the people, they consent that the seat of universal Empire shall be transferred to Constantinople, and renounce the right which they had nominally enjoyed, from the time of Augustus, of choosing their own Master. They state that the "republic" might safely confide in Odoacer, and humbly request that the Emperor of the East would invest him with the title o patrician and the administration of the diocese of Italy. Their request was granted, and Odoacer was ap-

If the terms of the vision had been adhered to, and the ten final kingdoms had been sought in the *whole* Roman empire, the modern theory of interpretation could never have existed; for it is based upon the extraordinary fallacy that *half* of the Roman empire *is* the Roman empire. Here, then, is a mistake sufficient to account for all the failure that has been found in result.

There are three criteria by which every interpretation of this chapter must be rigorously tested.

1st.—The ten kingdoms, represented by the ten toes of the image, are to be sought in the *whole* extent of the Roman empire—eastern as well as western.

2nd.—When once existent, they *continue till the end;* that is to say, until the stone smites them, grinds them to powder, and begins itself to fill the whole earth.

3rd.—Their development must be a plain and recognised development, analogous to that of the empires that have already been.

No one doubts that Chaldæa, Persia, Greece, and Rome have existed and ruled as sovereign empires. The development of the ten last kingdoms must be

---

pointed. Odoacer reigned from A.D. 476 to A.D. 492. Thus even barbarians acknowledged the supremacy of the Eastern branch. The superior importance of the East in Scripture will be abundantly apparent when we consider the eighth and eleventh chapters of Daniel. It will be the great sphere of Antichrist's coming glory.

no less decided. It will be a patent and unquestioned fact recognised by the whole earth.*

Such are the criteria. And, seeing that no division of the Roman empire answering to these conditions has ever taken place, it follows that this part of the vision remains to be fulfilled. We have seen the gold, the silver, the brass, and the iron ; but we have not yet seen the clay-iron *toes*. The seventh chapter, under the symbol of the fourth or Roman monster, equally fixes our attention on this ten-fold and last division of the *whole* Roman empire. *There* it is that that character of power, described as half-metal, half "pottery-ware," is to be found ; *there* is the sphere over which the power and blasphemies of the little horn are to spread: *there* are the countries whose atheistic evil is to cause the session of the Ancient of Days in judgment. It becomes, therefore, a subject of solemn interest to determine as accurately as we can, what countries were brought beneath the Roman power, for such countries we may soon expect to see revived in corporate though divided unity ; and they will hold the supreme controlling power of earth during the closing period of our dispensation.

* It should also be remembered that the Ten Kingdoms, when developed, will be *federally united*. Although distinct, they will not have the power of *separate* action. Accordingly, they are symbolised by the ten toes of *one* Image, and in the Revelation, by the ten horns of one Beast—that Beast in the Revelation representing an individual. In both these cases we have the emblem of distinctness, but also of *union*.

The provinces of Rome, at the most extended period of its power, may be enumerated thus :—

The most northern part of the Roman empire was Britain. It was first attacked by Julius Cæsar, but was not formally reduced into a Roman province until the time of Nero, under the name of Britannia Romana. This finally included England, and the greater part of Scotland. The Grampian hills may be taken as the extreme point to which the Romans penetrated. It was there that Agricola, in the reign of Domitian, fought his most northerly battle with the Caledonians. But his northern line of forts was drawn south of this point, across the narrow territory of about forty miles which is found between the Friths of Forth and of Clyde, a little north of the modern cities of Edinburgh and Glasgow. This line of forts was afterwards, in the reign of Antoninus, strengthened by a turf rampart, erected on foundations of stone, and was fixed as the limit of the Roman province. Ireland, though visited by Roman merchants, was never brought under Roman power. It is not to be regarded, therefore, as belonging to ἡ οἰκουμένη.

The Rhine, and the Vallum Romanum between the Rhine and the Danube, are the eastern boundaries of the Roman Empire in the direction of Germany. The Vallum Romanum left the Rhine near Bingen, and joined the Danube near Ratisbon.*

* The Vallum Romanum, after leaving the Rhine, first follows the line of the Taunus Mountains towards the N.E. ; then it turns southward, with a little east, and then more

The Romans possessed all Continental Europe west of this, viz., Portugal, Spain, France, Belgium, Luxemburgh, Rhenish Prussia west of the Rhine, Baden, Würtemberg, the chief part of Bavaria, and the whole of Switzerland.

In the south and south-eastern parts of Europe, the Romans possessed Italy, Greece, all the islands of the Mediterranean, including the Archipelago, and all other parts of Europe south of the Danube, that is to say, Turkey in Europe, and the Austrian dominions north of the Alps,* including that part of Hungary that lies south of the Danube. To this the Emperor Trajan added the province of Dacia north of the Danube. The boundaries of Dacia were: in the south, the Danube; in the west, the Vallum Romanum, remains of which are still visible. It left the Danube a few miles east of Belgrade, and running by Temesvar, continued its northern course until it met the Upper Theiss, which runs there from east to west. The boundary of Dacia then crosses the Carpathian mountains, and

---

easterly than southerly, before it joins the Danube. It is thus described by Gibbon:—" The Emperor Probus constructed a stone wall of considerable height, and strengthened it by towers at convenient distances. From the neighbourhood of Neustadt and Ratisbon, on the Danube, it stretched across hills, valleys, rivers, and morasses, as far as Wimpfen on the Neoker, and at length terminated on the banks of the Rhine, after a winding course of nearly 200 miles." Ch. xii.

* Austria held Lombardy and Venetia when this was first written. Italy was not then what she now is.

continues the line of the Dneister to the Black Sea. The whole province was about 1300 miles in circumference. Its modern divisions are: that part of Hungary which lies east of the Roman Vallum; Wallachia, Transylvania, Moldavia, and Bessarabia; which last is now occupied by Russia.* It may be here interesting to observe that the central part of Hungary, that is to say, that part of it which lies north of the Danube, and west of the Vallum Romanum just described, was never brought within the Roman Empire. Consequently the two parts which *do* fall within the Roman Empire, are, its western part south the Danube, and that part east of the Vallum Romanum which formed a part of Dàcia as just described. Dacia was retained as a Roman province for upwards of 160 years. It was relinquished about the year A.D. 270 by the Emperor Aurelian.†

In Asia, the Black Sea was the northern boundary of the possessions of Rome. A line drawn from the eastern corner of the Black Sea southward to the Euphrates, and then the Euphrates itself, would give its eastern limit in the time of Augustus. The dying request of Augustus was, that the Empire might never

---

* Since this was written, Russia has been compelled to relinquish the greater part of this province. The limits of the Roman Empire in this direction are almost, though not quite, restored.

† It should be observed that Bohemia, Moravia, in a word all *German* provinces now attached to Austria *north* of the Danube, do not fall within the Roman Empire.

be extended beyond that river; and until the reign
of Trajan, this request was regarded. That monarch,
however, ambitious of military renown, carried his
arms far beyond. But although he overran vast
districts, and the kings of Parthia consented to
receive their crowns at his hands, yet he only *retained
as provinces* three districts, namely, Armenia, Assyria, and Mesopotamia; but these countries were
regularly formed into Roman Provinces.* His suc-

---

* The era of Trajan is important, because it was he whose
conquests determined the final extent of the Roman Empire.
It was he, too, who added Babylonia to the provinces of
Rome. Whilst engaged (A.D. 115) in an expedition against
the Parthians, he advanced to Babylon, entered it, no one
withstanding him, reduced its large territory where the
Roman standards had never been before displayed, and
became master of Assyria and Chaldæa. At Babylon he
visited the house in which Alexander the Great died, and
performed there certain ceremonies in honour of his name.
Ammianus Marcellinus says that in his time Trajan's tribunal was still to be seen at a city in the neighbourhood of
Babylon. Trajan reduced Assyria to a Roman province, as
he had before done Armenia and Mesopotamia, so that the
Empire was extended to the Tigris and beyond. *See* "Universal History," Book III. ch. xx.

After the final limits of the Roman Empire in the East
had thus been reached, and Babylonia had become a Roman
province, Trajan returned to Antioch on the Orontes,—the
place which he had chosen as the basis of his operations in
the East, and which is now again likely to be selected as the
spot whence the civilisation of Western Europe is to commence its anticipated triumph in the East, by securing to
itself the control of the Euphrates.

Soon after Trajan's return to Antioch, that city was visited

cessor Adrian, however, resigned them all, and once more made the Euphrates the eastern boundary

---

by an earthquake, more terrible, perhaps, than any of which history supplies the record. Eusebius, Aurelius Victor, and Evagrius, all speak of it as "the greatest calamity recorded in history." *See* "Universal History," note, Book III. ch. xx. Dio Cassius, who gives a minute and vivid description of this earthquake, says that Antioch was at that time so crowded with troops and strangers from all parts of the Roman Empire, that there was scarcely a nation or province that did not share in the calamity, so that all the Roman world suffered in that one city—οὕτως εν τῃ Αντιοχειᾳ πασα ἡ οικουμενη ἡ ὑπο τοις Ρωμαιοις ουσα εσφαλη. Dio Cassius, Book LXVIII. ch. xxiv.

Dio Cassius states that the earthquake was preceded by thunder and strange portentous winds (αλλοκοτοι ανεμοι). Then came suddenly a terrible subterranean roar, which was followed by the earthquake. The whole surface of the earth was convulsed and thrown upward. The buildings seemed to leap from their foundations (τα οικοδομηματα ανεπηδα). Some fell with a mighty crash, whilst others were dashed one against the other as if by a surging sea. Trees were torn up by the roots. The heights of Mount Casius bowed and were broken off; other mountains were overturned; new rivers appeared, and others that had flowed before vanished. Nothing could be seen because of the dust of the ruins; no voice could be heard because of the crash and the subterranean roar. The earthquake continued, with brief periods of intermission, for many days and nights, so that destruction of life was vast, and Trajan himself was saved by a reputed miracle.

Such were the accompaniments of the inauguration of Roman sovereignty over Babylon. Was not this earthquake sent to remind us of that more terrible visitation which is to follow the future establishment of Western power at

of the Empire; but at a subsequent period they again became the subject of contest between the Romans and the Parthians, and afterwards between the Romans and Persians. "The generals of Marcus, the Emperor Severus, and his son, erected many trophies in Armenia, Mesopotamia, and Assyria."* Under the reign of Marcus, the Roman generals penetrated as far as Ctesiphon and Seleucia, which they captured. These places they never attempted to retain. By taking possession, however, of the kingdom of Osrhoene, which occupied the northern and most fertile part of Mesopotamia, the Romans again obtained "a firm and permanent establishment beyond the Euphrates."

In the reign of Diocletian, in his remarkable treaty with Persia, Mesopotamia, which had been the object of many wars, was ceded to Rome, and the Persians formally renounced all pretentions to that province. They also relinquished to the Romans five provinces beyond the Tigris. Four of these to the north of the river, were districts of inconsiderable extent; but on the east of the Tigris, the empire acquired the large and mountainous territory of Carduene, the ancient seat of the Carduchians. Their posterity, the Curds, with very little alteration, have acknowledged the nominal sovereignty of the Turkish

---

Babylon, when it shall fall never to rise again? "And there were voices, and thunders, and lightnings, and there was a great earthquake, such as was not since men were upon the earth, so mighty an earthquake, and so great." Rev. xvi. 18.

* *See* Gibbon, Vol. I. pp. 10 and 332, 8vo.

Sultan.   After this treaty (in which the Araxes was acknowledged by the Persians and by Rome as the eastern boundary of the Empire), Diocletian and Maximian celebrated the last triumph which Rome ever beheld.   Soon after this, observes Gibbon, the Emperors ceased to vanquish; and Rome ceased to be the capital of the Empire.

There can, however, be no doubt that in the time of Trajan, Babylonia was numbered among the provinces of Rome.   In defining the south-eastern limit of the Empire, Trajan would no doubt have drawn a line from Suez, skirting Syria and Arabia, carried it across the Euphrates so as to include Babylon and Babylonia, and continued it so as to touch the southern parts of Assyria Proper on the eastern bank of the Tigris.   Speaking generally, the possessions of Rome in Asia may be said to answer very nearly to that which we now call Asiatic Turkey.

In Africa the Romans possessed Egypt, and the whole northern coast, that is to say, the countries now known as Libya, Tripolis, Tunis, Algeria, and Fez. Sallè, a little outside the straits of Gibraltar, was their most westerly city.   A city also of their foundation may still be discovered near Mequinez, the residence of the Emperor of Morocco; but it does not appear that his more southern dominions, Morocco itself and Segelmessa, were ever comprehended within the Roman Province.*

* *See* Gibbon, chap. i.

Such are the countries which fall within the boundaries of that which was once the Roman Empire. From the earliest period to the present hour, these districts have ever been the centre of all that has influenced human life. The light of revelation first given to Israel, and then to the Christian Church, was set within these countries. All the civilisation of antiquity was centred there—*there* still resides the power which is at this moment forming the character of the world. It is the object of Daniel's prophecy to teach us *how* they use their power, and to record their end.

CHAPTER II.

THE HISTORY OF GOVERNMENTAL POWER AS TAUGHT IN THE VISION OF THE IMAGE.

OF all the divine interventions in judgment which have yet occurred, the most momentous has been the Flood. The next will not be until the prophecy which we are about to consider terminates—when the Son of Man having been brought before the Ancient of Days, and invested with the governmental power of earth, "all peoples, nations, and languages, shall serve him," and "the sovereignty of the world become the sovereignty of our Lord and of his Christ."

The long period which intervenes between these two limits, has already measured more than four thousand years. Within this period, three separate bodies have been called out into positions of corporate privilege and responsibility. The first of these was Israel. The second, that body of Gentile nations who are appointed to governmental supremacy in the earth, during the time of Jerusalem's punishment. The third is the professing Christian Church. The first originated in the call of Abraham; the second in the triumphs of Nebuchadnezzar over Jerusalem; the third commenced at Pentecost.

The histories of all are kept carefully separate in the Scripture. After they severally commence, they continue to that period called in Matthew "the end of the age," when the time for the intervention of God will have come, and when the history of the Jews as an unbelieving people, the history of the ruling Gentile kingdoms, and that of the professing Church, will *concurrently* end. The second of these bodies is that of which the Book of Daniel treats. His prophecy is concerned with the dynasty of the Gentiles.

There was one event connected with the establishment of this dynasty, which, though truly of momentous interest, seems scarcely to have been apprehended by any—I mean, the withdrawal of the Divine Glory, which, till then, had been visibly present with Israel in the earth. The Glory of God, which first appeared amid the solitude of the desert in the burning bush, had connected itself with Israel —extricated them from Egypt—gone with them through the wilderness—planted them in Canaan; and at last, entered into and abided in their Temple. The divided waters of the Red Sea—the fall of the cities of Canaan—the triumph over enemies like Sennacherib, bore witness to the resistlessness of its almighty power. The reigns of David and of Solomon supplied abundant evidence of the blessings which result to men when the wisdom of God is near, and is consulted: and when the springs of government are not touched without reference to Him. But as soon as the time was come for Israel to be punished, and for *Gentile* nations to be raised into supremacy, the Divine Glory, which till then had never forsaken Jerusalem, departed from the earth, not transferring itself to the Gentiles. " Thou never bearest rule over *them*: they were not called by thy name." Is. lxiii. 19. The great subject of the prophecy of Ezekiel (who lived at the same era as Daniel) is the departure of this Glory.* He saw it, under the symbol of cherubim, withdraw—hovering for a season over the Temple, and over the city, as if reluctant to depart; until at last, grieved away by the continued abominations of Israel, it retired into the heavens—there awaiting that hour when, judgment having wrought its work, it will return and depart no more for ever. Ezekiel in vision beheld its return; and as he was beholding its re-

---

* A comparison of the first with the tenth chapter of Ezekiel, shows that the expressions, "cherubim" and "living creatures" (the ζωα of the Revelation, see Rev. iv. and v.) are synonymous. There are few more faulty translations than that of "*beasts*" for ζωα, "living creatures." "*Beast*" (θηριον) is a word of well known meaning in Daniel and the Revelation. The moment when the "*beasts*" (θηρια) of Daniel begin their course, is the moment when the "living creatures" (ζωα) of Ezekiel and Revelation are withdrawn from the earth; and the "living creatures" will return when the "beasts" depart. One of the great objects of the Revelation is to contrast the condition of the earth while under the last great "beasts," with its condition when it shall again be brought under the "living creatures" or "cherubim." For some further remarks on the "living creatures," see "Thoughts on the Apocalypse," p. 51. It may be obtained as advertised at end of this volume.

entrance into the Temple, it was said unto him: " Son of man, the place of my throne, and the place of the soles of my feet, where I will dwell in the midst of the children of Israel for ever, and my holy name shall the house of Israel no more defile." Ezekiel xliii. 7. Thus, then, the *establishment* of the Gentile dynasty is marked by the withdrawal of the Divine Glory from the earth, the *fall* of their dynasty is followed by the return of that Glory. Nothing can be more significant than this. It distinctly marks the whole governmental system of the Gentiles as one that would act in alienation from God ; and .facts prove that it *has* been so. Nebuchadnezzar— Antiochus Epiphanes — Pilate — Antichrist — are names which sufficiently determine the tenor of its course : and even where better principles may momentarily have raised individuals like Darius above the habit of the times, yet even Darius, though desiring to act aright, found the stream of evil flowing so strongly, that he feared to breast it, and consented to cast the servant of God into the den of lions, in order that he might thereby save to himself his crown.

The Book of Daniel abundantly corroborates these things. In its seventh chapter, in describing the four Empires that were successively to arise among the Gentiles, the symbols employed are four fierce beasts ($\theta\eta\rho\iota\alpha$), the last of which, because of its blasphemies, is given to " the burning flame." And even in the vision of the Image, where the gold, silver, brass and iron, appear to be the symbols of that which is precious, rather than of that which is vile, yet here also the vision terminates, just as in the seventh chapter, with judgment. The Image is smitten, ground to powder, and made like the chaff of the summer threshing floor.

The reason of this difference between the symbols of the second and seventh chapters is very evident, when we remember that the Empires of which these chapters speak, must necessarily be viewed in two aspects : first, in respect of the *power* with which they are invested in the person of their rulers ; secondly, in respect of their *developed character and actions.* All who receive any special gifts or endowments from God, must be regarded in these two positions : the first attaching to them in virtue of the endowments they hold ; the second depending upon the manner in which they use those endowments, whether for good or for evil. The intrinsic value of a gift is not altered by its misuse. God invested Nebuchadnezzar and the Chaldean Empire with power. It was said to Nebuchadnezzar, "the God of Heaven hath given thee a kingdom, power and strength and glory." (Dan. ii.) Such investment was honourable and glorious ; therefore, Nebuchadnezzar and his Empire were, in respect of their power, *golden* ; although, in respect of their practical use of that power, their symbol was a fierce and devouring *beast.* The instruction would not be perfect unless we were taught the value and dignity of the position held ; and also the character of those who hold it.

The object of the second chapter of Daniel is to treat of the Gentile Empires, not in relation to their conquests, or their territorial extent, but *with reference to their governmental power.* These Empires were, in the person of their rulers, invested with a power the character of which is represented either by gold, silver, brass, iron, or by iron mixed with miry clay. In all these cases, the power with which they were invested was represented by *metal;* that generic character being still retained, even when the attempt is made to debase it by the admixture of miry clay. But the peculiar dignity and endowment of these Empires did not so much consist in their being possessed of power, whether golden, or iron, as in this—that they formed part of that wondrous Image. "Thou, O King, sawest, and behold a great image. This great image, whose brightness was excellent, stood before thee; and the form thereof was terrible." (Dan. ii.) It was glorious and terrible, and looked down as it were in proud and lordly supremacy upon the whole world. The Empires, therefore, represented by it, are not only endowed with power wherewith to regulate themselves, or to assail others (such power may be possessed by any nation, by Russia, for example, or by America—countries that fall not within the scope of the Image), but the distinctive characteristic of the Image-nations is, that authority has been granted to them by God to be *supreme* in such sort as for the mainsprings of influential power in the earth to be effectually under their control.* Even the clay-iron kingdoms are to inherit this supremacy. They too will be the centre of controlling influence in the earth.

This observation is intended to apply to the period in

The vision of the Image, therefore, enables us unhesitatingly to say, that nothing can prevent the nations of the Roman Empire being finally divided into *ten*: nothing can prevent the "clay-iron" principles of government from prevailing amongst them all: nothing prevent these ten last kingdoms from being *ultimately* possessed, in federal union, of that lordly supremacy which pertains to them as forming a part of this Image so marvellously endowed. God has appointed, and God has revealed these things, therefore they *shall* all be fulfilled in their season.

The subject, however, to which our attention is chiefly directed in this vision, is the *depreciation* of the metals. "The Image's head was of fine gold": and it was said to Nebuchadnezzar, "Thou, O King,

---

which the Empires or Kingdoms spoken of are existing in recognised development. For example, as long as the Roman Empire retained its iron power, it was *supreme;* and when the present long period of transition shall have passed, and the ten clay-iron kingdoms shall have been developed, they too will be *supreme.* It is true, however, that even during the period of transition from the iron legs to the clay-iron toes, supreme power has always been located in the Roman Earth. When barbarian nations have broken in, they have fixed their seats of power within the Empire. Two great examples are the Turks and the Germans. Constantinople was made the seat of Turkish power. The Germans, to whom the Imperial power of the West was given 900 years ago, made their seats of Empire within the Roman Earth, first in Suabia, and since in Austria. In the future (whatever may be the vicissitudes), it will be finally proved that the controll_ing power of earth, during the day of man, has been made the heritage of the Roman nations.

art this head of gold." We can easily apprehend, therefore, how wonderful a pre-eminence was assigned to Nebuchadnezzar. He was not only a part of this Image, he was its head; and not its head only, but its *golden* head. The power granted to this first Gentile monarch was perfect in its kind. It was not represented by silver, or brass, or iron, but by "fine gold." It was really precious as power.*

* It was said to Nebuchadnezzar, " Thou, O King, art a King of Kings, for the God of heaven hath given thee a kingdom, power, and strength, and glory ; and wheresoever the children of men dwell, the beasts of the field, and the fowls of the heaven, hath he given into thine hand and hath made thee ruler over them all." These words do not imply, as has well been observed by Dr. Tregelles, that Nebuchadnezzar "actually held and exercised this rule over every part of the inhabited earth, but rather that so far as God was concerned, all was given into his hand ; so that he was not limited as to the power which he might obtain in whatever direction he might turn himself as conqueror : the only earthly bound to his Empire was his own ambition." (See Tregelles' 'Daniel,' page 7.)

This gift was granted to Nebuchadnezzar in consequence of his being part of the Image, and was not dependent upon his power being "golden" in character. The endowment of all the successive Empires was similar to his. Hence their assumption of names or expressions implying universality of dominion ; and their title to do this is sanctioned in the Scripture. The Romans were accustomed to call their Empire "Orbis Terrarum ;" and in Scripture, the corresponding expression, πᾶσα ἡ οἰκούμενη, is used. "There went out a decree from Cæsar Augustus that *the whole world* should be taxed." Thus also Cyrus says, "the God of heaven hath given me all the Kingdoms of the earth." (Ezra, i. 2.)

Power, in order to have its own proper character, must be independent of all, excepting God, who gives it. The moment it becomes dependent, either as to its source, or as to its exercise on those whom it is intended to control, it ceases to have the true excellency of power. For him who holds authority, to rest on God—to consult and to obey Him is well; but for authority to lean for support on those who are beneath it, is to frustrate the object for which it is given, and ends at last in making government the mere expression of the human will—that very will which it is its office to control. There are some spheres in which men easily recognise such interference with authority, to be sin. In families, for example, what parent would not feel deprived of his proper place—the place that God had given him, if he were subjected to his children, or to his servants —if he were told that his title to rule originated in their choice, and that he should only govern according to laws appointed by *them ?* The parent would doubtless consider such authority to be no authority, and every one who was right-minded and feared God, would see in it a sinful perversion of the principles of His moral government. Is it less sinful when such perversion is attempted in the national sphere ? The principles of divine order are not mutable. In heaven, in earth, in every sphere, they are essentially the same. To adopt governmental principles on earth, which would be untrue in heaven, must morally dissociate earth from heaven. It must involve opposedness to Him who values His own principles because they are good, and who has determined that, finally, they shall be established in the earth; for His will shall be done in earth, as it is done in heaven. Accordingly, when God was pleased to endow the first of the Gentile dynasties with power, He gave it in its *golden* excellency. It was not derived *from* those beneath; neither was it responsible *to* them; nor was it legislated for *by* them. The first monarch of the Gentiles stood responsible to God alone. It was, as regarded man, irresponsible power. It had the proper preciousness of power: it was *golden*.

Irresponsible power is a word at which men have long learned to tremble. And not without reason; for it is an endowment too precious, too momentously important as to its results, for any but a perfect hand to hold. If any ruler could be found who would regard implicitly the will of God—using all his power for the good of others—swayed by no principles of selfishness or of pride—loving others as himself—having wisdom and understanding to appreciate and apply the principles of God to all the detail of human life, then nothing could be more desirable than that power—absolute power—should be placed in such a hand; and such an one *has* been found. There is ONE who came into the world, and "the world was made by Him, but the world knew Him not." He came unto His own, and His own received Him not. The Holy One of Heaven became the rejected-one of earth. And now, having been removed from the earth, He sits on the throne of His Father—waiting—waiting " till His enemies shall have been set as a footstool for His feet." There is no question of His competency to rule. The heavens, which He hath created, are subject to the order of His hand ; He upholdeth all things by the word of His power : the angels obey Him and praise His name : the universe is controlled by Him, and owes to His goodness every blessing it receives : His saints bless Him for His grace : all things in heaven and in earth declare His wisdom : and the gentleness and meekness, which were His characteristics when on earth, have not ceased to characterise Him now that He is exalted above every name. He is worthy therefore of " golden power." And such power *will* be assumed by Him. He will take it and exercise it as soon as these Gentiles have run their appointed course, and the time comes for the clay and the iron to be smitten.

It is the place of faith to wait for that hour, and to know that all things will be, and must be, out of course until then. The lesson taught by the whole history of man is this,—that the gifts of God are in vain given unless a PERFECT ONE be provided in whom they may be deposited and preserved. The headship of the first creation was in Adam, and it failed : the headship of the new creation is in Christ risen. So also with the priesthood: after failing in the hand of man, it now rests in Him who is " consecrated for evermore." (Heb. vii.) Nor is it otherwise with the administration of the nations upon earth. Governmental power over the earth was entrusted, first to the kings of Israel, and then to the Gentiles; and it has failed. The period of delegation to the Gentiles has, indeed, not yet terminated. They must first fully run their course of evil, and Israel be fully punished for the rejection of their king, and then the headship of creation, the priesthood and the administrative government of the earth will be manifestly concentrated in the person of ONE, who will be worthy to hold, and competent to execute, the office He bears. These are things for which faith has to wait. But the heart of man refuses to wait. Men became soon sensible of the danger of unlimited power being vested in the hands of those in whose goodness and whose wisdom they could not confide; and therefore, the dread of tyranny, the natural dislike of being controlled, and the desire of attaining influence themselves, became concurrent motives, inducing men to limit and modify, more and more, the actions of a power, which they regarded both with envy and with dread. Nor could any ruler stand in independency of the governed, save by leaning wholly and unreservedly on God. But this no ruler has done. No government has leaned upon God: and being too weak to stand alone, they naturally look for support to those who are lower than themselves, until, at last, they give up all *claim* to be possessed of the authority of God—quit the place in which they stand *officially* contrasted with other men, and mingle themselves with them. To use the language of Scripture, " they mingle themselves with the seed of men."

The progress, however, of the depreciation of power, was gradual, and manifested in distinct and successive periods. God appointed it so ; partly, doubtless, that the plans of human wisdom might have time to develop themselves, and their inefficiency be the more fully proved. As long as the Chaldæan successors of Nebuchadnezzar continued to rule, the power of the Monarch was, ostensibly at least, independent of those whom it governed. That it should so long have continued so, is a marvel that can only be accounted for by the secret agency of God. He secretly sustained it, until it had been sufficiently proved that absolute power, when used not in dependence on Him, could only produce effects such as those which the histories of Nebuchadnezzar and of Belshazzar show : man's happiness was *not* promoted thereby, neither God's glory. God was blasphemed—wickedness exalted.

The Medo-Persian Monarchy arose upon the ruins of the Chaldæan. Aristocratic Monarchy was the form that it assumed : the nobles, or men of birth being the sustainers, and, to a certain degree, the controllers of the crown. The extent of their influence is clearly shown in the narrative respecting the decree that consigned Daniel to the den of lions. It was proposed by the nobles, enacted by the Monarch. When once ratified, they insisted upon its being obeyed ; and Darius though he laboured hard to avoid its obligation, dared not resist their claim. The *golden* power of Nebuchadnezzar would have consigned *them* to the den rather than forego the exercise of his own will; but now other principles had come in; power had lost its full intrinsic excellence, and circumstances arose with which the depreciated power of the Monarch of Persia found itself unable to contend.*

We need not wonder, therefore, that the Persian Monarchy should be spoken of in the Scripture as *inferior* to that which preceded it. "After thee," it was said to Nebuchadnezzar, "shall arise another kingdom inferior to thee." It was represented in the vision by *silver*, not by *gold*. As to its territorial acquisitions and military prowess, it was *not* inferior. On the contrary, it subjugated regions (Asia Minor, for example), which the Monarchs of Chaldæa never reached; and in that respect, therefore, was far greater. But as to the *character* of its power, it was inferior; and this is the aspect which the vision of the Image presents. It is the history of the Gentile dynasty as regards the *character* of their power.

The third Monarchy was that of Greece, and was formed under Alexander the Great. In the eighth

* "In the case too of Ahasuerus, the King and the Princes act together, and the King could not undo what they had jointly decreed about Queen Vashti. In Ezra vii., we find authority given to that servant of God from the King and his seven counsellors. All this shows us, not a King acting in the right of his royal prerogative, but a King in a certain sense controlled by counsellors without whose advice and consent he could not act." (Tregelles on Daniel, p. 11.)

chapter, he is expressly stated to be the first king
of Greece. His conquests were vast, extending
across Asia Minor, Syria, and Egypt, to Affghanistan
and the Indus. His dominions, therefore, were far
more extensive even than those of Persia; but
nevertheless, the *character* of his power was only
worthy of being represented by *brass*; for his government was a military oligarchy. A conqueror
who has to rule subdued and reluctant nations,
must, if he lean not upon God, depend upon his
generals. They necessarily become the counsellors
and sustainers of the crown; and they are men who
are raised into these positions, not by birth (in
which there is more of the direct appointment of
God), but by their own energies, or by fortuitous
success. All who are acquainted with the human
heart, and have considered the lessons of history,
know that such are of all men most assuming—
difficult to be conciliated—hard to be satisfied—easy
to be provoked. Such were the men on whom
Alexander and his successors were obliged to lean.
Their thoughts and habits were, in no slight degree,
tinged with the doctrines that had been cherished in
the democracies of southern Greece. The aristocracy of birth gave way before the claims of military
prowess; and thus the Monarch possessed a character
of power too dependent upon the proud will of his
servants to be worthy of a higher symbol than that
of brass. This was a very decided step in the
depreciation of power; for brass is more removed

from silver, than silver from gold, and the further descent to *iron* was comparatively little.*

That further descent was taken when the Monarchy of the Cæsars grew out of the democracy of Rome. The Emperor was professedly the elected chief magistrate of the state, and the doctrine of power being originated from the people, may then be considered to have received its formal sanction.† The instability of that power—how dependent its tenure upon the will of prætorian cohorts or discontented armies, is too well known to need being recited here.

* At Rome, about this time, an ounce of *silver* was equivalent to about seventy pounds weight of *brass*. (See Gibbon, page 15.)

† See Address of Augustus to the Senate when he was appointed Emperor. The title "Imperator" instead of "Rex," was intended to imply that he was the chief magistrate of a Republic—not the hereditary occupier of a throne. Hence they shunned the regal "*diadem*," which was a fillet set with pearls, and wore only the laurel crown (στεφανος) of the victorious general. "Though with Augustus and his successors," observes Mr. Elliott, "the most absolute monarchical power attached to their emperorship, yet it was their policy to veil it under the old military and imperial badges." (Elliott, p. 129, vol. i.) It was this possession of absolute power when once they were elected, that places the "*iron*" in such direct contrast with the "*clay-iron*" that follows —in the latter case the *exercise* of the power being controlled.

I may here observe that vessels are made in France of clay mingled with iron, which to the eye have the appearance of being iron. Yet they are almost as fragile as pottery-ware. The particles will not cohere as in *metals* fused together.

It was not, however, under Imperial Rome that the great *adulteration* of power was effected. Indeed, the gradual descent from one *metal* to another less precious, is the symbol of the *depreciation* of power, rather than of its *adulteration*. The metal remained metal still, and no attempt was made to mingle with it a foreign substance. In other words, power, however it might be originated, or however supported, retained in itself a strength which was in danger of being utterly lost as soon as the theory of self-government was invented and the Monarch became controlled by the legislation of the people. During the reign of the Imperial Cæsars, though the people were supposed to originate the power of their sovereign, yet they were not entitled to *legislate for* that sovereign. *They were not made their own governors.* The Monarch had not then become the mere functionary of an authority, of which the real source and controlling power was vested in the people themselves. The Emperors of Rome, when once seated on the Throne, were Emperors. But that era has passed. Now, among the nations of the Roman World, we hear nothing except the theory of self-government extolled.

The present condition of some of the European nations, especially of France, affords a remarkable illustration of the earnest and laborious effort that is being made to mingle the iron and the clay together. But it cannot be satisfactorily effected. The iron and clay " will not cleave one to the other."* For men *to be governed*, and at the same time to *be governors of themselves*, is impossible. If there be any real truth in the theory of self-government, it must bear being carried out to its legitimate result. That result would be, the right of each individual member of society to govern himself; for what reason is there why the will of a majority should be submitted to more than any other will? Indeed, while man continues as he is, it is certain that both intelligence and truth will be with the few—not with the many. As human things now are, the path chosen by majorities cannot be the path of wisdom, truth, or peace.

That any power of government should continue to subsist where principles virtually subversive of all government are fostered, even by the governors themselves, is a marvel that can only be ascribed to the secret sustaining power of God, who has in mercy appointed, that power to govern shall, in spite of every effort to destroy it, continue in the earth until the end.

It has pleased God to say, "there *shall be* in it the strength of the iron," and therefore, every effort to extirpate the iron, or effectually to neutralise it

* If France afforded a melancholy example of this in 1849, when the above was written, how much more in 1872?

The late Emperor of the French returning, as he said, to "Cæsarism," wished to extirpate the clay and to restore the iron. But the era of the iron is passed. The Monarchs of the Roman World must be content to reign with a clay-iron sceptre, or else they must cease to rule at all.

by the admixture of clay must fail.   Yet the knowledge of this does not lessen the sorrow of beholding
those who hold authority from God, and therefore
stand in a place regarded as *officially* divine—it does
not lessen the sorrow of seeing such deliberately
quit that place, and mingle themselves with those
whom God has not officially raised from the ordinary level of man.   Either God, or the people, are
the source of power.   Both cannot be true.   The
voice of the people is either the voice of God, or it
is the voice of unregenerate man, guided by that
spirit who worketh in all the children of disobedience.   It is either the intention of God that men
should govern themselves, or it is His intention that
they should be governed by power emanating from
and directed by Him.   One of these things must be
true; and the other must be false.   The one will be
the truth of God; the other the lie of Satan; and,
therefore, I repeat, it is a sorrowful and evil thing to
see the governors themselves eagerly joining in the
general cry—disowning their title to authority from
God, and gladly owning the people as those who
confer the authority at first, and have the right to
control it when given.   " They mingle themselves
with the seed of men."*

---

* " They shall mingle themselves with the seed of men, but
they shall not cleave one to another, even as iron is not mixed
with clay."   If there were any doubt as to the reference of
" *they* " in the beginning of the verse, it is removed by the
concluding clause, where "iron" is used in explanation.
Throughout this vision, they who hold governmental power

But sorrowful as this is, it is even more sorrowful to see the indifference of the Church of God to these things. It is the privilege and duty of the Church to consider and to judge all things according to the Word of God, and to treasure His principles because they are His. There are certain principles connected with the established order of the universe; there are others connected with the moral government of God. Man as man, and nations as nations, have a certain relation to Him, and it is the duty of the Church as much to be vigilant against the perversion of the principles of God's go-

---

from God are represented by *metal*, and regarded as being in a place *officially* divine, whereas those who are ruled over are represented by clay, and as occupying a mere human place.

We are accustomed now to the words, "sovereign people;" and it is remarkable how distinctly the people are in this chapter recognised as *sharing* governmental power. "And whereas thou sawest the feet and toes partly pottery-ware, partly iron, the sovereignty shall be *divided*," and therefore represented no longer by iron merely, but by a mingled substance, partly of iron, and partly of clay. "*Sovereignty*" (answering to the use of βασιλεια in Greek), is the word I should adopt throughout this chapter instead of "*Kingdom*," because less ambiguous, and adapted to the character of the vision, as giving the history of governmental power, and not that of the Empire physically.

Clay may be combined with metal, but it cannot be infused into the metal so as to unmake it metal, or destroy the cohesion of its parts. Therefore, there is a strength of *metallic* substance even in this unnatural combination. A vessel made of this material will bear a heavier blow than one solely composed of pottery-ware.

E

vernment in these things, as to watch over the faith committed to themselves. A period when these principles are violated, and when men who have either ignorantly or carelessly violated them, are triumphing in the supposed success of their counsels, is one in which the Church is peculiarly called to watchfulness and to confession—confession both for others and for themselves. They may not, and, indeed, they will not be able to stem the tide of evil; nor is the government of nations a sphere in which they are now intended to act. " *Now* is my Kingdom not from hence." But they may weigh all things according to the Word of God: may keep themselves separate, and may testify. They may warn, and perhaps preserve others. But if, instead of this, even Christians despise the testimonies of the prophetic Scriptures, wander into the world's sphere, adopt and vindicate the principles of the day, and connect themselves with the very things that are to be made like the chaff of the summer threshing floor, how can there be any hope, I say not of the triumph of God's truth, but even of any testimony to it being maintained?

One result of the attempt to mingle the iron and the clay together is, that the sovereign power is partly strong, and partly "brittle," just as you might expect that to be in which pottery-ware is conjoined with iron. The effect of this is abundantly seen in the incapacity of governments to act unless they carry with them the will, not only of the majority, but of a large majority of those whom they govern.

There may be a crime of the deepest dye that loudly calls for punishment. A modern government fears to punish, except the feelings of the community be thoroughly enlisted on their side. Regulating ordinances are imperatively required; but it depends upon the will of the community whether or not they shall be enacted. How often the arm of government has thus been paralysed, those who have exercised its powers may best tell. But it cannot be wondered at. Who would venture to use a sceptre in which iron and pottery-ware are joined in precarious union, with the same confidence with which they would wield one that was formed of gold, or of iron?

If we suppose a government thus constituted to be imbued with all principles of truth—disposed to foster all that was good, and to check all that was evil, it evidently could effect nothing: for if it could, it would imply that the majority of men were wise and righteous, whereas the scripture declares that they are ignorant and evil. There can be no more decided evidence of a position being wrong, than when it enchains the energies of good, and renders its presence nugatory. As regards the individual character of those who exercise, or have exercised executive power amongst us, I desire neither to say nor to imply anything. But this I say, that none who really reverence and value the truth of God should ever consent to wear shackles—no, not if all the kingdoms of the world, and the glory of them, were given to them as the reward. They who carry into effect the governmental principles of the present hour are *constrained* to put truth on an equality with error; to flatter and cringe to falsehood; and to discourage every attempt to exhibit the lies of Satan in the real flagrancy of their evil. The governmental relation of England to Romanism in Ireland and elsewhere,* is a lamentable instance of this.

Unless we believe that the Most High has utterly abandoned the principles of His moral government, we can scarcely doubt that such violation of His laws must entail judicial visitation from His hand. The very circumstance of the springs of government being regulated by the hands of those who should be subject to the control and guidance of authority, must undermine the foundations of power, and finally entail its own chastisement. But when, in addition to this, we remember that the latter days are peculiarly marked by increase of evil—that perilous times are to come, and mockers to arise; and that government, instead of resisting such, is fettered by their influence,

* Seen also in the desire officially expressed by the British Government for the restoration of the Pope's *spiritual* authority at Rome. None of these things should tempt Christians to speak revilingly of any government whatsoever, but the knowledge of the channel in which the stream of things is flowing, and *will* flow, should cause them to take good heed that *they* do not accelerate its progress.

[The preceding note was written in 1849. The last twenty years have manifested a terrible fixedness of resolve to own no rule save *expediency*—especially in determining religious and moral questions. The cowardice and baseness of such a course seems utterly unrecognised.]

and becomes not unfrequently the organ of their sentiments—we can easily see that a harvest of iniquity must under such circumstances arise and inherit judgment. "Ye have heard," said the Apostle, "that Antichrist shall come." His coming will be an act of judicial visitation on the part of God. The "brittle" nature of the authority held by the Ten Monarchs who at that time will subdivide the Roman Earth, will be one reason why they will peculiarly welcome the advent of one who will strengthen them by the greatness of his wondrous power. The attractiveness of his intellect and his unrivalled glory will be added motives; and besides, there will be " the strong delusion " judicially sent by God. " God shall send on them strong delusion that they should believe a lie." God as a judicial infliction from Himself, will " put it into their hearts to fulfil His will, and to agree and give their kingdom unto the beast, until the words of God shall be fulfilled."

The increasing development of popular-monarchic principles through the countries which fall within the scope of that which was once the Roman Empire, is a fact which none can question. The wars which convulsed Europe under Napoleon Buonaparte broke up the connexions which had for ages subsisted amongst the Western European Kingdoms, partly, as remains of old institutions in the ancient Roman Empire, and partly as the result of later feudal and ecclesiastical arrangements. The settlement at Vienna which succeeded these convulsions, attempted to remedy the disorganisation, and to re-unite the scattered kingdoms. But that re-organisation could not last, for it was on principles entirely opposed to the revealed intentions of God. He has revealed that the whole body of nations which once composed the Roman Empire, shall be brought into a condition in which they shall answer to the clay-iron feet and toes of the great Image. The arrangements at Vienna in 1815, went far to hinder this; and accordingly, they have been set aside. Change after change has occurred, all tending to resuscitate the countries of the Roman Empire, and to bring them into a divided unity—a unity based upon similarity of institutions, interests and laws.

The establishment of governments that are virtually or actually democratic-monarchies, in England, Belgium, France, Algeria, Portugal, Spain, Italy, Austria and Greece, and the favour with which the principles of the Western European nations are regarded at Constantinople, Egypt and Tunis, indicate the approach of the period when clay mingled with iron, will fitly represent the character of governmental power throughout all the Roman Empire. The final sub-division into the Ten Kingdoms, denoted by the ten *toes,* is an event which will almost immediately precede the end, and will probably be contemporaneous with the national establishment of unbelieving Israel in their own land. The rise of him to whom the Ten Kingdoms give their power soon follows, and then the end will come. The Image is smitten; and becomes as the chaff of the summer threshing floors. The stone that smites it becomes a great mountain, and fills the whole earth. Of this I do not at present speak.

I would only further observe, that the Image is represented as existing in its integrity at the very end. The gold (although the Empire it represents has so long ceased to be) remains until the last, and is not destroyed until the Image is finally smitten. This could not be if the image had symbolised the Empires territorially and physically, instead of governmentally. The physical existence of men and nations is limited. It may be very brief. But if they have laid the foundations of governmental systems—if they leave behind them laws and institutions which penetrate successive ages, and abidingly affect human life—then, when viewed in connection with this prolonged and lasting moral influence, they are regarded as if still existent. Nations physically extinct may yet morally live. The legislative and governmental systems of Chaldæa infused a certain character into those of Persia; Persia in her turn, acted upon Greece; and Greece upon Rome. Chaldæa, therefore, Persia and Greece, lived on in Rome; and Rome will live again in the ten last kingdoms. Institutions are not necessarily destroyed because they are transplanted into another sphere, or are administered by other hands. The institutions of Chaldæa, when brought beneath the sovereignty of Persia, were subjected to a new control. They were directed by power that was " silver," and no longer " golden " in its character. But they were not thereby annihilated. Arts, laws and institutions *necessary* for the maintenance of civil and social order survive, not unfrequently, the very worse convulsions, and pass even from despotic into democratic hands, unscathed. The governmental system, therefore, of the Gentile dynasty is to be regarded as a connected whole. Many of the institutions and laws first promulgated in Chaldæa are operating still in the Roman world, and therefore do not receive their doom till the hour comes for the institutions of all these kingdoms to be annihilated for ever. Empires that have long passed away, may, as to their institutions, yet live. It is true of individuals also. Influence is a solemn thing, for it survives the grave.*

It is on the same principle that we speak of the Apostles as continuing, and to continue until the end. (See Eph. iv.) They indeed rest from their labours. But they were the legislators of the Church: their institutions and their written laws remain—and in this sense they live. "Lo, I am with you alway, even to the end of the age." The Church has indeed long ceased to be what it once was. *While the Apostles lived* it stood forth as the pillar and ground of the truth. But it is this no longer. It has lost its

* The blow falls upon the *feet* of the image, because they are regarded as being in *active* existence at the close. The ten kingdoms inherit from the empires that have preceded them. The whole Gentile system of power is one fabric; and the later parts could not be what they are apart from those which are anterior.

unity, and lost its separateness. It is enthralled, enfeebled, scattered, chastened. Nevertheless the truth which it once sustained remains in the written record of the Word of God. Whilst the Gentile image stands, as still it does, strong in its lordly strength, revealed Truth will continue to be despised and outcast. But when the time comes (and it is fast drawing nigh) for the image to be smitten and ground to powder, and made like the chaff before the whirlwind of wrath, then Truth shall arise out of its prison-house and stand forth in its excellency and beauty. Christ shall sustain it, and it shall reign for ever. To which then shall we cleave? Which shall we serve? Shall we cling to the image that is to be smitten, and share its doom? Or shall we seek humbly to cast in our lot with truth during the hour of its militancy in suffering, and await in patient expectancy the hour of its glory?

CHAPTER III.

FORMATION OF THE TEN KINGDOMS; CHANGES TO BE EXPECTED.

BEFORE we proceed, it is desirable to determine, with as much precision as possible, the changes which these visions would lead us to anticipate in the countries enumerated in a preceding chapter as falling within the Roman Empire. There are some things that we can infer with certainty—others with a probability almost amounting to certainty.

For example, we cannot doubt that the same governmental principles will prevail in all the ten kingdoms when developed, because all the toes of the image were alike formed of clay and iron. There will be in all therefore, the same adulteration of power. Again, seeing that the legs and feet of the image were two, and that the Roman Empire has existed in eastern and western branches, we may expect that five kingdoms will be formed in an eastern, and five in a western division of the Roman Empire, even as the toes were five on either foot.

Moreover, the ten toes, though distinct one from the other, are nevertheless, parts of one image. The one body from which they spring, gives to them a kind of corporate connection. The same may be said of the horns in the seventh chapter. They spring from the head of one beast. Consequently, the Roman Empire when finally divided, will as distinctly present a form of compact, though divided unity, as when it existed in undivided integrity. There will be therefore, in a certain sense, a restoration of the Roman Empire.

Lastly, we learn that the possession of supreme power in the earth is as much the endowment of the kingdoms represented by the toes of the image, as of those represented by its higher parts. The title to hold an authority, which no other nations should be able successfully to dispute, is the endowment of all the kingdoms represented by the image and by the beasts. Accordingly, however great and threatening the power of such nations as Russia, yet it shall not *finally* be able to take supremacy from those nations which fall within the Roman Empire. It shall neither succeed in introducing among them its principles, nor in preventing them from spreading "clay-iron" principles among themselves, nor in frustrating their final connection as similarly constituted kingdoms of the Roman earth. It may seem perhaps hazardous to venture such a prediction at a moment when Russia, by its late conquests in Hungary, has acquired more than ordinary influence over the arrangements of Western Europe.* But nothing can frustrate the Word of God. The power of Russia may act on the kingdoms of the Roman

* The Crimean war had not taken place when this was written, viz., in 1849.

earth. It may assist in preventing the undue pre-
ponderance of the "clay," and in preserving the
proper proportion of "iron." It may give a counter
influence against democracy, where the influence of
democracy has been inordinately strong. Dread of
the power of Russia may prevent the nations of the
west from warring with, and devouring one another,
as otherwise they might. It may lead them at last
to a more united defence of their common principles,
and so tend to consolidate their final union. All
this Russia may be used to effect, or to assist in
effecting. But it will not take from the countries of
the Roman earth their appointed supremacy, nor
prevent the development of their "clay-iron" power.

A river of lengthened course makes many a bend.
Sometimes, it may seem to be retracing its backward
way to the source whence it began to flow. Yet it is
not really so. All the time it is steadily advancing
toward the appointed end. So is it in the stream
of things. The course is steady, and the end sure,
however appearances may vary. In the early part
of the present century men thought that the world
was hopelessly passing under the despotic rule of one
great Conqueror. There was little apparent probability then of "clay-iron" principles being spread.
And when Buonaparte fell, and the restored governments re-constituted themselves at Vienna, the "clay
and the iron" still seemed unlikely to prevail. Popular
principles were little favoured at Vienna, and had then
but little spread. Even England had but partially
received "the clay," for the laws which have since

so extended the elective power of the people, and made them the virtual legislators of the land, had not then been enacted. But since that time how marked the progress of these principles has been ! Portugal, Spain, France, Algeria, Belgium, Greece, Austria, and Italy have received, or are receiving them—some we know, as if by the shock of an electric stroke. The return of the Jews into Syria (whenever that is effected) will probably be the means of establishing these principles in one most important part of the Turkish Empire. Indeed, at Tunis,* and at Constantinople, western principles are already favoured.

The separation of Belgium (which *was* in the Roman Empire), from Holland, which *was not* in the Roman Empire; the independence of Greece, and its acquirement of a constitutional government; the introduction of European principles into the north of Africa, by means of France, have been events suddenly accomplished against obstacles apparently hopeless, and strikingly evidence the sovereign power of God.

The sudden overthrow of the despotism of Austria, effected almost in a day, was a remarkable event; but its detachment from Germany (for Germany, with the exception of Baden, Wurtemburg and Bavaria, was *not* in the Roman Empire) will be more remarkable still. Many a tie has bound Austria to Germany. The claim of the fatherland—the ties

* Tunis is interesting as occupying the place of ancient Carthage. It will probably be the most westerly *African* part of the eastern division of the Roman world.

of affinity—the actual possession of power (for it has long swayed Germany) may seem bonds not to be relaxed; yet they are evidently been loosened. Austria is falling into the system of the Roman nations, and Germany is retiring into a peculiar system of her own. Finally we may expect the governmental system of Austria to be contrasted with that of Germany, almost as decidedly as that of England is contrasted with Hanover. It is remarkable also that Baden, Wurtemberg, and Bavaria, which *were* in the Roman Empire, and will finally, no doubt, be separated from the German confederation, are at this moment only kept down by the strong hand of Prussian power.*

We must, not indeed, attempt to predict the *time*, nor the *mode* of these and similar changes. A river, as I have already said, makes many a bend. A few months ago,* democratic fury seemed to be let loose upon the nations. It caused each throne to tremble. The "iron" seemed likely to be driven from the earth, and supplanted by "the miry-clay." But the tumult has been stilled, the mad and evil power bridled; and now despotism seems in some places to threaten. But we need only wait. The Word of God is sure. Monarchs shall not destroy "the clay;" neither shall the people rid themselves of "the iron."

It is true, indeed, that we can speak with certainty only of the end. We cannot predict the steps that lead to that end, because the Scripture supplies no

* This, it must be remembered, was written in 1849.

detail during the time that Israel ceases to exist nationally in their own city. For example, we are unable to say whether the political and territorial changes which must finally be effected in Europe, are to be produced by a general European war, or by other agency. We cannot say whether Russia may, or may not, be allowed to seize some of the Eastern provinces of the Roman world. But this we *can* say, if Russia, or any other power, were to become the mistress of the globe, they could not ultimately prevent the development of the clay-iron principles of power in all the countries of the Roman earth, nor deprive those countries of their final united federal supremacy.*

The changes, therefore, that may be expected in those nations which fall within the Roman Empire, may be classified under three heads :

First, the introduction of popular monarchic principles into those countries which have not yet received them.

Secondly, an alteration in the present territorial divisions throughout the whole extent of the Roman Empire, so as to form ten kingdoms therein.

Thirdly, the dissolution of governmental union between countries, one of which *did* fall, and the

---

* Although, on such a subject, no one can speak with certainty, we may be permitted to express an opinion. My *opinion* certainly is, that the moral and physical characteristics which are finally to attach to the Roman nations, are too far advanced in development for Russia, or any other power, effectually to hinder. Every day seems to show that the nations are *fast* falling into their final collocation.

other of which did *not* fall within the Roman Empire.

As regards the first of these, comparatively little remains to be accomplished. The countries in which popular monarchic principles are not yet established, are Morocco, Egypt, Turkey, Luxembourg, Rhenish Prussia on the west of the Rhine, Baden, Bavaria, Wurtemberg, Switzerland, Italy,* and Bessarabia. How the extension of the military power of France, or the commercial influence of England, and the return of the Jews to Palestine would effect or facilitate these changes, we can easily imagine. In Austria the change was effected even without such influences.

As respects the alteration of territorial arrangement, much more remains to be accomplished. The legs of the image, corresponding with the division of the Roman Empire into Eastern and Western, would lead us to expect that five kingdoms will ultimately be found in the Eastern, and five in the Western part of the Roman dominions. The eighth chapter of Daniel proves it beyond a doubt, that Greece, Egypt, Syria, reaching to the Euphrates and beyond, and the rest of Turkey, both in Europe and Asia, will form four of the eastern kingdoms.† As these are the only four out of the ten of which the Scriptures speak specifically, we cannot with certainty name any other kingdoms; but there seems

* This was written in 1849. Italy has since attained her independence, and is constitutionalised.

† See remarks on eighth chapter.

little doubt that France, Spain, and England, will continue kingdoms to the end. We must, however, as to these specific points, wait the unfolding of events. The accomplishment of the final division will, probably, precede very little the closing hour of the dispensation.

With respect to the third point, that is to say, the dissolution of unions at present subsisting between countries, one of which *did* and the other did *not* fall within the Roman Empire, there are two cases to be considered.

First, there is the case in which a country *external* to the Roman Empire, *holds authority over* a country that fell *within* the Roman Empire. Such was the relation of Holland to Belgium. It has been dissolved. We may expect to see a similar dissolution in all cases where the German Confederation exercises authority, west of the Rhine, or south of the Danube. Baden, Wurtemberg, the chief part of Bavaria, and Rhenish Prussia, are the countries thus circumstanced.

We may therefore expect their separation from Germany, and annexation to some of the countries that fall within the Roman Empire. We may also expect that Russia will resign Bessarabia,* and that her influence will be supplanted in Moldavia and Wallachia; that is, if the full extent of the Roman Empire is to be taken as it existed in the time of Trajan, and of this there can be no reasonable doubt.†

* Bessarabia, since this was written, has been resigned.
† If the extent of the Roman Empire is to be taken as it

F

But secondly, there is a more difficult question in cases where a country external to the Roman Empire is *subjected* to a country within the Roman Empire. The countries thus circumstanced are, Ireland in its relation to England; the central part of Hungary, which lies between the Danube on the west, and the Vallum Romanum on the east; also Bohemia, and all German Austria north of the Danube, and the colonies of England, France, Spain, and Portugal.*

This question cannot, perhaps, be answered with

---

existed in the time of Augustus, or as it was when divided under the two last emperors, then Dacia is not to be included. In that case the influence of Russia in these countries may be expected to increase. Since the above was written, I have seen an account lately published of that part of Hungary included in the Ancient Dacia. I have given some extracts in the Appendix. It appears that Dacian or Roman Hungary stands in marked contrast with those parts of Hungary west of the Theiss, which were *not* in the Roman Empire, and that constitutional liberty and civilisation, rejected by the feudalism of the Magyars are likely, through the influence of Austria, to be successfully introduced into Dacian or Roman Hungary.

* The course of the Vallum Romanum is described in Chapter II. It turns from the Danube to Temesvar, some miles east of the Theiss. Gibbon makes the Theiss the boundary, but this is not quite correct, for the Vallum Romanum can still be traced. The words of Gibbon are; "if we except Bohemia, Moravia, and the northern skirts of Austria, and a part of Hungary between the Teyss and the Danube, all the dominions of the house of Austria were composed within the limits of the Roman Empire." We may expect these districts to be in some way separated from Austria.

the same confidence as the preceding ; but I think there can be little doubt that the union between such countries will be dissolved, if not fully, yet to the extent of distinct and independent legislatures being granted, as indeed is already done, in the leading colonies of England. The importance of such separate legislation may not, perhaps, be fully apprehended now; but when the hour arrives for a decree to go forth enforcing the worship of Antichrist, and the rejection of Christ and of God, the value of a separate legislature will be more distinctly felt.*

As regards Germany, seeing that with the exception above noticed, it does not fall within the Roman Empire, the prophecy of Daniel says nothing respecting it. Its relation, however, to the Ancient Roman Empire was peculiar. Although never subjugated so as to be incorporated into the Roman Empire, it was greatly influenced by the contiguity of the Roman provinces, as well as by the inroads of their armies, and was therefore reached by principles which never penetrated either into the Scandinavian or Scythian districts beyond. Thus the German nations became interposed, as a kind of middle ground, between the rudest and the most civilised portions of the earth. They were not unreached by Roman influence, and there was also no inconsiderable influence exercised by them upon Rome.

There seems every reason to believe that they will

---

* The separation of Hanover from England may be regarded as an example.

occupy a similar relation to the ten Roman nations at the close. Although not incorporated with those nations, but on the contrary forming themselves into greater distinctiveness therefrom, the Germans have nevertheless imbibed not a few of the social and political principles of the Roman nations, and form a strong and broad line of separation between these and the Russian tribes. It is not to be expected, I think, that strict constitutional government, that is, the true clay-iron form, will ever prevail in Germany. If it be not democracy (which I do not expect), it will be, probably, representative government so connected with monarchy, as for the crown to be something more than the mere servant of the representative body; but in the clay-iron governments of the Roman world it is otherwise. There, the head of the government, whether president or king, is in fact merely the executive. The legislative power is really vested elsewhere, that is to say, in the representative body, which body is chosen *bond fide* by the people. I do not expect that this strict form of popular monarchy or democracy will ever subsist in Germany, although there is, no doubt, hidden there a dark philosophic sceptical republicanism, dreaming about the supposed perfectibility of man, that augurs ill for the future.

All this, however, is mere opinion, for in speaking of Germany, I quit the prophecy of Daniel, which is our only certain guide. That prophecy does not teach us whether there may, or may not be, other parts of the earth in which clay-iron principles may prevail; nor does it make the mere possession of that form of government, the *distinctive* characteristic of the ten kingdoms. Their distinctive characteristic is, their possession of this form, in corporate or federal connection with each other, and as *parts of the image*, whereby they receive that peculiar endowment of supreme controlling power to which I have elsewhere referred.*

Before concluding this part of my subject, it may be right to state, that it is doubted by some whose opinions are of weight on these questions, whether the prophecy before us pertains to the *fullest* extent of the Roman Empire when enlarged by conquest, or to its more limited extent when first constituted under Augustus Cæsar.

If we decide the question by the second chapter, the answer would, I suppose, be, that all countries in which the *iron* character of power was governmentally *established* by Rome—in other words, all districts that were formally *incorporated into* the Roman Empire during the period that its power was symbolised by iron, must be regarded as coming under the symbols used in that vision. Britain and other districts conquered subsequently to the time of Augustus were thus incorporated into the empire as provinces.

* I should expect the German tribes, especially those which the Romans overran, to be brought into very distinct contrast with the Scandinavian countries. The Romans penetrated as far as the Eyder, which divides Holstein from Schleswig.

The same answer appears to be supplied by the seventh chapter. The Roman Empire is there represented by a monster allowed to tread down and break in pieces certain nations of the earth. The question, therefore, seems to be, What nations were so brought under its power, as for their institutions and laws to be thoroughly subjected to its will? Such nations may fairly be regarded as composing the kingdom denoted by that monster, and it is said, that "*out of*"* that kingdom the ten kingdoms are to arise. If its "kingdom" were to be limited to that which it happened to possess at the very first moment of its existence, and if none of its subsequent conquests, however real, were to be included, we might certainly expect that a restriction so important would be clearly laid down in the Scripture.

No such restriction, however, is found. On the contrary, analogy of interpretation seems to require that the wider scope should be taken. For example, much more was included under the symbol of " the

* The expression "out of," which is very distinct in the original, is important, because it shows that no conquests of the ten kingdoms are regarded as forming part of the corpus of the Roman Empire. It is regarded as existing in its integrity first, and they are formed "out of it." It is on the *body* of the Beast that the destructive judgment called down by Antichrist's blasphemies is said to fall. "I beheld then, because of the voice of the great words which the horn spake: I beheld, even till the beast was slain, and *his body destroyed, and given to the burning flame.*" Dan. vii. 11.

bear," than was included under it when it first began to denote the Empire of Persia, for Egypt and various other places were annexed to that empire some time after its first formation. So also in the case of the leopard with four heads. It included under it much more than belonged to the Empire of Alexander when first represented by that symbol; and consequently, if we had been directed to divide the dominions of the bear, or of the leopard into ten parts, we must have divided more than was denoted by them at the first moment when they began to symbolise their respective empires. Why should we apply a different rule to the fourth or Roman beast?

One reason given for rejecting these later conquests as parts of the Roman Empire is, that some of them were voluntarily resigned. There would have been some force in this argument if, after these countries had been relinquished, the rest of the empire had retained its integrity until it passed as an undivided whole into the hands by which it is to be divided into its ten final parts. The history of such a whole, would in that case, stand in very marked contrast with that of the parts that had dropped off. This, however, was not the case. The Roman Empire has gradually been dissolved. The abandonment therefore of some of its provinces (which moreover was not really voluntary, but constrained by circumstances), was only the commencement of a gradual process of decomposition. How then can any argument be founded on a mere difference in the *mode* of dissolution? If· the *mode* of dissolution had been made thus *essential* to the exposition of the prophecy, it certainly would have been referred to in the Scripture; whereas it is passed over in entire silence.

Moreover, if we were to regard *relinquished* parts of the Empire, as if they had *not* been parts of the Empire, it would be difficult to draw any contrast between countries such as Parthia and Germany, which were merely overrun by Roman armies, but were never incorporated as Roman provinces, and countries which *were* incorporated, and of which some, like Britain, have abidingly received the impress of Roman institutions and laws.

Time, however, will make manifest this, and every similar point of detail. We shall probably soon see whether the clay-iron principles of government will, or will not spread throughout Dacia, or whether they will be strictly confined to the southern shores of the Danube. It will be interesting therefore to watch the progress of events in these countries, in the Euphratean districts, and in England. If Dacia is *not* to be included in the Roman Empire, it will probably be annexed to Russia, or become separated from Turkey in some other way. On the other hand, if it be included in the Roman Empire, we may expect Russian influence to diminish even in Bessarabia.*

There is yet one other subject on which it is

* Since this was written, Bessarabia has been resigned by Russia.

necessary to dwell a little before I conclude this section, viz., the division of the Roman Empire into eastern and western branches.

The Roman Empire was not the first of the four empires represented by a duplicate symbol. The arms also of the image were two, symbolising the empire of the Medes and Persians. But although the Medes were one nation, and the Persians another, yet they were combined in strict legislative union. They never acted but as one people. This is signified in the seventh chapter, where it is said of the bear which represents the Medo-Persian Empire, that it raised itself up " for one dominion,"* being herein contrasted with the leopard, which was destined for a fourfold dominion, and with the Roman beast whose dominion is finally to be tenfold. Regions, therefore, or nations, may be diverse from each other, and yet so combined as for their dominion to be one. This was the case in the empire of the Medes and Persians. Was it at first otherwise with Rome?

The empire of Rome, at the very first moment of its formation under Augustus Cæsar combined two very distinct portions of the earth—portions far

---

* In order to adopt "side" as the translation in Dan. vii. 5, it is necessary to suppose that שְׁטַר is put for שְׂטַר and that to be identical with סְטַר. But if we take the word as it is, it simply means "dominion." The participle of שְׂטַר is continually used in the Old Testament, and is always translated either "officer," "ruler," or "overseer." See Ex. v. 6, 2 Chrou. xxvi. 11.

more contrasted with each other than Persia was
with Media. Towards the east, Rome had wrested
from Carthage and from the successors of Alexander,
the fairest and the most civilised countries of the
earth. What could be more contrasted than the
great and ancient countries of the east over which
Greece had spread her language and her institutions,
and the half-savage districts which Rome acquired
in Western Africa, Spain, Gaul, and Britain? If
we mark out the countries in which, before they
were conquered by Rome, eastern civilisation had
effectually spread, we find a branch of the Roman
Empire utterly different from that which gradually
and slowly received civilisation through *Latin* institutions and the *Latin* tongue. This is to be
regarded as the reason why the Roman Empire is
symbolised as twofold, rather than because of its
actual division at a late period of its existence into
eastern and western governments, although, indeed,
the territorial division under the emperors is not
very different from that which would be suggested
by a regard to the extent of Greek or eastern
civilisation.

The formal division of the Roman Empire took
place under Valentinian and Valens. " In the castle
or palace of Mediana, they executed the solemn and
final division of the Roman Empire. Valentinian
bestowed on his brother (Valens) the rich prefecture
of the East from the Lower Danube to the confines of Persia, while he reserved for his immediate
government the warlike prefectures of Illyricum,

Italy, and Gaul; from the extremity of Greece to the Caledonian rampart, and from the rampart of Caledonia to the foot of Mount Atlas." *Gibbon*, chap. xxv.*

* The division under the two last Emperors Honorius and Arcadius, differed slightly from this. Arcadius had Thrace, Asia Minor, Syria, and Egypt, from the Lower Danube to the confines of Persia and Ethiopia. His younger brother Honorius assumed in the eleventh year of his age, the nominal government of Italy, Africa, Gaul, Spain and Britain; and the troops which guarded the frontiers of his kingdom were opposed on one side to the Caledonians, and on the other to the Moors. The great and martial prefecture of Illyricum was divided between the two princes; the defence and possession of the provinces of Noricum, Pannonia, and Dalmatia still belonged to the Western Empire; but the two large dioceses of Dacia (not Trajan's province) and Macedonia, which Gratian had entrusted to the valour of Theodosius, were for ever united to the Empire of the East. The boundary in Europe was not very different from the line that now separates the Germans and the Turks, and the respective advantages of territory, riches, populousness, and military strength, were fairly balanced and compensated in this final and permanent division of the Roman Empire. *Gibbon*, chap. xxix.

This arrangement, however, was altered a short time after, in A.D. 425, under Valentinian III., when the Western Illyricum was detached from the Italian dominions, and yielded to the throne of Constantinople. Dalmatia, Pannonia, and Noricum were thus added to the Eastern Empire, which thus possessed the greater part of the Austrian dominions. *See Gibbon*, chap. xxxiii.

[The Dacia mentioned in the above passage was not Trajan's Dacia, but a part of Servia—a division of the ancient Mœsia. When Aurelian relinquished Dacia, he transferred the Roman

This division does not very materially differ from that we should adopt, if we place in the eastern divi-

---

colonists to this part of Mœsia, which he called Nova Dacia, or Dacia Aureliana.]

The continual fluctuation in these territorial arrangements precludes our regarding it as an accurate guide. I therefore prefer being guided by the other principle—that of Greek possession—as determining the Eastern Branch. Moreover, since the vision of the Image represents the Empire as duplicate from its commencement, it seems scarcely possible to suppose this to be fulfilled in a late territorial division.

It is remarkable that when, under Justinian, in consequence of the victories of Belisarius, the Eastern Empire resumed for a little its integrity and strength, it spread from Illyricum in Europe, and Carthage in Africa, to the confines of Persia. These are just the limits to which we should be guided by the principle to which I have referred. Amida and Edessa, beyond the Euphrates, and other subordinate towns of Mesopotamia were fortified by Justinian. He also extended a series of fortifications from Belgrade (on the frontier of Austria) to the Black Sea, and from the conflux of the Saave to the mouths of the Danube.

The southern part of Italy, which was anciently called Magna Grecia, and was filled with Greek cities, of which Naples is one, was considered an adjunct of the Eastern Empire. The Eastern Emperor at Constantinople, till a very late period, claimed possession of Naples and the southern part of Italy. Although the Lombards held the greater part for 320 years, and had been confirmed in their possession by Charlemagne, yet in A.D. 891, Leo, the Greek emperor, succeeded in wresting it from them ; and it was not until 1157 the Greek Emperor Emmanuel acknowledged William the Norman as king. Time only will show whether Naples is to be connected with the Eastern or Western branch of the Roman Empire.

sion of the Roman Empire these countries into which civilisation had extended before they were incorporated with Rome. The Macedonian princes, as early as Philip and Alexander, claimed sovereignty over the provinces between Macedon, Thrace, and the Danube. "The Adriatic Sea and the Danube appear to have been the boundaries of Philip's empire in Illyria and Thrace." *Heeren*, p. 211. Whether therefore, we take the actual territorial division by the emperors, or follow the more satisfactory guidance of Greek civilisation as determining the extent of the eastern and western branches of the Roman Empire, the difference will not be material. In Africa, I feel little doubt, that the districts of Cyrene and Carthage [Tunis], in which civilisation was so early established by the Greeks and Phœnicians, will form the frontier countries of the eastern division. This will establish the boundary of the Turkish Empire as the limit in Africa also, between the east and the west. It would give Tunis, Tripoli, Barca, and Egypt, to the eastern division, and would make Algeria the first province of the western. Tunis, which answers to the ancient Carthaginia, would in connection with Tripoli, and Barca [ancient Cyrenaica] form one of the five divisions of the eastern part of the Roman Empire. When we consider the eighth chapter, we shall see that we can with much certainty affirm, that four out of the five are formed by Egypt, Greece, Syria, and the remaining part of Turkey.

In the long period of transition from the "*iron*"

of the ancient Roman Empire, to the "*clay-iron*" of the ten final kingdoms—a period not yet terminated —many things have occurred, which show that God has not forgotten to watch over the accomplishment of the vision of the Image. Although barbarians on every side inundated and overwhelmed the ancient empire, yet the home of governmental power has always been somewhere in the Roman earth. The Germans who established an empire in the west, and the Turks who became masters in the east, alike placed the seats of their authority within the Roman empire.

Nor has the distinction between the Eastern and Western branches been ever obliterated. In the days of Justinian and his great general Belisarius, the integrity of the Eastern part of the Roman Empire was so wonderfully restored, that some persons fancied it to be the second Beast of the Apocalypse. The crusades were in part undertaken to uphold, and for a time did uphold, the Eastern empire; and it was not until the year A.D. 1453 that the successors of Constantine finally fell before the Turk. Even then the effect was to preserve rather than to destroy the integrity of the Eastern branch. We may form a tolerably correct notion of what the extent of the eastern branch of the Roman Empire was, and is to be, by marking the limits of the Turkish dominions before Greece and Egypt were separated therefrom.

It is also worthy of notice, that long after the victorious barbarians had usurped the power of the

West, they continued to own the supremacy of the Eastern empire, and sought confirmation of their authority from it. The remarkable instance of Odoacer has been already noticed.* Even the Anglo-Saxon kings sought recognition from Constantinople, and are styled "Βασιλευς" on their coins.†

The fall of the Roman dynasty at Constantinople gave occasion to a more distinct development of western power. The ancient imperial name still continued to be borne by the chiefs of the German empire; and the names "Holy Roman Empire," and "King of the Romans" have descended to our own days.

But there has also been another difference in the dealing of the divine hand which has tended to preserve a marked distinction between the Eastern and

* *See* note to Chap I., p. 16.

† *See* Sir F. Palgrave's Anglo-Saxon Commonwealth. This seems another link between England and the Roman Empire. The notion of imperial appointment to association in the Empire was long maintained in the West. In 1338 the Emperor Lewis the Bavarian, met Edward III. of England, and constituted him *Imperial Vicar* of all countries on the left side of the Rhine. Edward III. used this authority with some effect against France. And this was not very soon laid aside. Queen Elizabeth at her coronation is said to have been crowned three times: 1st, the Queen of England; 2nd, of Ireland; 3rd, Sovereign and Lady Empress of all nations and countries from the islands Orcades, to the mountains Pyrenees. She helped the Huguenots in virtue of the Imperial authority.

Western divisions of the Roman Empire. The East was the early home of civilisation, and the place where the light of truth peculiarly shone; but these privileges were abused, and iniquity abounded. On this judicial visitation came. Desolation has fallen upon almost every ancient city of the East, from Babylon to Jerusalem, Egypt, north-eastern Africa, and Greece. The ruin of these countries has been so complete, that many have applied to the apostasy of Mahomedanism and the subsequent desolations, the prophecies respecting Antichrist, and the judgments of the final hour. Doubtless these things are to be regarded as premonitory. They speak in solemn warning to these Western kingdoms, which were so much later reached by civilisation and by truth, and establish another marked contrast between the East and the West. The early course of civilisation does not more distinctly define the Eastern branch of the Roman Empire, than do the later footsteps of desolation and apostasy.

While the East was thus sinking under judgment, the nations of the West were fast arising into power, and giving birth to new institutions. The principles of representative government were early found in the feudal nations, and thus new vigour was infused into the Roman earth, and those governmental principles introduced, whose full development is so especially to characterise the last condition of the Roman nations. The same century which saw the fall of the Roman Empire in the East, was marked in the West by events* which have in results entirely altered the aspect of human things, and made the Western kingdoms of the Roman world the depositories of a power whose influence has already reached, and will finally resuscitate, the fallen countries of the East.

Although the kingdoms of the West have never received any blow, resembling in severity that which has prostrated the countries of the East, yet, with only one exception, they have all been heavily chastened. The abominations of popery, entailing their own punishment, generated in Western Europe a wide-spread infidelity, of which the terrors of the French Revolution of 1792, and the desolating wars that followed, were the consequences—consequences which have not, even yet, ceased to operate. England alone escaped, and has for ages pursued a steady course of almost uninterrupted prosperity. Time was, when both its government and its people estimated in a measure this mercy, and were sensible of the privilege of its being a Protestant country. It recognised the Bible once as the authoritative. and the alone authoritative, standard of Truth; but it is otherwise now.

* These events were:
In A.D. 1440, the invention of printing.
In A.D. 1491, the expulsion of the Moors from Spain.
In A.D. 1492, the discovery of South America.
In A.D. 1497, India reached by the Cape of Good Hope.
n A.D. 1499, North America discovered by Cabet.
In A.D. 1453, the Eastern Empire ended, by the capture of Constantinople by the Turks.

G

At present this nation is holding a position of more effective influence than any other country in the earth. Its principles are fixed and determined, and it is earnest in propagating them. The governmental principles that it seeks to spread are those of popular monarchy. The pillar of its political and social system is commerce and commercial wealth. Its relation to the false religions of the earth is, that it *fosters* as well as protects all. It seeks to accommodate itself to influential institutions, rather than to supplant them by truth. These principles are, doubtless, well adapted to the character of the latter day, and are most sure to prosper.

England is at this moment seeking to convene to her metropolis an assembly of all nations, that they might there exhibit the riches of the earth, and the productions of their industrial skill. She well knows that no display of Imperial or Ecclesiastical pomp, no array of military greatness, could possess an influence equal to that which such an assembly represents: and *this* is the influence she seeks to wield. Such influence *appears* to be neutral in its character; but it is not really so. It can neither be retained, nor used, except by sanctioning, and, not unfrequently, employing the very systems which have sunk the world in superstition and idolatry. What then is more to be dreaded than a system *seemingly* neutral, which really sustains and gives effect to all Satan's ancient instruments of deception ? The final result of this influence, and what will be constructed under it, may be seen in the seventeenth and eighteenth chapters of Revelation.*

It is an affecting thought that England, so highly favoured as she has been, is using her advantages in nurturing the very principles out of which the last systematised form of human evil is to be formed. No city *at present* in the earth corresponds so nearly as London to the descriptions of the eighteenth of Revelation; no scene which the earth has ever yet beheld answers so nearly the twenty-seventh and twenty-eighth chapters of Ezekiel as that which is about to be presented in that city.† The energy

* It is not a mere question of displaying the inventions of men, or the riches of the earth. *That*, under certain circumstances, might be innocent enough. The question is, whether the commercial energy, of which such an assembly is the result, is not spoken of in Scripture as that which is to be the pillar of the world's last evil greatness. For further remarks on the character of this rising commercial system, see observations on the Ephah and the woman seated therein, in "Second series of Aids to Prophetic Enquiry;" also, "Thoughts on the Apocalypse," chap. xvii. and xviii.

† The object of the central part of Ezekiel appears to be this: to show *what* kind of power Israel finally seeks unto for shelter, now their iniquities have grieved away the cherubim power of God, under the shadow of which they once rested. The power which they select as their guardian is that which I have above described, viz., the energy that searches out and develops all the resources of earth—a power by and by to be again connected with Tyre, which was its ancient seat. Thus Tyre, as the representative of this energy, is described as occupying God's mountain—*i.e.* the Divine place of authority towards Israel, and being as Israel's oracle and cherub—

which visits every region, and develops and collects
all the riches of the earth, must be guided by some
definite principles; and if they are not the principles of Christ, they must be the principles of Satan.
England, in pursuing her favourite plans, is ever
ready, when *expediency* requires it, to smile on falsehood, or to frown on truth. Human fraternity is
everything in her sight, and she is beginning to
spurn at all that seems to interfere with the hoped-
for unity of men as men. She deems her latitudinarian commercial system to be the best remedy for
the convulsions of the nations; and she hopes, not
without reason, to force rival nations into fraternisation thereby, and to consolidate social and political institutions without unduly fettering the energies of men; but in the meanwhile truth is forgotten
or contemned. The legislation, as well as the influential speaking and writing of the day, afford
evidence of this, too plain to be gainsayed.

Would to God it were otherwise, and that these
sins were repented of and abjured ! But at present

---

the true cherubic power having been grieved away. There is
bitter irony in the expression, " I have set thee so." God has
appointed that this glorious but evil power should be the
cherub of Israel for a season.

The power now arising around us is of the same character
as that which Israel will make its " cherub" or guardian,
although, *as yet*, it only *exists* in embryo.

The several principles connected with this great commercial system are, as yet, comparatively undeveloped. The
Ephah is seen long before the woman or moral system hidden
therein is made manifest.

the moral features of England, no less than her geographical connection with the Roman World, mark her as one of those kingdoms that are to give their strength and power unto the Beast, and to engage in the last conflict against the King of Kings.

The following observations of Gibbon, respecting the difference that always subsisted between the Greek and Latin provinces of the Roman Empire, are of interest as bearing on the question of division :—

" So sensible were the Romans of the influence of language over national manners, that it was their most serious care to extend with the progress of their arms the use of the Latin tongue. The ancient dialects of Italy, the Sabine, the Etruscan, and the Venetian, sunk into oblivion; but in the provinces, the East was less docile than the West to the voice of its victorious preceptors. This obvious difference marked the two portions of the empire with a distinction of colours, which, though it was in some degree concealed during the meridian splendour of prosperity, became gradually more visible as the shades of night descended upon the Roman World. The Western countries were civilised by the same hands which subdued them. As soon as the barbarians were reconciled to obedience, their minds were opened to any new impressions of knowledge and politeness. The language of Virgil and Cicero, though with some inevitable mixture of corruption, was so universally adopted in Africa, Spain, Gaul, Britain, and Pannonia, that the faint traces of the Punic or Celtic idioms were preserved only in the mountains, or among the peasants. Education and study insensibly inspired the natives of those countries with the sentiments of Romans; and Italy gave fashions as well as laws to her Latin provincials. They solicited with more ardour, and obtained with more facility, the freedom and honours of the state, supported the national dignity in letters and in arms, and at length, in the person of Trajan, produced an emperor whom the Scipios would not have disowned for their countryman. The situation of the Greeks was very different from that of the barbarians. The former had been long since civilised and corrupted. They had too much taste to relinquish their language, too much vanity to adopt any foreign institutions. Still preserving the prejudices after they had lost the virtues of their ancestors, they affected to despise the unpolished manners of the Roman conquerors, whilst they were compelled to respect their superior wisdom and power. Nor was the influence of the Grecian language and sentiments confined to the narrow limits of that once celebrated country. Their empire, by the progress of colonies and conquest, had been diffused from the Hadriatic to the Euphrates and the Nile. Asia was covered with Greek cities, and the long reign of the Macedonian kings had introduced a silent revolution into Syria and Egypt. In their pompous courts those princes united the elegance of Athens with the luxury of the East, and the example of the court was imitated at an humble distance by the higher ranks of their subjects. Such was the general division of the Roman Empire into the Latin and Greek languages."

Whether, therefore, we take as our guide the provinces conquered by Rome from the successors of Alexander; or the formal division of the Empire under the Emperors; or the re-constitution of the Eastern branch under Justinian; or the extent of Turkish dominion; or the extent of modern desolation; we are brought pretty nearly to the same result.

It is obvious, too, that when the institutions and civilisation of the West shall have been introduced into, and shall have revived the East, there will be sufficient circumstantial differences to mark a very decided contrast between the Greek and Latin branches of the Roman Empire.

CHAPTER IV.

THE VISION OF THE EPHAH OF ZECHARIAH V., CONSIDERED IN RELATION TO THE PRINCIPLES OF MODERN LEGISLATION.*

HOMO SUM, NIHIL HUMANI A ME ALIENUM PUTO†— a sentiment long since promulgated by a Roman poet, has, from that moment to the present, maintained its hold upon the heart of man, and received the approbation of successive ages. It embodies, indeed, a great truth—a truth recognised and acted on by God Himself—one to which the conscience, as well as the affections of every human bosom responds. Philanthropy—real philanthropy is one of the great principles of God. The proof is, the Incarnation and the Cross.

And as Christianity is not intended to stand aloof

* This paper was written in 1851, and published as a tract, entitled, "What is the Ephah of Zechariah V.? or, the Exhibition of 1851 considered in relation to the principles of Modern Legislation." As the subjects treated of in this tract are of lasting importance, and as it illustrates much that has been said in the preceding chapter, I have thought it best to revise and introduce it here. It has gone through three editions, and is now nearly out of print.

† "I am a man—nothing that concerns man do I deem foreign to myself."

in heartless apathy, unmoved by that which is
affecting the human family around, so the spon-
taneous impulse of the rightly-ordered Christian
heart is to seek out, not that which it must differ
from and condemn, but that which it can join with,
sanction, and approve. One of the characteristics
of a heavenly and perfected condition of being will
be, that the interests and affections of the heart
will unrestrictedly flow out to, and delight in, every
thing. There will be no need of restraint where
everything is holy; no need of testimony *against*
any thing, where everything is worthy of being,
what it will be—everlastingly blessed. Antagonism
may be a duty, but in itself it affords no joy to the
Christian heart. Apart from the painful personal
consequences which it may involve, it is contrary to
the law of our new nature, which desires fellowship
—not conflict: nor could any thing but the plain
requirements of Truth reconcile us to the path of
perpetual strife and contention, where we seem to
employ ourselves in finding fault with every thing,
and earn for ourselves the character of a morose
and fanatical misanthropy.

Would to God that we could truthfully say, that
the tide of human things was flowing on in a course
of real prosperity and blessing ! It is a happy
thing to share in the interests of others, and to unite
one's activities with theirs. The very employment
of our energies is a pleasure, when the course is
right, and the end happy. It is painful, therefore—
very painful, in observing the development of civi-

lisation and social progress in which all are exulting, to be obliged to condemn, and to say that this progress is connected with certain moral principles which will finally bring it under judicial visitation from the hand of God.

Few will question that the great Industrial gathering which is about to take place in the metropolis of this country marks an era in human progress. There have been periods when assembled armies indicated the character of the power which chiefly swayed the nations. There have been other periods when assembled ecclesiastics have represented the dominant influence of the age. But such periods have passed away. If Russia were now to assemble her soldiers, or Rome her priests, neither would present a power so really potent—so really being, and about to be, the mainspring of the world's energies, as that assemblage which England has summoned to her shores. Accordingly, philanthropists are speaking of it as the indication of a power which is to regenerate the world; and even Christians are hailing it as the means by which the nations are to be knit together in amity and peace, and the millennial predictions of the Prophets fulfilled.

But surely the first thought that should be suggested to a Christian heart by such an assemblage, is, that it is *of the world :* and that which is of the world cannot be " of the Father." Whether it be a military, or an ecclesiastical, or a commercial spectacle that assembles men together, are not those so assembled essentially the world? Are not their habits of thought, and their practices such, that Christ's true principles, and doctrines, and laws, find no place among them? If it be so, how can a Christian view such an assemblage with complacency? How can he expect that it should result in overspreading the earth with Christ's truth, and with Christ's blessings?

Moreover, we have to remember that this is to be an assemblage marked by no ordinary characteristics. Never, since men first sought universal confederation on the plains of Shinar, when God interfered, and scattered them over the face of the earth—never since that hour has an assemblage been convened, so much resembling, in *some* of its features, that early gathering on the plains of Babel. It is true, indeed, that there is at present no intention of local centralisation; but a thought of moral centralisation *is* connected with this design. The Sun of human prosperity—the centre around which each part of the vast human system is to revolve—is supposed to be found in Commerce; and it is hoped that this coming gathering will aid the advance of commerce until it shall unquestionably become the paramount influence of the day. Moreover, one great moral feature that marked the assemblage at Babel was, a desire to make themselves illustrious and mighty, apart from God. This feature will not be wanting in the coming gathering of nations, for attainment of such greatness is the very idol of the hour.

As regards responsibility, the responsibility which

attached to those who assembled at Babel was but as dust in the balance, compared with that which rests upon the nations who will now meet in England. When men assembled at Babel, and there attempted the union of their race, experience had not yet taught her lessons. Israel had not yet received their light; Prophets and Apostles had not spoken; Christ had not taught; Christianity had not been prostituted; nor Infidelity come forth, like a viper nourished in the bosom of religious corruption. But now, all these things *have* been, and we have to do with their results. The Jew will come, hardened in pharisaic rejection of Christ, or else tutored in the school of neologian latitudinarianism; the Eastern ecclesiastic will come, the type of the early corruption of Christian Truth, and the witness of its present degradation; the Mahomedan will come, the representative of those who, mocking with bitter scorn the corruptions both of Judaism and Christianity, rushed with infidel fury upon both, and stamped out, as it were, the scattered and dying embers of Truth that lay smouldering in the midst of the fallen Churches; the Romanist will be there, as one who, by means of pretended Christianity, has led nations delivered from old idolatries back to idolatry again; Atheism, Deism, and all the various forms of Infidelity, will be there: Heathenism will be there. Such will be the component parts of that vast multitude, which Commerce and Civilisation are to "touch with their magic wand;" and finally binding them together in the bonds of philanthropic brotherhood, are to make them great, prosperous, and happy. But will such brotherhood and such greatness be of God?

That England should be the spot chosen for such a development marks it with a fearful pre-eminence. England is, necessarily, a country interesting to all men, for it has filled no ordinary place in the world's history. But the reason why it peculiarly interests those who search the Scripture, is, not because it is a great nation merely, but because it belongs to a certain circle of the earth respecting which God has been pleased to prophesy very definitely in His word. Two thousand five hundred years ago, when He first began to punish Jerusalem by subjecting it to the proud power of the Gentiles, He empowered the Prophet Daniel to give the prophetic history of certain Empires amongst whom civilisation and power were to find their centre and their home, throughout the long period of Jerusalem's punishment. Chaldæa, Persia, Greece, following each other in quick succession, transmitted their empire to Rome, and the extent of the dominions of Rome mark the limits of what is called by writers on prophecy—the Prophetic Earth. This portion of the earth has for ages been known, both in the East and in the West, as *H OIKOTMENH*—ORBIS TERRARUM. The countries which fall within its limits will be the peculiar seat of the world's energies and greatness in the latter day—and England is one of those countries.

I need scarcely say, that to give the history of

Chaldæa, Persia, Greece, and the Roman nations, is virtually to give the history of the world. Whatever enterprises have been undertaken, whatever inventions made, or colonisations effected, they have either emanated from these nations as their centre, or, if in any case the place of origin has been external to their limits, these countries have soon succeeded in attracting towards themselves the results. The effects of civilisation have ever gravitated, as it were, towards the Roman nations as their centre. God has so appointed that it should be.

Cain (in whose family the inventions of civilisation first appeared), and then Babel, Chaldæa, Greece, Rome, are names which mark darkly the moral character of human civilisation in this fallen earth. It has never moved as yet under the control of God. The giant idols which are now disinterred in Nineveh, the graves that are opened in Egypt, the fallen temples of Greece, and the ruined porticoes of Rome, all bear witness that the greatness of each of these nations has been directed against God. They all lifted themselves up against God, and He has withered them all. They have sunk beneath the blow of righteous retribution.

Civilisation, having its birth-place in the East, in the regions which surround the Euphrates, moved, as Daniel had foretold, with steady progress towards the West. Greece became the place of its meridian splendour. From Greece it was transferred to Rome, and through Rome reached the limits of Europe in the West. But judgment followed in its track. Chaldæa, Asia Minor, Egypt, Greece, and at last Rome, were smitten; and only a few centuries ago it seemed as if civilisation and power were likely to be driven from their ancient seats for ever, to find perhaps in another hemisphere a new sphere for their centralisation and development.

But God has said that it should not be so. He has said that the Roman nations shall to the end continue to be the centre of influence and controlling power in the earth;—by the end, I mean the period when He will forgive Jerusalem, and restore her to supremacy again. Accordingly, after the fierce inroad of the Turks had overspread with ruin more than two-thirds of the Empire of the Cæsars, and when, by other influences, even Rome herself was reduced to a settlement of cowherds—grass growing in her palaces, and oxen pastured in her streets,*—

* The following are the words of Ranke, vol. iii. p. 480 :—
During the absence of the Popes in Avignon, the Rome of the middle ages had sunk into equal decay with that ancient Rome which had so long lain in ruins. When Eugenius IV. returned to Rome in the year 1443, it was become a city of herdsmen; its inhabitants were not distinguishable from the peasants of the neighbouring country. The hills had long been abandoned, and the only part inhabited was the plain along the windings of the Tiber; there was no pavement in the narrow streets, and these were rendered yet darker by the balconies and buttresses which propped one house against another: the cattle wandered about as in a village. From San Silvestro to the Porta del Popolo, all was garden and marsh, the haunt of flocks of wild ducks. The very memory of antiquities seemed almost effaced; the Capitol was become the Goats' Hill, the Forum Romanum the Cows' Field, the

at that moment of dominant desolation, the Western corners of the Roman world, and, more especially, England, were permitted to become the rallying point of civilisation; the place where it has not only recovered its exhausted energies, but learned also to break ancient shackles, as well as to develop new powers.

Ecclesiastical tyranny had succeeded in binding many a fetter upon the hand of those wild nations that had broken in upon, and destroyed, the ancient Roman Empire. Priestcraft and degrading super-stitions had, for the most part, effectually crippled all mental energy; and if any developed itself it was doomed, as in the case of Galileo, to the dungeon and to death. But in England, during the reign of Henry the Eighth, ecclesiastical power, which under Wolsey displayed one great expiring blaze of bright-ness, suddenly sank. With Wolsey, ecclesiastical supremacy in England finally fell. Although Rome has not yet relinquished the hope of maintaining or restoring it in various countries, yet it may be safely said, that ever since the fall of Wolsey, principles have been in steady operation, chiefly through the instrumentality of England, which will finally de-prive both Popery, and every other ecclesiastical system within the Roman World, not indeed of influence, but of *supremacy*. All those parts of Scripture which describe the future history of the

strangest legends were associated with the few remaining monuments. The Church of St. Peter was in danger of falling down."

Roman Kingdoms during the coming period of their revived, but unsanctified glory, distinctly speak of the secular power as supreme, and of the ecclesiastical as subordinate. In England it has long been so; and it is to this that England owes, in no slight degree, her present position of influence and strength.

That, however, which is *most* of all distinctive in the present condition of England, is her Commercial system. Commerce, or the wealth and influence thence arising, has become the mainspring of England's energies—the chief bulwark of her social institutions—the pillar of her government. When ecclesiastical power fell, and the feudal aristocracy became gradually enfeebled; and when the steady advance of the people seemed to make democracy (perhaps revolutionary democracy) the sure end of the social movement, there was gradually being formed, in this country, a new aristocracy, more potent than any, whether ecclesiastic or hereditary, that had preceded—the aristocracy of wealth. The expressions, commercial interest; manufacturing interest; moneyed interest; Indian interest; and the like, suggest sufficiently intelligible ideas to English minds. The ramifications of these interests are so various and so extended, that the mass of society is effectually reached and controlled by their influence; and thus a power has been consolidated, the like to which has never before existed. The tranquillity with which England passed through the late period of European convulsion in 1848 is an

H

evidence of the strength of this power. The State
and its institutions consigned themselves to its protection, and rested quietly under its shield. In
France no such consolidated power exists, and
France has been shaken to her foundations.

In England this power is learning to work in
harmony with the State. Indeed, the State has
virtually become its organ. Plutocracy is a com-
prehensive, not an exclusive system. Its elasticity
is great. It can adapt itself to the changing circumstances of the hour, and, receiving within its
circle both the aristocrat and the democrat, it pro-
vides a place of honour and influence for both. In
its relation to ancient systems it seeks, not to annihilate, but rather to modify, adapt, harmonise, and
employ. It possesses, therefore, not only its own
intrinsic weight, but is acquiring also all the weight
which governmental authority can give. No other
interest, whether royal or ecclesiastic, aristocratic
or popular, is allowed to throw any effectual impedi-
ment in its course. Virtually, its will is paramount.
The appropriate device of England would not be,
either the crown or the mitre; the coronet or the
sword, but some emblem of Commerce. An "Ephah"
should be emblazoned on her banners. Our government is a Commercial government, not because
England happens to be a mercantile country, but
because manufacturing and trading interests supremely sway her councils, and all other interests
are being made subordinate. Such are the features
which characteristically mark the period during

which the powers of civilisation have been renovated in this western corner of the Roman World. The abasement of ecclesiastical *supremacy*, the establishment of constitutional monarchy, and the rise of commerce into sovereign influence may be regarded as accomplished facts. They distinctively characterise England ; and finally they will equally characterise every other kingdom that falls within the Roman World. The success of England naturally causes her to be imitated. Her influence, which is great, is exerted, as might be expected, for the propagation of her principles, and the circumstances of the hour favour these principles. We cannot marvel at this, for the Scriptures plainly declare that such shall be the principles of the closing period of our dispensation. Whatever opinion may be formed as to the particular City indicated in the eighteenth of the Revelation, this at least is evident, that that chapter describes a closing scene in the world's present history, and speaks of " merchants being the great men of the earth," and of a commercial city being " queen " of the nations.

Our first feeling when we review the rise of England's greatness, is commonly one of satisfaction and triumph. Civilisation, we say, cannot be in itself wrong. It cannot be wrong to rejoice that the fetters of ecclesiastical and royal tyranny are broken. It cannot be wrong to develop the natural resources of the earth ; to encourage the inventions of science and art ; to call forth the various powers of the human mind, and to employ its energies. All

this may be true : but still the question recurs,
Can the Christian rejoice in the means by which
England has acquired her power, or in the principles she is adopting in its use ? That question
can only be answered by considering the governmental relation of England to God's revealed Truth.

When Protestantism struck off from England the
shackles of Popery, the Bible was put into her hand,
and for a season she seemed to rejoice in the gift.
In her political conflicts with Popery she used it ;
but, as the dread of Popery lessened, the Bible was
less and less regarded ; until at length, ignorance
and indifference so prevailed, that there have been
few periods of deeper darkness than that which
reigned in England during the greater part of the
seventeenth and the commencement of the eighteenth
century. In the meanwhile, various new forms of
nominal Christianity, and at last Popery and
Judaism, increased in political power : and when at
length the theory of constitutional government
was matured, and government (ceasing to stand
between God and the people, as holding authority
from Him) became avowedly the organ of the
people's will, it was of course requisite that the acts
of government should correspond with the relation
in which it stood to the manifold varieties of Creed
found among those whose will it had undertaken to
express. This, of course, necessitated latitudinarianism. All who were ambitious of power, found
it needful to be officially, if not personally, latitudinarian.

But there were other influences, more potent even than these, tending to the same end. England and the merchants of England began to conquer, to colonise, or to visit, all lands. They found these lands teeming with the various forms of idolatry and evil which the ingenuity of Satan had devised throughout the earth, in order to dishonour God, and to ruin souls. Has England taken her stand in the midst of these abominations, and given faithful testimony to the truth of the word of God ? Has she steadily and practically declared that there was one God and one Lord Jesus Christ—and has she carefully avoided rendering her aid to any except to those who simply preach the Gospel of the GRACE of God ? No : she found it more expedient to con- ciliate than to testify ; more advantageous to honour falsehood than to contend for Truth ; and, therefore, she practically laid aside the Bible, and determined to sanction, whenever expedient, every creed alike. Accommodation to existing systems became her rule. Accordingly, she has presided over the priesthood of Buddha ; offered gifts at the shrine of Juggernaut ; flattered the Mahomedan in the East; honoured the idols of Popery in the West, endowed their Colleges, paid their Priests, and frowned upon all who have sought, in the midst of these things, to act aggres- sively for the Truth of God. In Ireland, especially, she has scowled upon the Truth, and upon its servants.*

* See facts stated in the late reply of the Bishop of Cashel to his Clergy. The administration of Ireland has afforded a

There has been one individual (he too acted on by the love of influence) who has trodden a like path ; and that person, more than any one else in modern days, has foreshadowed the actings of the last great Antichrist—I mean Napoleon Buonaparte. Buonaparte, avowedly reckless about truth, and fearing neither God nor Satan, honoured, as it suited him, every thing. In Holland, he pleased the Protestants, elsewhere, the Pope. When meditating schemes of conquest in the East, he flattered the Jews; and when in Egypt, acknowledged Mahomet. His Egyptian proclamations bear the Moslem motto—"There is one God, and Mahomet is His prophet:" and one is yet extant, in which he solemnly avers that he had received a commission from God to destroy the Cross, and to plant the Crescent in its stead. I do not say that England has, as yet, equalled this blasphemy; but she has entered the same character of path. She has bowed before more idols than did Buonaparte, and that, after having been favoured with more light than he—for he was born in idolatry, and nurtured in atheism. The lust of extended power tempted

---

fearful exhibition of reckless Latitudinarianism, and the doctrines lately avowed at Manchester show how completely the Commercial School have adopted similar principles. It is true that real Christianity may, and does, flourish more without the support of such, than with it; but this does not lessen the guilt of those who see no honour in assisting the distribution of the Holy Scripture, and no sin in crushing it, and delivering over the souls of the people to devouring priests.

him: the lust of extended commercial influence has seduced England. Some time ago, when England was charged with these things, her rulers seemed, in measure, sensible of their shame; they pleaded necessity, and the like. But now we hear less of that plea; now, it is openly said and written, that the Bible is not intended to be used in human legislation, and Truth is declared to be a phantom too subtle for our grasp.

If the shackles of Popery had remained on England she could not have pursued her present path. Popery would not have permitted it. Popery would have forbidden her to follow a course that so compromised its own supremacy. But when human shackles are removed, and not replaced by the golden chain of Christ's truth, the hand that is liberated is liberated only for transgression. England has ceased to be the slave of Popery, but her liberty is becoming the liberty of deistical forgetfulness of God.

It is true, indeed, that the course of the old ecclesiastical or Popish party, which is struggling to regain ascendancy, is at present opposed to these things. If we examine the present condition of society in England, if we observe the books they read, and watch the sentiments avowed by the pulpit and the press generally, we shall find that the influential principles of the day distribute themselves under one of two classes. They either lead back to the ecclesiastical corruption of past ages, or, under the pretence of philosophic superiority to prejudice, and philanthropic desire after peace, they lead to the apathy, if not to the activities, of latitudinarianism. If Dr. Wiseman delights in the tyrannical uniformity (for we cannot call it unity) of Rome; we find, on the other hand, a professedly Protestant statesman delighting in the thought that his town presented the form of a happier unity, produced by negation of truth ; for there he beheld Socinians, Dissenters, Churchmen—sects that once fiercely contended, content to forget their differences, and to live harmoniously together. If Dr. Pusey and his Tractarian followers wish again to bind on governments and nations the ancient manacles of superstition and priestcraft, Lord Macaulay, on the other hand, and the liberal writers of the day, whilst seeming only to break the bonds which man has imposed upon his fellow-man, break with them also the bonds which God's own hand has formed—assert that the Bible is no more to be regarded by the governor in governing than it is by a mechanic in making a machine—ask scornfully whether any *certain* truth can be attained, and advocate principles which, when they have taken their full effect, will cause the nations to say, both of Jehovah and of Christ, "Let us break their bonds asunder, and cast away their cords from us." The advocates of modern Liberalism point, and not without reason, to the Exhibition of 1851 as the symbol of their principles—benign, they say—philanthropic—fraternal. But are their principles at all nearer God than the principles of those, the symbols of whose creed are found in cloisters, cathedrals, and priests ?

Are they not even more distant? Yet, doubtless they will attain supremacy; for they knit together the units of mankind on *natural* principles, without constraining any to forego their individual peculiarities; and when that supremacy has fully been attained, we shall see even Popery herself abating her pretensions, and falling as a handmaid (and an honoured handmaid) into the train of her mighty Mistress.

Would that I could see in "the Exhibition" the symbol of a power that had, benignly indeed, but firmly, entered all lands with the oracles of God in its hand — refusing fellowship with corruption, whether found in the darkness of heathenism or the abominations of pretended Christianity; and seeking to encourage all who should declare to a lost world, that God was ready, through the *finished* work of the Lord Jesus, to accept, in His name, the perishing sinner—to forgive him freely and to clothe him with the robe of Christ's righteousness for ever ! Would to God that England, Protestant England, had thus traversed the nations—that she had marked well the difference between Judaism, Mahomedanism, Popery (which all talk of God and obedience to God), and Christianity, which testifies not only of God and God's *righteousness*, but of His GRACE abounding where sin hath abounded—imputing righteousness without works—justifying freely, through faith, on the sole ground of the imputation of the righteousness of ANOTHER. "We are reputed righteous before God ONLY because of the merit of our Lord and Saviour Jesus Christ, by means of faith, not because of our own works, or deservings."—Eleventh English Article.*   Would that she had imitated her first true Protestant King, and judged it to be her chief honour to exalt the Word of the living God against the traditions of men, to find out Christ's servants and to help Christ's truth!   But alas! her course has been far otherwise.   She has ignored Christ's Gospel; she has found it convenient to strengthen Christ's enemies; her conscience seeks relief from the sin in the easy doctrines of latitudinarianism; she calls it charity; and whilst confirming those systems, which like so many iron barriers keep the nations from the bread of life, she amuses them by a display of earthly riches (things for the sake of which she has virtually sacrificed their souls), and by asking them to behold her greatness, invites them to adopt her principles—principles whereby Truth perishes.   Let any Christian think of these things, and rejoice in " the Exhibition " if he can !

The seeming innocency of the spectacle will doubtless deceive many.   It stands apparently in very advantageous contrast with other forms of the earth's greatness.   Armies of warriors, or armies of priests might terrify us.   They remind us bloodshed and death; of the chains of the conqueror, or of the

---

* Tantum propter meritum Domini et Servatoris nostri Jesu Christi, per fidem, non propter opera et merita nostra, justi coram Deo reputamur."

racks and fires of the Inquisition. But Commerce seems only to hold forth the olive branch of peace, and beneficently to subserve the necessities of human life. Few care to distinguish between Commerce and the *principles* Commerce may adopt; and whilst enjoying the results of the former, willingly forget to enquire respecting the latter.

There is a remarkable prophecy in the Book of Zechariah (a prophecy distinctly unfulfilled) which bears very closely on the circumstances of which we speak. The object of the vision shown to Zechariah is to instruct respecting the character of the influence which shall be dominant over Israel, and over the nations at the closing period of their evil history. It reveals where the master-power shall reside, which, in the latter days, shall "go forth" with pervading influence, to control the energies of the earth. And what is the symbol of this power? It is not a sceptre, nor a sword, nor a mitre, but it is an Ephah. "Then the angel that talked with me went forth, and said unto me, Lift up now thine eyes, and see what is this that goeth forth. And I said, What is it? And he said, This is AN EPHAH that goeth forth." An Ephah is the symbol of Commerce. There is to be a period, therefore, during which Commerce is to rule the earth; a period when an Ephah might fitly be emblazoned on the banner of each Kingdom of the Roman World as the device best suited to indicate where the secret of its influence lay. "This," said the angel, speaking of the Ephah—" This is their eye (עֵינָם)* through all the earth."

In the outward appearance of the Ephah there was nothing to terrify. Men have learned to dread the sceptre, the sword, and the mitre; but the Ephah presents an aspect than which nothing can be more innocent or peaceful. The Prophet, however, was commanded to look again. A heavy weight of lead rested as a lid or covering on the mouth of the Ephah. The Angel raised it, and directed the Prophet to look within. He looked within, and beheld a Woman sitting in the midst of the Ephah. A Woman, when used symbolically, is in Scripture the emblem of a moral system. When we speak of the reign of Commerce, we do not

---

* This word literally means "*eye;*" thus the Vulgate " Hæc est oculus eorum in universâ teriâ." "Eye" may either mean *aspect, appearance,*—as in Numbers xi. 6, where it is said of the manna, that "the colour or appearance thereof was as the colour of bdellium"—or, "eye" may mean that to which we look for guidance, favour, or any supply of blessing. This, no doubt, is its meaning here. If the eye of a father or friend rest benignly on us, we look to its kindness as a source of supply to all our requirement. Hence, "eye" is continually used of fountains in the wilderness, and wells of water. See Gen. xvi. 7. Also Deut. xxxiii. 28: " Israel then shall dwell in safety alone; the fountain (literally *eye*) of Jacob shall be upon a land of corn and wine; also his heavens shall drop down dew." Thus we have to contrast the "eye" of unbelieving Israel and the nations, viz., the Ephah in the land of Shinar, with "the eye" of forgiven Israel in the land of Emmanuel, when Jehovah shall be their strength and their song.

mean merely that commercial activities are to be increased, and that the nations will begin to trade one with the other more energetically ; but we mean that the influence of those whose commercial wealth enables them to touch and control the secret springs of government will be directed to the sustainment of certain *formed* principles—political, educational, religious, and the like—as definite and precise as any which have heretofore characterised Popery, or any other similar system.

If old principles are abandoned, new principles must be supplied in their stead, or else the world must be left ungoverned : and as these new principles are formed and brought into operation, so, of course, a new system of moral agency is created. For example, it was once taught as a principle that all power was from God ; and it was deemed a kind of Atheism to teach that the people were its source : but now the latter principle reigns, and the former is utterly abjured. Once it was thought fit to maintain the truth of Holy Scripture, so far as to refuse to sanction idolatrous and corrupt religions ; but now such sanction is freely and systematically given. Once it was thought desirable to encourage those who circulated the word of life ; but, now, they who circulate it in some of the districts where it is most needed are crushed, and their enemies honoured. The Bible was once thought to contain principles which it was the duty of the Governor to recognise ; but now the Bible, in legislation, is to be ignored. It was once thought that all right fraternity must be based on Scripture; but now fraternisation, apart from Truth, is to be the panacea of the world's disorders. It was once thought that the ruler should encourage Truth where he discerned it; now he is not to believe that certain Truth is anywhere to be discovered. Such are some of the principles. It is impossible that they can be adopted without a system being formed, as definite, and probably more definite, than any of the systems which it supersedes.

The vision, however, plainly indicates that this system is formed secretly, for it is represented as *hidden* in the Ephah. And nothing can be more true. Sheltering itself under the excuse of expediency, this nation, which more than any other owns the sway of the Ephah, has secretly and stealthily adopted principles which it is still ashamed to avow as the fixed acknowledged rule of its conduct. Many a sentiment has dropped from the lips of legislators and statesmen, which, although welcomed by multitudes, and acted on, have not yet become the recognised principles of the State. Who, for example, would dare to enter on the Statute-Book of England that tribute should be paid to Juggernaut; all Mahomedan festivals honoured; Popish priests duly paid; Protestant testimony, in certain spheres, forbidden? Who would at present dare to propose that it should be registered as a principle amongst England's laws, that Truth cannot be ascertained; that the Bible is not to be regarded in legislation; that all religions have in them a measure of truth, and that consequently all may, without sin, be encouraged? It is but lately that the voice of the Dragon has ventured to mutter this last sentiment in our ears, and no one just at present would dare to claim for it public authorisation. These, and such like principles, separately and cautiously enounced, and slowly becoming systematised under the protection of Commercial power, are at present a kind of "mystery" hidden. The time has not yet come for them to be presented to the world in a systematised and ordered form, nor, indeed, are they as yet brought into that form: but when that time does come, they will no longer remain a "mystery" *hidden:* they will be seen in the manifested, displayed attractiveness of the scarlet Harlot of Babylon. Her *hidden* existence in the Ephah precedes her *manifestation* "IN THE LAND OF SHINAR."

As soon as the leaden lid was removed from the mouth of the Ephah, the Prophet beheld the Woman, who had been hidden within it, preparing to spring up from her imprisonment. But she was not permitted to arise, the angel, exclaiming "This is Wickedness" ($\alpha\nu o\mu\iota\alpha$), thrust her down into the midst of the Ephah and "cast the weight of lead upon the mouth thereof." Thus "Wickedness" was hidden within the Ephah. "Wickedness," when thus definitely used in prophetic Scripture in relation to the closing events of our dispensation, is a word of very precise meaning. "The Wicked One" is both in the Old and New Testaments, the designative appellation of "The Antichrist." Compare הָרָשָׁע of Isaiah xi. 4, and ὁ ἄνομος of 2 Thess. ii. 8. "Wickedness," therefore, as used in this passage, is a word that expresses the fulness of those principles of lawless evil that will finally be embodied in Antichrist, and make him what he will be. But Antichristianism exists before Antichrist. That system of lawless Infidelity to which he will ultimately give full effect, becomes a formed, though not a manifested, system, during the time that Commerce is advancing to her place of sovereignty. When the time comes for that sovereignty to be displayed, and the Ephah be transferred to its resting-place in the Land of Shinar, then the Woman shall be no longer hidden. Then she shall be displayed in all her attractiveness as the Harlot of Babylon, and Antichrist, for a season, will become her servant and her minister. We cannot marvel that Antichrist, personally, should at last be sent as a scourge upon nations that have deliberately adopted for their own advantage the principles of a practical Deism.

How long this system will remain *hidden* in the Ephah we are not told. Its *manifestation* will certainly, I believe, follow, not precede, the return of Israel, in unbelief, to their own land. Whenever the religious systems of the Roman World—Judaism, Mahomedanism, Romanism, and the like, shall unite with one another, and with the secular Governments in adopting this system, then, with every influence favouring, it will be transferred from the place of its origin to the Euphratean countries—the earliest home of civilisation—and there established. *There* the Woman of the Ephah will be displayed as the Harlot of the Revelation, admired by all, delighted in by all, giving the cup of joy and gladness to all nations—wine that will gladden for a season, but the wine of everlasting wrath. Into these things, however, as I have elsewhere considered them very fully, I do not now enter.* I will only observe that this administration of the cup of gladness is very distinctive of this last System. Previous systems, such as Popery, have been oppressive, and caused sorrow ; they have bound heavy burdens and grievous to be borne, and have been any thing rather than dispensers of universal joy.

The course which England has, for many years, been governmentally pursuing, tends steadily towards the end which the seventeenth and eighteenth chapters of the Revelation delineate. England is silently, but efficiently acting on all the countries of the Roman World by negation of Truth, and by an idolatrous devotion to the "material interests" of men,—thus paving the way for the advent of that system which is to reign in the Harlot City. Asia Minor, Syria, Egypt, are all feeling the effects of England's influence. Israel, too, will soon be added to the list. They also will join the system that deifies civilisation and ignores Truth ; and then the end will quickly come. "The Exhibition of 1851" is the

* See "Babylon," and "Thoughts on the Apocalypse," second edition, Houlston and Sons, 7, Paternoster Buildings.

1

exponent of a power which is silently effecting these. things.*

As regards the various degrees of responsibility attaching to those who are leading, or being led in these paths, I say nothing. There is One only who can determine to whom responsibility attaches, and

---

* The reaction towards Romanism which has taken place in England, has, to a certain extent, impeded the progress of pure Latitudinarianism. It is a hindrance that will operate for a time, but for a time only. It is necessary to the full establishment of Latitudinarianism that dominant religious influences should be so far neutralised as to be deprived of their dominancy. Thus the ancient dominancy of Mahomedanism is being destroyed in the. East by the introduction of other influences. So also in Spain, Italy, and France, the dominancy of Popery is departing. In England, where Protestantism has ruled, the dominancy of Protestantism is being destroyed, and Puseyism (as it is called) is one of the instrumentalities by which this is being effected. But, apart from the temptations of self-interest, no man of intelligence or character has long consented to be the tool and slave of Ecclesiasticism. Self-interest is now leading men in another path. The exclusiveness of Sacerdotalism, even if men were not disgusted by the transparency of its falsehoods, is ill-suited to the temper of the present hour. Ecclesiasticism may become Latitudinarian, but Latitudinarianism will not resign the throne to Ecclesiasticism. But whilst Ecclesiasticism and Latitudinarianism are thus warring, even as the Pharisees and the Sadducees did of old, we must remember that it was said unto both, " *O generation of vipers*, who hath warned you to flee from the wrath to come ?" May it be remembered, before it is too late, that the one way of salvation as declared in Scripture, through faith in the one finished Sacrifice, is alike rejected by the Ritualist and the Latitudinarian.

in what proportion. We have to remember, however, that it attaches to the *people* of this country, more, perhaps, than to its Governors; for the theory of modern Government is, that the Governor is the servant, not the master, of the popular will. The hour of "civil and religious liberty" proves the truth of its pretensions, by so fettering the hand of the Sovereign that she can neither governmentally maintain the sole supremacy of the Word of God, nor refuse to pay and honour the ministers of a ystem at which her conscience trembles. Practically, however, it often happens that individual Governors, by force of skill and talent, sway the minds of the people, so as to mould the spirit of the age. On such, of course, the deepest responsibility rests. There may be some, however, who, like Darius, when he prayed for the liberation of Daniel, feel overpowered by circumstances too strong for them, and yield because they fear to resist. To yield is indeed not weakness merely, but sin; nevertheless, the heart of Darius was not so far from God as that of those who constrained him into a path in which *their* hearts indeed delighted, but which *his* heart and *his* conscience abhorred. Such, of course, plead no necessity in excuse; for they acknowledge no sin. They are not like Naaman, who confessed that it *was* a sin to bow in the temple of Rimmon, and meekly asked forgiveness; on the contrary, they exult in their principles; and if they remember God at all, they declare that they are honouring Him, and doing Him and His creatures service.

Can there be any remedy for blindness such as this?

Some, perhaps, will say, that it is better for the people of God to dismiss all questions respecting the world and its government, and to concern themselves only with those things which immediately affect their own condition. It is true, indeed, that it would be most wrong for the servants of Christ to quit their own peculiar sphere and to attempt the government of nations; but it is not wrong for them to search the Scripture, that they might be able to admonish and advise all men according to the truth therein revealed. To admonish and warn is their *duty*. Both Prophets and Apostles have testified many things concerning the nations, their prospects, and their end : and are the servants of Christ to quench that light, or to put it under a bushel? In that case their own condition will soon become fatally affected. They will soon begin themselves to stumble. He who at the midnight hour casts away his torch and buries himself in darkness may have a seeing eye, but, practically, he is little better than the blind; and whether the blind be led by the blind, or by those who have thus darkened themselves, matters little as to all present consequences. They must both grope in darkness, and nothing but undeserved sovereign grace could prevent either the leaders or the led, from falling into the ditch at last. Present facts justify the strength of my expressions. Many who profess to lead in the paths of Christ are speaking of this gathering as being a kind of second Pentecost, and request that it may be remembered in prayer as one of the great instruments whereby God intends to accomplish His work of final blessing in the earth.*

* "Electricity is not an insulated jar, geology is not a mere boulder on the earth, astronomy is not a lofty and lone observatory, music is not a mere solo strain, poetry is not a mendicant minstrel, art is not a solitary tradesman set up for himself; but a grand unity binds them all in one, bringing them day by day to be more and more the echo of the Christian's anthem—'Glory to God in the highest, and on earth peace, good will toward men.' Steam and lightning are not secular, but Divine powers. They are inspirations from on high, preparing the way of the Lord. All science, worthy of the name, is either a messenger to man proclaiming God, or a servant coming down from God to prepare the way of the Lord. All the sciences, like the Magi of old, will come not only to the cradle, but to the Cross of our exalted Redeemer."—*Dr. Cumming's God in Science*, p. 40.

"There is before us an Exhibition connected with science. I rejoice, I must say, in spite of the prophecies of some, in the prospect of that noble evidence of peace and harmony among mankind. It seems to me a very noble idea, and such I pray that it may prove to be, being a lover of science as I am, next to a lover of my Bible—I pray to God that it may fulfil the promises of the sanguine, not the vaticinations of those who augur ill. It will teach us Britons, perhaps, to be more humble, and to cease from measuring ourselves by ourselves, which the Apostle says is not wise. It may be a contribution to the peace of nations, by showing a nobler rivalry than arms, better trophies than banners and garments rolled in blood, and a warfare whose field is the Crystal Palace in Hyde Park—whose artillery are steam-engines and hydraulic presses—whose soldiers are philosophers, and engineers, and spinners, and dyers—and its protocols treatises

How little would the heart of John in Patmos have responded to such thoughts as these! He was set there, not to prophesy peace to the nations —not to bid them "God speed" in their evil course, but to prophesy *against* them, to predict their impenitency and final doom : and his prophecy, be it remembered, is not yet spent, for it is terminated only by the Coming of the Lord in glory. If we shrink from or scorn the Patmos-place of testimony; if we refuse to eat the bitter book of prophecy— "sweet in the mouth, but in the belly bitter"; if we

---

on science, and its traces good feeling, amicable rivalry, and social and universal advancement. Such great movements have always been connected with the elevation and progress of mankind. It was when the Medes and Parthians and dwellers in Mesopotamia—and I speak it with a deep sense of the solemnity of that event—were all assembled at Jerusalem, that the Holy Spirit came down, and made them the ambassadors of God and the benefactors of mankind. It may be, that during this great assembly of the nations of the earth, of Jew and Gentile, Greek and barbarian, bond and free, God may have in store unknown to us—I pray that it may be so—social blessings that the world shall not be able to exhaust. It may be a new era. At all events, we may feel persuaded that multitudes will witness here what they never dreamt of. Muftis and Sultans may return to Constantinople, to make known what Christianity has done—for it alone has done it for this great land of ours. Yes; despots and tyrants from afar may go home to their capitals, never to forget the impression of liberty without license, loyalty in the subject without despotism in the ruler, the omnipotence of law, the majestic might of order, of harmony, and of peace."—*Dr. Cumming's God in Science*, p. 42.

will *not* maintain the truth of the words that he prophesied "against (επι) many peoples, and nations, and tongues, and kings," we forfeit the place of honour which God's mercy assigns us in the great battle-field of Truth, and shall probably be permitted so to mistake His foes for His friends, that our energies will be spent in cheering on His adversaries in their last assaults on all that He counts precious in the earth.

It is marvellous how readily mercies and words of mercy are, in the thoughts of men, separated from Him, through whom and by whom these mercies come. Men, for example, like to be reminded of the words, "Glory to God in the highest, on earth peace, good will towards men :"* and some have

---

* The words which the angels really sang were, "Glory to God in the highest, and on earth the peace of complacency (or well-pleasedness) in the midst of men" ἐν ανθρωποις.

As commonly understood, these words are regarded as expressing nothing more than God's kindness and beneficence towards all His creatures. We have indeed to thank and praise Him, for that benificence. Truly He is good to all and His tender mercies are over all His works. He hath "so loved the world, that He gave His only begotten Son, that whosoever believeth in him should not perish, but have eternal life." But the words which the angels sang express something different from this. They speak of something being found in *the midst of men*, in which God could rest in satisfied complacent peace. In the midst of the darkness of earth One stood, around whom a circle of heavenly light was drawn. Of Him God could say, "This is My beloved Son, in whom I am well pleased" (ευδοκησα). "The peace of well-pleasedness" (ειρηνη ευδοκιας) was in the midst of men, because Jesus

proposed that they should be multiplied in ten thousand various forms of inscription in every known
language of the earth, and placed on all the arches
of that vast edifice, which is now being builded as
the Tabernacle—the Congregation-place—of all nations. Men love to hear these words, but do they
remember the earth's present relation to Him over
whom those words were sung ?   Have the nations
repented of their rejection of Him—of their persecution and corruption of His truth? Have they fled
to Him and to His blood for refuge ? Have they
confessed His name, and gathered round the banner
of His Truth? Has the Jew done this, or the
Mahomedan, or the Romanist, or the Heathen, or
the Infidel ? Has England remembered Him, owned
His servants, favoured His truth, or is she ready to
barter it all away—to sell it for influence and for
gain ? Perhaps the words which the angels sang
may be sung again : perhaps they may again herald
Christ's return unto this earth; for when God
" again bringeth the First begotten into the world,"
He will say, " Let all the angels of God worship
Him." Would the nations welcome these words so
employed, or would they be as words of thunder in

---

was in the midst of men. A circle of acceptance, and peace,
and love, was drawn around Him ; and all who by faith were
brought within that circle, were received within that circle,
and were rested in with " the peace of well-pleasedness." The
being objects of this complacency is something very different
from being the objects of kindness and beneficence merely,
and is the portion of believers only.

their ears, awakening the wail of everlasting anguish?

We have indeed reason to thank God as we remember these things, that He is pleased still to continue in the earth the message of His GRACE. Whilst His Holy word exposes and denounces the path which the nations tread, it speaks also of a refuge: it proclaims a fountain opened for sin and for uncleanness in the blood of the Lamb. There God receives the humbled sinner, receives him in his guiltiness, asks from him no character, (for he has none to bring), justifies him freely, imputes to him righteousness without works, accepts him in the Beloved. Have we not then reason, whilst we consider the abounding evil, to thank Him that the master of the house has not yet risen up and shut to the door?—although the hour now draweth near, when it will be finally said, "He that is unrighteous let him be unrighteous still."

The last book of Scripture, which more than any other is concerned with the closing scene of the world's evil, and which chiefly sets God's holiness in contrast therewith, does not conclude without the fullest and most explicit testimony to the freeness of GRACE. The Spirit and the Bride—names whose holiness stands in living contrast with the earth's abominations—the Spirit and the Bride, holy though they be, nevertheless say, "Come. And let him that heareth say, Come. And let him that is athirst come. And whosoever will, let him take the water of life freely." Blessed words of grace, when we think of that coming Day of visitation!

Not one, be it remembered, of the Old Testament prophecies which speak of the coming of the Day of the Lord is as yet fulfilled. "The Day of the Lord of Hosts shall be upon every one that is proud and lofty, and upon every one that is lifted up; and he shall be brought low: and upon all the cedars of Lebanon that are high and lifted up, and upon all the oaks of Bashan . . . . and upon all the ships of Tarshish, and upon all pleasant pictures. And the loftiness of man shall be bowed down, and the haughtiness of man shall be made low: and the Lord alone shall be exalted in that day. . . . . And they shall go into the holes of the rocks, and into the caves of the earth, for fear of the Lord, and for the glory of His majesty, when He ariseth to shake terribly the earth." (Is. ii.) Chapter after chapter in the Old Testament speaks in language similar to this; and when we turn to the New Testament, the closing book of prophecy there describes the last great City of human greatness—that City which is especially to evidence what modern Civilisation and Commerce are able to effect. We read of "the merchandise of gold and silver, and precious stones, of pearls and fine linen, and purple and silk, and scarlet, and all thyine wood, and all manner vessels of ivory, and all manner vessels of most precious wood, and of brass and iron and marble"—in a word, all that modern art and science are able to effect in developing the resources of the earth, and making them available for the purposes of man, will be developed in that great City. "Her merchants" are to be "the great men of the earth, waxing rich through the abundance of her delicacies." But what is to be the end of these things? Is this the City of which it shall be said, "Arise, shine, for thy light is come, and the glory of the Lord is risen upon *thee*"? Is this the City that "shall call her walls Salvation and her gates Praise"?—or is the word of the Lord *against* her, saying, that she shall be "the habitation of devils, and the hold of every foul spirit, and a cage of every unclean and hateful bird:" and that they who rejoice in her are to wail the wail of everlasting anguish, when the Alleluiahs of Heaven are sung over her destruction? "The sovereignty of the world" will then, at last, "become the sovereignty of our Lord and His Christ," and "He shall reign in Mount Zion, and in Jerusalem, and before his ancients gloriously." "Therefore wait ye upon me, saith the Lord, until the day that I rise up to the prey: for my determination is to gather the nations, that I may assemble the kingdoms, to pour upon them mine indignation, even all my fierce anger: for all the earth shall be devoured with the fire of my jealousy. For then will I turn to the people a pure language, that they may all call upon the name of the Lord, to serve him with one consent." Civilisation will cease then to be the servant of pride, and shall no longer ripen the nations for destruction.

It is true, few, very few, believe these things.

Even Christians are falsely prophesying peace, and encouraging the nations in their prosperous course of ruin. Man's expectations are found increasingly at variance with the predictions of God. But which shall we follow—the words of men, or the testimonies of the living God?

CHAPTER V.

ON THE FOUR BEASTS OF DANIEL VII.

IN the second chapter of Daniel, we find the history of the four successive Gentile Empires, with respect to the *character* of their power. But their personal history, if I may use the expression, is not there given. We are taught that they are endowed with power which progressively sinks in excellency, until at last it becomes adulterated even by the consent of the rulers themselves: but the *character* of the Empires and *how* they use their power, and *why* so destructive a blow falls upon the image at the close, we are not, in the second chapter, told. Instruction respecting this is reserved for the chapter we are now about to consider.

The vision of the image was sent, not to Daniel, but to Nebuchadnezzar. Whenever great and important endowments are received, a corresponding responsibility is contracted; and it is not likely that One who is merciful and gracious, would leave men uninformed as to the position in which they are set, or uninstructed as to their responsibility. The visions, therefore, of the image and of the tree (both of which refer to the greatness and responsibility of the position occupied) were given to the ruler. But in the seventh chapter, the ordinary method of instruction is resumed, and the vision is sent, not to the king, but to God's servant; for none but His servants really value and use His instructions, especially such instructions as this chapter gives. No eye except the eye of faith—an eye that has learned to behold the things of earth in the light of God, is likely to understand *why* fierce and devouring "beasts" should be the symbol chosen to represent Empires, so glorious in the world's eyes, so distinguished by every thing that this world counts precious. It is to faith, therefore, that the vision of the beasts is given.

The symbols chosen by God to represent the four successive Empires of the Gentiles, are a lion, a bear, a leopard, and a nameless ten-horned monster. There were specific differences in these symbols. The lion was different from the bear, and yet more different from the fourth shapeless monster. But there was this common likeness among them, that they were all fierce and evil beasts, having a common birth-place in the midst of convulsion and strife, symbolized in the vision by waters of the deep, on which the four winds of heaven together strove. "Daniel spake and said, I saw in my vision by night, and behold, the four winds of the heaven strove upon THE GREAT SEA. And four great beasts came up from the sea, diverse one from another." (Dan. vii. 2, 3.)

There is a time coming of which God hath said, "I will be as the dew unto Israel: he shall grow as the lily, and cast forth his roots as Lebanon. His branches shall spread, and his beauty shall be as the olive-tree, and his smell as Lebanon. They that dwell under his shadow shall return ; they shall revive as the corn, and grow as the vine : the scent thereof shall be as the wine of Lebanon." (Hosea xiv. 5—7.) Such are the blessed and peaceful agencies under which Israel and the nations by and by shall find the birth-place and the home of their holy prosperity and glory. They shall be "as a field which the Lord God hath blessed." How different a picture from that of the waters of the unquiet deep, which under no circumstances rest ; but which in this vision are seen as the scene of conflict between the four winds of heaven.

There appears, however, to be something more specific than this. It was not the sea *generally*, but one particular sea, THE GREAT SEA, that was chosen as the symbol. "The great sea" is, in Scripture, the name of that which we now call the Mediterranean.* *That* was the sea on which the four winds of heaven were seen to strive. *That* sea has ever been the peculiar sphere of the world's energies. In earliest ages it was the highway of nations—the

* Thus, when the boundaries of Israel are appointed in Numbers xxxiv. 6. "For the western border ye shall even have *the Great Sea* for a border. And this shall be your north border; from the Great Sea ye shall point out for you Mount Hor." "The Great Sea," says Dr. Tregelles, "is always used in every other passage of Scripture in which the phrase occurs, as meaning distinctively the Mediterranean Sea."—*Tregelles on Daniel*, p. 21.

pathway of their intercourse, whether for commerce, friendship, or war.

> " Thy shores were Empires,
> Changed in all save thee."

Chaldæa did not assume her place as the first of the four ruling Empires, until her conquest of Jerusalem, Tyre, and Egypt, had made her mistress of the Mediterranean Sea. Persia did not assume her place as the second Empire until the subjection of Asia Minor, and of the Greek cities there, together with the acquisition of that which had belonged to Chaldæa before, had given her possession of all the Asiatic coasts of the Mediterranean. The Mediterranean was the home of the Greek and Roman Empires. The Roman Empire viewed on the map, forms the coast of the Mediterranean; enclosing it on every side. The present importance of that sea is great; but it is little in comparison of that which it *will* be when the nations of the Roman Empire shall have regained their vigour, and when the return of Israel and other agencies shall have reawakened the energies of the East.

The Chaldæan was the first of these Empires. Its symbol is a lion. "The first was like a lion, and had eagle's wings. I beheld till the wings thereof were plucked, and it was lifted up from the earth, and made stand upon the feet as a man, and a man's heart was given to it." (Dan. vii. 4.) We might expect a lion to be chosen as the symbol of this first Empire, because there was attached to it a dignity

and a majesty never attained by the Empires that
succeeded. They were more warlike, and their
dominions more extended; but they had not the
same dignity of power. Indeed, in this, the fourth
Empire was peculiarly deficient; and accordingly
the fourth beast, though it had great iron teeth, and
nails of brass, stands in marked contrast with the
majesty of the winged lion. The lion had eagle's
wings. The eagle is the monarch of birds. The
wings denote, no doubt, the energy and rapidity of
this first Empire's movements in extending its conquests, and diffusing its power. Energy and rapidity were markedly the characteristics of the
Empire of Nebuchadnezzar. The whole duration of
the Empire of Babylon was only from B.C. 604 to
B.C. 538—that is, 66 years—and out of this Nebuchadnezzar reigned from 604 to 561—that is, 43
years. In the early part of his reign he made Babylon what it was—the marvel of subsequent ages.
" Is not this great Babylon that *I have built ?* " His
power over Assyria was established by the ruin of
Nineveh, the previous metropolis of Assyria, and he
conquered also Syria, Tyre, and Egypt, thus making
himself the master of Ἡ Οικουμενη, the civilised
world.* All this was rapidly effected; and then the

* He was titularly the monarch of Spain, in consequence,
no doubt, of his having succeeded into the place occupied by
Tyre, which had extensively colonised that country. Indeed,
the Colonies of Tyre had even at that early period marked
out the extent of the Roman World. They had settlements
at Marseilles and in Cornwall.

conquests of Babylon ceased. "The wings were plucked." It ceased from conquering, and addicted itself to the humanising pursuits of peace. The rude and savage power of the Medes had, in conjunction with the father of Nebuchadnezzar, utterly destroyed Nineveh, which till then had been the centre of Eastern civilisation. But it found a new home under Nebuchadnezzar in Babylon ; and even the science and civilisation of modern Europe look back to Chaldæa as the nursery, if not the birthplace of the arts which have since humanised the nations. This, I suppose, is the reason why the characteristics of "man" are so remarkably connected with the Chaldæan Beast. "It was lifted up from the earth ;" that is, it became erect, and was "made stand upon the feet as a man, and a man's heart was given to it." It had the attitude and reflectiveness of *man ;* yet with all its intelligence, it ceased not to be a *beast* in the estimate of heaven. It never glorified God. Meekness and gentleness it knew not. When weighed in the balances it was found wanting. Belshazzar, only twenty-three years after the death of Nebuchadnezzar, saw on the night of his wicked revelry, the handwriting on the wall announcing that the sovereignty was taken from him and given to the Medes and Persians. "In that night was Belshazzar, the king of the Chaldæans, slain. And Darius, the Median, took the kingdom." (Dan. v. 30.)

The Medes were a people who for some centuries previous to Nebuchadnezzar had ruled over the wild hordes which lay east of the Tigris, and extended

indefinitely towards the central parts of Asia. They
had originally been subject to the Assyrian monarchs
of Nineveh, but revolted from them about the year
B.C. 717.* For some time they remained in a wandering, nomad condition, without a king ; but about
the year B.C. 710, Deioces obtained the sovereign
power, and founded the Median monarchy. From
this time to that of Cyrus, in B.C. 560 (that is, for
150 years), their annals, private and public, were
peculiarly marked by bloodshed and savage cruelty.
During this period they were for twenty-eight years

* This century, the eighth century before the Christian
era, was a very remarkable period in the history of the world.
In this century the kings of Assyria carried the ten tribes of
Israel into captivity. This event was the forerunner to the
overthrow of Jerusalem, and the commencement of the times
of the Gentiles. Accordingly, in this century all those arrangements among the nations which have since given a
character to the whole period of Gentile pre-eminence commenced.

In B.C. 761, Menahem began to reign over Israel. In his
reign, Pul, the king of Assyria, first attacked Israel.

In B.C. 722, the kingdom of Israel was finally destroyed by
Shalmaneser, King of Assyria.

In B.C. 710, the kingdom of Media was founded by Deioces.

In B.C. 729, the kingdom of Macedon was founded, according to Herodotus, by Perdiccas.

In B.C. 754, Rome was founded.

Thus in the same century preparations were made for the
rise of the four successive Empires, for Babylon inherited the
power of Assyria, and became its chief city. The migrations
also of the Cymmerians and Scythians, on which all the arrangements of modern Europe are founded, commenced *in
this century*. See Turner's History of Anglo-Saxons.

subjugated by the Scythians, whom at last they treacherously massacred at a feast. The reign of Astyages, the grandfather of Cyrus, was marked by almost unheard of cruelty. Two years before the accession of Astyages, viz., 597, they united with Nabopulassar, the father of Nebuchadnezzar, governor of Babylon, in destroying Nineveh. But they did not *then* succeed to the Assyrian name and power. Although Babylon was at that time comparatively an insignificant place, and the father of Nebuchadnezzar had been but a dependent governor, yet it pleased God to repress Media, and to give to Babylon and to Nebuchadnezzar, not only the headship of Assyria, which Nineveh had previously held, but to make them supreme in the earth. Hence the emphasis of the words addressed to Nebuchadnezzar, "Thou, O King, art a king of kings; for the God of Heaven hath given thee a kingdom, power, and strength, and glory. . . . Thou art this head of gold."

The reigns of Nebuchadnezzar at Babylon and of Astyages, the grandfather of Cyrus, commenced nearly at the same time. During the reign of Astyages the foundations of Persian supremacy over Media were being laid, until at last Cyrus, who had been cruelly treated by his grandfather, headed a rebellion of the Persians against the Medes, and, succeeding in his attempt, established the Medo-Persian dynasty. The Medes, wearied by the tyranny of Astyages, were not displeased at his success, and a united kingdom was formed, named

Medo-Persian, in commemoration of the union. The Bear, which symbolised them, raised itself up, not for a twofold dominion, but for "one dominion." (See note on page 73.)

I have detailed this early history of the Medes (more minutely perhaps, than is needful) because the more accurately we are acquainted with their history, the more we discern the marked intervention of God in giving to Nebuchadnezzar and to Babylon precedence over a nation so much older than themselves; and the better we appreciate the fitness of "the Bear" to denote this empire when it arose under Cyrus, and was commissioned "to devour much flesh." It had already made three empires its prey (viz., Nineveh, the Empire of Crœsus, and Babylon) when it succeeded to the supremacy of which Babylon had been deprived. On this account it is represented on its first appearance as having between its teeth three ribs, the flesh of which had apparently been just devoured. The conquest of Egypt, Libya, the Archipelago, Macedonia, and Thrace, as well as of other vast districts in the East, prove how truly it afterwards performed its commission to "devour much flesh."

The empire that succeeded the Medo-Persian was that of Greece. It was symbolised by a winged Leopard. The rapidity and extent of the conquests of Alexander exceeded anything that the world had ever before seen. Not only did he subject Asia Minor, Tyre, Egypt, and possess himself of all that had belonged to the Medo-Persian Empire as far as

the Jaxartes,* which was its north-western limit, but
he advanced his conquests across the Indus, into that
very district which England is now subduing. This
was accomplished in about ten years. But although
Greece was thus warlike under its first great king,
yet it was even more distinguished by its refinement
and taste. The Leopard was its symbol—a fierce and
subtle beast, but elegant and beautiful. Its heads
were four; for Alexander's four victorious generals
divided his dominions. For some time these kingdoms, especially Syria and Egypt, maintained themselves in considerable power; but they were all
successively assailed and subdued by the Romans.
The last representative of the Empire of Alexander
was Cleopatra of Egypt, and when she was conquered at Actium† by Augustus Cæsar, the Roman
Empire assumed its position as the fourth and last
of the universal empires.

How truly that empire has answered to the symbol of a Beast, "dreadful and terrible, and strong
exceedingly," I need not say. Its conquests have
been detailed in the previous chapters. Its relation to God has been, that it has crucified His Son;
persecuted, and then perverted His truth; and it
has utterly crushed Jerusalem. But its course is
not yet terminated. The Ancient of Days has not
yet sat in judgment on its blasphemies, nor has the
Son of Man been invested with the sovereignty
which he is to exercise in the earth. These events

* Modern Sir or Sihon, in Turkestan.
† Fought September 2nd, B.C. 31.

must *precede* the hour when the body of this Beast is to be "given to the burning flame."   But these are subjects which I reserve for another chapter.

The closing hour of this dispensation is, of course, materially influenced by the character of the Empires that have already been, and therefore their history is not passed by in silence ; but the main burden of this prophecy is obviously directed to a time yet future—"the time of the end."   The blasphemies of the Little Horn, and the consequent Session of the Ancient of Days in judgment, are the great theme of this vision.

As regards the *futurity* of this Little Horn, I may be allowed to refer to what I have elsewhere written.*   Unless it can be shown that ten kingdoms are at *this present moment* existing in the Roman Earth, and that the power of these ten kingdoms is *at this moment* vested in one mighty hand, and that all that is written in the thirteenth chapter of Revelation respecting the Image, its worship, and its decree (for the decree is spoken of as emanating from the Image, see Rev. xiii.), are *at this moment* being fulfilled, and that all the saints of God throughout all the Roman World are *at this moment* suffering persecution unto death, unless these things, and many other like things can be affirmed to be *present subsisting* facts, it follows that the rise of this last great Monarch of the Gentiles is *yet to come.* If these things be not present, they must

* See *First* Series of "Aids to Prophetic Enquiry," chap. vi.; also tracts entitled, "Antichrist Future ;" and "1,260 Days of Antichrist's Reign Future."

be future, for they cannot *have* existed and *have* passed away, because it is expressly said in this chapter that they are *terminated by* the Session of the Ancient of Days, when "the time comes for the saints to possess the Kingdom." (See verse 22.)

The special subject of this chapter should also be observed. It is the history of those who hold, under delegation from God, the *secular* power of earth until the Lord comes. It is the history of *Kings*— not of priests. The power committed to the Gentile Empires was not ecclesiastical power : *that* God never delegated to the rulers of earth. But *secular* power has been delegated; and this vision tells us that *all* the secular power of the Roman Earth will be concentrated at last in the hands of one great Blasphemer. Since Rome fell, has any individual, or any system, ever possessed such universal power? *Division* of power, not its *concentration*, has marked the history of the Roman Empire ever since it began to crumble. The predicted period, therefore, of final concentration *must* be future.

When we remember the fearfulness of that closing hour of evil, we might expect that the mercy of God would shorten it. Accordingly, it will be limited to three years and a half. This is expressly revealed in the 24th and 25th verses. "The ten horns out of this kingdom are ten kings that shall arise; and another shall arise after them; and he shall be diverse from the first, and he shall subdue three Kings. And he shall speak great words against the most High, and shall wear out the saints of the High Places, and think to change times and laws : and they shall be given into his hand until a time and times, and the dividing of time."*

As the succeeding chapters will necessarily lead us to recur to this subject, I avoid enlarging on it here. I would only further observe that it is a solemn thing, at this present crisis in the world's history, to persist in concealing what Scripture has revealed respecting the closing history of *secular* power in the kingdoms of the Roman earth. *Secular* power is to control the systems of the Roman earth ; and when we speak of those systems we virtually speak of everything that has influenced, or will influence, man as man. It is an influence which acts alike on the Mahomedan and on the Jew ; on the Greek and on the Western Roman ; on the nominal Christian and on the infidel. To teach that the potency of this evil is confined within the limits of any one particular system ; to lead men to suppose that they have escaped the danger if they happen to be disconnected from a particular form of ecclesiastical corruption, is effectually to co-operate with that great Deceiver who anxiously desires to divert attention from the new and wider paths of evil that he is now engaged in opening. It is the SECULAR power that will *lead* and *head* the evil, although *the false ecclesiastical will follow in its train.*

And as it is the SECULAR power of earth which is spoken of in this chapter as about to become *apostate*, so it is the SECULAR power which is spoken of as

* See notes appended to this chapter.

recovered. It is taken from those to whom it had been so long delegated, and is *not* given to "another [earthly] people" (לְעַם אָחֳרָן Dan. ii. 44), but to the Son of Man, and to the saints of the High Places. Their designation—saints of the High Places, sufficiently indicates that the home of the kingdom, and the dwelling-place of those who hold it, will be above the skies, although the sphere of its exercise will be below: or as it is said in the 27th verse, "UNDER the whole heaven." The kingly power and the priesthood shall be united then in " the Prince of Peace." " Of the increase of His government and peace there shall be no end, upon the throne of David and upon his kingdom, to order it, and to establish it with judgment and with justice from henceforth, even for ever. The zeal of the Lord of Hosts will perform this." (Isa. ix. 7.)

NOTES ON DANIEL VII.

I beheld till the thrones were cast down, &c. More properly, " till the thrones *were set.*" So rendered by the Septuagint, Theodoret, and Vulgate, ετεθησαν and " positi sunt." Gesenius renders it " *to put,* to *place,* as for example, *seats.*"

The scene is judicial, not regal. No *crowns* were seen in the vision. The snowy whiteness of the garment of the ancient of days, and the hair of his head being as the pure wool, indicate his fitness for the office of a judge: the qualifications being purity, and the wisdom and calmness which age gives. "Fire " is the emblem of the Divine holiness; here brought into opposition to the condition of the nations under Antichrist.

" Behold the day cometh that shall burn as an oven ; and all the proud, yea, and all that do wickedly shall be stubble : and the day that cometh shall burn them up, saith the Lord of hosts, that it shall leave them neither root nor branch."

" *Wheels,*" as in the vision of the cherubim (Ezek. i.), denote the resistless course of the Almighty power of God, which was now *again* about to be manifested in the earth. The " saints " were about to be invested with this character of power, and then would answer to the symbol of the cherubim, guiding the symbolic *wheels*, as seen in Ezekiel. (See "*Thoughts on the Apocalypse*," chapters iv. and v.)

These thrones of judgment are *not* to be set for passing sentence on the dead, nor on Christendom, nor on the heathen nations. They were set in order that inquisition might be held, and sentence passed on the kingdoms represented by the ten-horned beast, that is, the Roman Empire finally divided into ten kingdoms. The eleventh verse shows very remarkably how entirely the *whole* body of the Roman Empire will be involved in the blasphemies of Antichrist; for it is said, that " the beast was slain, and his body destroyed and given to the burning flame," "*because of the voice of the great words which the horn spake.*" "The infliction of this judgment on the ten kingdoms and their head, is frequently described in Scripture. See conclusion of Rev. xix. and Joel iii. The judgment is inflicted by the hand of Christ. Wrath and desolation, such as the world has never yet beheld, will fall on *all* the ten kingdoms, and especially on the flower of their strength that will have been gathered under Antichrist at Armageddon.

In this respect the end of the fourth Empire will stand in very marked contrast with the end of the Empires that have preceded it. They had "their dominion taken away," and fell into a subordinate place, but they were not visited by any utterly destructive judgment. Their "lives were prolonged" for an indefinite period, and the great means of their extinction at last was, not sudden destructive judgment from God, but gradual decay or absorption into the Empires that respectively followed them.

It is the habit of Scripture, after carrying us by its instruction to a certain point, to retrace, and adding fresh instruction, to bring us to the same point again. Thus the first chapter of Genesis brings us to the conclusion of creation; the second *retraces*, and after describing the mode of Eve's creation, brings us to the same period again. So also in this chapter; the destruction of the fourth Empire is mentioned in the eleventh verse, and there the narrative 'pauses. The next verse retraces and adds an additional circumstance, viz., the investiture of the Lord Jesus with the sovereignty of earth. This investiture takes place *before* the judgment is inflicted on the fourth Empire, although, in the order of narration, it is *mentioned* after. The order of the events here noticed is this:—

I. The session of the ancient of days.

II. The examination into the condition of the ten kingdoms, for it is said, "the books were opened."

III. Investiture of the Son of Man with the power of earth.

IV. Destruction of the fourth Empire and its kings.

We know that this is the order of these events, because we are expressly told in the 19th of Revelation, that the Lord Jesus comes forth crowned as " King of Kings, and Lord of Lords," and *afterwards* destroys Antichrist, and the kings who are gathered with him. Antichrist, it should be observed, is represented as wearing *ten* diadems, but the Lord Jesus as having *many* diadems, for the sovereignty of *all* nations will be given unto Him. "ALL kings shall fall down before Him; ALL nations shall serve Him."

These great beasts, which are four, are four kings; they will arise from the earth. But the saints of the High Places shall take the kingdom. The object of this passage is to contrast the four Empires which have their origin *from earth*, with the saints of the High Places, whose power is *from above*.

Some have found a difficulty in this passage because it speaks of *all* the four Empires as *future*, whereas one had already arisen. But the reason obviously is, because the four Empires are looked upon conjointly, and have their sovereignty as a *whole* contrasted with the sovereignty of the saints which is to follow.

The future tense is constantly used in Hebrew to denote an action which has commenced, but is still *in process of accomplishment*. The use of the form successive Gentile Empires, though it had commenced, was still unaccomplished when Daniel saw this vision. In the Greek Testament, this Hebraistic use of the future to denote a progressing but unaccomplished course of action, is frequent. See, for example, that notable instance, "On this rock I will build (I will go on building) my Church." The building had commenced, but it was not completed.

It should be observed, that "kings and kingdoms" are used in an interchangeable sense in this vision. Thus it is said, " four *kings* that shall arise ;" and " the fourth beast shall be the fourth kingdom." The Empires, however, were not considered as formed *until* they were brought under their respective heads, viz., Chaldæa under Nebuchadnezzar; Persia under Cyrus; Greece under Alexander; and Rome under Augustus Cæsar. We may therefore expect that the Ten Kingdoms will not have an existence that *Scripture recognises*, until they have their respective heads.

The expression "saints of the High Places," is used *four* times in this chapter.

In verse 18, " The saints of the High Places shall take the kingdom."

In verse 22, "Judgment was given |to the saints of the High Places."

In verse 25, " And he shall speak great words against the MOST HIGH, and shall wear out the saints of the High Places."

In verse 27, " The people of the saints of the High Places."

This last expression I understand to mean, that the sovereignty is to be given to a people *composed of* the saints of the High Places. They are regarded as " a people," although a *heavenly* people, having a heavenly city. This agrees with the second of Daniel, where we are told " that the kingdom shall not be again given to another people "—that is, to another *earthly people*.

We learn from other parts of Scripture, that during the millennium heavenly glory (which will have its *home and place of perfect development* only in the heavenly city and in the heaven of heavens) will be manifested partially on Mount Zion, as it was for a season on Sinai of old. Thus there will be three distinct spheres in which heavenly glory will be displayed, viz., Mount Zion, the Heavenly City, and the Heaven of Heavens. They who shall rise in the first resurrection, constituting "the Church of the first-born ones," will have as their own proper place of existence and action, these three spheres of glory, and therefore will be distinctively known by Israel on the earth as "saints of the *High* Places." This expression includes the places of heavenly glory that are to be manifested *below* the heavens (on Mount Zion, for example), as well as those which are to be *above* the heavens. "High Places" is, therefore, an expression of wider scope than that of "heavenly places;" the latter applying *only* to that which is to be *above* the heavens. In other respects they may be considered identical with each other, and with the title "host of the heavens" *prospectively* given to the saints in the eighth chapter.

Time, times, and the dividing of time. This period is elsewhere expressed by 42 months, and by 1,260 days—thirty days being reckoned to the month. (See Rev. xi. and xii.)

"Time" is not a word of ambiguous meaning. It had before been used in Daniel to denote a year, when it is said, that "seven times" should pass over Nebuchadnezzar whilst he remained in his state of madness. No one in this case, pretends that a day is to be understood as meaning a year, for then Nebuchadnezzar's madness must last 2,520 years, and consequently must be continuing still. Therefore, what "time" means when it is used to denote a period avowedly definite in the fifth chapter, *that* it must be supposed to mean in a passage equally definite in the seventh chapter. In Leviticus the corresponding Hebrew word is used to denote the interval between one set feast and another—that is, one year.

"This period," that is time, times, &c., says Dr. Tregelles, "has been commonly taken (and I have no doubt rightly so) as signifying three years and a half. Now we know that it must mean a period exactly defined, and not about such or such a time; for had it been merely an indefinite statement, the mention of 'half a time' would be useless. It is impossible to be definite and indefinite at one and the same time. The word rendered 'time' is that which denotes either a stated period, or else a set feast, or else an idea blended as it were of the two; namely, the interval from one of the great set feasts to its recurrence—*i.e.*, a year. Thus, then, we find a time, *i.e.*, a year; times (the smallest plural, as the statement is definite) two years; and half a year; that is, three years and a half."—*Tregelles on Daniel.*

The early Christian writers uniformly gave the same interpretation. Thus *Cyril of Jerusalem.*— "Antichrist will reign three and a half years only. We say this, not on the authority of apocryphal books, but of Daniel, for he says, 'and it shall be given

L

up to him until a time, times,' &c.   Now a time is one year."—Cyril, Catech. xv.

So also *Jerome*, in his Commentary on Daniel : "a time signifies a year;" times, "according to the idiom of the Hebrews, who have themselves a dual number, signify two years, but half a time signifies six months."

So also *Theodoret*, commenting on this chapter of Daniel, speaks of the period being three years and a half, and observes that it is the time of tribulation mentioned by our Lord in Matthew xxiv.; the same likewise as is spoken of in 2 Thess. ii.

Mr. Gresswell most truly observes that the early Christian writers were unanimous in believing "that before the end of the world Antichrist must be expected to appear. It made no difference whether they were advocates or opponents of the doctrine of the millennium in particular; in the reception of this opinion there was a perfect agreement among all parties. The Fathers are likewise agreed in considering Antichrist himself to be a real person, and no merely figurative or symbolical character."— *Gresswell on Parables*, vol. i., p. 369.

Even Mede allows that, until the twelfth century, no one suspected that the Pope was THE Antichrist. "All," he says, expected one who would last for three years and six months" (triennalem et semestrem expectabant).

The strong temptation under which Christianity now labours, is to conceal from itself the *real character* and END of the secular power with which it has thought fit to connect itself. This is a sufficient reason for its departure from the simple exposition of such a prophecy as that we are considering, and a reason why we should be watchful in receiving its later interpretations.

CHAPTER VI.

THOUGHTS ON THE HISTORY OF PROFESSING CHRISTIANITY, AS GIVEN IN THE PARABLES OF MATTHEW XIII.

THE subject of the book of Daniel is the *secular* history of the Gentile Empires in their relation to Jerusalem, and *not* the history of Christianity. In considering, therefore, the history of Christianity, we deviate from the strict course of this prophecy. But it is a deviation that may be permitted. Not only is the subject in itself unspeakably important, but it is closely connected also with all we have been considering. The full character of evil that attaches to the Roman Empire cannot be understood unless its false relations to Christianity be in some degree appreciated. Moreover, although the ripened evil of Judaism, and of the nations governmentally, will largely contribute towards the final development of Antichristianism, yet it will be aided no less by an apostasy from among professing Christians. Thus also we answer an objection often urged, viz., that by our interpreting the Old Testament prophecies so exclusively of Israel and of the Gentiles, we leave nothing in Scripture that bears directly on Christianity. We show that the Scripture *does* speak prophetically of Christianity, and of its corruptions.

There are many parts of the *New* Testament which very distinctly supply the prophetic history of Christianity during the present period—the period, not of its triumph, but of its weakness—a period in the commencement of which it met with hatred and rejection, and then became itself the subject of corruption and decay.

It must not, however, be expected that the moral history of Christianity can be given with the same minuteness as the outward history of kingdoms. Its prophetic history is *mainly* one of failure and of corruption; but the forms of its corruption are so various, and so widely diffused (for nominal Christianity has extended over nearly a third of the globe), that if all the ways of its evil were detailed, who would be able to read the books that should be written? If some of these forms of evil were noticed, and others passed by in silence, it would be pleaded that those which were unnoticed must be exempted from the condemnatory descriptions. The Scripture avoids these difficulties by making its statements general, and by dwelling not on the *specific*, but on the *generic* features of corruption. Every form, therefore, of evil that falls under these *general* descriptions receives thereby its condemnation.

The germs of the corruptions of Christianity were manifested before the Apostles died; consequently, every word written by the Apostles in condemnation of these early manifestations, remains as a record against them when they reach a more developed form. Besides which, much of the Epistles are prophetic, and professedly describe corruptions then future. The Epistles, therefore, do by themselves supply a large fund of prophetic instruction. But *the* part of Scripture which most distinctly refers to the corruptions of Christianity in its *corporate* form is the Gospel of Matthew. The corporate testimony that had been committed to Israel was succeeded by another corporate testimony committed to the professing Church. The setting aside of the one, and the introduction of the other, is one of the especial subjects of the Gospel of Matthew. It speaks of the presentation of the Lord Jesus to Israel, and their corporate rejection of Him both as teacher and King. It records also His solemn rejection of them. It then proceeds to speak of others who should succeed into the place of corporate testimony, but intimates that among *them* also false profession and corruption would be found. This instruction is generally conveyed in prophetic parables, of which the marriage-supper, the wise and foolish virgins, the servants trading with the talents, the sheep and the goats, are examples. All these parables refer to the professing Church.

But the thirteenth chapter affords the most important example. The twelfth chapter records the solemn denunciations of the Lord Jesus against the wickedness of the Jewish teachers, and concludes with the following description of the *final* condition of unbelieving Israel. " When the unclean spirit is gone out of a man, he walketh through dry places seeking rest, and findeth none. Then he saith, I will return into my house whence I came out; and when he is come, he findeth it empty, swept, and garnished. Then goeth he, and taketh with himself seven other spirits more wicked than himself, and they enter in and dwell there: and the last state of that man is worse than the first. EVEN THUS SHALL IT BE ALSO UNTO THIS WICKED GENERATION."*

One part of this prediction is at this present moment being fulfilled. The Jews are not now *in any especial manner* inhabited by the energy of evil. They are much as other men; indeed, not unfrequently their characters stand in favourable contrast with those of professing Christians around them. Idolatry, to which they were once peculiarly addicted, seems extirpated from among them. There is much natural kindness, much benevolence displayed by many. One of the leading philanthropists of the day, adored almost by his own nation, and extolled both by Mahomedans and Christians, is a Jew. Thus they are not only freed for a season from that terrible power of evil which once carried them into vile idolatries and other frantic excesses of evil, but they possess much that is amiable and attractive—much that naturally adorns.† They are as a house swept

* The word "*generation*" is frequently applied to the whole family of Israel. Thus, in the Song of Moses, which includes their history for 4,000 years—" And he said, I will hide my face from them, I will see what their end shall be: for they are a very froward *generation*, children in whom is no faith . . . . they are a nation void of counsel, neither is there any understanding in them."—Deut. xxxii. 20, 28.

† Their freedom from idolatry is boasted of by the Jews

and garnished, but *empty*. The truth and Spirit of Christ are not there. It is a mansion unoccupied; open therefore to be entered, as it soon *will* be entered, by that unclean spirit, which, after long wandering up and down, and finding no other people so suited for his designs, will, with seven other spirits more wicked than himself, again make that people his peculiar habitation. *Then* will be developed the full iniquity of the closing hours of our dispensation.

These words have almost entirely failed to arrest the attention of real Christians. Many appear not to know that the Lord has spoken them. Else they could not as they do, " cleave to Israel with flatteries," and tell them that they are advancing into their millennial rest, when in truth, they are fast approaching the great hour of their anti-Christian evil and final visitation from the hand of God.

The chapter, however, which thus records the doom of unbelieving Israel, does not conclude without referring to another family which the Lord Jesus *could*, and *did* own as His, at the very moment when

themselves. Thus, in a letter published in the "Jewish Chronicle," dated November, 1849, it is said : "The principal and greatest sin our forefathers committed against God was *idolatry*; the wrath of heaven was kindled against them, and the first Temple was destroyed. . . . Again the Jews sinned, and the second Temple fell in ruins before the Romans' merciless torch ; the Israelites suffered the penalty of their transgressions. But they are *idoluters* no longer. In this wide world there is not a people or a class which is freer from idolatry, bigotry, or immorality."

He was thus rejecting Israel. "He stretched forth his hand toward his disciples, and said: Behold my mother and my brethren! For whosoever shall do the will of my Father which is in heaven, the same is my brother and sister, and mother." All, therefore, in whom the spiritual characteristics of Abraham shall be found—all who shall believe and obey, shall be owned as the family of God, whilst Israel nationally are rejected.

It were happy, indeed, if the Church had remained what it once was, the obedient family of faith. In that case, the parables of the thirteenth of Matthew would never have been spoken. But seeing that it was to be otherwise; that the family of faith on which, at first, grace rested so abundantly, was to be invaded by false profession, and to become the seat of worldliness and evil, instruction respecting these things was needed; and this instruction the parables of the thirteenth of Matthew supply.

The object of our Lord in this chapter is, as He Himself says, to teach us respecting the "mysteries of the kingdom of Heaven," that we might be as scribes well instructed, able to bring out of our treasures things "new and old." The Old Testament had revealed much respecting the establishment of Christianity in the earth when the hour of Christ's and of Israel's millennial glory shall have come; but it had revealed nothing plainly respecting the introduction of Christianity by the foolishness of preaching, or respecting its subsequent corruptions. These were the "new things," "the *mysteries* of the

kingdom;" the knowledge of which is here added
by the Lord to the "old things" which the Prophets
had already declared.*

* "The kingdom of heaven" is to exist in the earth at two
very different periods.   First, while the world remains under
the power of *Satan*, as it now is; secondly, when it shall be
sustained by the manifested and glorious power of Christ
after Satan has been bound.

These are conditions *circumstantially* very different; but
the *essential* points of similarity are paramount to any of the
circumstantial differences; and therefore those who profess
the name of Christ *now*, and those who *will* hear that name
in the millennium, are *alike* regarded as subjects of the *same*
kingdom.   They have the same king; the same legislator;
the same spirit; the same priest; the same redemption.
They differ only *circumstantially*.   The spiritual blessings of
those who belong to the family of faith now, and of those
who will belong to it in the millennial dispensation, are
essentially the same.   They differ only in the mode and
degree of their development.

The kingdom of heaven is also called the kingdom of Christ,
because He is its Head.   Thus Christendom—*i.e.*, Christ's
kingdom — is an equivalent expression to "kingdom of
heaven" as used in this chapter of Matthew.   The season of
His *return*, therefore, will neither be the period of its *introduction* (for it has been *already introduced*), neither will it be
that of its *destruction*.   So far from destroying it, He says
that He "will gather *out of it* all things that offend;" that is,
He will purify it; and taking His saints who are in it into
the heavenly branch of the kingdom, He will at the same
time bring Israel and others converted in the earth, into its
earthly branch.   Instead, therefore, of being *destroyed*, it will
be *enlarged*, part of its subjects *glorified*, and itself *established*
in undisputed *supremacy of glorious power*.

The heaven of heavens, and all that existed previously to
the Adamic creation, is *not* included in that which is *dis-*

The first in this series of parables (*seven* in number) refers to the *mode* in which our dispensation was introduced. "Behold a sower went forth to sow." The humble place of one going forth to sow, was that which the Lord, in introducing it, consented to fill. Nor was this all. The sowing for the most part failed. There were *four* kinds of ground on which the seed was scattered, but only *one* in which it prospered. The agency by which the disciples expected the "kingdom of Heaven," to be introduced was *glorious power*, but instead of this it was *lowly testimony*. The result was, *not* universality of success; it was almost universal *failure*. This first parable, therefore, fixes a character upon the whole period of which it commences the history; for surely, no dispensation, thus introduced, could be intended to be otherwise than lowly, nor could it, *universally* prosper. It could not be that dispensation in which the Messiah of Israel, no longer seen as an humble and despised sower, "shall stand and feed in the strength of the Lord, *in the majesty* of the name of the Lord his God." It could not be the same with that period of which it is written, "that *all* kings shall fall down before him, *all* nations shall serve him . . . . and men shall be blessed in him, all

---

tinctively the kingdom of the Son; and seeing that the saints when changed are not to be restricted even to the heavenly city, but are to be admitted also into the highest heavens, it is said, "that they shall shine forth as the sun," not merely in that which is distinctively the kingdom of the Son, but also in the kingdom of His and "their Father."

nations shall call him blessed." Strange that the
saints of God should ever have confounded between
periods so dissimilar. It could only have been because our eye had ceased to be single; because we
had sought to reign as kings when we should rather
have desired to be " as the offscouring of all things."

The first parable, then, teaches us, that even when
the Lord was Himself the minister, effectual hindrance to the progress of the Gospel was permitted.
But Satan was allowed to do more than this. Secretly,
he gained access to the *good* ground where the sowing
had prospered, and sprinkled evil seed over it. He
could not change the nature of the wheat. Wheat
must ever remain wheat: nor was he allowed to root
it up. But he could spoil the general aspect of the
field, and hinder the healthful, happy growth of
each individual blade, by planting strange plants
among them. And this he did. "Certain men crept
in unawares;" and these were found, after a little,
" to be ungodly men, turning the grace of our God
into lasciviousness, and denying the only Lord God,
and our Lord Jesus Christ." This is the instruction
of the *second* parable. It is the record of the second
great event that occurred in the dispensational history of Christianity.

The introduction of false professors greatly, of
course, affected the appearance which the Church presented to the world. A field intermingled with tares
cannot *appear* as one in which wheat only grows.
The loveliness of its aspect must be gone. Nevertheless, the corporate standing of the Churches was

not thereby forfeited. They were still regarded by the Lord as worthy of being represented before Him by their original and proper symbol—"candlesticks of gold." The steadfastness even of individual saints, although endangered, was not necessarily destroyed by the approximation of evil, however near. Neither was the executive agency of the Churches necessarily perverted; and it is by the acts of its executive that the character of every corporate body is determined. Holy discipline might have been exercised. There were still means whereby the evil might have been met, so as for the claims of holiness to have been answered, and the standing of the Churches preserved. Accordingly, the Epistle of Jude (which was one of the last admonitions which the Spirit of God addressed to the Churches) whilst it fully recognises the introduction of these tares, does not speak as if there were no hope. On the contrary, it exhorts the faithful to strengthen themselves, to be mindful of their own spiritual health, to build themselves up in their most holy faith, that so, as in the natural body, when the energies of remaining health are strengthened, there might be power to conflict with and throw off disease. If the spiritual had obeyed this commandment, the others would either have been put away, or have separated themselves and gone away; or would in some manner have succumbed to the faithfulness and holy zeal of those who feared God. But these last commandments were, as others, not obeyed. The people of God did not strengthen themselves. They did not set themselves against these intruders.   Instead of repressing, they cherished them, so that the Apostles had scarcely died, when false professors so increased in numbers and in power, that the executive government of the Churches fell almost entirely into their hands.*

This sealed the ruin of professing Christianity. The doctrines of Christ, and the order of His Church, were thus subjected to the will of evil and unconverted men, whose object was, not to be the servants of God, but to command influence, by pleasing men. The truths of Christ were modified and altered, so as to be moulded into adaptation to the minds and tastes of the world.

There was no longer any simple testimony to the fulness of God's grace in the blood of the Lamb. The great truth that we are justified and saved simply and only on the ground of the meritoriousness

---

* Although St. Paul so imperatively enforces the exercise of church-discipline in 1 Cor. v., yet the parable of the tares is often quoted as if it forbade discipline. All that the parable forbids is such a *mode* of separating from the Church as would be a putting out of the earth. It forbids that kind of separation which it belongs only to the holy angels to effect when the Lord comes. It is not for us to take the sword of destruction.

No doubt tares would have remained in the Churches even if discipline had been faithfully exercised. But the Church would not have been condemned for that, seeing that they are only expected to deal with *ostensible* and *proved* contrariety to the doctrines and ways of Christ. But they have sanctioned and retained *proved* evil that has not been repented of; and it has ended in their not seeing evil, even where it most palpably exists.

of another being imputed to us was repudiated. The believing people of God were not taught respecting their union with the Lord Jesus in the heavens, nor the sureness of their inheritance *there*, and therefore were not strengthened to rise above the attractiveness of circumstances *below*. Nor, indeed, did many desire it. The path of the Lord Jesus in humiliation was no longer regarded as one desirable for the Church to follow. They saw something more attractive in flourishing as the green bay tree, than in being as "a root out of a dry ground, having no form or comeliness." It was found far more profitable to gratify men than to please God.

It was not wonderful, when the distinctive truths of Christianity were thus either discarded or adulterated, that the heads of the Roman Empire should no longer despise a system which they saw to be possessed of moral influence, and therefore capable of being advantageously used in the government of men. Accordingly, in the fourth century, the Empire of Rome and the Church united. The Courts of Cæsar indeed, had not changed their character or become like the little upper chamber in Jerusalem, where the lowly Church, small as the "grain of mustard seed," first congregated. It was the Church, not the world, that had changed. The so-called servants of Christ had long forsaken that chamber, and coveted the honour of kings' courts: and God caused it to be given them. He gave Saul to Israel; and He gave a worse than Saul to that fallen body that still arrogated to itself the name of Church.

It was no wonder that, under such circumstances, the so-called Church should become great in the earth—so great, that the very emblem employed in Scripture to denote the imperial greatness of the Gentile kingdoms—the emblem of a fair and wide-spreading tree, should become applicable to her. The greatness of Nebuchadnezzar and of the Gentile Empires, of which he was the head, is represented by a tree "which grew, and was strong, whose height reached unto the heaven, and the sight thereof to all the earth." Dan. iv. 20. The Church could now be represented by a kindred symbol. Though little as the "mustard seed" once, it had grown, and become a tree, so as for "the birds of the air to lodge in the branches thereof." *

But it may be asked, Why should not the "mustard seed" grow? Does it not in growing, merely fulfil the law of its nature? Why then may not the Church, which like its Master is well suited to rule, and to rule supremely, why should it not rise into greatness here? The answer is, Because of the *character of this present age.* So long as it pleases God to permit that Satan should continue the "prince of this world;" "the ruler of the darkness of this present age," so long must it be true that

---

* As soon as the Church became linked to the Roman Empire, the glory of the nations being given to it, was mistaken for the glory of Christ's coming kingdom. The great ecclesiastical structures of the Gentiles, in which idolatry or worldliness are hallowed, still bear the once despised names of Peter and Paul.

Christ's kingdom "is not from hence," and therefore abasement, not "the reigning as kings," must *now* be the characteristics of His servants on the earth. It is a question of time. Accordingly, every principle given to the Church in its present standing below, must necessarily check its growth as to all that could promote its exaltation in the earth. The taking up our cross daily and so losing our lives in this world, the spending and being spent for others, the following Jesus *of Nazareth*, are principles sufficient to deprive the Church, while it adheres to them, of all governmental influence *now*. Besides which, the active agency of Satan is against those who really cleave to the Truth of Christ. No wonder, therefore, that they should be blighted; no wonder that in their measure, they should be like Him, who, although He was indeed a tender plant, worthy of being cherished under every kindly influence, yet flourished not in the earth, but was "as a root out of a dry ground." No plant that remains in the spot where God's Truth would keep it, can flourish here. The nourishment that God gives is for the *new* creation—heavenly, and not of earth. If therefore it do flourish here, it can only be by having been transplanted into other circumstances, where "the prince of this world" can foster and direct its growth, and use it when grown, for his own purposes of evil.

That the Church in the fourth century did attain to greatness in the earth, is a fact that cannot be disputed. It is equally plain that that greatness

M

was neither held, nor exercised according to God. Intoxicated by their exaltation, they began to speak and to write as if the Millennium were already come; and appropriated to themselves not only the national blessings of Israel in the latter day, but even the descriptions of the New Jerusalem.*   As the in-

* When Heathenism had been cast down from its supremacy, and Christianity established in the Roman World, the changes consequent were immense and universal.   Now, throughout its vast extent, the *cross*, once so despised, was everywhere in honour, and the preserving and conquering virtue celebrated that everywhere attended it.   Now, the righteousness of the slaughtered martyrs that had been gathered under the altar was acknowledged in public edicts, and the living confessors restored to their homes in triumph from the mines and dungeons where they were suffering. Now, instead of vaults and catacombs for the sacred assemblies of Christians, and other hiding places shut out from the light of heaven, to which, like their earlier Christian brethren, they had been reduced during the late persecution, there arose in the cities and towns churches of magnificence, and the ritual was celebrated with a pomp corresponding.   Now, instead of desertions and apostasies from the Christian body, such as had been the case with not a few under the fiery trial, the daily accessions to it were innumerable. Candidates in throngs applied for baptism; and at the Easter and Pentecostal festivals, the newly-baptised Neophytes, in their white vestments, grouped conspicuous around each Christian sanctuary.   Now, moreover, under Imperial auspices, the Christian professing Church Catholic was gathered for the first time in Œcumenical Council.   Representatives attended from every province, and nation, and tongue in the vast empire.   The palace gates were thrown open to the holy delegates.   The emperor bowed in respectful deference before them.   If in the use of his power he was to the Church

fluence of the Church increased (and it increased rapidly during the fourth and fifth centuries), so it

---

as a nursing father, his behaviour was respectful as that of a son. Can we wonder then at the exultation that was felt at this time by many, perhaps by most that bore the Christian name, or at their high-raised expectations as to the future happy destiny of the Roman, now that it had been changed into the Christian nation ? It seemed to them as if it had become God's covenanted people, like Israel of old ; and the expectation was not unnatural—an expectation strengthened by the remarkable tranquillity which, throughout the exten of the now re-united empire, followed almost immediately on Constantine's establishment of Christianity—that not only the temporal blessings of the ancient Jewish covenant would henceforth in no small measure attach to them, but even those prophesied of as appertaining to the latter day. Hence on the medals of that era the emblems of the phœnix, all radiant with the rising sunbeams, to represent the empire as now risen into new life and hope, and its legend, which spoke of the happy restoration of the times. Hence, in forgetfulness of all former prognostications of Antichrist and fearful coming evils, the reference by some of the most eminent of their bishops to their latter-day blessedness, as even then about fulfilling. The state of things was such, Eusebius tells us, that it looked like the *very image of the kingdom of Christ*. The city built by the emperor at *Jerusalem*, beside the new and magnificent church of the *Holy Sepulchre*—the sacred capital, as it were, to the new empire—might be perhaps, he suggested, the *new Jerusalem*, the theme of so many prophecies. Yet again, on occasion of the opening of the new church at Tyre, he expressed in the following glowing language, not his own feelings only, but those, we may be sure, of not a few of the congregated Christian ministers and people who heard him : " What so many of the Lord's saints and confessors before our time desired to see and saw not,

became more and more the corrupter of truth, until in the seventh century the establishment of Popery in the West, and similar corruptions in the East, set Christianity in a position which the next parable too truly delineates. It is likened unto leaven which a woman took and hid in three measures of meal till the *whole* was leavened.

It cannot be denied by any who take Holy Scripture as the test, that the doctrines and practices of the professing Church had, at the period of which we speak, become like leaven, corrupt and corrupting. She had indeed "*meal*" also. She had not renounced all the good and wholesome truths of God. She could boast of her creeds. Abstractedly she acknowledged, and her lips recited many holy and precious verities which were as meal—wholesome and good food: but she had leaven too, and this leaven she infused into all her meal, until the whole became a poisoned and corrupted mass. This she dispensed; this she dealt out to all who came to her for food. There are countries, such as America and India, which have received their influences from Christi-

---

and to hear and heard not, that behold now before our eyes! It was of us the prophet spake when he told how the wilderness and the solitary place should be glad, and the desert rejoice and blossom as the lily. Whereas the church was widowed and desolate, her children have now to exclaim to her, 'Make room! Enlarge thy borders! The place is too strait for us! The promise is fulfilling to her,—in righteousness shalt thou be established: all thy children shall be taught of God: and great shall be the peace of thy children." —*Elliott's Horæ Apocalypticæ.*

anity since it occupied this exalted but evil place. Have they been fed with fine wheat, or have they eaten of this leavened meal? Have the pure doctrines of Christ been disseminated there, or do falsehood and idolatry and worldliness reign under the shelter of that which *professes* to be the spouse of Christ? I speak not of what holy individuals may have done. I speak of the corporate action of professing Christianity on the wide world.

The parables of our Lord are addressed chiefly to conscience. If our consciences are perverted we shall either give no heed to the instruction, or else mistake, and probably, *reverse* the meaning. For example, he who conceives the honour and dignity of this present age to be according to God, and therefore well suited for His Church, will be sure to find in the parable of the "mustard seed" an encouragement to aspire after worldly greatness. He who admires the present condition and influence of professing Christianity, will not be hindered by the mere circumstance of leaven being *uniformly* used in the Scripture as the type of *evil*, from interpreting it as the symbol of the *diffusiveness* and diffusion of *good*. Parables, if they do not enlighten, blind.*

* They who object to the interpretation that has been given, would do well to consider whether they can suggest any other. "The kingdom of heaven," in this series of parables, cannot be interpreted of the *millennial* kingdom, for *there* Satan will not be present to steal away the seed, or to sow tares; nor can it refer to the elect of the present dispensation only, for if they *alone* were indicated, then *tares* could not be among them, nor *bad* fishes as well as good. For

At this point, the series of parables divides. Those which we have been considering were spoken publicly; those which follow, to the disciples apart. In

---

the same reason it cannot refer to heaven. Neither can it represent any inward condition of soul; for neither the parable of the Tares, nor of the Fishes, can have any accomplishment in a *believer's soul*. The expression, therefore, as used in this chapter, can refer to one thing only, that is, the Professing Church.

As regards the parable of the Woman spreading Leaven, we cannot suppose that there is inconsistency in the manner in which Scripture employs its emblems. In every other place throughout the Bible, leaven, whenever mentioned, is always used to indicate corruption. It would be strange, therefore, if in this passage it should represent the *diffusive power of good*. Moreover, it is not true that Christ's truth spreads throughout the earth in this present Dispensation. It is not to be infused into all nations, nor are their institutions to be transformed thereby. If so, there would not remain at the end of the Dispensation any ten-horned Beast to be "given to the burning flame," nor any Image to be "ground to powder."

As regards the application of this parable to a believer's soul, that is impossible. In the first place it must not be interpreted except in harmony with the rest of the parables with which it stands connected; and they respect a kingdom in which the righteous and the evil are together found, *until* separated by the angels of God. Moreover, leaven as being the type of evil, cannot represent the new principle of life and righteousness which is implanted in the believer, nor does that principle infuse itself into our old nature. Our old nature ever remains evil, and struggles against the Spirit. A power *resisting* and *bridling* evil in us, is a very different thing from that which is so *infused*, as to bring everything into which it enters into assimilation to itself.

the former, our minds have been chiefly directed to the power of Satan and of evil in marring the blessings introduced by God; in the latter we learn the goodness of God in interfering to counter-work the power of evil.

In every dispensation hitherto, God has allowed His great enemy to triumph for a season against His truth; and professing Christianity has exhibited more terrible results of that enemy's corrupting influence than any sphere in which he has yet acted. But God retains a power of counter-working Satan's evil. In the previous dispensation, when Israel had buried truth in corruption, He mercifully interfered, and the light kindled in the times of Ezra and Nehemiah was the instrumental means of preserving a remnant, who were witnesses of Truth until the Lord Jesus came. So also in our dispensation: God has been pleased to interfere by what may be termed a secondary action of His grace; and when the darkness was very deep, rekindled a light, the effects of which will be discernible until the Lord Jesus comes in glory. The next parable of " the treasure " directs our thoughts to one of these interferences of God in blessing.

For more than a thousand years after the professing Church had assumed her place of evil pre-eminence, there was little to counteract her influence: and it spread almost unresisted over the most civilized of the nations of earth, who fed carelessly on her leavened meal. In the sixteenth century the triumph of her evil was so complete that Truth seemed to have perished from the earth. In the east and in the west priestcraft and idolatry, superstition and wickedness reigned, just as much when Christ's name was mentioned as when it was ignored. But it pleased God to interfere, and into these Western countries—countries, indeed, which the *pure* Gospel of His grace had never visited—He sent that Gospel, and also His own Holy Word.

The doctrine of justification by faith alone—that doctrine which Popery hates, still teaching that they who hold it " are accursed," was the centre-truth of the Reformation. It made the love of God in the sacrifice of His Son the one object of *saving* faith. It presented as the refuge of a sinner's soul the living love of God and of Christ, instead of dead ritual ordinances—ordinances, which (even if they had been appointed to that end, which they never were) would have been powerless in the hands of those who were not the Church of God at all, but the ministers of Satan. The power of the Reformation, therefore, was in *owning* this doctrine, and in *owning* it practically: in maintaining the title of all who had believed to be regarded as the Church of the living God: but in denying the title of fellowship in that body to all who rested their claim on mere ritual ordinances, whilst they showed both in doctrine and in practice, that they were strangers to the Gospel of Christ.

The Reformation, however, would have failed in producing any alteration in the visible aspect of Christianity, unless the Reformers had been led to discern, in the light of the word of God, the real condition of the professing Church. They, like others, had long conceived it to be their duty to own as the Church, that which *professed* itself to be the Church. They had therefore served the woman who had mingled leaven with her meal. They had sanctioned her position, had aided in dispensing her corruptions, and had owned all her ministrations. For a long time, even Luther feared wholly to reject her claim, and shrunk from saying, that they who showed that they had received and been sanctified by the Truth were the only Church which God recognised for blessing. But when the eyes of the Reformers were at last opened to discern the fearfulness of their error in having ascribed the attributes and functions of the Church of the living God to a body that was efficiently serving the god of this world, they turned away from that synagogue of Satan, denounced its ordinances, rejected its authority, retired from within its confines, and learned for the first time practically to distinguish the *real* Church for which Christ died, from that false body which had usurped her functions.

In recognising this, they recognised the principle on which Christ had ever acted. The parable speaks of "treasure hid in a field; the which when a man hath found he hideth, and for joy thereof goeth and selleth all that he hath, and buyeth that field." The *outward* professing body was *not* "the treasure" for which Christ resigned all in order to buy both it and the spot in which it was hidden—that is, this earth. "The treasure" which He valued were His elect—

His own believing people to whom alone the holy name and standing of the Church properly pertained. This was the principle of Christ; and the real strength of the Protestant Reformation was in cleaving to this principle, and practically giving it effect. It was the true power of its earlier testimony; and whenever in later times the distinction between the elect Church and the corrupt professing body has been faithfully recognised, there has seldom been wanting a measure of the Divine blessing.*

High and honourable is the service to which Protestantism has been called. Like Moses, when he returned to the idolatrous camp of Israel, it has had to gather without the gate those who were on the Lord's side; to fold them as the sheep of Christ and to teach them,—but only from the word of God. Such is its calling. It has to remember that the nations governmentally, even if not controlled by the

* No one who valued or understood the Gospel of grace could interpret the parables of "the treasure," or of "the pearl," of believers, for what is there that they *purchase?* Christ, however, purchased the earth for the sake of His Church that was hidden in it, and purchased the Church, and in purchasing it, purchased "a pearl;" for like "a pearl" it will one day be.

These two parables are placed late in the series because they apply to the periods when, in consequence of some of the servants of Christ recognising the principles taught by "the treasure" and "the pearl," two fresh eras are marked in the history of Christianity.

It should be observed that when either of the seven parables have once commenced, they continue on to the end of the dispensation.

woman, are represented both in Daniel, and in the Revelation, by the horns of fierce monsters that know not Christ: and likewise, that the individuals of whom those nations are composed, are, for the most part, men who have showed by their doctrines, and by their lives, that they are enemies to the Gospel of Christ, unfit therefore to be recognised as His, however loudly they may protest against ecclesiastical corruptions. It was the place of Protestantism to distinguish between "the treasure," and that which was discerned *not* to be "treasure." But in this Protestantism has failed.

It is most painful, after witnessing the clearness and power with which many of the Reformers wrote on the privileges and everlasting separateness of God's believing people, to observe how entirely they seem to have forgotten these things when called upon to act. They might almost be suspected of holding these truths as abstract principles, incapable of being followed on earth, for they practically denied them in their arrangements for the corporate order of the Churches. Not only worldly and wicked individuals, but whole provinces and nations have been welcomed into the Protestant fold, so that even Popery has been scandalised by the facility with which the Governors of the nations were made, in virtue of their office, governors also in the Church of God.

It is painful thus to write of that which we would desire not to censure, but to praise. Yet we dare not close our eyes to the fact that Protestantism early

compromised its fundamental principle. As a necessary result it became *nominal* Protestantism: and it
now teems with worldliness and infidelity. It pro-
tested against the corruptions of the body to which
it found itself attached; but it used its light and its
advantages, in forming *another* body which has also
proved itself to be " of the world." It fled from the
woman, but it purchased for itself a refuge by placing itself under the power of that ten-horned monster, whose character, and whose doom, Daniel and
the Prophets had foretold. But the testimonies of the
Prophets were either slighted or perverted. Popery
had concealed the real character of that beast, and
pretended to have made it the servant of the truth of
Christ. Protestantism, equally concealing its real
character, was in not a few instances content to receive that ten-horned monster for its master.

When we consider how deliberately Protestantism
has secularised itself in all its corporate arrangements, it is wonderful that any thing like vitality
should have remained. Yet it is a fact, that tens of
thousands, quickened by the spirit of God, have been
found among Protestants, whilst Popery has been
sleeping the sleep of death. This is mainly attributable under God to its recognition and diffusion of
Holy Scripture. Until of late years, Protestantism
has not consented to mutilate them, or to hide them
from the people.* By means of the Scripture, myriads

* I refer to the educational system adopted by the legislature in Ireland. The Educational Board mutilates: Popery
hides, and substitutes its traditions.

who, if they had been left to the human systems around them would have fallen uninstructed into the grave, have been enabled to learn immediately from God, and have become wise unto salvation.

Nevertheless, the effects of the errors of Protestantism are becoming every day more manifest. Even in England, where Protestantism has had such favourable opportunity to develop itself, and in such various forms, multitudes, partly scandalised by its corruptions, partly hating its truth, are becoming its avowed enemies; deny that any distinction should be made between the professing, or, (as they call it) apostolic body, and the real Church, and are rushing back to Popery again. Others are wandering into the mazes of German Philosophy and Pantheism, and are industriously disseminating principles, which, if they be true, the Scriptures must be a lie. In their case it is a simple question whether or not the mind of man shall succeed in defying the revelation of God.*

---

* Since the above was written, Neology by means of the judgment pronounced by the judicial committee of the Privy Council in the case of the " Essays and Reviews," has attained a legalised immunity in the Anglican Establishment for some of its most extreme statements — statements which might well satisfy the desires of the most advanced infidel. A similar standing has now been accorded to the Romanist party by the judgment in the Bennett case. Adoration of the elements, that is to say idolatry, may now be taught by a minister of the Anglican Establishment, and his lips be unsilenced. The great Evangelical party have, for the most part, submitted to

It is plain from every sign around us, that we are living at a period of crisis, not only in the world's

---

the decision; and not a few avow that they see in it a triumph for Truth, because, say they, many right principles were enunciated by the judges, although by their judgment they not only abstained from giving practical effect to those principles, but by their refusal to condemn have established a precedent which will, for the future, secure immunity to those who trample these vaunted principles under foot.

What should we think of a nation that boasted of the exceeding excellency of its laws, but when asked whether those laws were enforced, was obliged to answer, no—that there would be danger in enforcing them, and that consequently systematic disobedience was allowed, and immunity granted to crime?

To know what is good, and to know what is evil, and yet to shelter the evil, what is this in the sight of God? If the triumph of that accursed latitudinarianism which is fast leading on to matured Antichristianism and Antichrist be the triumph of Truth, then the Evangelical leaders do well in saying, that Truth has triumphed. But if it be the triumph of the principles by which Satan is bringing on the last great hour of darkness and apostasy, what must be the position of those who speak respecting it, "smooth things"? Let the history of the relation of the prophets of Israel to Jeremiah be read before that question is answered.

Would to God that the leaders of evangelical Christendom could have their eyes opened to discern the signs of this present hour. Nothing can be more certain than that God is presenting to them a roll in which is written "lamentation, and mourning, and woe." They may refuse to read it. They may seek to hide it, but they cannot destroy it. Jehoiachim succeeded for a time in burning the roll which God sent to him through Jeremiah. But it was written again; "and there were added besides many like words." Jer. xxxvi. 32.

PARABLES OF MATTHEW XIII.

done by those who fear God? Shall we forsake those
blessed principles of Truth which Protestantism,
under God's own power, restored: or shall we rather
cleave to them with ten-fold tenacity? Only, we
must separate the precious from the vile. "If," as
was said to Jeremiah, who himself lived at a period
when all things were out of course, "if thou wilt
take forth the precious from the vile, thou shalt be
as my mouth." If Protestantism at the Reformation
failed to judge the primeval corruptions of Christianity—if, thinking only of the Woman and her evil,
it forgot the sin of the Church in forsaking her lowliness, and becoming like the fair-spreading Tree—
if it neglected to search into the prophetic word, and
consequently remained in ignorance of all that Israel
is to be, and of all that the nations are, then have we
to avoid these quicksands. We have to carry our
thoughts back over the long train of corruptions,
until we reach the Apostles of our Lord and Saviour.
We have to remember that the kings of the Gentiles
exercise lordship, but not we—that neither the condition of Israel under the Law, nor of Israel
in millennial rest, is to be the condition of
Christianity now; and that the nations, symbolised by evil monsters, are in God's sight, contrasted in every possible sense with her who is the
Bride of Christ, and who once occupied in the earth
a position worthy of being represented by "candlesticks of gold." Attention to those things would
not only materially affect our practical position, but

would lead us also to a right "division" of the Scriptures, without which they can neither be interpreted nor applied aright.

We feel shocked when we read the description of Christianity in the days of Constantine. We see the fearfulness of the error into which *they* fell who mistook the hour of the Church's ratified evil for the hour of Christ's millennial kingdom, and who applied to the season of the Church's deadly sin, Scriptures which belong to the season of the Truth's final triumph. Yet from that hour to the present, the self-same principle has been followed in the interpretation of Scripture. Parts of the Word of God which belong only to a time when Christ shall have stopped the present dominance of evil, and established His own righteous and peaceful reign, are interpreted of a period when the secular power of earth is advancing to its final doom; and when Christianity refusing to suffer, has desired to unite itself with the very nations who are hastening into the final Apostasy.

If through the mercy of God His servants should be led to see that the Epistles, and *not* millennial Scriptures prescribe the condition of the Church's present calling; if the secular prospects of the nations should be judged of by the prophecies of Daniel and of the Revelation; if the *contrast* between the present position of believers and that of Israel in the millennium, and that of the nations now, were acknowledged; and if the spiritual and other blessings of Israel when at last brought into the

Church, were duly recognised as they are revealed in Scripture, then not only would our minds be freed from many dangerous and delusive thoughts, but the Scripture would be understood because rightly divided, and would become available for our united guidance. If it should please God, in pity to our present circumstances, to grant to His people an insight into the general bearing of His Holy Word as clear as that which many do possess as to the doctrines of salvation, then new and momentous subjects would instantly be before us, which, under His blessing would give to our hearts common interests, and to our mouths common testimonies. We should begin to think and speak alike, because we should be drawing from the same source, and be directed by the same rule. If believers, instructed immediately from the Scripture, were to think and speak of their own prospects, and of the nations' prospects as they are written *there*, they would soon acquire a character of practical unity in their own and in the world's estimate, such as they have never had since they first departed from the guidance of those holy oracles.

The Church has for ages lost all right apprehension of its relation to the nations, and thus been led into circumstances which have despoiled it of its purity, and its testimonies of their value. In the days of Constantine it welcomed union with the nations, a union which it must long before have desired, otherwise it would not have so rejoiced in it when it came. During the days of Popery, the

N

effort of Christianity was to rule the nations. The desire of national Protestant Churches is to be ruled *by* them. Other forms of Protestant Christianity have adopted a middle course. They teach that the Church in its corporate character should not rule, but that Christian individuals *may* rule the nations. But surely *that* cannot be individually right which is corporately wrong; nor can the Christian sustain a double character, so as in the Church to adopt the Scripture as his guide, and out of the Church to adopt some other rule. It is not too strong to say that modern Christianity has not read the history of the nations in the Book of God. If the light of God's word, so long neglected, should again be sought unto and followed, a position of separateness and of purity would, in principle at least, be attained, such as the Church has never held since it first entered on its path of declension. It would be a position in some degree answering to that emblem which appears to be given in the parables we are considering as the fit measure of our condition. The last parable had compared the elect Church to a " treasure;" the next parable likens it to "a pearl" —one pearl, pure and precious.

The Lord Jesus when He died for His Church regarded it as hidden " treasure," but not as "a treasure " merely: He viewed it as a treasure, the preciousness of which should be displayed and recognised. No one doubts that a pearl is pure, or that it is precious. The unity, the purity, and the preciousness of the Church, will alike be manifest in the day of its glory; and if the principles which will determine its relations *then* should be made through the Scripture influential *now*; if true Protestant Christianity should adopt and openly avow principles which separate *from* the systems of the world as distinctly as the principles they have hitherto avowed unite them *to* the world, then we might expect to see a position unitedly assumed, which, although perhaps feebly held, would as regards the principles maintained, be pure, precious, and therefore pearl-like, and so estimated by the graciousness of Christ.

If at the Reformation a few, by recognising that the elect Church was the " treasure " for which Christ died, and acting on that recognition gave thereby a new phase to Christianity and marked a fresh era in its history, would not a similar recognition of these further truths, even within a comparatively narrow circle, produce a similar result? Would it not give a new aspect to Christianity in the earth? The mere fact of this parable respecting " the pearl " forming one of the links in this evidently connected chain, would lead us to expect that, before "the mysteries of the kingdom of heaven " conclude, there would be yet once more an interference of God on behalf of His neglected Truth, resulting in some of His people being caused to teach and to act according to the principles illustrated by " the pearl." This, indeed, is what other parts of Scripture would lead us to expect. We read in the Book of Revelation of some who are said to " keep the commandments of God, and the faith of Jesus," at the very moment of the Church's last trial; and their faithfulness is such that it is made the subject of thanksgiving, even in heaven. "They overcame him because of the blood of the Lamb, and because of the word of their testimony; and they loved not their lives even unto death." In Daniel also, some are mentioned who are expressly designated "the wise or understanding ones" at that same hour. "The wicked shall do wickedly, and none of the wicked shall understand, but the understanding ones shall understand." Even then, as at the close of a day of tempest and gloom the sun sometimes struggles for a moment through the resisting clouds, and darts one parting ray of brightness over the troubled scene, so may we believe that it will be in this our dark dispensation of sorrow and of failure. A testimony will for a short moment be given, raged against by Satan, crushed by the governments of the Roman earth,* hated by all men, a feeble few excepted, yet honourable and precious in the sight of God. After this testimony has been given, the net, which has through God's patient grace so long been toiling in the great deep, will be drawn to shore. In every age it will have enclosed some "fish." Their character will then be determined: "the good will be gathered into vessels," "the bad cast away."

Thus ends this series of parables. When they finish, *"the mysteries* of the kingdom" end, and the

---

* See Rev. xii. Satan by means of the Ten Kingdoms of the Roman World, seeks to destroy those who are represented in that vision as the children of the TRUTH.

time of its glories, according to all that the Old Testament Prophets have revealed, at length comes. We have to remember both these things: its humiliation, and its glory. We have to bring out of our " treasures, things new and old."

If any should hesitate to regard this chapter as the intended prophetic history of our dispensation, let them use it simply in the way of illustration. Let them consider what the great cardinal events in the history of Christianity have been, and let them see how far they can be illustrated from these parables. The instruction will still remain.

It has not unfrequently been asked, whether the woman with the leaven in the thirteenth of Matthew is the same as the woman first seen *concealed* in the Ephah, (Zech. v.) and afterwards *displayed* in the attractiveness which the seventeenth of the Revelation describes.

This question may be answered by asking another. Suppose a system were now to be formed with the view of uniting the Ten Kingdoms of the Roman World, and commanding a moral influence over them; would that system be *ecclesiastical*, and therefore necessarily narrow in its scope, or must it be a system wide enough to embrace the many minds which it would have to influence, whether Jew or Greek, Mahomedan or Heathen, Papist or nominal Protestant?

Few will hesitate in answering this question. Whether such a system were collocated at Paris or Constantinople, at Rome or Jerusalem, at London or Babylon, it must be *wide* enough to embrace men as men.

Such is the system at present *hidden* in the Ephah, but soon to be displayed in the land of Shinar, in all the attractiveness which the seventeenth of the Revelation describes. False Christianity, as exhibited in the Roman and Eastern Churches, has, by feeding the nations with leavened meal, prepared the way for the seductions of that coming system, which is symbolised by a woman holding in her hand a cup, with the wine of which the nations are made drunken—a cup of intoxicating joy. No ecclesiastical system has ever yet spread universal gladness among the nations. On the contrary, the rule of such systems has been oppressive, and their yoke grievous. But the very power of the coming system will be, that it makes the nations glad with her wine, and with her delicacies.

Those who are now turning from the Scripture, and discarding the precious truths which the Protestant Reformation restored, may be distributed into two great divisions. The one class are retracing their way back to forsaken superstitions, and are seeking to become as near as possible what the Church was when she first became like the woman spreading the leaven. Another, and an increasing class, both in Germany, Switzerland and England, are throwing off all real regard to Scripture, and enamoured of schemes about man's powers, and man's destinies, are preparing themselves and others to welcome a system based on principles of *human*—not *Christian* fraternisation.

No two paths therefore, can be more thoroughly opposed than those which these two classes are at present following. *But they will be found capable of being bent round to the same point at last.* The attractiveness, and still more the influence of the woman of the seventeenth chapter of the Revelation will (at any rate throughout the Ten Kingdoms) entirely eclipse the attractiveness of the woman with the leaven. The latter will yield to the superior power of her rival, and become her servant. Her present votaries will follow in her train, and be transferred to the palaces of the Harlot. Symptoms of this yielding on the part of professing Christianity to the rising system of commercial and secular power are already manifest.

But the woman with the leaven, and the woman hidden in the Ephah, are not the *only* symbolic women of whom we read in the Scripture. We read also of another woman "clothed with the sun and with the moon under her feet and on her head a crown of twelve stars." She represents the system of God—the system of His revealed Truth now present in the earth *—His Truth as revealed in the Holy Scriptures.

* The character of glorious power which will attach to God's system of truth in the millennium, is clearly expressed by these symbols. It will be sustained by the presence

When we remember that God's truth is finally to be exalted, so as to be supreme over all nations, and that it is to be sustained by the full power of Christ's manifested millennial glory, we might expect that it would be represented, even whilst yet despised and outcast, by symbols expressive of its essential excellency—an excellency which in God's estimate, and therefore in the estimate of faith, attaches to it under all circumstances.

There is reason to hope that some, through increased acquaintance with the Scriptures, are becoming more sensible that there is such a system of Divine Truth now present in the earth. They are beginning to understand its character and its prospects in contrast both with those of the woman with the leaven, and with those of the Harlot of the Revelation. To such these questions are no matter of curious speculation.

Their estimate of the worldliness and falsehoods and idolatries of the professing Church, and of the yet more terrible wickedness of the rising latitudinarian system that will culminate in the Harlot of Babylon and Antichrist—their estimate of these things in contrast with the holiness and purity of DIVINE TRUTH, as revealed plainly, fully and sys-

---

of Christ's personal glory, that is symbolised by "the sun." The glory of the risen saints is continually represented by "stars." Hence her crown. "The moon," as shining with reflected light, is the emblem of ecclesiastical position—a position that will then be held by Israel, made subservient to God's truth. "The moon" was under her feet.

tematically in God's written word, is to them no barren abstraction. It supplies the influencing motives of their conduct. It enters into all their meditations, affects every prayer, and determines, more or less, all the practical arrangements of their lives. They see in Ecclesiasticism and in Latitudinarian Secularism, SATAN; in revealed TRUTH, that which Prophets and Apostles have written, they see GOD. They feel and they act accordingly.

CHAPTER VII.

ON DANIEL VIII.

CONNEXION OF ANTICHRIST WITH GREECE AND JERUSALEM.

THIS chapter may be regarded as commencing the second division of the Book of Daniel. The preceding chapters have, in a manner very unusual in Scripture, been almost appropriated to Gentiles. We have been shut up as it were into a Gentile sphere, and Jerusalem and the land of Israel have been left. Our thoughts have been directed either to the governmental principles that prevail among the Gentile empires, or to the characters of the Gentile monarchs, as in the narratives respecting Nebuchadnezzar, Belshazzar, and Darius, or to the history of the empires as fierce beasts trampling down and devouring the earth; but nothing is said of Jerusalem. If any of Israel are 'mentioned, it is only as being, like Daniel and his companions, strangers in a Gentile sphere. Even the last great monarch of the Gentiles, who will be so especially concerned with Jerusalem and the land of Israel, is, in the chapters we have been considering, only mentioned in his own Gentile connexion.

Accordingly, the very language marks this peculiarity. In the first seven chapters, it is not Hebrew but Chaldee—the language of Babylon, the great destroyer of Israel; but the eighth and subsequent chapters resume the Hebrew of the other Scriptures, and return to the language of the land of Israel. The great Gentile oppressor is indeed still mentioned, and is in fact the great theme of the prophecy, yet it is not any longer to the exclusion of Jerusalem. On the contrary, Jerusalem and the land of Israel are the theatre on which his evil is displayed. If in the former chapters the *Jew* is seen in the land of the *Gentiles*, in these chapters the Gentile is seen in Israel: Jerusalem is the place of his acting: the period is, "the time of the end."* Even in the second and seventh chapters, which are diffusive, we find that the prophecy is directed mainly to the concluding events of the dispensation; but this is more peculiarly the case in the eighth chapter. Thrice in this chapter the vision recorded in it is emphatically declared to point to "*the time of the end.*"

"He said unto me, Understand, O son of man; for at THE TIME OF THE END shall be the vision." (v. 17)

And again: "Behold, I will make thee know what shall be in the LAST END OF THE INDIGNATION; for at the time appointed the end shall be." (v. 19).

And again: "In the LATTER TIME OF their king-

---

* This, and all kindred expressions, such as "consummation" in Is. x. and Dan. ix. may be understood to refer to the same period, viz., that in which God, by means of Antichrist, is punishing Jerusalem for the last time. For the proofs of connexion between Dan. vii., viii., ix. and xi. see "Aids to Prophetic Enquiry, First series," Ch. vi.

dom, when the transgressors are come to the full, a king of fierce countenance . . . . shall stand up." (v. 23)

The seventh chapter reveals that this great person will arise out of the Roman Empire, for he is symbolised by an eleventh horn springing from the head of the Roman monster. We might indeed be sure that those mighty energies of evil which ever characterised Imperial Rome, *must* be connected with him who is to give to that evil its *last* form of concentration. Accordingly, his power will be exercised through the ten subordinate kings of the divided Roman World; and the limits of his authority are marked by the extent of the dominions of Rome. He will thus concentrate in himself the power of that empire, which, after inheriting the strength of the empires that preceded it, and adding thereunto new glories, has disappeared for a season from the world's view. But it will rise again in a federally united form, invested with new powers, and endowed with fresh energies to give effect to the evil engendered in its own course and that of the three empires which preceded it.* The empire which crucified Christ, which persecuted Christianity when pure, perverted it when fallen, and which will at last grow

---

* There were some in the early centuries who believed that the Roman Empire would grow torpid, and then revive. See Elliott, Horæ Apoc., quoting from some of the Oxford Tracts. "Another expectation of the early Church was, that the Roman Empire, remaining torpid for centuries, would wake up at the end of the world and be restored."

weary of it, and cast it off as a loathed and worthless thing, is the Empire from which the last great "desolator" will derive his *imperial* characteristics. Hence the Romans (when, under Titus, they destroyed Jerusalem) are described as "the people of the prince that shall come;" literally, "the prince, the coming one." Dan. ix. 26.

But there was a nation that preceded Rome—a nation with which Rome was never able to vie, either in taste, intellectual refinement, or in anything that adorns, or gives attractiveness and fascination to human life. That nation was Greece. It was there that the *mind* of man was allowed, in a special manner, to develop its powers. It exerted itself to throw a deceptive halo around the condition of humanity. Its deficiencies were concealed—its miseries veiled—its vices hallowed. Idolatry was made attractive by all that taste and refinement could draw around it to adorn. The powers of oratory and poetry were put forth to dignify evil, and to commend licentiousness: and if occasionally a philosopher or a moralist arose whose manners were austere, or whose teaching condemned the grosser flagrancies of vice, yet it was but the substitution of one evil for another. Pride and self-complacency were the results, even in the best of their schools of philosophy. "Professing themselves to be wise, they became fools," and brought their own hearts, and the hearts of others, even into deeper distance from God. From Greece this tide of evil poured into Rome. The foul and bitter streams have thence descended to these later

days, and have done more to fix a character on the
Gentile World, than Rome, unaided, would ever
have effected by all her extended and long protracted power. It was Greece that gave to Rome
her chief ability to fashion *morally* the nations.

It is not wonderful, therefore, that the name to
which Scripture has given precedence, when speaking of the Gentiles, should be that of Greece. "Jew
and Greek," is an expression continually used in the
Scripture as equivalent to "Jew and Gentile:" and
at a time yet future, when Israel shall be forgiven,
and again be strengthened against her Gentile
enemies, we find Greece still used as the great de-
nominative name for Gentilism. "When I have
. . . . . raised up thy sons, O Zion, against thy
sons, O GREECE."* Zech. ix. 13.

We might expect, therefore, that he who is so
peculiarly to concentrate in himself the power of
the Gentiles, who is to lead " the sons of Greece "

* Lactantius, who wrote at the commencement of the
fourth century, has a remarkable passage respecting the rise
of the East into dominion over the West: he says, "The
Roman name by which the world is now governed (I tremble
to say it, but I will say it, for it is to be) will be taken from
the earth, and the dominion will be restored to Asia; and
the East will again rule, and the West obey." Lactan. lib. vii.
These expectations of Lactantius will, in a qualified sense be
verified. It will not be true that the Eastern branch of the
Roman Empire will rule the Western; for they will form
parts of one great federation; but the Greek or Eastern half
will be infinitely the most important. Signs of this are even
now beginning to appear.

against "the sons of Zion," who is also to be so distinctly marked by intellectual power as to be noted by a peculiar symbol * such as no other earthly monarch ever had, and who in the Revelation is symbolised by "a leopard" (in Daniel, the symbol of Greece)—we might expect that such an one, though *Roman* as to the geographical extent and the iron character of his power, would in some especial manner be connected with *Greece*.

Accordingly, this chapter reveals that he will, as a king (at first a petty king), spring from that part of the Roman Empire which the Romans gained from the successors of Alexander. That this chapter treats of Alexander and his conquests is a fact which scepticism itself hardly dares to question. "The ram which thou sawest having two horns, are the kings of Media and Persia. And the rough goat is the king of Grecia: and the great horn that is between his eyes is the first king. Now that being broken, whereas four stood up for it, four kingdoms shall stand up out of the nation, but not in his power. And in the latter time of their kingdom, when the transgressors are come to the full, a king of fierce countenance, and understanding dark sen-

---

* "A horn having eyes." Of all the Empires, and all the individual monarchs who yet have been, none are regarded as having "eyes" united with their strength; and yet, some have not been deficient in wisdom. Nothing but *Satanic* power could give to Antichrist the superhuman perceptiveness and power of surveillance, devoted by the "eyes;" for God would not endow him with such power.

tences, shall stand up." The first king of Grecia
has arisen and has fallen: his four successors also
have reigned: but they too have passed away, and
their kingdoms have vanished without the king of
fierce countenance having appeared of whom it is
declared that he shall arise "in the *latter* time of
their kingdom." Has then this prophecy been
falsified?

It has *not* been falsified. The chapter throughout
its whole course declares that its burden respects
"the time of the end, when the transgressors shall
have come to the full," and regards the four kingdoms of Alexander's successors as *existent* at that
closing hour. "*The latter time of their kingdom*"
agrees with the time "*when the transgressors shall
have come to the full.*" See verse just quoted. These
four kingdoms therefore must be revived.

We know from the preceding chapter that the
whole Roman Empire, and therefore, that part of it
within which these kingdoms fall, is to be revived.
We know also that its Eastern, as well as Western
branch, is to be divided. All therefore as to this
that we learn additionally from the eighth chapter
is, that four of these divisions will be kingdoms
which passed from Alexander's successors into the
hands of Rome; that is to say, Greece, Egypt,
Syria, and the rest of the dominions of Turkey.

A few years ago, perhaps, this would have been
thought impossible. The maintenance of the integrity of the Turkish Empire was made the object of
such anxious effort on the part of the ruling king-

doms of the West, that nothing seemed more unlikely than its partition. Yet it has been in part dismembered; and Egypt and Greece have already separate governments of their own. It is also a fact that a similar separation of Syria has been in contemplation. Such a separation would be an almost certain concomitant of the return of the Jews to Palestine; and as soon as that separation is accomplished, the four kingdoms will re-exist.

And here I would remark that the mere fact of Egypt and of Greece being now existent as recognised governments, is a proof that the prophecy before us is *not* fulfilled. The king spoken of is said to arise " in the *last* time of *their* kingdom." Now, nothing that occurred previously to their disappearance as kingdoms, or previously to the late separation of Egypt and Greece, could be the LAST TIME OF THEIR KINGDOM, because sovereigns in Egypt and Greece *are at this moment ruling;* and seeing that the king predicted has *not* arisen *since* the separation of those kingdoms, it follows that his rise must be *future.*

That Antichrist is to arise from the Eastern part of the Roman Empire, and from that part of the East which fell under the rule of Alexander's successors, is rendered unquestionable by this chapter. But, seeing that in the eleventh chapter he is mentioned as conflicting with the king of the North (*i.e.* the king of Syria), and also with the king of the South (*i.e.* the king of Egypt), it is plain that he does not arise either from Egypt or Syria. He must

O

therefore arise either from Greece or from the districts immediately contiguous to Constantinople. It is true that if he arose from the latter, or indeed from either of the four, he would be esteemed Greek in origin, because all the four were divisions of the Greek Empire; but it seems far more probable that Greece Proper will be the place of his rise. He is described as "waxing great toward the South and toward the East, and toward the pleasant land;" that is, toward Egypt, Syria, and Palestine—a description that would geographically suit the position of one who was supposed to be in Greece.

Moreover, a "*little* horn" (an emblem not of that which he is as an individual, but of that which he is as a monarch) is a symbol that well suits one who should arise from one of those petty principalities which once abounded in Greece, and have even still their memorial in the throne of the sovereigns of Montenegro.

Since the time when the Gentiles first began to tread down Jerusalem, almost every one who has arisen among them illustrious for conquest or for power, will be found to have foreshadowed some of the distinctive features that are to characterise the last great Monarch of the Gentiles. This is especially the case whenever Jerusalem or the East is the scene in which the glory of such conquerors has been displayed. The two monarchs of Grecian origin, whose connection with Jerusalem in past time has been attended with circumstances of more than ordinary interest, are Alexander, and one of his successors, Antiochus Epiphanes; and they are the two to whom our attention is specifically directed in reading this chapter. It is necessarily directed to Alexander, because he is expressly mentioned as the first king of Grecia, and the overthrower of Persia; and because he was the *first king of Greece connected with Jerusalem.* It is directed to Antiochus, because he went far towards fulfilling all that is terrible in this chapter in relation to Jerusalem. Both Alexander and Antiochus, therefore, may be considered as foreshadowing the last great inheritor of the Gentile power.

The kingdom of Macedon (of which Alexander was the chief) was insignificant until suddenly raised by Alexander's father and himself to the headship of Greece. The education of Alexander under the leading philosopher of his day, his talent, his taste, and his power of conciliating and fascinating even his enemies, are too well known to be narrated here. For the most part dignified and self-possessed, it was but occasionally that he manifested the fierce and degrading passions that slumbered within. He came to Jerusalem in all the pride of victory and triumph—was met by the High Priest and priests in a supplicatory procession — forgave them—made a covenant with them—offered sacrifice —gave gifts to the Temple, and in everything became their friend. We can scarcely fail to discern in this a foreshadowing of him who, surpassing Alexander in attractiveness and power, will, for a season, present himself to Jerusalem as its protector and friend. "By peace he shall destroy many" (Dan. viii. 25).

Some years after Alexander came Antiochus.* No one can read in the first Book of Maccabees the terrible description of his actings in Jerusalem without seeing that he must have been especially intended to foreshadow the last great Destroyer. The mild-

* Jerome, speaking of this vision in the 8th of Daniel, says: "Most of our people (plerique nostrorum) refer it to Antichrist, and say, that what was done under Antiochus in type, is to be fulfilled under the other in reality."

The following passage from a recent historian shows how many of the plans and features of the last great Gentile King were foreshadowed in Alexander.

"Proportionate to the simplicity of Alexander's plans for the commencement, was apparently the immensity of those forecast for the sequel. Babylon was to be the head city of his empire, and consequently, of the world. The union of the East and the West was to be brought about through the amalgamation of the dominant races by marriages, by education; and, more than all, by the ties of commerce; the importance of which, far ruder conquerors in Asia itself soon learned to appreciate. In nothing, probably, is the superiority of his genius more brilliantly displayed than in his exaltation above national prejudice, particularly when we consider that none of his Macedonians could in this respect approach near to him. To refuse him that quality is impossible, whatever the judgment formed on his general character. Sudden death, by fever, of Alexander at Babylon, under the circumstances of the time, was the greatest loss mankind could experience. From the Indus to the Nile, the world had been shivered: and where was the architect that could gather up the scattered fragments and restore the edifice?" *Heeren.*

ness and fascination of the first King of Grecia was gone, and nothing remained but destructiveness and fury. Here was the result of the link that bound Jerusalem to Greece. And so it *will* be again. They will be captivated by one more attractive and mighty than Alexander, but will find in him, at last, a terror and a power of destruction, such as Antiochus but faintly pre-figured.

By thus considering the past, and recalling the remembrance of individuals and empires that have departed, we are able to apprehend more clearly the character of him in whom all human glory will be concentrated, and all energy of evil dwell. But one chief use of regarding the future history of this last great monarch is, that we might read in the light of that history the character of all human glory in this present age. The concentrated blaze of this evil glory will not burst upon men without their having been before familiar in their embryo forms with the *elements* of its brightness. If we learn not to judge the character of such glory in the fragmentary and divided forms in which it has been heretofore presented, how can we expect to escape the dazzling power of its *concentration* when the appointed hour of strong delusion comes?

The character, therefore, of Greece and Rome, and of everything connected with their greatness, may be learned in him who finally unites their characteristic glories. But there is another people who, though less attractive, have been equally influential for evil. The JEW, the Greek, and the Roman, were the three from whom the generation in which the Lord Jesus lived derived its characteristic features. The title of His cross was written in Hebrew, in Greek, and in Latin. These had been, and were, the influential languages of the earth ; and their union in that inscription too clearly indicated that light, intellect, and power, abused by man, were united in the attempt to crush the only One in the earth that was holy and acceptable before God. And when again the last great assault is made upon the Truth of God and of Christ, it is by one, Greek in origin and character, Roman in power, but located in Jerusalem, and associated with transgressing Israel there. The scene of the chapter we are now considering is Jerusalem ; for he is mentioned as profaning the "sanctuary," and "taking away the daily sacrifice ;" and in the chapter that follows he is described as making "a covenant with many for one week," which covenant he afterwards violates.

What the iniquities of Jerusalem have been in days that are past, need not be told to them that know the Scripture. What it *will* be, may be judged of both from Scripture and from present facts. The present condition of the Jews, their wealth, their intellect, their energy, their readiness to gather around one who should unite the greatness of Rome with the attractiveness of Greece, show too plainly that they are fast ripening for the great transgression. In this state they are to be re-gathered to Jerusalem, *there* to be the prey of the last great Destroyer. "I will send him against an hypocritical nation, and against the people of my wrath will I give him a charge, to take the spoil and to take the prey, and to tread them down like the mire of the streets." In Jerusalem they will become the victims first of his delusions, and then of his cruelties; *there* also they will be made partakers of his plagues. "Thus saith the Lord God: Because ye are all become dross, behold, therefore I will gather you into the midst of Jerusalem. As they gather silver, and brass, and iron, and lead, and tin into the midst of the furnace, to blow the fire upon it, to melt it; so will I gather you in mine anger and in my fury, and I will leave you there, and melt you. Yea, I will gather you and blow upon you in the fire of my wrath, and ye shall be melted in the midst thereof. As silver is melted in the midst of the furnace, so shall ye be melted in the midst thereof; and ye shall know that I, the Lord, have poured out My fury upon you." (Ezekiel xxii. 19) The words also of our Lord respecting the final inhabitation of Israel by the sevenfold power of Satan will be remembered by those who have read the preceding remarks on the thirteenth chapter of Matthew.

The earliest period at which Antichrist brings himself into connexion with the Jews as a people in Jerusalem, is mentioned in the *ninth* chapter. He is there said to make a covenant with many for seven years. This, no doubt, is the period of which it is said that "by peace he shall destroy many." But there is too much of the order and ostensible worship of God connected with Jerusalem, for him long to remain satisfied with the arrangements which for a time he will sanction there. The Jews, when they return to Jerusalem, will re-build their temple and re-institute their sacrifices: and although such worship will be hateful to God, and "he that killeth an ox will be as if he slew a man," and "he that offereth an oblation, as if he offered swine's blood;" yet there will be enough that reminds of God in these things to excite the enmity of him who intends to "exalt himself above all that is. called God, or that is worshipped." Antichrist will little care whether God does, or does not own the Temple and accept the sacrifices. He will be the servant of Satan; and Satan knows that those sacrifices and that Temple, however prostituted and misused, stand before angels and before men—before God and before Christ, as a memorial of truths precious and everlasting: and therefore he will desire to sweep such memorials utterly away. God, because of the transgression of His people, will not interfere to hinder. "An host," *i.e.* power, will be given him against the daily sacrifice, and he will cause it to cease.*

But Judaism will not be the only object against which he will direct his fury. He will "magnify himself against the Prince of princes," *i.e.* against

* The relation of Antichrist to Israel will, in some respects, resemble that of Judas to the Lord. They too will prove the bitterness of betrayal and desertion by a pretended friend. Hence, in Psalm lv. there is evidently a double allusion to Judas and to Antichrist.

Christ. He will not, indeed, be able to reach Him personally, for He is high above all heavens; but Christ's Truth, and Christ's people will yet be within his grasp, and them he will persecute and trample down. He "waxed great, even to the host of the heavens (עַד־עְבָא הַשָּׁמָיִם); and cast down some of the host and of the stars to the ground, and stamped upon them." Prospective titles of glory are here given to the believing people of Christ whilst yet the hour of their militancy in suffering is being continued. As in the seventh chapter we have seen them called "saints of the high places" whilst they were yet travailing in the earth, so here they are called "stars," and "host of the heavens," even whilst the fell power of the great Destroyer is allowed to prevail against them. To the outward eye they will appear to be but a feeble few, despised for their ways, and hated for their testimony, but God seeth not as man seeth. He knows them, and He names them according to that which they will be when the hour of their sorrow shall have passed, and when bright in the radiancy of unearthly glory "they shall shine as the stars for ever and ever." As soon as the "morning star" shall arise upon the dark night of evil, they too shall be called up to share its glory. "To him that overcometh will I give the morning star." But during *the time of the end*, whilst Truth is being trampled on and cast down, they will be privileged to share its sufferings : they will be cast down together with it. It will be to them an honour and a joy. It will not repent them in the day of Christ's glory, that they have suffered for and with Christ's Truth.

Many attempts have been made to nullify the testimony of this chapter as to the future. Some have sought to find " the king of fierce countenance" in the Pontiff of Rome; others, ashamed of the folly of such an interpretation, have suggested Mahomet. But to which of the criteria supplied by this chapter does Mahomet answer ?

First, Mahomet did not spring from one of the divisions of Alexander's broken Empire (see verse 22); he was an Arabian. Secondly, he did not arise "in the latter time " of the kingdoms spoken of (see verse 23), for both Greece and Egypt are even at this present moment, existent, recognised powers. Thirdly, he did not live at a time when " the transgressors had come to the full " (see verse 23), for there has been advance in transgression ever since, and the culminating point of the triumph of evil is even yet in the future. Fourthly, he did not live " at the last end of the indignation " against Israel and Jerusalem (see verse 19), for that hour is still to come. Fifthly, Mahomet neither visited Jerusalem, nor took thence the daily sacrifice (see verse 11), nor did any daily sacrifice then exist. Sixthly, although Mahomet may be said (though not in the sense in which the words are used in this chapter) to have " exalted himself against the Prince of princes," yet he was not " broken without hand," *i.e.* by the direct interference of almighty power from heaven. Nor, seventhly, must the characteristics ascribed to the last great Head of transgression in the preceding chapter be disregarded. He is to reign not over the East merely, but over all the Ten Kingdoms of the Roman World. The very words "king of fierce countenance" mark him as being imperially *Roman*. Do these characteristics attach to Mahomet, or to anyone else whom the earth has seen since Daniel wrote these words? Antiochus Epiphanes is doubtless the person whose course most nearly assimulates itself to the descriptions of this chapter, yet even he (although so remarkably fore-shadowing the relation of Antichrist to Israel and Jerusalem) did not live "in the last end of the indignation," nor did he (as Antichrist will) stand up against the Prince of princes, for Christ had not then come; nor did he live when the transgressors had come to the full; nor was he broken without hand.

When, therefore, the appointed time arrives for "the transgressors to come to the full," that is, when all those who are to unite in the last great Apostasy are ready, a Head shall be provided for them. He shall be "strong [or mighty] in countenance"* like the Romans of old; for it is of them that

---

* Such is the literal translation of עַז פָּנִים He will be a king mighty in countenance. The same expression, "strong or mighty in countenance" is in Deut. xxviii. 50, used of the Romans, when they are first mentioned as the appointed desolators of Jerusalem. It is an expression therefore that seems peculiarly applicable to the crushing *iron* strength of the *Roman* power, of which Antichrist will be the last inheritor.

this expression is used in Deuteronomy xxviii. 50,
where the Romans are first mentioned as the
desolators of Jerusalem.   It is an expression that
denotes especially the iron strength of the Roman
power.   But his wisdom and intelligence shall be as
marked as his power.   He shall understand dark
and hidden things,* and be able to solve questions
which baffle the powers of other men.   What
Solomon was through wisdom given from God, that
Antichrist will measurably be through intelligence
communicated by Satan.   The word translated
"policy," is a word strongly indicative of understanding and wisdom.   Thus David said to Solomon,

---

* "Understanding dark sentences."   The word translated
"dark sentences" means, properly, something twisted or involved and therefore difficult.   The same expression is used
when it is said of the Queen of Sheba that she went to prove
Solomon with "*hard questions.*"   It again occurs in Psalm
lxxviii. 2. "I will open my mouth in a parable, I will utter
dark sayings of old"—a passage applied in Matthew to the
Lord Jesus.   Again, we read in the Proverbs of "the words
of the wise and their dark sayings."   "Understanding dark
sentences" is therefore a description indicative of supernatural wisdom.   This last great Monarch of the Gentiles,
described in the Scripture as one that "cometh up out of
the bottomless pit," will rival Solomon in wisdom, and men
will admire and venerate that wisdom, little caring to enquire
whence it comes.   It will come from the indwelling energy of
Satan.   This and the preceding clause will well explain the
reason of the symbol—"a horn having eyes"—*i.e.* strength
and supernatural intelligence combined — but it will be
intelligence that will come from, and lead unto, Hell.   The
only One who can deliver from these things is "the great
Shepherd of the sheep."

"Only the Lord give thee *wisdom;*" and again it is said of Solomon, "endued with *prudence*"—the same word שֵׂכֶל being used in all these passages. But his wisdom will be accompanied by "craft" or "subtilty." It is the word which is used of Jacob when Isaac said, "thy brother came with subtilty." Deceit therefore, sinuosity, and lying, will habitually mark all the applications of his power and of his wisdom. The Leopard which is his symbol (Rev. xiii.) and the symbol of Greece (Dan. vii.) is especially characterised by subtilty. Yet his strength, though so mighty, will not be his own, for he will rule as the elected federal head of the Ten Kings who shall divide the Roman World. It is they who concur and give their authority unto him "until the words of God shall be fulfilled." See Rev. xvii. 17. He will stand up against the "Prince of princes," for he will be the head of that confederacy that shall say of Jehovah and of Christ, "Let us break their bands asunder, and cast away their cords from us." He will continue to stand up against Him, even at the moment when He cometh forth in His glory as King of kings, and Lord of lords; but he shall be "consumed by the spirit of His mouth, and destroyed by the brightness of His appearing." "Thus he shall be broken without hand." No human power shall grasp and overcome the "sons of Belial." They shall be utterly burned with fire kindled by Him who kindleth Tophet. See Is. xxx. 33, and 2 Sam. xxiii. 6, 7.

Such is the Monarch with whom Israel in Jerusalem shall enter into covenant (see Dan. ix.)—that covenant of which God has said, "Your covenant with death shall be disannulled, and your agreement with hell shall not stand." Yet it is a covenant under which they will rest for a short season.*

It is but too evident that Jews, Mahomedans and Christians, whether in the East, or in the West, are alike ready to welcome the advent of such an one as this chapter describes. There appear to be many tokens that "the time of the end" is approaching. The disposition among many of the Jews to return to Palestine, the separation of Egypt and Greece into recognised sovereignties, the introduction of

* The entering into this covenant is, as I have already said, the first event which Scripture records of Antichrist's connexion with Jerusalem. He makes it for seven years. This we learn from the *ninth* chapter. About seven months after he has made this covenant he begins to " practise " in Jerusalem, probably then visiting it for the first time. This we learn from the *eighth* chapter—the vision which avowedly respects *the whole period during which he practises in Jerusalem and has power over the sanctuary.* That period is said to be 2,300 days, *i.e.* seven years wanting about seven months. At the half of the seven years, and therefore about two years and five months after he begins to practise in Jerusalem, he takes away the daily sacrifice, and sets the abomination of desolation in the Holy Place; and this continues for 1,260 days, or three years and a half. Thus we have three points in his history. *First,* the formation of his covenant. *Secondly,* the commencement of his actings in Jerusalem. *Thirdly,* his violation of his covenant, and establishment of the idol. The covenant is for seven years: the practising for six years and five months: the worship of the Idol for three years and a half.

Western principles and of Western material prosperity into the Eastern parts of the Roman World, and the wondrous spread of latitudinarian scepticism may be numbered among the signs of the end drawing nigh. They show that the kingdoms are, morally and physically, falling into the form which we know from Scripture to be that which they will bear when the conclusion comes.

The four-fold partition of the Empire of Alexander is our guide to a corresponding division that will appear within the dominions over which Turkey once ruled. Whenever Syria is separated from Turkey, whether by convulsion; or by more quiet agency, it will probably be said by many that the vials are being poured out, and that the waters of the Euphrates are being dried up. But, instead of this it will be the hour when the Euphratean regions will begin to arise in renovated strength; and when Constantinople herself, or the kingdom of which she will be the seat, will attain to a rank among the Ten Kingdoms of the Roman World, greater than she has ever held as the head of the crumbling Empire of the Turks.*

* In the final division of Alexander's dominions, Ptolemy possessed Egypt, Cyrene, Cœle Syria, and some of the southern parts of Asia Minor. Cassander; Macedon and Greece. Lysimachus; Thrace and Bythynia. Seleucus; all the rest. His dominions extended from the Mediterranean across the Euphrates to India, including Babylon.

This division may give us a general notion of the territories to be comprehended within these four kingdoms when they again exist. We must remember, however, that no provinces

But this revival, and all that is consequent thereupon, will be a revival by man and by Satan—not
by God. He has in present human energies no
power of life or of blessed renovation; they are in
His sight agencies only of woe and desolation.
Before He renovates, He will cause death to pass
upon every hope and anticipation of man. All shall
be as the valley of bones which Ezekiel beheld:
bones that were "very dry." But God is accustomed to make the place of death the sphere of the
operation of His power in blessing. He will at last
speak the word, and life shall enter into the scene
of death ; and men will at length discern the difference between the presence of the life-giving glory
of God, and the presence of that other glory which
had been kindled from the pit, whose course had
been desolation—its end, wrath.

---

are to be included in the final division *except those that were
subjugated by Rome*. The kingdom of Syria, therefore, will
not extend much beyond Babylon. Greece and Egypt will
no doubt be considerably augmented by accession of territory.
The latter probably will annex to herself Ethiopia (Abyssinia).
In Albania and the northern provinces of Ancient Greece,
there has been for many years a strong desire to separate from Turkey, and to unite with southern Greece. It is
probable, however, that among the kingdoms of the Roman
World, Greece is that which will develop itself latest. As in
ancient times, Egypt and the coasts of Asia Minor and Syria
are at the present moment forestalling Greece. Στασις και
λησ̄τεια, "faction and robbery" hindered Greece ancient, and
στασις και ληστεια are hindering her now. Yet her time of
meteor-like brightness will again come : it will last for a
moment : and then she shall fall never to rise again.

CHAPTER VIII.

THE SEVENTY HEBDOMADS. DANIEL IX.

THE prophecy of Daniel dwells so much on the evil glory of the Gentiles, and on the divine "indignation" against Jerusalem, that he is regarded by the Jews as peculiarly their prophet of woe. On this account they are accustomed to separate his prophecy from the rest of the prophetic writings, and to place it by itself at the end of their Bibles, not because they value it less than the other Scriptures, on the contrary, they value it most highly. They do this in token that they recognise in the Book of Daniel the history of Israel's chastisement, degradation, and woe. It is the book that treats of Gentile supremacy and Jewish debasement.

The vision of the ninth chapter, however, may almost be regarded as an exception to the general character of this prophecy. The humiliation of Daniel and his confession of the sin of his people were accepted, and an angel was sent to instruct and comfort him. The punishment of Jerusalem is indeed still spoken of, but the mention of that punishment is so tempered by a reference to the mercies that are to follow, that the darkness of the present is almost lost in the light of the future. "Seventy weeks are determined upon thy people, and upon thy holy city, to finish the transgression, and to make an end of sins, and to make reconciliation for iniquity, and to bring in everlasting righteousness, and to seal up the vision and prophecy, and [to anoint the most Holy." Dan. ix. 24. These are the thoughts that predominate in this vision, and cast over it the light of bright and peaceful anticipation.

It was granted as a reward to the humiliation and confession of Daniel. He had remembered and used the prophecy of Jeremiah. It was a prophecy *unfulfilled;* but *unfulfilled* prophecy was not despised by Daniel. By using it, he learned that the time was drawing nigh for God again to show favour towards Jerusalem, in terminating the seventy years of her then present desolation. The knowledge of this led him to confession and prayer, and his faith was answered. 'Not only was he taught respecting the approaching restoration of God's city, but instruction was vouchsafed even concerning things about which he had not asked; and he was carried on into ages yet to come, when Jerusalem "shall not be plucked up, nor thrown down any more for ever." Jer. xxxi. 40.

As the passage, however, which contains this prophecy, is imperfectly rendered in our present version, it is necessary, before we proceed, to consider it in some detail.

The word translated in our version "*weeks,*" means simply a septenary number or *hebdomad.* It stands in the same relation to *seven,* as our English word dozen does to twelve, or as decad to ten. Thus as we may say, a dozen of days, or a dozen of weeks, or a dozen of years, so we may say, a hebdomad of days, *i.e.* seven days ; or a hebdomad of weeks, *i.e.* seven weeks ; or a hebdomad of years, *i.e.* seven years. In the case before us, the expression "seventy hebdomads" being used alone, and not followed by the word days, or weeks, or months, or years, it is necessary to determine by other means which of these is intended to be supplied.

The next word, translated in our version " *determined*," is not elsewhere used in the Old Testament. It means, according to Gesenius, *to cut, to divide*, and is rendered by Theodotion συνετμηθησαν, and by others, τετμηνται. *To sever into a divided portion, or portions*, is evidently the meaning. Seventy hebdomads have been *severed from the rest of time*, that in these hebdomads God, acting definitely in Jerusalem, might there accomplish His work.

The word translated "*finish*" means "*to shut up*," or "*imprison*," answering to the Greek κλειω or κωλυω. It is used thus 1 Sam. vi. 10, "*and shut up their calves at home :*" and again, Ps. lxxxviii. 9., "I am *shut up*, and cannot come forth." The thought is analogous to burying, or hiding out of sight. The transgressions of Israel will then be hidden for ever.

The word translated "*to make an end of*" means literally "*to seal up*," in the sense of effectually and authoritatively shutting up. God will then *shut up* the transgression, and *seal up* the sins of Israel. The same thoughts are similarly connected in the Revelation—there applied to the imprisonment of Satan. The angel was seen to "*shut him up*, and *set a seal* upon him." Rev. xx. 3.

The words "to make reconciliation," adopted by our translators as the translation of לְכַפֵּר in the next clause, is not a satisfactory rendering.

The Pihel of כָּפַר when used with reference to the expiation of sin, is employed in two very distinct senses. Its first and great use is when it is applied to *the act of the priest in presenting atoning sacrifice to God.* This is its prevailing meaning in the Old Testament, and when thus used it is followed by עַל, בְּעַד, or some other preposition either expressed, or else associated with it, in the context. When thus used it should always be translated, "*make*, or *offer atonement*"—atonement meaning, not at-one-ment, *i.e.* reconciliation, but denoting the atoning offering itself presented to satisfy the claims of God.

In its second use it is applied, not to the priest as making atonement, *but to God as applying it*, and so forgiving and cancelling the iniquity. In this sense it is used in the passage before us. It here directs our thoughts not to the making atonement by the Priest (*that* was finished on Calvary), but to the application of that atonement to Israel, when they shall have believed, and their sins be cancelled and remembered no more. For the use of כָּפַר in this sense, see Deut. xxxii. 43, and Deut. xxi. 8, where it is translated "*be merciful unto;*" 2 Chron. xxx. 18, where it is translated "*pardon;*" and Jer. xviii. 23, where it is translated "*forgive*," all these and like passages referring, not to the making of the atonement by the priest unto God, but to the application of the atonement by God, or by the Priest as representing God, to the persons or things purged by it.

To seal up the vision and prophecy. This is not a satisfactory translation. It is indeed the same word that is used in the previous clause, and which I have translated *seal up*. But "to seal" is used in three senses in the Scripture :—

I. In the sense of hiding, confining, or securing, because we are accustomed to *seal up* that which we wish to hide, confine, or secure. The ancients were accustomed to put a seal on many things for which we use a lock.

II. In the sense of confirming, or ratifying; because we seal that which we wish to ratify.

III. In the sense of *terminating;* because we affix a seal to a document or letter as our concluding act.

Either of the two last meanings may be taken in the present passage. Past vision and prophecy will then be both terminated and ratified by fulfilment.

To anoint the most Holy—that is, the most Holy Place, the Holy of Holies. Whether this be understood as referring to the place of Israel's earthly worship, or to the antitypical heavenly sanctuary not made with hands, in either case it speaks of the time of Israel being forgiven and brought under the applied power of redemption. This expression is nowhere used as signifying a person.*

* See Tregelles on Daniel, p. 98.

Abominations. This word is continually used for "idols." Our translators have so rendered it in 2 Chron., xv., 8—"Put away the *abominable* idols." Again, we read of "Chemosh the *abomination* of the Moabites;" and so in a multitude of other passages where the same word is used. The answering word in Greek, βδελυγμα, is similarly used.

Overspreading. The word thus translated means . simply "a wing." It is customary in all languages to apply this word metaphorically as when we speak of the *wing* of an army, or of the *wing* of a building. In Hebrew this is done more than in our language. Thus it is applied to the earth, and translated *corners:* "From the four *corners* (literally *wings*) of the earth." We cannot be surprised, therefore, that it should be applied to the *"pinnacle"* of a building. The Greek word πτερυγιον, translated *pinnacle* in the New Testament, exactly corresponds with it. Christ was placed by Satan on a pinnacle of the Temple. Gesenius thus translates כָּנָף in this place. The expression *pinnacle of idols* is a Hebraism, and means *idolatrous pinnacle.* The Vulgate does not translate, but paraphrases the passage by saying, "et erit in templo abominatio desolationis"—"and the abomination of desolation shall be in the temple." Theodotion* does the same: και επι το ιερον βδελυγμα των ερημωσεων—"and on the temple shall be the abomination of desolations."

As regards the words מְשֹׁמֵם and שֹׁמֵם, which are merely different parts of the same verb, they are

* See Appendix.

rightly rendered by Gesenius in the active sense "desolating" or "desolator." * See also Tregelles, Stonard, and Faber.

The translation of the whole passage may be given thus :

"Seventy hebdomads are severed [or divided off] upon thy people and upon thy holy city, to shut up transgression, and to seal up sins, and to bring under atonement iniquity, and to bring in everlasting righteousness, and to ratify [literally to seal] vision and prophet, and to anoint the most Holy Place. Know therefore, and understand, from the going forth of the commandment to restore and to build Jerusalem unto the Messiah, the Prince, are seven hebdomads, and sixty and two hebdomads; the street shall be built again, and the wall, even in pressure of time [i.e., in times of straitness or pressure]. And after sixty and two hebdomads, Messiah shall be cut off, and there shall be nothing to him ;† and the city and the sanctuary shall the

---

* The expression occurs in the following passages :—

Dan. viii. 13. "Transgression that desolateth."

Dan. ix. 27. "On the pinnacle of abominations shall be the desolating one."

Idem. "Until that determined be poured upon the desolating one."

Dan. xi. 31. "The abomination that desolateth."

Dan. xii. 11. "The abomination that desolateth."

The expression of our Lord in Matt. xxiv, βδελυγμα της ερημωσεως is equivalent to that in Dan. xii.—ερημωσις being the active form of the verbal noun.

† There shall be nothing to, or for Him, i. e. in Jerusalem and Israel. Israel was not gathered.

The end of Antichrist is to be in "the overflowing." "Overflow" is a word applied with peculiar definiteness to

people destroy of the prince that cometh; and his end shall be in the overflowing, and until the end there is war, even that which is determined for desolations. And he [the prince that cometh] shall confirm a covenant with the many [*i.e.*, with the multitude] for one hebdomad; and at half the hebdomad he shall cause sacrifice and oblation to cease, and upon the pinnacle of abominations [*i.e.*, the idolatrous pinnacle] shall be that which causeth desolation, even until the consummation, and that determined shall be poured upon the causer of desolation."

This, I believe, is as exact a translation of this remarkable passage as can well be given. The two periods on which it principally dwells are—the time when the sins of Israel shall be forgiven; and the time that immediately precedes their forgiveness, when, for seven years, they shall be under the hand of the great destroyer. Both these periods are of course future. The prophecy does not terminate at the crucifixion, nor at the destruction of Jerusalem by the Roman armies; it mentions both these events, but it does not conclude with them. Like the rest of Daniel, it goes on to the termination of the desolations of Jerusalem, and does not cease until "THE CONSUMMATION," when the Holy of Holies is anointed, and that determined is poured upon the desolator. The past periods of the devas-

the *last hour* of visitation on Israel. Thus it is said, "The consumption decreed shall *overflow* with righteousness," *i. e.*, with righteous judgment. Is. x. 22. And again: "When the *overflowing* scourge shall pass through, then shall ye be trodden down by it." Is. xxviii. 18.

tation of Jerusalem by Roman armies were not periods of which it could be said that her sins were forgiven and everlasting righteousness brought in. On the contrary, they were times when her sins were had in remembrance; and in consequence thereof her people have been led captive into all nations, and scattered towards the four winds of heaven. But an hour is coming, when the blood of atonement that has been already shed shall be *applied* to repentant Israel, and when, the evil having been taken from their heart, they shall recognise Him whom they have despised as being Jehovah their Righteousness. Then everlasting righteousness shall be brought in; then, at last, it shall be said: " Speak ye comfortably to Jerusalem, and cry unto her that her warfare is accomplished, that her iniquity is pardoned; for she hath received of the Lord's hand double for all her sins." Is. xl. 2.

The seventy hebdomads of *years* * mentioned in this passage are distributed into three divisions.

* The use of the word " hebdomad" without an adjunct (especially in a chapter where years had been spoken of see ix. 2.) is, of itself, sufficient to show that " years" are intended. There is no doubt that Daniel and the Jews would so understand it. Grotius says : " Seventy hebdomads, that is of years ; for so the Talmudists were accustomed to speak, as they still do : consequently, when a hebdomad of days is, meant, the word days is wont to be added." So also Aben Ezra, who lived in the twelfth century: " It was said by our honourable master Saadias that those weeks are weeks of years. In proof of this may be quoted the saying of Daniel x. 2. ' I Daniel was mourning three weeks of *days*.' Now Saadias expounds correctly and well . . . . Know also

The first consists of *seven* hebdomads, *i.e.* 49 years.

The second of *sixty-two* hebdomads, *i.e.* 434 years.

The third of *one* hebdomad, *i.e.* 7 years.

The first of these divisions—viz., of 49 years—commenced when the commandment went forth to restore and to build Jerusalem, and ends by "the street being built again, and the wall, even in troublous times." The wall, therefore, begun by

that in Holy Scripture days are always days, and never years. Yet it is possible that the word 'days' may mean an entire year, since the repetition of the days produces a return of the year, as when it is said in Ex. xiii. 10, from days to days, *i. e.* from year to year, days meaning a complete year. But when the number is stated, as two days, three days, it cannot mean years, but must mean days as it stands." See Aben Ezra quoted by Maitland in his Apostles' School of Prophetic Interpretation.

But even if we were to admit that the expression was ambiguous, they to whom it was addressed could not long have remained in doubt whether hebdomads of days, or weeks, or months, or years, were intended. If they imagined that the wall could be completed in 49 days, or 49 weeks, or 49 months, they would soon be undeceived when they came to the end of those periods, and found that it was not completed. Its completion at the end of 49 years would demonstrate to them that *years* were intended. The Septuagint in their translation actually insert " years."

As few now quote this passage in support of the extraordinary theory of " days " meaning " years," perhaps nothing need be said respecting it. It is very obvious that since the word "days" does not occur in the passage, that which does not exist cannot be put for anything, nor mean anything. For further remarks on the hebdomads, see Tregelles on Daniel, p. 91.

Nehemiah, was not completed until 49 years from its commencement.

The second division commenced from this completion of the wall, and extends to the "cutting off" of the Messiah. After threescore and two hebdomads *i.e.*, 434 years, shall Messiah be cut off.

The third division, *i.e.*, seven years, will commence when "the prince that shall come," *i.e.*, Antichrist, "shall make a covenant with the multitude," and ends by wrath being sent upon the Desolator, and blessing on Jerusalem.

The hebdomads, therefore, do not commence as soon as the prophecy was given to Daniel. It was given in the first year after the conquest of Babylon by Cyrus, B.C. 537, but it did not commence to be fulfilled until the decree given to Nehemiah to restore the wall of Jerusalem in the twentieth year of Artaxerxes, B.C. 454 or 455. Eighty-three years therefore passed away before these hebdomads commenced their course. These eighty-three years were years of much interest to Israel, for in them the labours of Ezra and others restored the Temple. Nevertheless, these years are not included in the seventy hebdomads severed, or divided off, on Jerusalem. The reason evidently is this: the prophecy respects not Israel merely, but *Jerusalem*. "Seventy hebdomads are divided upon thy people, and *upon thy holy city*." They were not to commence until the commandment should go forth to restore and to build *Jerusalem:* and that commandment was not given to Ezra, but to Nehemiah. Ezra rebuilt

the Temple merely, but Nehemiah builded the
wall, and restored the *nationality* of Israel in Jerusalem.

The "seventy divided hebdomads," therefore,
are not concerned with any or every period in the
history of Israel.   They concern only periods in
which God regards Israel as nationally gathered in
their own city ; and in which His hand is directly
engaged in forwarding His great plan of overthrowing the Gentile oppressor, and delivering His people.
Consequently, the progress of the seventy hebdomads is stopped at the Crucifixion ; for then Jerusalem was virtually set aside when the Lord Jesus,
four days before His death, said, "Your house is
left unto you desolate."   The plans for its national
blessing, and the destruction of its enemies, which
till then the hand of God had steadily carried forward, were suspended ; and soon after, Jerusalem
was utterly blotted out.   The course of the hebdomads will not be resumed until Israel, under a
covenant formed with Antichrist, shall again assume
a *national* existence in Jerusalem.

Then again they will become in Jerusalem the
subjects of direct dealing from the hand of God
" set to," as He Himself expresses it, to effect His
own designs of final blessing.   That blessing, however, is to be reached through judgment and fiery
indignation that will consume the transgressors.
Jerusalem is to be " the furnace" before it is the
City of Peace.   "The Lord's fire is at Zion, and his
furnace in Jerusalem."   "Because ye are all become

dross, behold, therefore *I* will gather you into the midst of Jerusalem. As they gather silver, and brass, and iron, and lead, and tin, into the midst of the furnace, to blow the fire upon it, to melt it; so will I gather you in mine anger and in my fury." Ez. xxii. 19. "Therefore saith the Lord, the Lord of Hosts, the mighty One of Israel, Ah, I will ease me of mine adversaries, and avenge me of mine enemies: and I will turn my hand upon thee, and purely purge away thy dross, and take away all thy tin: and I will restore thy judges as at the first, and thy counsellors as at the beginning: afterward thou shalt be called, The city of righteousness, the faithful city. Zion shall be redeemed with judgment, and her converts with righteousness." Is. i. 24.

I quote these verses in order to show how peculiarly the closing period of unbelieving Israel's existence in Jerusalem is marked as one in which the Divine hand begins again, in an especial manner, to act in Jerusalem for the effectuation of its own purposes. The great " Desolator" is only an instrument commissioned of God to effect this end: "I will send him against an hypocritical nation, and against the people of my wrath will I give him a charge, to take the spoil, and to take the prey, and to tread them down like the mire of the streets." Is. x. 6.

Yet this fearful treading down will end the indignation and usher in the morning without clouds. " It shall come to pass in that day, that the remnant

of Israel, and such as are escaped of the house o f
Jacob, shall no more again stay upon him that
smote them; but shall stay upon the Lord, the
Holy One of Israel in truth. The remnant shall
return, even the remnant of Jacob, unto the mighty
God." Is. x. 20, 21.

The progression therefore, of the hebdomads,
which was suspended at the crucifixion, has not yet
been resumed. During this long interval, all *detailed*
history respecting both Israel and the nations is
suspended, not only in Daniel, but in all Scripture.
During this period no dates are given—no names
recorded. Many kings and mighty conquerors have
arisen among the Gentiles since Jerusalem was
extinguished, but none of them are mentioned in
Scripture, because none are connected with God's
nation in Jerusalem.

But as soon as Israel is again gathered back to
Jerusalem for judgment, and nationally re-exist in
their land and city, prophecy resumes its detail.
The covenant made with Antichrist, that covenant
of which it is said, "Your covenant with death shall
be disannulled, and your agreement with hell shall
not stand," (Is. xxviii. 18) will be a sign of their re-
constitution as a nation, and then the hebdomads
will again resume their course. To this period
belongs the concluding part of every vision of every
prophet that speaks of judgment on Jerusalem.
All the visions of the Revelation, from the sixth
to the nineteenth chapter inclusive, belong to this
period, especially to its latter half. The latter half

of this last hebdomad is the "1260 days," or "forty-two months," or "time, times, and a half time," so often spoken of in Daniel and the Revelation.

The hope that Israel cherishes of protection and rest under this covenant with Antichrist, will after a time be dissipated. "Wherefore hear the word of the Lord, ye scornful men, that rule this people that is in Jerusalem. Because ye have said, we have made a covenant with death, and with hell are we at agreement: when the overflowing scourge shall pass through, it shall *not* come unto us : for we have made lies our refuge, and under falsehood have we hid ourselves: therefore . . . . when the overflowing scourge shall pass through, then ye *shall* be trodden down by it." They will think to escape desolation by making a covenant with the Desolator; but it shall not stand. They will soon have to say, "he hath put forth his hands towards such as be at peace with him, he hath broken his covenant." We have seen, in the eighth chapter of Daniel, that not six months elapse after this covenant has been made, before he begins to practise evilly in Jerusalem, and at the half of the hebdomad, he causes the sacrifice and oblation to cease, and the pinnacle of Israel's temple becomes the pinnacle of an idol—his own idol. The wonderful history of this idol is given with unusual minuteness of detail in the New Testament. He who commands it to be formed, will have power to give life unto it, that it "should both speak, and cause that as many as would not worship it should be killed."*   Rev. xiii. 15.   The Desolator, represented by this animated image, stands upon this pinnacle.   The temple of Israel becomes the place of his worship and of his power, and the world, throughout all the appointed sphere, bows before him until the consummation, when " that determined is to be poured upon the desolator."

. Here the vision of sorrow ends.   Then comes the hour for everlasting righteousness to be brought in, and for the pinnacle of idolatry to be supplanted by the Holy of Holies, anointed for the worship and government of the Lord God of Israel.   Then, at last, it will be said, " Jehovah is in his holy temple: let all the earth keep silence before HIM."

* *Victorinus*, in the third century, speaks of this. His words are : "The false prophet will cause a golden Image to to be set up to Antichrist in the Temple of Jerusalem ; and into this image, the Apostate angel will enter, emitting voices and oracles. He will also cause both bond and free to receive a mark in their foreheads, or on their right hands even the number of his name, that none may buy or sell without it."

Lactantius, who wrote in the fourth century, says, speaking of the same period, "He shall command fire to descend from heaven, and the sun to stop in its course, *and the image to speak.*"

CHAPTER IX.

ON DANIEL X., XI., AND XII.

WE are now arrived at the last vision of the Book of Daniel, recorded in the tenth, eleventh, and twelfth chapters, which should be read continuously, as forming in reality one chapter. This portion of the prophecy is more minute in its detail than any of the preceding parts.

It is uniformly the case in books of prophecy that minuteness of detail increases in the later visions. The commencing visions are not specific. They pass rapidly over the whole period of which the prophecy treats, and supply an outline which is filled up by subsequent visions. Thus the first chapter of Isaiah brings us to the period of Israel's forgiveness after their last punishment. None of the subsequent visions exceed as to time the circle which the first chapter draws. So also in Daniel. The vision of the Image leads us to the time when the Gentile power is smitten, and the kingdom of heaven established. No subsequent vision exceeds this boundary. Like the Revelation, the Book of Daniel consists of a number of distinct visions, each complete in itself; not chronologically following each other, but each tracing either the whole or a part of the same period,

Q

and adding fresh circumstances. Enquiries awakened by the commencing visions are, for the most part, answered in the visions that succeed.

We are told, in the tenth chapter, that Daniel still continued to enquire. He again set his heart to understand, and to chasten himself before his God. And further instruction was vouchsafed, although Satan resisted, and for one and twenty days resisted successfully. Dan x. 13.

It is not the least important effect of enquiry into prophetic Scripture, that it draws aside the veil which hides that wonderful agency which is being perpetually carried on around us, partly by holy, and partly by evil spirits. Holy Angels are employed as "ministering spirits, sent forth for ministration on account of them who are to inherit salvation." * Heb. i. 14. Their ministry is not confined to the care which they continually exercise toward each individual saint in guarding him from danger in his going out and in his coming in ; there are many other things to which their ministry is directed, but all for the sake of those " who are to inherit salvation."

The appointed progression in the empires of the earth, as they successively rise and fall, is not unconnected with the final glory of God's people. This progression holy and evil angels watch ; holy angels, that they may assist ; evil angels, that they may hinder the purposes of God. The time of the con-

* Εἰς διακονίαν ἀποστελλόμενα διὰ τοὺς μέλλοντας κληρονομεῖν σωτηρίαν.

tinuance of each successive Empire, and the order of their succession, God has appointed with minute precision.　As they successively fulfil their course, so the period of Satan's reign is shortened, and the time of his punishment and of the long-predicted glory of the saints draws nearer.　On every account, therefore, the devil and his angels desire to obstruct the appointments of God.　They hate them because they are His; because each successive step is made needful to the great result, and because, as each change occurs, it brings nearer the period of their own doom.　They seek, therefore, to hinder the progress of these changes, to hinder also the instruction which God vouchsafes to His servants respecting them.

We have an instance of this in the chapter before us.　An angel was sent from God to instruct Daniel, but for one and twenty days he was hindered. "Then said he unto me, Fear not, Daniel: for from the first day that thou didst set thine heart to understand, and to chasten thyself before thy God, thy words were heard, and I am come for thy words. But the prince of the kingdom of Persia withstood me one and twenty days: but, lo, Michael, one of the chief princes, came to help me; and I remained there with the kings of Persia."　Dan. x. 12, 13.

No power of man could have resisted for one and twenty days the angel of God, and that so successfully, that, until Michael the Archangel came to help him, he could not prevail.　"The prince of Persia," therefore, must be some evil angel appointed under

Satan to watch over the realm of Persia, in order to check and to hinder the counsels of God. When the power of the first king of Persia was established upon the ruins of Chaldæa, the angel of God was needed to confirm and strengthen him. "Also I, in the first year of Darius the Mede, even I, stood to confirm and to strengthen him." Dan. xi. 1. And although when Daniel saw this vision the time was as yet distant for the second transfer of authority from Persia to Greece, yet even the very attempt to make known to Daniel that transfer, and the events that were to follow, was resisted by the angel of Satan. How sure we may be that this resistance is continued still against every attempt to understand or to unfold these things.

This vision was given in the third year of Cyrus. Before, therefore, the Empire of Persia had achieved its victories, or enlarged its boundaries to their destined extent, its overthrow was foretold. But it was not the immediate object of the vision to foretell the overthrow of Persia, nor even the rise of Greece. Its object was to reveal what should befall Israel *in the latter days* through him who should inherit the Grecian name. "Now I am come to make thee understand what shall befall thy people in the latter days: for yet the vision is for many days." Dan. x. 14.

Accordingly, the history of Persia is passed over in one single verse: "And now will I shew thee the truth. Behold, there shall stand up yet three kings in Persia; and the fourth shall be far richer than they all: and by his strength through his riches he shall stir up all against the realm of Grecia." Dan. xi. 2. This was Xerxes. His successors are not mentioned, but the prophecy hastens on to the king of Grecia. "And a mighty king shall stand up, that shall rule with great dominion, and do according to his will. And when he shall stand up [shall have stood up], his kingdom shall be broken, and shall be divided toward the four winds of heaven; and not to his posterity, nor according to his dominion which he ruled: for his kingdom shall be plucked up, even for others besides those." Dan. xi. 4. This was Alexander. His posterity was cut off, and four of his rapacious generals divided his dominions, and became sovereign princes. But the history of two out of the four is not pursued, because they were not connected with Jerusalem. But the two who were connected with Jerusalem— that is to say, the kings of Syria and of Egypt— have their histories given with considerable minuteness. The king of Syria, having the seat of his empire at Babylon and its neighbourhood, is called the King of the North; the king of Egypt, is the King of the South—north and south giving the respective positions of Syria and Egypt in their relations to Jerusalem.

It is not necessary to follow the history of all the kings of Syria and Egypt in their perpetual conflicts with each other, and their contests respecting Jerusalem. This has been already done by Rollin, Bishop Newton and others, with all the accuracy that is now possible, for the writings of many historians have perished, and others remain only in fragments. The history, however, of one of the kings of Syria, Antiochus Epiphanes, was so remarkably connected with Jerusalem, that it is necessary to consider it with some minuteness.

The object of the prophecy of Daniel is to detail the facts of Gentile history, so far as they are connected with Jerusalem. It seems, therefore, impossible to suppose that the history of a monarch like Antiochus, who so wonderfully foreshadowed Antichrist, (for he defiled the temple for 1,260 days, and placed "the abomination of desolation" there,) should be omitted in Daniel. We must not, however, expect that the detailed accounts of Scripture can in every minute particular be confirmed by the records of secular history; nor is it wonderful that we should be required to trust God for the accuracy of statements that He makes on His own authority. We have no evidence, except from Scripture, that the wall of Jerusalem was finished forty-nine years after its commencement by Nehemiah; yet we do not doubt the correctness of that date any more than that of the Crucifixion, which is afterwards given, although the latter can be corroborated from other sources. So also in the case before us. We cannot expect that uninspired history should furnish us with anything more corroborative of the great leading facts recorded in this prophetic history of Antiochus Epiphanes.

Uninspired history distinctly informs us that

Antiochus Epiphanes was a "vile person,"* who, not being the legitimate heir to the kingdom of Syria,† and therefore not having it given to him in due course, did, by "flattering" the Romans and others,‡ acquire the kingdom peaceably; and after overpowering all obstacles, overthrowing one and deceiving another of the High Priests of Israel,§ plundered whole provinces; exceeded all that had preceded him in mad profuseness;‖ attacked and

* Polybius says, his name should have been Epimanes, the madman: not Epiphanes, the illustrious.

† His nephew Demetrius was the rightful heir.

‡ His address to the Romans is recorded in Livy. He begs the Romans to "enjoin on him whatsoever should be enjoined on a king who was their good and trustworthy ally, and promises them he never would be found wanting to his duty." Livy. l. 42, ch. 6. Eumenes also, the King of Pergamus, and Attalus, were gained over by him.

§ The High Priest overthrown by him was, according to Theodoret, Onias. By prince, or leader of the covenant, he supposes to be meant the High Priest, who was at that time the chief office-bearer in Israel. Onias was removed, and afterwards murdered. His brother Jason, by immense sums obtained the Priesthood, but was immediately after supplanted by his own brother Menelaus. These things may be trivial in Gentile history, but they are important as proving the entire subjection of Jerusalem to the Gentile oppressor.

‖ His extravagant liberality is recorded both by Polybius, and in the first book of Maccabees. Polybius relates, that sometimes accidentally meeting with persons whom he had never seen before, he would enrich them with unexpected presents; and sometimes standing in the public streets, he would throw about his money and cry aloud, "Let him take it to whom fortune shall give it." In I Maccabees iii. it is

conquered the King of Egypt ;* treated him with
apparent kindness but deceived him, and was in
turn deceived by him ;† returned from Egypt with
great riches and punished the Jews ;‡ came against
Egypt; was met on the shores of Egypt by the
Ambassadors of Rome, who had just landed from
their ships ;§ was compelled to retire from Egypt;

---

said ; "He [Antiochus] feared that he should not be able to
bear the charge any longer, nor to have such gifts to give
so liberally as he did before, for he had abounded above the
kings that were before him."

* For account of his victory over Egypt, see I Maccabees i.
appended to this chapter.

† No one doubts, says Jerome, that Antiochus made peace
with Ptolemy, feasted with him, and laid plots against him.
Jerome, *in locum.*

‡ See I Maccabees i.

§ The following is the account given in Jerome of the
retreat of Antiochus from Egypt at the bidding of the Roman
Ambassadors. "Again after two years he collected an army
against Ptolemy, and came towards the south. And when
the two Ptolemies, who were brothers and whose uncle he
was, were besieged in Alexandria, Ambassadors from Rome
arrived, one of whom, Marcus Popilius Lenas, having found
him standing on the shore, gave him the decree of the senate
by which he was commanded to retire from the friends of
the Roman people, and be content with his own dominions.
When the king sought to postpone his final resolve until he
could consult his friends, the ambassador is said to have
drawn a circle in the sand with a staff which he held in his
hand, and to have enclosed therewith the king, and said,
'The senate and Roman people demand that you should in
that spot declare what your determination is,' whereby he
being alarmed, said, 'If it so please the senate and the

marched into Palestine and assailed Jerusalem; con-
federated with apostate Jews; placed the idol of
Jupiter in the Temple; and commanded that all who
would not worship it should be killed. Compare
this account with Dan. xi. 21-26.

These events in the life of Antiochus are capable
of satisfactory proof from history. But even if all
of them were not corroborated by profane history,
yet no one doubts that the great cardinal events
which this prophecy records, viz., an invasion of
Egypt, the intervention of the Roman Ambassadors,
a going to Jerusalem, and a placing an idol in the
Temple of God, are events which did occur in the
history of Antiochus. And when we remember
that the writer of the first book of Maccabees virtually quotes the words of the eleventh of Daniel,
and calls the idol placed by Antiochus " the abomina-

Roman people, we must retire,' and so immediately he drew
off his army." Jerome *in locum*.

As regards the expression, ships of Chittim, there can be
no doubt that it refers to the coasts of the Mediterranean.
" This plainly appears," says Bishop Newton, " that where-
ever the land of Chittim or the isles of Chittim are mentioned
in Scripture, there are evidently meant some countries or
islands in the Mediterranean." Dissertation v. " The
Hebrews," says Jerome, " interpret it of Italians and Romans
Hebræi Italos volunt intelligi atque Romanos." In the first
chapter of Maccabees it is applied to Greece. It is probable
that the Roman Ambassadors crossed into Egypt from Greece,
for Emilius, their Consul, had just subjugated Macedon.
The real Septuagint (not Theodotion) render Chittim by
Romans.

tion of desolation," we can scarcely doubt that this
passage in the eleventh of Daniel was considered to
belong to Antiochus at the time when the book of
Maccabees was written.

I am aware that some, whose judgment I greatly
value, and from whom on any subject I differ with
regret, are accustomed to apply this description to
Antichrist. But the reasons which forbid its application to Antichrist appear to me not less strong than
those which require its application to Antiochus.

In the first place, every description which Scripture elsewhere gives of Antichrist, would lead us to
regard him as exceeding all other kings, both in
intellect and in power, from the first moment of his
manifestation. Other kings may be symbolised by
horns, but he is represented by a "horn having
eyes." From the first moment of his appearance,
his look is "more stout than his fellows';" nor do we
ever read of anything but prosperity and triumph
—nowhere of anything approaching to failure or
reverse, until he is finally smitten by the hand of
God. But in the passage before us, the description
of the "vile person" who obtains his kingdom by
flatteries, is below rather than above the level of the
descriptions given of the ordinary kings of Egypt
and Syria that have preceded. The person spoken
of is decidedly unsuccessful, and is turned back by
ships from the Mediterranean, that very sea of
whose ships and whose coasts Antichrist will be
sovereign lord from the first moment he has assumed
his power.

Moreover, nothing appears to me more certain than that the kingdom obtained by the "vile person" is the kingdom of the north, *i.e.*, Syria. As king of the north, he is represented as conflicting with and conquering the king of the south, *i.e.*, Egypt. See verse 25. If therefore he be the king of the north, he cannot be identical with the king mentioned suddenly in the 36th verse, as "the king who shall do according to his will," because this wilful king is NOT king of the north, inasmuch as he is mentioned immediately afterwards as conflicting with, and overcoming the king of the north. See verse 40.

Moreover, we are told that only 1,260 days are to elapse between the "setting the abomination and the end;" and this period is expressly spoken of in Scripture as a shortened period. How would it be possible for all the many and diverse events mentioned from the 31st to the 45th verses, inclusive, to be accomplished in this period? One of these events is that "Israel is to fall by the sword and by flame, captivity, and by spoil, *days*." Now, although this last expression is not definite, yet it seems to signify a period too long to be included in a remnant of the 1,260 days.

Moreover, it is evident from the thirteenth of Revelation, and other parts of Scripture, that Antichrist is at the very height of his power, and is wearing the ten diadems of the Roman world at the time when he sets the abomination of desolation. Consequently, he cannot be the person who sets "the abomination" mentioned in the eleventh of Daniel, for that is set by a person who is returning from an *unsuccessful* expedition against Egypt.

For these and other reasons it is utterly impossible to apply this passage to Antichrist. A consideration of the verses that follow, viz., 32, 33, and 34, afford additional proof that it belongs to Antiochus Epiphanes (that remarkable foreshadower of Antichrist), whose history is given in the following chapter of the first book of Maccabees. His relation to Jerusalem should especially be observed.

"And it happened after that Alexander, son of Philip the Macedonian, who came out of the land of Chittim, had smitten Darius, king of the Persians and Medes, that he reigned in his stead, the first over Greece, and made many wars, and won many strongholds, and slew the kings of the earth and went through to the ends of the earth, and took spoils of many nations, insomuch that the earth was quiet before him; whereupon he was exalted, and his heart was lifted up. And he gathered a mighty strong host, and ruled over countries, and nations, and kings, who became tributaries unto him.

"And after these things he fell sick, and perceived that he should die. Wherefore he called his servants, such as were honourable, and had been brought up with him from his youth, and parted his kingdom among them, while he was yet alive. So Alexander reigned twelve years, and [then] died. And his servants bare rule every one in his place. And after his death, they all put crowns [upon themselves]; so did their sons after them many years: and evils were multiplied in the earth.

"And there came out of them a wicked root, Antiochus (surnamed) Epiphanes, son of Antiochus the king, who had been an hostage at Rome, and he reigned in the hundred and thirty-seventh year of the kingdom of the Greeks. In those days went there out of Israel wicked men, who persuaded many, saying, Let us go and make a covenant with the heathen that are round about us: for since we departed from them, we have had much sorrow. So this device pleased them well. Then certain of the people were so forward herein, that they went to the king, who gave them license to do after the ordinances of the heathen: whereupon they built a place of exercise at Jerusalem, according to the customs of the heathen: and made themselves uncircumcised, and forsook the holy covenant, and joined themselves to the heathen, and were sold to do mischief.

"And now when the kingdom was established before Antiochus, he thought to reign over Egypt, that he might have the dominion of two realms. Wherefore he entered into Egypt with a great multitude, with chariots, and elephants, and horsemen, and a great navy, and made war against Ptolomee, king of Egypt, but Ptolomee was afraid of him, and fled; and many were wounded to death. Thus they got the strong cities in the land of Egypt, and he took the spoils thereof. And after that Antiochus had smitten Egypt, he returned again in the hundred forty and third year, and went up against Israel and Jerusalem with a great multitude, and entered proudly into the sanctuary, and took away the golden altar, and the candlestick of light, and all the vessels thereof, and the table of the shew-bread, and the pouring vessels, and the vials, and the censers of gold, and the veil, and the crowns, and the golden ornaments that were before the temple, all which he pulled off. He took also the silver and the gold, and the precious vessels: also he took the hidden treasures which he found. And when he had taken all away, he went into his own land, having made a great massacre, and spoken very proudly. Therefore there was great mourning in Israel, in every place where they were; so that the princes and elders mourned, the virgins and young men were made feeble, and the beauty of women was changed. Every bridegroom took up lamentation, and she that sat in the marriage chamber was in heaviness. The land also was moved for the inhabitants thereof, and all the house of Jacob was covered with confusion.

" And after two years fully expired, the king sent his chief collector of tribute unto the cities of Juda, who came unto Jerusalem with a great multitude, and spake peaceable words unto them; [but all was] deceit: for when they had given him credence, he fell suddenly upon the city, and smote it very sore, and destroyed much people of Israel. And when he had taken the spoils of the city, he set it on fire, and pulled down the houses and walls thereof on every side. But the women and children took they captive, and possessed the cattle. Then builded they the city of David with a great and strong wall, [and] with mighty towers, and made it a stronghold for them. And they put therein a sinful nation, wicked men, and fortified [themselves] therein. They stored it also with armour and victuals, and when they had gathered together the spoils of Jerusalem, they laid them up there, and so they became a sore snare: for it was a place to lie in wait against the sanctuary, and an evil adversary to Israel.

" Thus they shed innocent blood on every side of the sanctuary, and defiled it, insomuch that the inhabitants of Jerusalem fled because of them; whereupon [the city] was made an habitation of strangers, and became strange to those that were born in her, and her own children left her. Her sanctuary was laid waste like a wilderness, her feasts were turned into mourning, her Sabbaths into reproach, her honour into contempt. As had been her glory, so was her dishonour increased, and her excellency was turned into mourning. Moreover, king Antiochus wrote to his whole kingdom, that all should be one people, and every one should leave his laws; so all the heathen agreed, according to the commandment of the king. Yea, many also of the Israelites consented to his religion, and sacrificed unto idols, and profaned the sabbath. For the king had sent letters by messengers unto Jerusalem and the cities of Juda, that they should follow the strange laws of the land, and forbid burnt offerings, and sacrifice, and drink offerings in the temple; and that they should pro-

fane the sabbaths and festival days; and pollute the
sanctuary and holy people: set up altars, and groves,
and chapels of idols, and sacrifice swine's flesh, and
unclean beasts; that they should also leave their
children uncircumcised, and make their souls abominable with all manner of uncleanness and profana-
tion: to the end they might forget the law, and
change all the ordinances. And whosoever would
not do according to the commandment of the king,
[he said,] he should die. In the self-same manner
wrote he to his whole kingdom, and appointed over-
seers over all the people, commanding the cities of
Juda to sacrifice, city by city.

"Then many of the people were gathered unto
them, to wit, every one that forsook the law; and
so they committed evils in the land, and drove the
Israelites into secret places, even wheresoever they
could flee for succour.

"Now the fifteenth day of the month Casleu, in the
hundred forty and fifth year, they set up the abomination of desolation upon the altar, and builded idol
altars throughout the cities of Juda on every side,
and burnt incense at the doors of their houses and
in the streets. And when they had rent in pieces
the books of the law which they found, they burnt
them with fire. And wheresoever was found with
any the book of the testament, or if any consented
to the law, the king's commandment was, that they
should put him to death. Thus did they by their
authority unto the Israelites every month, to as
many as were found in the cities.

"Now the five-and-twentieth day of the month they did sacrifice upon the idol altar, which was upon the altar of God. At which time, according to the commandment, they put to death certain women that had caused their children to be circumcised. And they hanged the infants about their necks, and rifled their houses, and slew them that had circumcised them. Howbeit many in Israel were fully resolved and confirmed in themselves not to eat any unclean thing. Wherefore they chose rather to die, that they might not be defiled with meats, and that they might not profane the holy covenant; so then they died. And there was very great wrath upon Israel."

CHAPTER X.

REMARKS ON DANIEL XI.—(*continued.*)

In the days of Antiochus, ruin seemed to be settling in upon Jerusalem. The faith and labour of Ezra and Nehemiah, in restoring Jerusalem, appeared likely to have no other result than that of providing a place in which the enemy might the more effectually insult God, and destroy His people. But God had not forgotten that Jerusalem was His city, and Israel His people. He had yet left among them a remnant. Accordingly, when they were all brought very low, and " all the house of Jacob was covered with confusion," it pleased God to raise up some to know and to serve Him; so that whilst the wicked in Israel were gained over by the flatteries of this evil persecutor, there were a few who stood boldly forward for the name and truth of the Lord God of Israel. They were the family of Judas Maccabæus, a private and almost unknown Israelite.

No former period of Israel's history affords a more distinct example of Divine interference on their behalf than the days of the Maccabees. God, indeed, was not visibly present with them as He had been with Moses and with Joshua: there was no hand of power manifestly stretched out in signs and mighty wonders, but He was not less truly nigh. Faith sought and obtained His help; and accordingly the Maccabees are numbered among those "who through faith subdued kingdoms, wrought righteousness, obtained promises, . . . escaped the edge of the sword, out of weakness were made strong, waxed valiant in fight, turned to flight the armies of the aliens, . . . of whom the world was not worthy." Heb. xi. 33-38.

It is not likely that an event so remarkable, and so indicative of the grace and goodness of God, would be unnoticed in this continuous prophecy. Accordingly, as soon as the great act of blasphemy performed by Antiochus in placing the abomination of desolation had been mentioned, the next verse records two things: first, that the wicked in Israel would be corrupted and gathered around the blasphemer by his flatteries; secondly, that corresponding energies should be awakened in those who did know their God, and that they should be strengthened and do exploits. "Such as do wickedly against the covenant shall he corrupt by flatteries: but the people that do know their God shall be strong, and do exploits." It will be remembered how entirely the statements of this verse are confirmed by the chapter just quoted from the Book of Maccabees. That chapter says that "there had gone out wicked men who persuaded many, saying, Let us go and make a covenant with the Gentiles that are round about us: for since we departed from them we have had much sorrow. So this device pleased

them well. Then certain of the people were so forward therein, that they went to the king, who gave
them license to do after the ordinances of the Gentiles: whereupon they built a place of exercise at
Jerusalem, according to the customs of the Gentiles,
and made themselves uncircumcised, and forsook
the holy covenant, and joined themselves to the
Gentiles, and were sold to do mischief." Thus when
Antiochus came to Jerusalem, he found already
there men who had long been "doing wickedly
against the covenant," and who were ready therefore to be led into deeper corruptions. This is just
what Daniel states, and so will it again be when
the antitype of Antiochus visits that city.

But when Antiochus thus brought an increased
power of evil into Jerusalem, it was met by an increase of power granted by God to His servants.
Daniel says, "the people that do know their God
shall be strong, and do exploits." The historic
record of the Maccabees says, speaking of Judas
Maccabæus, that "he fought with cheerfulness the
battle of Israel; that he pursued the wicked and
sought them out, and burned up those that vexed
his people; wherefore the wicked shrunk for fear of
him, and all the workers of iniquity were troubled,
because salvation prospered in his hand. He grieved
also many kings, and made Jacob glad with his acts,
and his memorial is blessed for ever." Thus the
testimony of the Prophet is abundantly confirmed
by the record of history.

But it is seldom that the faith of God's people

retains the vigour of its early energy. The later days of the Maccabæan family were clearly marked by declension. The power of Rome was arising in the West, that power which had successfully controlled their persecutor and driven him back from Egypt. It is a melancholy fact that the Maccabees coveted and sought Roman protection, and were the means of first bringing into connexion with their people the power of the great destroyers of Israel. "Now Judas had heard of the fame of the Romans that they were mighty and valiant men, and such as would lovingly accept all that joined themselves to them . . . . . and that they were men of great valour. It was told him also of their wars and noble acts that they had done among the Galatians, and how they had conquered them and brought them under tribute . . . . . . also that whom they would help to a kingdom, those reign; and whom again they would, they displace; finally, that they were greatly exalted . . . . . In consideration of these things Judas chose Eupolemus and Jason, and sent them to Rome to make a league of amity . . . . . and to entreat them that they would take the yoke from them, for they saw that the kingdom of the Greeks did oppress Israel with servitude. They went therefore to Rome, which was a very great journey, and came into the senate, where they spake and said, Judas Maccabæus, with his brethren and the people of the Jews, have sent us unto you to make a confederacy and peace with you, and that we might be registered your confederates and friends.

So that matter pleased the Romans well. And this is the copy of the epistle which the senate wrote back again in tables of brass and sent to Jerusalem, that there they might have by them a memorial of peace and confederacy: Good success be to the Romans and to the people of the Jews by sea and by land for ever; the sword also and enemy be far from them . . . . . . According to these articles did the Romans make a covenant with the people of the Jews."

The Romans were the nation of whom Moses had said: "The Lord shall bring against thee a nation from far, from the end of the earth, as swift as the eagle flieth: a nation whose tongue thou shalt not understand, a nation of fierce countenance, which shall not regard the person of the old, nor show favour unto the young, and he shall eat the fruit of thy cattle, and the fruit of thy land, until thou be destroyed; which also shall not leave thee either corn, wine, or oil, or the increase of thy kine or flocks of thy sheep, until he have destroyed thee; and he shall besiege thee in all thy gates." Deut. xxviii. 49. This also was the nation symbolised in the vision of Daniel by " a beast exceeding dreadful, whose teeth were of iron, and his nails of brass; which devoured, brake in pieces, and stamped the residue with his feet." Dan. vii. 19. Yet Judas forgot the testimonies both of Moses and the Prophets; saw nothing in this people but grandeur, strength and excellency; sought and received their benediction, and hoped that thereby *"prosperity would be to them, and to the people of the Jews by sea and by land for ever."*

I need not say how soon the dreadful consequences of this recourse to Rome became apparent. But before the full result was reached by "the Romans coming and taking away both their place and nation," a new act of mercy was directed towards Jerusalem. The verse which speaks of the holy energy of the Maccabees, is followed by another which says : "They that understand among the people shall instruct many, yet they [the people] shall fall by the sword, by captivity, and by spoil many days," or, to translate more closely, " the understanding ones of the people shall instruct *the* many, yet they [the people] shall fall by the sword, by captivity, and by spoil [many] days."

This verse teaches us that soon after the Maccabæan period, there should arise in the midst of, and out of Israel, persons to whom the name of " wise or understanding ones " would in some marked manner apply. They were not to " do exploits," like the Maccabæan family who preceded them, but only " to instruct." They were not to be THE people, but to arise from the people—" the understanding ones *of* the people." They were to be found in the midst of Israel, but they were only to be a few. Moreover, Israel as a people not receiving their testimony, it was therefore to be sent to others. It was to go to *the* many :* לָרַבִּים, εἰς τοὺς πολλούς, *i. e.*, to the Gentiles. The people of Israel, unreached by

* The word הָרַבִּים *whenever contextually contrasted with*

this testimony thus marvellously sent among them, were to "fall by the sword, by captivity, and by spoil many days."

I scarcely need say how minutely this verse has been fulfilled in the mission of the Lord Jesus and His Apostles, and in the rise of the Pentecostal Church. Light, such as never yet had been, was suddenly sent into the midst of Israel. They to whom it was committed might well be called "the wise, or understanding ones," for "the day-spring from on high" had visited them. They belonged to the people, and they taught *amongst* the people, but the nation was not reached thereby, nor its doom averted. They rejected the light, and it was sent to "the many." Wrath came on the people, and they have "fallen by the sword, by captivity, and by spoil many days." The words of this verse seem to have been referred to by the Lord Jesus when, speaking of the rejection of His truth by Israel, He said: "They shall fall by the edge of the sword, and shall be led away captive into all nations; and Jerusalem shall be trodden down of the Gentiles, until the times of the Gentiles be fulfilled." Luke xxi. 24.

For 1800 years the sword, spoil and captivity have marked the general condition of scattered Israel. Through long successive ages the Gentiles maintained towards them a relation of cruel and unrelenting oppression. But of late the feelings of the

---

Israel, always denote Gentiles. See further remarks on this in " Thoughts on Scriptural subjects," pages 160 and 161.

Gentile nations, especially within the limits of the Roman world, have undergone a marked change in relation to the Jews. They are now being favoured rather than oppressed; they are acquiring rights of property and of freedom, even in Rome itself; they are courted for their wealth, and sought after because of their influence, which is increasing daily.* This is just what the next verse teaches us: "When they shall fall [shall have fallen] they shall be holpen with a little help: but many shall cleave to them with flatteries." If we watch the aspect of events, we can scarcely doubt that we are at this moment entering on the period to which these words belong. Each year will more and more show the aiding, fostering hand of Gentile power directed towards the unbelieving House of Israel, until it helps them back to their own land, with their sins still resting on them; and then, more than ever, "many will cleave to them with flatteries."

It were well if these "flatteries" came only from the world. We cannot be surprised that the world should worship wealth, or admire ingenuity, or be captivated by the amiability and philanthropy that may be found among the Jews. But it is wonderful that any who understand and value the truths of

* On the Jewish Day of Atonement in the year 1849, the Legislative Assembly in Jamaica suspended its sittings out of respect to the Jewish members of their body, who were eight in number. The members are in all forty-seven. A Jew recently inaugurated with prayer the session of Congress in America.

Christ, should be blind to the present condition and prospects of that people, a people who, during the many long years of their chastisement, have ripened in the iniquities which caused them to be driven from their land, and whose return in unbelief is in Scripture spoken of in language more fearful than any that has yet been applied to Israel. There could not be this blindness among Christians unless *their* light also had become dim, and unless the testimonies of Scripture had also ceased to be their guide.

It is indeed sorrowfully apparent that Gentile Christianity is not in a condition rightly to instruct any inquiring heart in Israel. How often have we seen converted Israelites, as soon as brought under the power of Gentile teaching, deprived of the hopes which the reading of the prophets had kindled in their souls! We have seen the expectation of the Advent of the Lord and of their own nation's millennial glory taken from them by the instructions of Gentile Christians. And even in cases where the millennial blessings of Israel have been allowed, how often have they been taught to hail the present progress of the nations in civilisation and refinement under Satan, as the dawn of the day of millennial blessing? The dark future has been hidden from their eyes; and Christian Jews have been taught by Christian Gentiles to prophesy peace where there is no peace. If the Jews were at this moment to return to Jerusalem, and if any converted from among them were induced to sustain the principles now generally favoured in the Gentile churches, it would not be too much to say that their testimony would contradict the words both of Prophets and Apostles, and that they themselves would be, in many things, servants to those corruptions and worldlinesses which are conducting both Israel and the nations to their final doom.

Such Christianity, before it could render any effectual service to the truth, must be chastened. It is of this that the next verse speaks. "And some of the understanding ones shall fall, to try them, and to purge, and to make them white, even to the time of the end : because it is yet for a time appointed." We are not told what this fall of " the understanding ones " is to be. It will, no doubt, be something very terrible. But the effect will be their purification as a body, the purification and strengthening of their brethren, if not of themselves. They shall be "made white." This is the period of which it is said in the Revelation, that there are some who " will overcome because of the blood of the Lamb, and the word of their testimony ; and who will not love their life even unto death." When we remember the identity of the periods and the similarity of circumstances (for both periods are mentioned as connected with the hour of Antichrist's glory) we are necessarily led to the conclusion that they of whom Daniel and the Revelation speak are the same body ; and that they who are described in Daniel as " *purified, and made white, and tried,*" are the same who in Revelation " *love not their life even unto death.*" To this period also the parable of " the pearl " is especially intended to apply.

Blessed in the sight of heaven and in the estimate of faith, will that hour be (however dark outwardly), when " the understanding ones of the people " shall again arise in the midst of Israel. Marvellously have these verses up to the present point been fulfilled. We have seen Antiochus; we have seen the Maccabees; we have seen the understanding ones appear in Israel; we have seen them rejected by Israel, and going forth to teach the Gentiles. For eighteen hundred years Israel have fallen by captivity and spoil. It is equally certain that they are favoured now, and will finally be established in their land and " cleaved unto with flatteries." Christianity will certainly again find a sphere for itself in the midst of Israel, and will again give a brief but pearl-like testimony in the land of its nativity, re-awakening the voice of Prophets and Apostles in the midst of the triumphant evil of the hour of Antichrist. That testimony will be the result of " the understanding ones " of the people again appearing, who shall be chastened, purified, and made white. This is the only bright spot that appears in the future of this present dispensation, otherwise it is a future of unrelieved blackness. Yet this bright spot will be only temporary. The blackness of darkness will overwhelm it also. Nevertheless, it shall not be in vain. Its record shall abide in heaven.

The verses we have been considering, that is to

say, the thirty-third and the two following verses, stand in remarkable contrast with the rest of the eleventh chapter. The part that precedes abounds in detail in a manner unusual in Scripture; so also do the verses that follow, from the thirty-sixth to the end. But these intervening verses, although extending over a period six times exceeding that of which the rest of the chapter treats, are only three, and are as general in their statements, as the others are specific and minute.

There is in this respect a considerable resemblance between the prophecy of the hebdomads and this chapter. That prophecy, as we have already seen, divides at the Crucifixion. It gives no further detail until Antichrist appears. So likewise in the chapter before us. Its detail continues until the period of the rise of Christianity is mentioned; then the time having come for Jerusalem to be nationally extinguished, all detail ceases, and is not resumed until Antichrist appears.

His history is the principal subject of this chapter, as, indeed, of all the concluding visions of Daniel. In the seventh, eighth, and ninth chapters, his character and his actings have been so fully described, that in this vision he is suddenly spoken of without preface as THE king, as being a person already well known to those who have considered the previous visions.

In former chapters we have seen him described as Roman in the nature and extent of his power. He will lead the Ten Kingdoms of the Roman World.

In origin and in character we have seen him Greek; but the sphere in which this Greek sovereign of the Roman World will chiefly display his greatness will be the East. Oriental is a word well nigh synonymous with majesty, magnificence, and splendour. His glory will be Oriental. Its seat will be partly Jerusalem, and partly Babylon.

If we conceive of the chief of some petty principality, perhaps in northern Greece, appointed or becoming the head and the functionary of that great federal system which I have elsewhere described as located in Babylon, and thence ruling for a season all the Ten Kingdoms of the Roman World*—if we think of him in this place, proudly conscious of the superiority which intellect and position give; devising schemes for his further elevation; attaching to himself the Jews, and practising in Jerusalem; exciting at last the enmity, or alarming the jealousy of three of the monarchs over whom that federal system rules; attacked by those monarchs, over-

* See "Babylon; its revival and final desolation." The destruction of Antichrist is described in the 10th and 14th chapters of Isaiah. In the 10th chapter he is described as "the Assyrian;" in the 14th chapter he is called "the King of Babylon." But, as I have elsewhere dwelt fully on the subject, I do not enlarge upon it here.

In the early centuries it was a current opinion that the Chaldæan Babylon would be the place of Antichrist's birth as well as the place of his destruction. See Hoveden, quoted in Collyer's Ecclesiastical History, vol. ii., pp. 387—390, 8vo., 1840. See also *Hippolytus*, quoted in "Babylon; its revival and final desolation."

coming them, and appointing others in their room; elected by all the monarchs of the Roman World to be their sovereign head, after they had united with him in destroying the system, which till then they had subserved; despising everything which naturally or religiously controls other minds; inventing for himself in everything new paths, and finding even new demons to adore; entering into the Land of Israel; stretching out his hand upon the countries, and grasping their riches and their power; alarmed, at last, by adverse tidings from Central Asia, and therefore gathering the hosts of his kingdoms into the Land of Israel, where he had already set the tents of his palaces in Zion, the glorious holy mountain, and then smitten by the Lord, when Michael shall arise and deliver Israel; if we conceive of these things, we shall be not far from apprehending what this passage, read in connection with the rest of Scripture, reveals respecting this last great monarch of the Gentiles.

Roman, as being the master of the Ten Kingdoms of the Roman World; *Greek*, as arising from one of the four divisions of the ancient Empire of the Greeks; *Chaldæan*, as bearing the title of King of Babylon, and having that city as the centre of his power; *Head of Israel* by election, or by conquest, he will thus revive and concentrate in himself past powers and past energies, to operate with more intensity than ever against God. By him, and by his END, we have to measure the past and the coming prosperity of the nations. All is to terminate in

THE King; and what is prepared for THE King?
"Tophet is ordained of old, yea for THE KING it
is prepared: he hath made it deep and large, the
pile thereof is fire and much wood; the breath of
the Lord like a stream of brimstone doth kindle it."

Names and titles of the past are not in vain given
to this great monarch of the future. They are
intended to mark a continuity in the progress of
human evil. Antichristianism is not the sudden
creation of a moment; it is the consequence of
principles long operating, of which the final climax
of evil is the due and well-merited result.

In the early centuries of Christianity, after the
Apostles died, a sense of the awfulness of the character and reign of Antichrist prevailed widely in
the professing Church. But they dwelt so exclusively on the truth of his being the agent and
emissary of Satan, and invested him so much with
Satanic characteristics, that they almost forgot to
think of him as a man endowed with human attractiveness, and human powers of thought and action.
They were even accustomed to pray that the power
of Pagan Rome, though bitterly persecuting them,
might be prolonged, that so the dreaded reign of
Satan might be postponed. The period of Antichristianism was looked upon as something *altogether*
new, rather than as the result and offspring of circumstances long existent; and thus the evil of the
future was set in such undue contrast with the present, that all adequate apprehension of the moral
connection between the present and the coming

period was lost. It was virtually forgotten that there must be a seed-time before the harvest. It was forgotten that Rome, whether Pagan or nominally Christian, and the nations that had preceded her, as well as the nations that were to follow, had sown, or would sow seeds, of which Antichristianism would be but the legitimate result; and thus anticipations of future evil were made to destroy right apprehensions of *present* iniquity.

There is reason to fear lest the *mode* in which the expectation of Antichrist is now being revived should lead to our minds being similarly diverted from right judgment of present evil. If the links which unite the present with the closing period of iniquity be seen as revealed in Scripture, then few things will be found more profitable than an acquaintance with the character of the closing hour. But if these links are neglected, and the closing period be looked upon as one altogether new in character, and detached from its connection with the circumstances now around us, then nothing would be more likely to sink us into lethargic and careless acquiescence with the very evils that are bringing on the great final consummation of apostasy. We may even be tempted to defend present evil, and to say, as many have said, that everything which Antichrist will when he comes destroy, should be by us *now* defended and cherished as good. But it is far otherwise. God chastens evil by evil. Why of old was the godless blaspheming power of Babylon sent to crush Jerusalem? Was it not because of the long continued

s

corruptions and abominations of Israel? So now, what is it that will move God to send that hour of temptation, with all its attendant judgments, that is coming "to try them that dwell upon the earth?" It will be sent *mainly* because of those falsehoods and worldlinesses and idolatries that are being cherished in defiled, tainted, leprous, apostatising Christendom.

CHAPTER XI.

NOTES ON PARTS OF DANIEL XI. AND XII.

[*The understanding ones of the people.*] It is interesting to observe that this body of "understanding ones," after they once appear, continue to the close of the Dispensation. They are mentioned as still existent in the darkest season of Israel's evil. "None of the wicked shall understand, but the understanding ones shall understand." And when the time of sorrow is past, and the long-expected glory has come, it is said, "the understanding ones shall shine as the brightness of the firmament." The Revelation, when treating of the same period of Antichristian evil, speaks of some, who shall at that time "keep the commandments of God, and the faith of Jesus" (Rev. xiv. 12), and "who loved not their life even unto death." They will *chiefly*, no doubt, be composed of converts from Israel brought into the faith of Jesus. Gentile Christianity has so long been wise in its own conceits, and so unconscious of its doom, that it seems scarcely likely that the last "pearl-like" testimony of Christianity should be entrusted to it. It will revert to "understanding ones *of the people.*"

The King shall do according to his will.] This

person has already been mentioned three times in
this Prophecy as a King : viz.

In Dan. vii. 24.—"The ten horns out of this
kingdom are ten kings that shall arise, and
ANOTHER shall rise after them; and he shall be
diverse from the first, and shall subdue three kings."

In Dan. viii. 23.—"A king of fierce countenance
and understanding dark sentences shall stand up."

In Dan. ix. 26.—"The Prince that cometh,"
whose " end shall be in the overflowing."

Having thus been made the great theme of the
Prophecy, he is introduced without preface in this
chapter as THE King "who is to prosper till the
indignation be accomplished, for that which is determined shall be done." The two expressions,
" till the indignation be accomplished," and, " that
determined shall be done," identify this passage
with the eighth and concluding verse of the ninth
chapter, where the same expressions occur, as also
with Isaiah x. 22, 23.*

As in the eighth chapter we suddenly pass from
the period when Alexander's Empire existed in its
fourfold condition on to the "latter time of their
kingdom when the transgressors are come to the
full," so likewise this prophecy passes rapidly over

* In Isaiah xxx. 33, we have a similar instance of sudden
and abrupt reference to this last great oppressor of Israel.
"For Tophet is ordained of old, yea, for the KING it is
prepared ; he hath made it deep and large ; the pile thereof
is fire and much wood ; the breath of the Lord, like a stream
of brimstone, doth kindle it."

all the events that intervene between Antiochus the forerunner of Antichrist, and Antichrist himself: so as to connect as much as possible in our thoughts, the Greek King of Syria and of Babylon (which Antiochus was) with his last great successor and antitype.

The 36th and three following verses, refer to the personal *religious* relations of Antichrist—especially those which he will hold when in the plenitude of his power during the last 1260 days. He will exalt himself above every god that has hitherto been worshipped—and will blaspheme the God of gods—and will think to change times and laws, that is, will endeavour to alter the whole social and political arrangements of human life. But, although thus "magnifying himself above every god" that had hitherto been known, there will be some demon or demons unknown before, whom he will himself worship in strong holds. "Thus shall he do in the most strong holds with a *strange* god." The Devil will not tolerate in his servants absolute independence of himself. The four verses we have been considering, from the 36th to the 39th inclusive, describe the religious history of Antichrist on to the end of his course. In the next verse (*i. e.* the 40th,) the prophecy, after having brought us to a final point, retraces—and gives us the history of this person as a Warrior King.

[*And at the time of the end.*] Literally, "in the time of the end." This and kindred expressions, such as "*consummation*," have especial reference to the conclusion of Jerusalem's punishment, and therefore would not be applied to Antichrist, except in his connexion with Jerusalem. The time of the end therefore, may be said to commence when Antichrist becomes the scourge of God upon Jerusalem, and begins to oppress Israel there. *After* this period has commenced, (for it is said IN the time of the end) Antichrist is fiercely attacked by the King of Syria and the King of Egypt—both of whom would be necessarily interested in the condition of Jerusalem, where Antichrist is at that time practising. (See chap. viii.) He overthrows them both, and becomes master also of Lybia and Ethiopia. The Kings of Syria and of Egypt are doubtless two of the three kings, whom in the seventh chapter are said to be overthrown by him.

It must be remembered, that at this time Antichrist is holding power over the Ten Kingdoms, in virtue of his being the servant and sustainer of that mighty Commercial System, described in the seventeenth of Revelation—a System which will at that time be supreme over the Ten Kingdoms. (See " Babylon, its future history.") After overthrowing three kings out of the ten, and appointing others in their room, he becomes possessed of sufficient power to destroy the sovereign System, which till then he had served. The Kings of the Ten Kingdoms unite with him in this—and assuming independent kingship after they have destroyed their former mistress—do, at the same moment agree to

give their united support to him. Then it is, that
he is for the first time represented in Scripture, with
his ten horns "crowned"—before this, they were
not crowned. *Systems*, not *individuals* rule till then.
Till then, he is the functionary of those systems,
through the one great Sovereign System located in
Babylon. After this he becomes *supreme*. The *seventeenth* chapter of Revelation describes Antichrist in
the earlier part of his course, whilst sustaining the
Babylonish system. At that time the ten horns are
not represented as crowned—because, at that time,
the monarchs are the *functionaries*, not the masters
of the systems from which they derive their power.
In the *thirteenth* chapter Antichrist is described as
the Sovereign King—and then the ten horns are
crowned: for they and he cease to be mere functionaries. They receive power as kings at one hour
with him. See Rev. xvii. Thenceforward, in his
relation to Jerusalem, and to the countries immediately connected therewith, he becomes peculiarly
"the Desolator." Hence Daniel in this passage
speaks only of war and convulsion. Nevertheless,
Edom, Moab, and the chief of the children of
Ammon, are not allowed to fall under his hand.
Idumea or Edom is always mentioned in Scripture as
strong and flourishing at that time: which shows,
therefore, that its utter desolation, as described in
Isaiah, is still future, and not to be fulfilled till "the
day of the Lord" comes.

As the conclusion of his course draws nigh, "tidings" out of the east and out of the north trouble

him. We find from other Scriptures, that the Median hordes and the kingdoms of Ararat, Minni, and Aschenaz unite in attacking Babylon, which is his chief city; for he is distinctly called "King of Babylon" in Isaiah x. He gathers the strength of his Ten Kingdoms to Armageddon in the Land of Israel (Rev. xvi.)—attacks Jerusalem (Zech. xii.)—is confronted by the manifested glory of the Lord (Zech. xii. and Rev. xix.), and is destroyed in the Valley of Jehoshaphat. (Joel iii.)

[*And there shall be a time of trouble.*] More properly, *it shall be a time of trouble;* that is, the period in which Michael stands up will be a period of unequalled tribulation; but it is *terminated*, not commenced, by the rising up of Michael. It will have lasted 1,260 days *before* he arises. These are the days of unequalled sorrow spoken of by our Lord in Matthew xxiv.

[*At that time thy people shall be delivered, every one that is found written in the book.*] Thy people, *i. e.*, Daniel's people—Israel. Yet only a remnant of Israel is to be saved in that day—those whose names are written by the *grace* of God in the book of salvation. Thus it was said to Isaiah, "Though the number of thy people Israel be as the sand of the sea, yet [only] a remnant shall return." (Isaiah x. 22.) "Short work shall the Lord make upon the earth." (Rom. ix.) The word translated "short" does not mean short as to time. It is a figure taken from that which you pare or cut round again and again, until a very small portion remains. In the Land of Israel itself, one third is to be spared. (See Zech. xiii. 8.)

[*And many of them that sleep in the dust of the earth shall awake, some to everlasting life, and some to shame and everlasting contempt.*] We know from other parts of Scripture, that all the righteous dead will then awake to life—"LIFE," and not "*awake*," being the word which implies the possession and exercise of the power of resurrection-being. The souls of the departed saints whilst in a disembodied state, although in Paradise, and perfectly conscious of their blessing, are not in the exercise of the *functions* of life—those functions requiring the presence of the body. Hence our Lord in his reply to the Sadducees who denied the resurrection of the body, proves it by saying, that if there were no resurrection, God would not be called the God of Abraham : for that He is not the God of the dead, but of the living. The *soul* of Abraham is now consciously receiving blessings *from* God; but Abraham will not be able to *live unto* God until he again receives his body, and in this sense is still regarded as dead, not as living. So also it is said of David : "David is not ascended into the heavens" (Acts ii. 34); yet David's soul is there in conscious blessedness with Christ, though he, in the integrity of his personal condition, is not there—his body being in the grave. Nor are the departed wicked represented in Scripture as living, although their souls exist in torment.

Hence it is said, " the rest of the dead lived not (ουκ εζησαν) until the thousand years were finished;" " live," being here used not in the sense of " *exist*," but as denoting the possession of those powers also which are connected with the body. Man, therefore, is not said to live, *i. e.*, in the sense of exercising the functions of life, either when he is dispossessed of his body, or when, having his body, he is placed in the second death.

There are, however, some of the wicked who are to have a peculiar doom. They will not, like the rest of the wicked dead, be raised again at the close of the Millennium to be judged, but will awake at the commencement of the Millennium, not to life, but in torment. They are those who have been involved in the blasphemies of Antichrist, who have borne the mark of the beast, or worshipped his image. Such have their doom already pronounced. "If any one worshippeth the beast and his image, and receiveth his mark on his forehead, or on his hand, he also shall drink of the wine of the wrath of God, which is poured out without mixture into the cup of his indignation; and he shall be tormented with fire and brimstone in the presence of the holy angels, and in the presence of the Lamb; and the smoke of their torment ascendeth up for ever and ever, and they have no rest day nor night, who worship the beast and his Image, and whosoever receiveth the mark of his name." (Rev. xiv. 9, 10, 11.) Such will not live again in order to be judged. They have, in the words just quoted, received their sentence. The following passage in Isaiah refers to the same period:—"They" (*i. e.*, those who are spared through the judgments of the Day of the Lord) "shall go forth and look upon the carcases of the men that have transgressed against me: for their worm shall not die, neither shall their fire be quenched; and they shall be an abhorring unto all flesh." (Is. lxvi. 24.)

[*But thou, O Daniel, shut up the words and seal the book, even to the time of the end.*] This is a repetition of the commandment given in the eighth chapter, where it is said to Daniel: "The vision . . . which was told is true; therefore, shut thou up the vision; for it shall be for many days." Because the vision is true, THEREFORE shut it up—that is, preserve it carefully and for a long time, seeing that it is to be for many days. Documents of value which are intended to extend to a distant period, are commonly "sealed," and "shut up" in a place of security, in order that they may be preserved, and be always ready for reference when needed by those whom they concern. This is evidently the force of these words in the present passage. They have no reference whatever to "shutting up" in the sense of rendering inaccessible.

We find a similar passage in Isaiah, "Bind up the testimony, seal the law among my disciples." The word צָרַר here translated "bind up," is sometimes used in the strong sense of shutting up. But that it only means in this passage to shut up in the sense of securing is manifest from the verse which follows, where commandment is given to consult the Law thus "bound up" and "sealed." "To the Law and to the testimony if they speak not according to this word." We could not be commanded to consult that which was hopelessly concealed.

[*Many shall run to and fro, and knowledge shall be increased.*] The word translated "run to and fro," is used of the Israelites when they went up and down to gather manna, when it first fell around their camp. It is used also of Joab when directed by David to go through the coasts of Israel to number the people, and of Satan "*going to and fro*" in the earth, making his observations for evil. It is used also of the eyes of the Lord which "run to and fro" throughout the earth, to show Himself strong in behalf of them "whose heart is perfect towards Him." (2 Chron. xvi. 9.) It is a word therefore that indicates diligence and activity of observation and search; and seems to teach us that there shall continue unto the end, servants of God who shall diligently observe the signs of the times, and seek after and glean truth, whereby knowledge shall be increased. This progressive increase of knowledge could not be if the book were hopelessly sealed.

[*When he shall have accomplished to scatter the power of the holy people, all these things shall be finished.*] It is remarkable how the name "holy people" is still given to Israel, even in the midst of their apostasy and sin. So also Zion is called the glorious holy mountain, even when the tabernacles of Antichrist are there; and the Court of the Temple still called the Holy Place, even when the abomination of desolation is there, and the Temple deserted by God.

Israel is represented at that time as having power that needs to be scattered. At this moment they are gathering to themselves great power. "When they go back in their sins to Jerusalem, their land will be full of silver and gold, neither will there be any end to their treasures; their land also will be full of horses, neither will there be any end of their chariots." (Isa. ii. 7.) All this greatness must be scattered by the Lord, until they are brought very low, and have no strength left.

[*Then said I, O my Lord, what shall be the end of these things?*] This was evidently a request for minute and specific instruction respecting the things spoken of, such as Daniel had before received in some of the previous prophecies respecting the Chaldæan Empire; for he had been able specifically to point out Nebuchadnezzar, and to say, "Thou art this head of gold." If the things prophesied of in this vision had been in the same manner present, no doubt Daniel would have been enabled to understand and explain them specifically; but seeing that the vision was to be "laid up" for many days, and was to receive its accomplishment only at the time of the end, no specific interpretation could be given. Even we, for whom Daniel and the prophets prophesied (1 Peter i. 12), cannot at this moment specifically name the Ten final Kingdoms, or tell the exact place or period of Antichrist's rise. The prophecy is "preserved," and we consult it from time to time, and by means of it watch the progress of events; but it is only when "the time of the end" comes, when Antichrist appears in Jerusalem, that we shall be able to explain its specific references, and point out by name each individual, and each kingdom to which they apply. Use of the prophecy, and understanding its specific details, are two different things.

[*Many shall be purified and made white and tried: but the wicked shall do wickedly and none of the wicked shall understand; but the understanding ones shall understand.*] This has no doubt a continuous application to the whole period from Daniel to the present hour, but will be peculiarly true at "the time of the end." Antichristianism as it increases will so blind the eyes of men, that they will not understand any of these things; but there shall be "understanding ones."

[*And from the time that the daily sacrifice shall be taken away, and the abomination that maketh desolate set up there shall be 1,290 days.*] This evidently refers to some event of blessing on Jerusalem, because the destruction of Antichrist, which will occur *thirty* days previously, will be the termination of Jewish chastisement. What this event of blessing may be, is not revealed; but as it appears to have some connexion with the sanctuary, and since the sanctuary is cleansed, and the idolatrous worship there ended, at the conclusion of the 1260 days from the fixing the abomination, it is not improbable that this further date may refer to the renewal of accepted worship in the sanctuary thirty days after.

Again, forty-five days after this, some further event of blessing will occur; but what it is, is not revealed. The return of the Divine glory to the Temple, and the inauguration of the government of Christ in glory on Mount Zion, are some of the events which are to occur about this period; but as it is the object of the prophecy of Daniel to reveal the sorrows, and not the glory of Israel, the vision here closes.

CHAPTER XII.

ON 2 THESSALONIANS II.

THE literal translation of this chapter may be given as follows :—

"But we ask of you, brethren, on behalf of the coming of our Lord Jesus Christ, and our gathering together unto Him; that ye be not soon shaken from your understanding, or be troubled, neither by spirit, nor by word, nor by letter, as from us, as if we had said, that the day of the Lord* had commenced. See that no one deceive you by any means: for that day will not commence, except there first come THE Apostasy; and the man of Lawlessness† be revealed, the son of perdition, who opposeth and exalteth himself against every one that is called God or that is worshipped, so that he seateth himself in the Temple of God, showing himself that he is God. Remember ye not that whilst I was yet with you I told you these things? And ye know that at present there is that which restraineth in order that he

* Του Κυριου. See Tregelles and all critical editions.

† 'Ο ανθρωπος της ανομιας. I here follow the reading of א and B. placed by Dr. Tregelles in his text, although he places της άμαρτιας in the margin as nearly equal in authority.

might be revealed in his season [and not before]. For the mystery of Lawlessness is already working (only there is at present one that restraineth) until it become developed out of the midst, and then shall the Lawless One be revealed whom the Lord shall consume with the breath of His mouth and destroy by the brightness of His coming: even him whose coming is after the working of Satan with all power and signs and deceiving wonders, and with all deceivableness of unrighteousness in them that perish, because they received not the love of the truth that they might be saved."

We learn from this passage, that the Thessalonians were being deceived by some who had told them, that the Apostle had said, that the Day of the Lord had commenced in heaven.

I say in heaven, because they well knew from every sign around them, that it had not commenced in *earth*. The world was prospering—their persecutors were strong—they themselves were worn out by suffering. All these, and many other like things, daily reminded them that the Day of Christ had *not* commenced below. They well knew, that as soon as it was manifested in the earth, they would be taken to the Lord, and sudden destruction would fall upon their persecutors. (See First Epistle to the Thessalonians.)

They understood therefore, that it had not commenced in the earth, but they were not indisposed to believe that it had commenced secretly in heaven; where indeed it *will* first commence, unseen by the eyes of men, whenever the time shall come for the

T

Ancient of Days to sit, and for the Son of Man to be brought before Him, to be invested with the power of earth.

They were not wrong therefore, in thinking that the Day of the Lord will commence in heaven, before it is known or manifested to any on the earth. But they ought not to have believed that it *had* commenced, or that St. Paul had said that it had commenced, because he had before told them that it would *not* commence, even in heaven, until the apostasy and the Man of Lawlessness had first been manifested in the earth. The teaching of St. Paul could not contradict the Old Testament Scriptures; and it had been expressly revealed in Daniel, that the blasphemies of Antichrist would not only precede, but also be the immediate cause of the Session of " the Ancient of Days," and the investiture of Christ with the sovereignty of earth.

The Apostle therefore besought the Thessalonians, not to believe that he had ever said (either when speaking under the immediate inspiration of the Spirit, or in any of his communications either in letter, conversation, or otherwise) that the Day of Christ had commenced. He besought them not "to be shaken from their understanding," nor disturbed by the excitement of untruthful expectation.

It is well to observe the earnestness with which he beseeches them not to be deceived as to these things. "Let no man deceive you by any means." "Remember ye not, that when I was yet with you, I told you these things?" We can easily appreciate the value of these warnings, when we consider the evil that has again and again been produced in the Church by false and excited expectation on these subjects. We must ever remember that truth only sanctifies—error never can. And when one seed of error has been sown and fructifies, incalculable results of evil (unless God mercifully interferes) are sure to follow.

" Let no man deceive you by any means, for that day shall not commence, except there come THE apostasy first, and THE Man of Lawlessness be revealed," There is only one event to which the expression " THE Apostasy " is applied in Scripture, viz. the open renunciation by Israel, and by the Roman nations, of all acknowledgment both of God and of Christ. All Scripture reveals this as about to be before the return of the Lord Jesus in glory.

But although THE Apostasy and THE Antichrist were then as they still are—future; yet the principles which were to end in this manifestation of evil were even then secretly working. " The mystery of lawlessness," said the Apostle, " doth already work."

What this "Lawlessness" will be, at the period of its full development, may be gathered by considering the course of him whom the Devil will be permitted to raise up to defy God. By him the institutions and laws of the Most High will be for a season effectually trampled under foot. The Lawless one will " think to change times and laws, and they shall be given into his hand until a time and times and dividing of time." Dan. vii.

But even at the time when the Apostle wrote, the falsehoods and abominations of Jewish Sacerdotalism, and Sacerdotalism as exhibited in Gentile Paganism, had disgusted the hearts and consciences of men, and given them an excuse for becoming sceptics. Many besides Pilate were saying, "What is Truth?" When the soul has learned proudly and scornfully to ask this question, "lawlessness" is sure to follow; for if the heart recognises in nothing the authority of God, self-will must become its master. In the time of the Apostle, scepticism was becoming so prevalent among the Sadducees and the educated Gentiles, and also among those, who, after tasting the pure truths of Christianity, had turned away and blasphemed them (See Hebrews vi. 4 and x. 26), that the seeds of a godless infidelity had become widely scattered—so widely and so successfully, that nothing except the restraining power of God could account for the repression, through so many ages, of the open avowal of atheistic Lawlessness. Professing Christianity by its priestcraft, idolatries and worldliness, has now, in its turn, produced wide results of hardened infidelity. As soon as the renovated voice* of infidelity

* German Neology, works like "Good Words" and "Ecce Homo," and the "Essays and Reviews," and the writings of such men as Jowett, Stanley, Maurice and others of the like school, have given an impulse to Infidelity more potent than any afforded by the efforts of Bolingbroke, Voltaire, or

among the Gentiles shall be responded to by latitudinarianised Judaism, the hour of " THE Apostasy " will be very nigh. The mystery of lawlessness which has been long working under the surface will "become developed out of the midst," and the most cultivated, civilised, and advanced section of mankind, will be allowed to develop what it has gained to itself by its abandonment of God.

There are two *contrasts* to be noted in this passage. The period during which the wickedness spoken of works secretly, is contrasted with the time of its palpable development, when, to use the language of the Apostle, it " becomes out of the midst:" (γιγνεται εκ μεσου) : and the period during which God is the Restrainer (ὁ κατεχων) is contrasted with the period when the restraining power (το κατεχον) which He instrumentally employs is stayed—I say stayed, because it is no where said to be *taken out of the earth.*

It has been imagined by many that the Thessalonians were acquainted with the agency, by which God was restraining the manifestation of the wickedness. But we have no authority for saying that they knew anything more respecting it than we ourselves know. *They* knew, and *we* know, that there *is* a restraining power, but what that power is, and how and by what instrumentality it works,

Proudhon. Those men were open blasphemers, but in most of the modern neologian school we have "the horns of a lamb" connected with the voice of the Dragon. Few, however, detect the latter.

they were even as we are now ignorant. * To understand this, would be to understand the secrets of the providential government of God, and these He does not reveal even to His saints. Who has ever known the manifold agencies by which God acts upon the hearts of men, in restraining their evil and in restraining the power of Satan? We know that there *is* a Restrainer, and restraining agency. But who that Restrainer is, whether it be God Himself, or an angel, or a power appointed by Him, we know not.

Many have also supposed that this Restrainer, or restraining agency, is to be taken away; but this notion arises from a wrong apprehension of the meaning of the word γιγνεσθαι εκ μεσου. See notes that follow. It is true indeed, that restraining power will no longer be *exercised*, when the appointed hour of the manifestation of the *mystery* of iniquity shall have come. But for the *intervention* of God's power in checking the progress of lawlessness to cease, is a very different thing from the power itself ceasing to exist, or being withdrawn altogether from the earth. Even if the words γιγνεσθαι εκ μεσου be understood to imply removal, it would be removal of INTERVENTION, and not removal from the earth. The power of God, which is now being employed in hindering, will, when it ceases to hinder, be employed in accelerating.

The Apostle speaks of "the *mystery* of lawlessness as already in his day working, and he tells us

* See Notes subjoined to this paper.

also respecting its future *development* under Antichrist as its head, when it will be a mystery no longer; but of the history of this "mystery" during the period which intervenes between its commencement and development, the Apostle says nothing.

In Zechariah, however, we find, that at a period between the limits just mentioned, "wickedness" becomes identified with the Woman hidden in the Ephah. That the system of mercantile greatness finally to be established in the East, and which is now arising around us, will be infidel when developed, is plain from Scripture, and from facts. The connexion therefore of this special form of "wickedness"* with the Ephah, will be the precursor—

* "And he said, This is wickedness. And he cast it into the midst of the Ephah." (See preceding paper on Ephah.)

'Ο ἄνομος, rendered by our translators " the wicked one," as answering to the הָרָשָׁע of Isaiah xi. 4, should be rather rendered "the Lawless one," for רָע is the word by which the Hebrews were accustomed to denote the turbulence and rebelliousness of manifested evil. The Hebrews seem to have imagined that a person might commit "sin," (ἁμαρτιαν) and yet be altogether free from the guilt of that advanced form of evil which is denoted in the Old Testament by רָע *rebellious wickedness*, and in the New Testament by ἀνομια *lawlessness*. But this cannot be. There is a connexion between youth and age; between incipiency and maturity. The most matured form of development is nothing more than the manifestation of that which is hidden in the germ. Hence the Apostle says, "Every one that is a doer of sin is likewise a doer of lawlessness, and sin is lawlessness"— πᾶς ὁ ποιῶν τὴν ἁμαρτίαν καὶ τὴν ἀνομίαν ποιεῖ, καὶ ἡ ἁμαρτία ἐστὶν ἡ ἀνομία. I. John iii. 4. 'Ανομία is not to be rendered as if it were ἡ παράβασις τοῦ νόμου.

almost the immediate precursor, of its development. The Land of Shinar will be the place—the Ten Kingdoms the sphere—and Antichrist the functionary and Head of the developed Apostasy.

At present we may see signs of the infidelity of Jew and Gentile finding a common centre, in the rising system of commercial greatness. The time, therefore, cannot be far distant when "Lawlessness," still working as a mystery, and at present hidden in the Ephah, will come forth out of its hiding place, and take its stand in lordly strength in the land of Shinar, and be cherished and sustained by Antichrist, and gather to itself the allegiance and affections of mankind. It will be a mystery no longer then.

NOTES ON 2 THESSALONIANS II.

Verse i.

"*But we ask of you, brethren, on behalf of the coming of our Lord Jesus Christ, and our gathering together unto Him.*"

Ἐρωτῶμεν δὲ ὑμᾶς, ἀδελφοί, ὑπὲρ τῆς παρουσίας, &c. The preposition ὑπέρ is not here used in the sense of obtestation ; nor would it be accurate to say that it is used like περὶ in the general sense of "*concerning.*" Inclusion of an object within the scope of our inquiries or remarks, is implied by περὶ ; but ὑπερ indicates more than this. It implies that we feel a kindly interest respecting that which is included in our remarks. We speak not only *concerning* it, but we speak *in its interest*, or *on its behalf*. Thus in the present case, the Apostle implies that the truth respecting "the coming of the Lord Jesus, and our gathering together unto Him," had been *wronged* by the false thoughts which had come into the minds of the Thessalonians. Therefore he asks, *on behalf* of these injured and outraged truths, that they should correct these thoughts.

It should be observed that the expressions "coming of the Lord" and "our gathering together unto

Him," are placed in the original under the same
article; whereby these two events are associated as
to time. They are similarly associated throughout
Scripture.

Verse ii.

"*That ye be not quickly carried away from your
understanding* [or mind], *or be perturbed* [excited],
*either by spirit or by word, or by letter as through us,
as if we had said, that the day of the Lord had set in*"
[or commenced].

Carried away from your understanding]. "Shaken
in mind" is a very faulty translation of σαλευθῆναι
ἀπὸ τοῦ νοὸς. Ἀπὸ is "*from*," not "*in*." The
figure is that of a vessel tossed and driven by
the surge, and so carried away from its anchorage.
Our understanding, that is, our new spiritual understanding, should ever be to us as an anchor. When
prejudice, terror, fear, or even affection, act strongly
on the feelings, then the exercise of the understanding is peculiarly needed as the stay. Our spiritual
state can never be otherwise than unhealthful, if
there be not the concurrent exercise of the understanding, the conscience, and the affections. The
Thessalonians were not duly exercising their understanding. They were drifting, therefore, from their
anchorage.

Or be perturbed.] Or "excited." Θροεῖσθαι
means the being thrown into a tumultuous condition

of thought and feeling. *Ταρασσέσθαι*, not *θροεῖσθαι*, is used for the perturbation of distress. *Θροεῖσθαι* occurs twice besides, in Matt. xxiv. 6, and Mark xiii. 7, where it is similarly used of perturbation and excitement caused by wrongness of expectation as to the end being immediately nigh, when it was not.

As through us.] *Ὡς δι' ἡμῶν ὡς ὅτι*, &c.   The ellipsis must be supplied by *λεξάντων*—*ὡς δι' ἡμῶν ὡς λεξάντων ὅτι ἐνέστηκεν*, &c., " as through us, as if we had said," &c.   If, says the Apostle, any one should affirm that we, either when speaking authoritatively in the Spirit, or in conversation, or in a letter, have declared that the day of the Lord had " *set in,*" and so become a present existent reality, believe them not.   We have constantly affirmed the very reverse.

The translation of *ἐνέστηκεν*, given in our version, is most faulty.   It never means " *is at hand.*"   It is never used to signify the approach of anything not yet existent.   " Hath set in " is its literal meaning, as when we say, " the tide has set in," or " the winter has set in :" the question " Where ?" still remaining to be asked.   And seeing that that which has set in *upon us* is *present* to us, this word may, in certain cases, be regarded as equivalent in meaning to the being present, and is not unfrequently so rendered in our version.   See, for example, Heb. ix. 9, " for the time then present " [*εἰς τὸν καιρὸν τὸν ἐνεστηκότα*], literally, " for the time that had then set in." So in Rom. viii., "Things present (ἐνεστηκότα) or things to come"—things that have set in and things future. So also in 2 Tim. iii., " In the last days perilous times shall come (ἐνστήσον-ται)—literally, "shall set in." It is frequently used in the Apocryphal books, and always in this sense. St. Paul would never have said that the day of the Lord was not at hand. *It is at hand.* What he said was, that it had not " set in," or commenced. In the Latin translation of the Arabic version it is rightly rendered, " *advenerit,*" hath come.

Verses iii., iv., v.

See that no man deceive you by any means, because that day shall not set in, etc.

Whatever word we employ as the translation of ἐνιστήμι in the second verse, we must also use when we supply the ellipsis in the third verse.

I have already observed that the Thessalonians were not wrong in believing that the day of the Lord, when it does commence, will commence *in heaven ;* and that the event by which it is commenced will be unseen on earth. The event by which the day of man will end, and by which the day of the Lord will be commenced, will be the Session of the Ancient of days in heaven. That Session is fully and solemnly described in the seventh chapter of Daniel; and yet there is, perhaps, no event so little believed in, or expected by the Church of God. Their eyes seem utterly blinded as to this great coming act of God. The object of that Session will be to pass sentence on the matured iniquities that will mark the closing period of Gentile dominance, to take for ever from the hands of men the administration of the governmental power of earth, which the Throne of God has delegated to them for a season, and to invest it in the hands of the Son of Man, "whose dominion is an everlasting dominion, and of His Kingdom there shall be no end." This is the period of which the Lord spoke when He said that He was as a nobleman going "into a far country to receive for himself a kingdom [or sovereignty], and to return." This is the time to which the words of Rev. xi. 15 belong: "There were great voices in heaven, saying, The sovereignty of the world (ἡ βασιλεία τοῦ κόσμου) hath become the sovereignty of our Lord, and of his Christ. . . . We give thee thanks, O Lord God Almighty, because thou hast taken to Thee Thy great power, and hast reigned." Whenever the Son of Man shall be brought, before the Ancient of days in the manner described in Daniel, *then* will He take unto Him His great power, and *then* the day of the Lord will *in heaven* begin.

The Thessalonians, in their carelessness, had been induced to believe that the Apostle had said that the day of the Lord *had* thus commenced; not indeed on earth (they knew that it had not commenced *there*), but in heaven. In believing this they had drifted away from the anchor of their understanding. If the day of the Lord had commenced, the day of

Gentile dominance and of Jewish rejection must have terminated : the last great apostasy must have been consummated : Antichrist must have reached the end of his career, and all that Daniel had prophesied respecting the proud course of Gentile prosperity and power must have been accomplished. But it was altogether otherwise. No wonder, therefore, that the Apostle was grieved at the facility with which the Thessalonians had been beguiled. Aptness in receiving error is a symptom of great spiritual unhealthfulness in God's people. If they lay aside the lamp of God's revealed truth they will receive no other, and will (until recovered to repentance) go on to grope and stumble in darkness.

What can be more express and emphatic than the Apostle's testimony? "LET NO MAN DECEIVE YOU BY ANY MEANS : for that day shall not commence unless there shall have come THE APOSTASY first, and the man of lawlessness shall have been revealed, the son of perdition : who opposeth himself and exalteth himself against every one that is called God, or that is worshipped ; so that he taketh his seat in the temple of God, showing himself that he is God".

This is that of which Daniel testified—that which the Lord Jesus Himself confirmed. He said that He would not return until *after He had received* the sovereignty which He went to heaven to receive. " They thought that the kingdom of God should immediately appear. He said, therefore, A certain nobleman went into a far country to receive for himself a kingdom, and to return." He cannot receive this kingdom until the Ancient of days shall sit; and the Ancient of days will not sit until THE APOSTASY shall not only have commenced, but shall have run its course. See Dan. vii. *Then*, but not before, the day of the Lord will commence in heaven, and (seeing that the day of man will then end) the manifestation of the power and glory of the day of the Lord on earth will *immediately* follow its commencement in heaven. To imagine (as some in these later days have done) that Christ will take to Himself His great power, and that after that Antichrist will be revealed, and reign gloriously over Israel and dominate in the earth, is to suppose that man would triumph most after the day of man had ended. The Ancient of days does not sit, and the Son of Man does not take to Himself His great power until the three years and a half of Antichrist's glorious power have ended.

The Apostasy]. Men may apostatise, that is, depart and remove themselves away from certain truths and positions which God has commanded them to maintain, and yet may not reach that culminating point of rebellion which is termed in Scripture THE Apostasy. THE Apostasy will be marked by the rejection and abandonment of every thing that God has ever revealed respecting Himself, whether through Christ, or previously. He will be rejected both as the Jehovah of Israel, and as God the Creator. Even in Protestant England creation is now pronounced to be "an unphilosophical thought:"

yet they who utter this blasphemy are not discarded by society, but rather cherished and honoured. "The wicked walk on every side when vilenesses are exalted over the children of men."

As God]. These words should be omitted. (See Tregelles, and other critical editions). Such words might be applied to a person who, like the Pope, blasphemously assumes to be the *vice-gerent* of God: but Antichrist will do more than this. He will assume *to be* God. "So that he in the temple of God taketh his seat, showing himself that he is God."

Verse vi.

" *Ye know that at present, there is that which restraineth, in order that he may be revealed in his own season*" [or appointed time].

There are many reasons that compel us to reject the rendering of this passage as given in our English version. If St. Paul had said, " *At present ye know*," it would have implied that a time would come when they would cease to know—which is impossible, for such knowledge, if once communicated, would not be subsequently withdrawn. The object of the passage is not to contrast a *present possession* of knowledge with a *future cessation* of knowledge, but to contrast a period during which an appointed restraining power would repress and keep back the concealed working of "lawlessness" with another period when such repressive power would cease to act.

In the concluding part of this verse, the connection of the word "*now*" (ἀρτι) with "*one that restraineth*" ["Ye know that there is *now* one that restraineth"] proves that the corresponding word "*now*" (νῦν) in the commencement of the verse must also be connected with "*restraineth*," and not with "*know.*" The second "now" (αρτι) in the concluding clause is nothing more than the representative of "now" (νυν) in the first clause. The word opposed to this twice repeated "*NOW*" is THEN (τοτε), the contrast being between the period during which "Lawlessness" is restrained, and works secretly under the surface of society as a mystery hidden, and another period during which it is to be no longer restrained, but ceasing to be a mystery, becomes "revealed," as a developed organised system under a recognised Head—"the man of Lawlessness," Antichrist.

If the Thessalonians had been made acquainted with the agency by which God restrains the working of evil, they must have been taught respecting all the methods of His providential government—methods, that are, for the most part entirely hidden from our view. The Thessalonians did not know, and it was not intended that they should know, the manifold agencies by which God counterworks and restrains Satanic and human evil. The sentence only requires the supply of εἰναι or ὑπαρχειν, and should be translated, "And ye know that there is at present that which restraineth."

Verses vii. and viii.

" *For the mystery of Lawlessness doth already work,
only there is at present One that restraineth, until he be
removed out of the way, and then shall the Lawless One
be revealed,*" etc.

Or,

" *For the mystery of Lawlessness doth already work
(only there is at present one that restraineth)* [and as a
mystery it will continue to work] *until it become
developed out of the midst, and then shall the Lawless
One be revealed,*" etc.

Such are the two translations that have been
given of this passage. My reasons for preferring the
latter are given in "Notes on Greek of the First
Chapter of the Romans" (page 89), as advertised
at end of this volume.

Here I would merely observe that the words ἕως
ἐκ μέσου γένηται, simply taken, do not mean "*donec
de medio tollatur,*" but "*donec e medio fiat*"—*until it
become out of the midst*—a sense eminently suited to
the subject of which the whole passage treats, for it
speaks of something that is now working secretly in
the midst of society, becoming developed. When
we speak of a person who had been hidden in a
crowd appearing "out of the midst" of that crowd
or of a horn springing out of the head of an animal,
there is in neither of these cases any thought of
removal or *taking away*, but simply of *manifestation*.
So it is in the present instance. That which is now
working secretly in the midst of men, is soon to

come forth in palpable development, and then it will cease to be a mystery.

There is nothing in the words εκ μεσου, to signify removal, or taking away. They mean simply "e medio"—out of the midst. In other passages they are connected with the verbs ἁρπαζω—to snatch away (Acts xxiii. 10); αιρω, to take away (1 Cor. v. 2); εξερχομαι, to come out from (2 Cor. vi. 17), and in these cases there is of course the sense of separation or removal, a sense derived entirely from the verb which is appended to εκ μεσου, and not from εκ μεσου itself. The word with which it is here united, viz., γενηται, has not in itself at all the sense of removal, but rather of origin or existence.

If the translation be thus corrected, "the mystery of iniquity" becomes the nominative to γενηται. The words — "only there is at present one that restraineth," are in a parenthesis; το γαρ μυστηριον ηδη ενεργειται της ανομιας (μονον ο κατεχων αρτι) ἑως εκ μεσου γενηται και τοτε, etc. for the mystery of Lawlessness is already working (only there is at present one that restraineth) *and will continue to work* until it be developed out of the midst and then shall the Lawless One be revealed.

Many most unsatisfactory attempts have been made to explain this passage, on the mistaken supposition of its implying the removal from the earth of some power now present. Some have supposed that it means that the Holy Spirit is to be taken from the earth; but this is untrue, for Christ said— "Lo, I am with you alway, even to the end of the age." Others have supposed that all the saints are to be taken away, but this also is untrue. It is contradicted by the words of our Lord just quoted; and we also read of those, who " keep the commandments of God and the faith of Jesus" during the terrors of Antichrist's reign. Moreover, the tares and the wheat, the wise and foolish virgins, are not separated until the end of the age, when the Lord comes. Besides this, the expression used, viz., "He that restraineth" (ὁ κατεχων), being masculine and in the singular number, is a word inapplicable to the saints collectively.· Nor can the word κατεχω, which, properly signifies *to hold fast forcibly*, be ever applied to the relation which either the Saints or the Holy Spirit hold towards the mystery of iniquity. They testify, but they never use violence or compulsory power.

Others have interpreted this passage of the Roman Empire, and have supposed that the Head of the Roman Power was the Restrainer. But the whole body of Roman power is to be concentrated in Antichrist;—he is the eleventh horn of the Roman Monster, and that Monster is not to be destroyed, nor the Image to be smitten, till Antichrist falls. How, then, can it be spoken of as removed? But I need not pursue this question, if these thoughts arise from a mistake in the translation of the passage.

The expectation of the removal of the Roman Empire, and the habit of representing the Antichristian period as one, manifestly and palpably *Satanic*, operated most injuriously in the early ages.   Satan, in this dispensation, acts in and through men : and although faith, guided by the Scriptures, discerns Satan, yet to the outward eye the actings appear to be those of Empires or individual men.   Thus the symbol by which God represents the condition of the ten Roman nations, at the commencement of the last 1,260 days, is a ten-horned dragon; the dragon representing Satan, Faith, therefore, understands that Satan will be guiding then the action of the Ten Kingdoms; but to the eye of man nothing will appear, beyond the ordinary action of ten human governments, concurring to persecute Christianity.

The nominal conversion of the Roman Empire—its gradual dissolution—the establishment and wane of Popery—the history of nominal Protestantism—the subjection of the Ten Kingdoms (when they shall have been formed) to a federal commercial system sustained by Antichrist—the destruction of that federal system—and the assumption of all the power of the Ten Kingdoms by Antichrist alone: are all connected events consequent one on the other, as links in a chain.   Throughout the whole period there is a moral connection in the progress of the evil most important to be watched.   If the moral connection be not seen, if it be expected that the present condition of things, is, in *such* sense to be removed as to be succeeded by something that has not originated in, and grown out of present circumstances, then, the moral power of prophecy is lost, as bearing practically, on the circumstances now around us.

CHAPTER XIII.

ON THE NATURAL RELATIONS OF MEN AND GOVERNMENTS TO GOD.

In the preceding papers, it has, I trust, been sufficiently shown, that it is the desire of God that His Church, throughout the whole of the present Dispensation, should neither individually nor corporately, be entangled with the administration of secular power. They who are connected with "the Stone" that smites the Image, should be dissociated from all which that "Stone" is to destroy. They who through God's marvellous grace are united with the Son of Man now, and will be associated with Him in the glory of His Kingdom hereafter, should be separate from all that that Kingdom will destroy with judgment, when it is manifested in its glory.

But because the Church is to keep itself separate from the administration of power that is not directed by the principles of Christ, it is not, on that account, to stand apart in listless or hard-hearted carelessness, as if it could in nothing act toward the nations for good. The being beneficent to all men—the hearing, like the good Samaritan, the cry of distress simply because it is the cry of distress, are features of character for the display of which the present condition of the nations affords increasing opportunity. The Lord Jesus fed unbelieving multitudes, and was kind to the unthankful and to the evil.

But the Lord Jesus did more than this. He was the Minister of grace, and has entrusted His Church also, with the ministration of grace to every lost child of Adam. The Church is instructed to say, "God hath so loved the world, that He gave His only begotten Son, that whosoever believeth in Him might not perish, but have eternal life." The antitypical Serpent of brass, is placed as it were in their hands. They can bear it into every dwelling, and place it before the eyes of every sinner. They can speak of Jesus as the Saviour appointed by God, and say to all, that "through this man is preached unto you the forgiveness of sins, and through Him all who believe are justified from all things."* Behold, the Lamb of God."

Every one who casts himself on God, thus testifying of Christ, as the Lamb *slain*, is immediately placed in new circumstances. The value of Christ's name—the preciousness of Christ's blood is imputed to him. Union is granted to him with Christ risen,

* It is most important to observe in John iii. the connexion between regeneration and faith in Jesus crucified. Nicodemus said, "How can a man be born again?" The Lord does not seem to answer the question, but turns apparently to another subject; for He suddenly speaks of the Serpent of Brass. But in speaking of it, He does answer the question most fully; for He says, that whosoever shall look

whereby he is associated with all the peace and all the glory of the new creation of God. He "has passed from death unto life"—he "is born of God." He is accepted in the meritoriousness of Another. But because of this new relation to God (the only one of unchanged and everlasting blessing), we must not forget, that there is also another relation in which man, as man, stands to God. There is a *natural* relation, which man, as the creature of God, holds before Him.

The air we breathe, the sunshine, the rain, the fruitful seasons, are proofs that the natural relation in which God stands towards His guilty creatures, is one of beneficence and goodness. His providential interferences likewise, as "when they cry unto the Lord in their distress, and He bringeth them into the desired haven"—His warnings also, and His chastisements are results of the relation which He bears towards man, as their Creator. It is of this relation, that His servant Jonah said: "I knew that thou art a gracious God and merciful, slow to anger, and of great kindness, and repentest thee of the evil." Jonah iv. 2.

to Him and to His Cross, as the dying Israelite looked to the Serpent of Brass, "hath eternal life"—in other words, is born again. If, therefore, the soul says, "Have I been born again?" it may ask itself another question, "Have I looked at Jesus crucified as the Israelite looked at the 'Serpent of Brass?'" If we say, "Is there anything that I can place before others dear to me, that they might be regenerated?" —the answer is, "Yes—speak to them of Jesus as the Serpent of Brass, and whosoever believeth, hath everlasting life."

Mercies such as these, are, it must be remembered, the purchase of Christ's blood. The necessary holiness of God prevents the extension even of temporal mercies towards a guilty world, except on the ground of the intervention of One, who, having honoured and sustained the governmental holiness of God by that which He has rendered unto Him, does, in consequence thereof, receive from God mercies for others, which could not be granted or dispensed, unless the claims of God's essential holiness had first been adequately met. Many a mercy, many a bestowment of the Divine goodness, visits the path of the careless and unbelieving world; but all such mercies are purchased mercies—purchased by the blood of Jesus. Noah builded an altar, offered sacrifice, and "the Lord smelled a sweet savour," in consequence whereof summer and winter, day and night, seed-time and harvest, recur in their seasons—all purchased mercies. And yet they for whom these mercies are purchased may despise the sacrifice that purchased them (that sacrifice which Noah's offering prefigured) and never be themselves brought under its saving efficacy. Every one that is born into the world momentarily receives (though he may be utterly unconscious of it) blessings *through* Christ; but none except those, who are brought into personal reliance on His blood, have a title to say that they are brought into His Church, or that they are under Him as "the Mediator of the new covenant," or that they are under the new covenant, or that they are under Christ as their

Priest, or that they are under the value of His atoning blood. His blood is preached to men as a refuge from the wrath to come ; but as men they are not personally under it. To receive blessings through it, and to be under it, are far different things. To be *under* it is everlasting salvation.

If the conscience of any bear witness to these things—if they recognise that countless mercies have thus been bestowed upon them, but that their responsibility has been increased thereby, and their guilt aggravated because of the unprofitableness and ingratitude, and rebellion with which, on their part, these mercies have been met, then, we can preach to them the Gospel of the grace of God. We can tell them that God, who well knows that all mercies received by men as men (seeing that they are sure to be misused) only aggravate condemnation, has been pleased to appoint that that same holy and most precious blood, through which He is able to bestow these mercies, should also be made the ground of pardon and everlasting acceptance to every one who, as a sinner, casts himself thereon. " Christ is exalted as a Prince and a Saviour *to give* REPENTANCE (for repentance is needful) and REMISSION of sins." Thus, even that wonderful relation of grace which God has assumed, in that He Himself undertakes the ministry of reconciliation and " preaches peace through Jesus Christ," is to be numbered amongst the other relations of love in which God stands towards man as man. We can say to every man, that natural mercies, providential

mercies, and the preaching of *everlasting* forgiveness
of sins through Christ crucified, are all results of a
relation of goodness and mercy which God occupies
towards men as lost sinful children of Adam.

We must indeed be careful, as I have already
said, not to confound these relations of God *to men*,
with those spiritual relations which subsist only between God and those who are brought by faith into
His Church. The relations of the Church are alone
those of abiding blessing : nevertheless the relations
of man are not on that account, to be forgotten.
Let us suppose the case of the father of a family,
who, having received the Gospel, has himself been
brought by faith into the Church of God. He may
perhaps be surrounded by children, who have *not*,
like himself, received the Gospel, who are therefore,
not capable of answering to *Christian* responsibilities.
Whilst in this condition, he cannot treat them as if
they had been brought into the spiritual relation-
ships of the Church : but shall he on that account,
say that there are no *natural* relations of God, respecting which he can teach them? Although he can
not expect them to receive truths, or act on principles
which none but Christians can appreciate, yet, he
must not keep back from them such truths, or such
principles as their consciences are able to understand. He has to teach them, that there is one God,
and to show to them the proofs of His holiness, His
power, and above all, His goodness. He has to tell
them that the Bible is the Book of God, and that in
love He has sent it into the world, that men might

have a light to guide them into the way of peace.
He must teach them who Jesus of Nazareth was,
and why He was led as a Lamb to the slaughter.
He must tell them of the desire of God to receive
sinners and to grant to them forgiveness of sins
through Christ's blood. He must speak to them
also of the holiness of God, the universality of
human sin, the coming of the day of wrath and the
everlasting torment of the wicked. He has to tell
them also of the everlasting peace and glory and
blessedness of those whose garments are washed and
made white in the blood of the Lamb. The actually
subsisting relations between God and all His creatures, whether believers, unbelievers, angels, or
devils, should form the subject of his instructions.
He has to teach them these things as truths and
facts, fixed and sure, because revealed on the authority of God: and although it be true that the
mere acknowledgment of such facts does not make
men Christians, yet the repudiation of them places
them in double distance from God. It makes them
atheists, infidels, blasphemers, adversaries.

Again, if we suppose the head of a family who is
not brought by personal faith into the Church of
God, to have, nevertheless, such regard to God and
to the Scriptures, as to make him desirous of guarding himself and his household against the denial of
certain truths which his conscience has apprehended
as revealed in those Scriptures — would not such a
father, and such a household be, and be regarded by
God as being, in a condition different from one in

which the Scriptures were scorned, and the facts, which God had asserted respecting Himself and His Son, blasphemously denied? The former would not indeed be a condition of salvation. Perhaps nothing more might result from it than certain transitory blessings here, which God, in the order of His moral government, not unfrequently connects with the observance of His natural laws. But still the conscience of such might be expected to be less hardened against the appeals of God. At any rate, it would be a condition not marked by the same characteristics of obdurate guilt as when the scornfulness of the scorner is added to the transgression of the sinner.

And now, let us consider these principles in relation to the government of nations. There are governments which have for ages endeavoured to act as if they and their subjects were really brought into the Church of God. They have, in consequence, found themselves entangled in many a difficulty, from which they are now seeking to free themselves. They see that for a Legislature to pretend to act on the principles of the Church of God, when they and those for whom they legislate do *not* belong to the Church of God, is hypocrisy. They find also, that nothing is gained by the fiction. They have discovered that modern principles of government, most especially, are hindered rather than assisted thereby*.

* It is not difficult to expose the weaknesses and follies into which real as well as pretended Christians have fallen,

The withdrawal of governments from a Church position, and their resolution to free themselves from principles, which, however binding on the Church of God, are neither applicable to, nor understood by *them*, cannot be regretted. However much we may deprecate the motives of that withdrawal, and the manner in which it is being effected, we cannot wish to maintain a fiction, nor to induce

in their endeavour to maintain governments and nations in a fictitious church position. The falsity and hypocrisy of such a position, and the disastrous consequences resulting therefrom, have been exposed skilfully and very unsparingly by a popular historian of the present day. His work suits the temper of the hour, and many are rejoicing in it. True, as well as professing, Christianity, has exposed itself to these rude assaults, by its follies and its sins.

It is easy for such writers to destroy; but what do they substitute in the room of that which they overthrow? Nothing, except virtual infidelity. They have no desire to lead men to the Bible. They scorn and hate it.

We are told by these writers, that revealed truth has no more to do with right government than with the right manufacture of a machine by a mechanic; in other words, we are asked to believe, that although governors stand in a *moral* relation to God, and in a *moral* relation to their subjects, yet they are in nowise concerned with the *moral* principles revealed by God, and can rule better without the Bible (which alone declares what those principles are), than with it!

Such is the path by which governments, pretending to retire merely from a church position, are, in reality, retiring from all truth, and wooing the darkness by which Satan is exultingly quenching the light of the Scriptures of Truth, and leading society blindly onward to the day of wrath and revelation of the righteous judgments of God.

men to profess to be what really they are not. But the withdrawal from a Church position, is made the excuse for withdrawing from something more. It is made the excuse for renouncing other principles, which, in virtue of *natural* relation to God, are binding both on them and on their subjects, not because they are God's Church, but *because they are God's creatures.*

It cannot be indifferent to God, whether or not governments encourage principles which subvert such truths as men by natural conscience are able to recognise. There are some truths, which can be recognised by the converted only; but there are other truths, which men, as men, can and do acknowledge. They belong to a sphere in which man, as man, is placed; and although the acknowledgment of such truths does not bring into a spiritual relation to God, yet the rejection of them involves in the guilt, either of Infidelity, or Idolatry. The consequences of the rejection of the Gospel of salvation, may be seen, perhaps, only in another world; but the rejection of truths, which even natural conscience recognises, and which it is one of the great offices of government to maintain, meets with visitation even here; if not in the way of outward chastisement, yet surely in a judicial hardening of the heart.

A government is not asked to act as if it belonged to the Church of God, when we seek of it, that it should not cherish, or give effect to principles that destroy the natural relations in which man stands to God—relations that man is able to recognise in the Word of God, and sometimes in the works of creation.

The eternal power and Godhead of God, are borne witness to, both by the Scriptures and by the works of creation. It is a fact which man's conscience is capable of recognising. Consequently, the denial of His existence, or the acknowledgment of other gods, or idolatry, *i. e.* the ascription to creatures of attributes that belong only to the Creator, is a breach of a *natural* relation in which man stands to God. The shutting up the Book which God has written, and the refusal to allow Him thereby to speak immediately to His creatures, is an interference with His prerogatives as God, as well the breach of a natural duty.

Again, to deny that the Lord Jesus is God, and that He is now administering the goverpment of the Universe, is to deny an actually subsisting fact. Men may, to use the language of Scripture, count themselves unworthy of everlasting life, and spurn the salvation of their souls through faith in the great Sacrifice. They may reject Him as their Saviour, and refuse to submit to the principles on which He guides His Church. But they need not, on that account, plunge deeper into sin, and unite with the Jew or the Infidel, in denying His present existence and government at the right hand of power. The Lord Jesus has been made "both Lord and Christ;" and in that character, is administering the government of the Universe on the Throne of

His Father. To deny this, now that it has been revealed as a subsisting fact, has the same character of sin as a denial of the government of God.

Whenever, therefore, a government fosters any system, or forwards the influence of any individual that assails such truths as these, it forsakes the duty which it naturally owes to God. It is not a Church question, or a spiritual question—it is a question of *natural* duty. It is a question, whether, after that God has plainly declared certain things to be facts, men shall be encouraged to say, that they are *not* facts. Heathenism—Romanism—Judaism—Infidelity—are all systems which assail, not only the truths belonging to God's Church, but those also which concern His government of man, as man. Heathenism denies the eternal power and Godhead of the One God, and fixes men in idolatry. Romanism hides the Book of God, says that the traditions of men are "equal" in authority with the Scriptures of God, and, in bearing on the idolatrous Gentile world, whilst making war on *heathen* idols, leads back by pretended Christianity, to idolatry again. Judaism denies the existence (save as of a malefactor who has perished in his sins) of Him, who is now controlling the Universe and upholding all things " by the word of His power."

There was a time, when this country governmentally maintained a testimony against idolatry, and refused to cherish institutions, or to pay the ministers of a system that practised idolatry and kept the Scriptures of God from His creatures. This

x

testimony was given at a time when the fiction was
maintained of the government being so one with
the Church, that no one could hold a legislative or
magisterial appointment who did not receive the
symbol of Church communion. And yet, notwithstanding this fiction, we know that the testimony of
of England against idolatry, and her national
acknowledgment of the Word of God, were so far
owned of God, that the desolating wars, which for
nearly half a century swept over Europe, were
averted from these shores. The history of Protest-
ing England supplies many an evidence of the providential interferences of God on her behalf. But
she has become weary of Him now. She is aban-
doning God more and more every day. His word
is honoured no longer as the one repository of
Truth. Lies are welcomed; and idolators and blasphemers honoured. Antichrist and Armageddon
await her. England will be numbered among those
nations that shall "drink, and be drunken, and spue,
and fall, and rise no more." (Jer. xxv. 27.)

Those who wish to banish all regard to the truths
of God from the governmental arrangements of
human society, have said much respecting the natural rights of men; but surely, no one can have a
right to require of another, under whose authority
God has placed him, that he should be raised into a
position where he might more effectually labour for
the destruction of God's governmental verities. On
the contrary, the Governor has a right to expect of
such an one, that he should respect the fundamental

principles of God's natural government, no less than those of the human government under which he may be placed. No one in this land is deemed fit to hold authority, who disowns the Sovereign as supreme—who refuses to promulgate her. laws, or who assigns to others allegiance or homage that is due only to her. Is less due to the Sovereign who rules in heaven? Less cannot be due. How then, can we avoid the necessary conclusion, except by saying, that God has never promulgated one principle that affects human society upon earth, nor revealed one fact that can be understood by them? Few, I trust, would venture on the expression of such a sentiment. What remains, then, except to say, that His principles are first of all to be regarded—if from no higher motive, yet that there might be escape from consequences of sorrow and judicial visitation here.

Let it not however be supposed that I mean, that the mere refusal to cherish Infidelity or Idolatry is all that should be expected from a government that recognised these *natural* responsibilities. It might in many things act positively as well as negatively: it might promote, for example, the spread of the Holy Scriptures. Nevertheless, as things now are, there would be a joy in seeing any government refrain, because it feared God, from nurturing and encouraging antichristian evil. It might refuse to uphold the idolatries of Ritualism and the blasphemies of Neology.

The condition of Agrippa was doubtless very far from satisfying the desires of the heart of Paul.

Yet evidently it was with a certain joy that the Apostle said: "King Agrippa, believest thou the prophets? I know that thou believest." His acquaintance with the Holy Scriptures did not make Agrippa all that he should have been; but it *did* place him in favourable contrast with the infidelity of Festus, and the careless and ignorant levity of Gallio. The light of Scripture had reached the conscience of Agrippa. It afforded a ground of hope to the Apostle that the testimony of Christ's truth might yet fasten upon his soul; and it did prevent his becoming the persecutor of the servant of God. Who, therefore, would not rejoice to see a reverence for the word of God so far at least awakened in the bosom of rulers as to save them from the abyss into which they are now hastening. It is vain to hide from ourselves that the governmental system of England has of late made rapid progress in renouncing the principles of God. The endowment of Popish seminaries—the deference and adulation shown to Popish Ecclesiastics—the honour paid in India and elsewhere to Popish and Heathen ceremonies—the determination to uphold and honour in the Anglican Establishment, the patent idolatry of the Sacerdotalist, and the no less open infidelity of the Neologian, are evidences of this departure. The Jews recently have been invested in this country with governmental power. The Jews are a people who pronounce Him by whom "Kings rule and princes decree justice," to be accursed. They are themselves under a peculiar judicial visitation from the hand of God. They have said, in reference to the Holy One, "His blood be on us and on our children." A curse more terrible than the curse upon Cain rests on their heads. They are in a peculiar manner driven out from the presence of God. Will, then, investiture with magisterial and legislative authority bring governmental power nearer unto God, or will it remove it into yet further distance, where it will go on ripening for the hour of Antichrist? The influence of the Church (I speak now of real Christians) has rather accelerated, than repressed, the tide of evil. Some, with godly intentions, but with a zeal undirected by the word of God, have urged on the governmental body the maintenance of a Church-position. Such appeals, however, fell powerless on the consciences of those to whom they were made. The position was seen to be fictitious, and the attempt to maintain it, to be a kind of hypocrisy; consequently, the moral influence of those who advised it was gone. In addition, not a few who have argued on these questions have used against their opponents weapons not taken from the armoury of God. Recrimination and bitter revilings have not unfrequently marked their controversies, as the recent history of Protestantism in Ireland too plainly shows. Can we wonder that the hearts of the rulers should resolutely steel themselves against such appeals as these? Again, another large section of the Church (and they have been chiefly found among the Dissenters) have strenuously opposed the efforts of their fellow Christians in these things, and have vehemently maintained that it is unlawful for the governmental body, *under any conceivable circumstances*, to hold a Church-position. Many among them, in doing this, have not feared to speak evil of dignities, and have united with men, to whom those well-known and awful passages in Jude and Peter emphatically apply. Moreover, in their anxiety to compel the relinquishment of a Church-position, they have entirely overstepped the limits of truth. They have drawn no distinction between truths that pertain to the Church, and those that belong to men, as men, and have advanced principles which, if they were true, would render the coming reign of our Lord and Saviour impossible. For, although not now, a time *is* coming, when the Church-position shall be held by the governing power of earth—when the Kingship and the Priesthood shall be united in One; and the Headship of Power shall be identified with the Headship of Truth. That cannot, therefore, be *abstractedly* wrong which is to be effected then. Christianity has tried, in the title of a Church-position, to govern the world. It has also tried, in a Church-position, to be governed by the world. Thirdly, it has tried to keep its Church-position separate from the world,—and while it has exhorted the Church corporately not to seek to rule the world, has encouraged the *individual* members of the Church to covet secular greatness, as one of the surest means of ensuring the universality of the Kingdom of Christ. But if Popery has displayed the evil of the first of these attempts, and the established churches of Protestantism the second, surely the days of Cromwell, when the principles of dissenting Christianity were allowed full scope for their development, exhibit a no less deplorable failure. It was, indeed, an attempt to put a new patch upon an old garment. Strange that it should not be instantly apparent to every Christian heart, that that which is corporately wrong cannot be individually right, and that a Christian may not act upon Christ's principles in the Church, and adopt the world's principles for his guidance in the world. Christ lived, even as we, at a time when the "fourth beast" of Daniel was ruling in the earth. He sought neither to destroy it, nor to control its course. He owned its authority in the person of Pilate, as being from God, and was content to suffer. His Apostles followed in His steps, and why should we adopt other principles now? *

If any one can rule now with the Bible in his

---

* I have already referred to the attempts that are being made by some, to substitute for the systems of Christian or church-fraternisation which have failed, a system of mere human fraternisation. Certain of the principles and precept of Christ, selected at discretion, are permitted to form part of the code of this new fraternity of man. See the principles avowed in the French Assembly by the *Protestant* M. Coquerel and others, and the writings of many in our own country.

This movement is essentially infidel in its character, but it is assisted by many misguided philanthropists, who, though not infidels, are not only endeavouring to make the world act

hand, guided by that alone, by all means let him
rule.   But if he cannot do this (and how soon must
the impossibility become apparent to any one who
tries), then what can he do except retire—retire and
wait for the time of rectification; when He who is
now hidden in the heavens shall return, and establish righteousness and judgment in the earth, and
" the isles shall wait for His law."   Yet, whilst in
patience of hope waiting, we may (and it is our
duty) warn, admonish, and plead with those in
power.   We may beseech them not to spurn the
authority of God, or trample under foot His holy
word.   We may rejoice if we find an Agrippa who

---

upon principles intended solely for the Church of God, but
are also taking away from the world the principles which
pertain to it by the express appointment of God, whilst it
remains in its present condition.   For example, the Scriptures say, that the magistrate is " a *revenger*"—the minister
of God for wrath," that "he beareth not the sword in vain "
(Rom. xiii.); but this, misguided philanthropy joins the infidel
in denying. "The penalty of death," say they, "is a vengeance, and vengeance is an illegitimate act."   In vain has
God said (not at Sinai, but to Noah) " Whoso sheddeth man's
blood, by man shall his blood be shed."   The human mind,
when under certain influences, is unaffected by the plainest
statements of Scripture Truth.

Results of mercy are far more likely to be attained by
adhering to the enactments of God, than by substituting for
them devices of our own.   A murderer's soul is far more
likely to be driven to the one Rock of Refuge by being subjected to the terrors which God has appointed to bear on
him here, than by having those terrors removed by the unauthorised and disobedient action of a human hand.

believes the Prophets, even as we weep when we see a Herod rage, or a Gallio carelessly and contemptuously turn away.

If, instead of forcing half-Christian principles on an unchristianised world, the Church were to draw its own principles from the Word of God, and, taking its own separate place, were thence to act upon the world wisely—making the right distinctions between things that differ, there would certainly be restored to the testimonies of Christianity a truthfulness and a vigour which have been long absent from them. We might become the means of saving many individuals, and it may be governments, from association with the coming Apostasy. Individuals, if not nations, might be saved from joining the hellish compact into which, under Antichrist, Israel and the Ten Kingdoms of the Roman world are about to enter, and might refuse with them to say of Jehovah and of Christ, " Let us break their bands asunder, and cast away their cords from us."

CHAPTER XIV.

ORDER OF EVENTS CONNECTED WITH THE APPEAR-ING OF CHRIST AND HIS MILLENNIAL REIGN.

EACH of the visions we have been considering attests that which, indeed, all Scripture teaches—the gradual but steady progress of iniquity, until the day of visitation from the Lord revealed in His glory. Whether we consider the Jews, or the Ten Nations of the Roman Earth, or the Heathen, or the Professing Church *as a body*, we find them all unprepared—evil having abounded in all. But the Ten Nations, and a large portion of the Jews, will be not only unprepared: they will also be involved in the blasphemies of Antichrist, having said both of Jehovah and of Christ, "Let us break their bands asunder, and cast away their cords from us." (Psalm ii. 3.)

All the descriptions of the antichristian period that we have read in Daniel show that the blasphemies of Antichrist will be allowed to ripen into full maturity before the Lord interferes in judgment. God will be denied, both as to His creative and providential power, and the truths, both of Jewish and Christian revelation, will be alike blasphemed. Antichrist "will exalt himself above *all* that is called God, or that is worshipped." He will change times and laws, and they are to be given into his hand for an appointed period. All the arrangements of human life, throughout the whole sphere of his dominion, are to be remodelled by his Satanic skill. The saints (as many as are within the scope of his power) will be persecuted; and not a few will seal their testimony by their blood. "He shall wear out," it is said, "the Saints of the High Places." But they will be strengthened to endure, and "will not love their life even unto death." Such will be the character of the evil, which God's own mercy will confront with the Almighty power of Christ, that it may be swept away for ever. For this, even the saints will pray, saying, "Lord, how long?"

The matured blasphemies of Antichrist and of the Roman Nations are the immediate cause of the Session of "the Ancient of Days." In the vision in the seventh of Daniel, thrones were seen to be set, and the Ancient of Days came, and inquisition was made into the condition of the nations who had given themselves over to the blasphemies of Antichrist. The thrones were *judicial* not *regal*. It was not the court of God's government, but of His solemn assize, appointed especially for inquisition on the governing nations of the earth. Nations, not individuals, are to be the subjects of that enquiry. Neither the dead nor the living were placed before the Throne to be individually judged. The whole chapter belongs to the Ten Nations governmentally. The effect produced upon the earth, by means of the power which had been so long entrusted to those Nations, is the subject of the enquiry. They will be weighed in the balances, and found more than wanting: they will be united in blasphemous rebellion against God.

The Session of the Ancient of Days, will be a scene manifest only to heaven. No eye beneath will discern it, no heart be conscious of it. They who watch the signs of the times will know, from the condition of the nations and from the duration of Antichrist's blasphemies, that the hour is nigh. But the Ancient of Days will sit in heaven, and inquisition into the condition of the blaspheming antichristian nations be made, and sentence be passed upon them, and the Son of Man will be brought before the throne of' the Ancient of Days and solemnly invested with the governmental power of earth, without any of these things being made manifest to any earthly eye.

The withdrawal of governmental power from those to whom it had been delegated in the earth, and its transfer to the Son of Man, is the event which terminates the Day of man, and commences "the Day of the Lord." It is in heaven that "the Day of the Lord," will commence, unseen and unknown by any on the earth. It is in heaven, not on earth, that it will be first said, "The sovereignty of the world hath become the sovereignty of our God and of His Christ, and He shall reign for ever and ever.".

The first visible intimation which the earth receives of "the Day of the Lord" having commenced in heaven is conveyed by the signs in the heavens, mentioned in the gospels. "There shall be signs in the sun and moon and stars." "The sun shall be darkened, and the moon shall not give her light, and the stars shall fall from heaven, and the powers of the heavens shall be shaken, and then shall appear the sign of the Son of Man in heaven." These signs will be the immediate precursor of the descent of the Lord Jesus into the air. All the holy angels will attend Him when he descends from heaven into the air; but His saints will not be with Him, because it is said, they shall be taken up "to meet Him in the air." (1 Thess. iv. 17.) There His descent will be *for a short period* stayed. Thence He will send forth His angels to gather together all His believing people—"all who are Christ's at His coming." They shall be caught up in the clouds to meet the Lord in the air, before He has reached the earth—and when He descends from the air to the earth, they come with Him, and surround Him when His feet stand on the mount of Olives. That is the moment of which it is said in Zechariah— "The Lord my God shall come, and all the Saints with Thee." *

---

* The word in Thessalonians translated, "*meet*" (απαντησις) means properly, to meet and come back with the person met. It is used of those who went out to meet St. Paul at Appii Forum, and accompanied him back to Rome. Thus the saints meet the Lord in the air, in order to accompany Him in His further descent to the earth. Απανταω and its deriva-

The condition of the earth at the period of the Lord's descent into the air is to be regarded in four aspects.

First, there will be the Jews partly in their own

---

tives are never used in the New Testament in any other sense than that of "to meet and come with." This will be seen if the *corrected* readings are observed. Thus, in Matt. xxv. 1, ὑπαντησιν, not απαντησιν, is the true reading.

It is very commonly said, that *the rapture* of the saints will take place "in a moment, in the twinkling of an eye;" but this is not so. *The resurrection* of the saints who have fallen asleep, and the change of those who are alive, will take place "in a moment, in the twinkling of an eye;" but between the resurrection, or change, of the saints, and their rapture to meet the Lord in the air, a certain period is to intervene. The interval will be doubtless very brief—to be measured by minutes rather than by hours—nevertheless, there will be an interval. This is distinctly taught in the Scripture, by the use of the word επειτα, in 1 Thess. iv. 17. Επειτα means "afterwards," not *then*, as it is wrongly rendered in our version. "*Afterwards*, we who are alive and remain shall be caught up," &c.

The existence of such an interval is necessary to the accomplishment of Matt. xiii. 49; for after the true professors of the name of Jesus are changed, holy angels descend, and separate from amongst them the false professors of the name of Jesus, who remain unchanged. "So shall it be at the end of the age : the angels shall come forth, and sever the wicked out of the midst [εκ μεσου] of the just." These words, it must be remembered, are, by the context, limited to those who are found professedly "in the kingdom of heaven," *i.e.*, the professing church. It is of that body only that the parables in 13th and 25th of Matthew treat. The "tares," "the bad fishes" enclosed in the same net as the good, the "foolish virgins," "the goats," do not represent either

Land, as at the time of the Crucifixion, partly scattered throughout the nations, and many of them in captivity.

Secondly, there will be the Ten Nations of the

---

heathens, or Jews, or Mahomedans, or anti-Christian infidels. They represent only those who are professedly the subjects of Christ's kingdom. He will gather "*out of His kingdom* [not out of the whole world] all things that offend, and them that do iniquity.*"* Matt. xiii. 41. He will not thus act towards the whole world, for He will spare and convert many Jews and many heathen.

If, in any part of the world, a true believer should in that day be found standing by the side of a heathen, the believer would be taken, the heathen left. If one of Christ's true people were standing by a Jew, he would be taken to the Lord, the Jew left; if by the side of a Mahomedan, the believer would be taken, the Mahomedan left. Some of those left amongst the Jews, and amongst the heathen, and those of irresponsible age, would be spared and converted; the others would be destroyed by some visible judgment, inflicted on them before they were removed into the unseen world.

On the other hand, if ten professing Christians were at that time assembled together, of whom five had really, five nominally, believed, those who had truly believed would, at the sounding of the trumpet, be, "in the twinkling of an eye," changed : the other five would remain unchanged. Immediately holy angels will appear, and separate those who are unchanged "out of the midst" of those who are changed, *after* which the latter will be caught up, together with the saints who have been raised, to meet and come with their Lord.

Moreover, after the true saints ("sheep") have been thus separated from those who only nominally profess the name of Christ ("goats"), both will be presented before the Lord whilst He yet remains on the Throne of His Glory in the air.

Roman World—all owning Antichrist—all apostate from God—their armies gathered around Antichrist at Armageddon, and advancing upon Jerusalem. (Rev. xvi. 16 ; Joel iii.).

Thirdly, there will be many countries still sunk in the darkness of heathenism—countries, of which it is said, that up to that moment they have not heard the fame of Jehovah, nor seen His glory. (Isaiah lxvi. 19.)

Fourthly, there will be throughout the earth vast

He will then declare the reason why the one are adjudged to be " sheep," and the others " goats." The latter have never discerned, nor desired to discern, between those who are truly, and those who are nominally, Christ's people ; and consequently never given even a cup of cold water to a disciple in the name of a disciple. On the other hand, each of the " sheep " will be found to have ministered, on some occasion or other, to Christ's people, on the ground of their being His people. How important to mark well this principle ! *Mere* philanthropy will not be recognised in that day ; only such philanthropy as is combined with the recognition of Christ in His people.

It should further be remembered, that this is not the final judgment of those denominated " goats ;" it is merely a declaration of the ground on which they are adjudged to be what they are. At the last resurrection (see Rev. xx., 11), each of those here denominated " goats " will be called before the Great White Throne, to be judged individually—each one according to his works. After having been adjudged to be " goats," they will be taken to the unseen place of punishment, there to await the judgment of the final day. The saints, on the other hand, after having been adjudged to be sheep belonging to the fold of the Great Shepherd, will fall into the train of the Lord's glory, and will come with Him.

multitudes of Gentiles, who will retain the profession of the name of Christ. Few that acknowledge the name of Christ will be found in the Ten Kingdoms of the Roman World; for *there,* profession will, for the most part, be swallowed up by Apostasy. But throughout the rest of the earth, wherever Christianity has penetrated, multitudes will be found still bearing the name of Christ. Some will be His in truth; others only in profession. The first He has named in one of His own Parables, " wheat "—the others He has denominated " tares." These together compose what is called in Scripture " the kingdom of heaven " or "*His* "—that is, Christ's kingdom. It is named according to its profession. (See Matthew xiii.)

This—His kingdom, will be the first subject of visitation from the Lord. We learn in the Gospel of Matthew that as soon as the Lord has descended into the air He will send His angels to gather out of His kingdom all things that offend, and them that do iniquity.* At the same time, His saints will be gathered to Himself, and will shine as the sun in the kingdom of their Father.

* It is *not* said that He will gather *out of the earth* all that offend—for that would not be true, inasmuch as many of the unconverted Jews and Heathen will be spared and converted. Neither is the earth regarded as *having been* His Kingdom, though it is *about to become* such. The expression, " His Kingdom," is limited in this passage *to the Professing Church*—out of *that,* He gathers all that offend. Neither Jews, nor Apostates, nor Mahomedans, nor Heathen, are in this kingdom; and, therefore, cannot be gathered out of it.

Y

The gathering of the living saints to the Lord is preceded by the change of their mortal bodies, as also by the resurrection of all who have ever fallen asleep in Jesus. The same moment that changes the living saints—the moment of the last trump—is also that which awakens the dead that have died in the Lord. They arise in bodies incorruptible, and, together with the living saints in whom also mortality is swallowed up of life, are caught up to meet the Lord in the air.

We should accustom ourselves to consider the realities of that hour as they are revealed in the Scripture. It will be an hour solemn and terrible to nature; although the feeblest Believer may wait in peaceful expectation, as knowing that grace, and only grace, is to be brought unto him at the revelation of Jesus Christ. The signs in the heavenly bodies are spoken of in Scripture as occurring before the saints are changed. They will be yet on the earth, and behold these premonitory signs before the trumpet sounds. "When these things [*i. e.*, signs in the sun, and in the moon, and in the stars] begin to come to pass, then look up and lift up your heads, for your redemption draweth nigh." But as soon as the Lord descends into the air, the same trumpet that announces His presence changes them, and angels are sent to gather them to the Lord. Angels are also sent to seize on those who are unchanged, and to gather them from among the righteous (Matt. xiii.). But the saints are changed, and cease to be the subjects of mortal feelings before that separation is effected—otherwise they might be unable to bear its agony. "Herein is love made perfect in its dealings with us (in order that we might have confidence in the day of judgment), because as He [Christ] IS, so are we in this world." (1 John iv. 17.)

Few living saints, and few mere professing Chris-

---

* The day of God's judgment begins as soon as the Lord Jesus returns. The principles of God's holiness are then manifestly applied to the condition of human things. The raising all who have fallen asleep in Christ, and the leaving all the rest of the dead unraised, is an act of discriminative judgment. Another is the separation of the "Tares" and the "Wheat"—another the destruction of the anti-Christian nations, and the visitation on Israel. Indeed, the whole of the Millennium has, more or less, the character of discriminative judgment. Then also, " He will give reward to His servants the Prophets, and to the Saints, and those who fear His name, the small and the great."

In order that we might have confidence in the day in which the principles of His holiness are applied to the condition of human things below, the love of God has been pleased already to grant to the feeblest Believer union with, and acceptance in, His Son: in other words, to make him, even whilst here, what Christ IS. We are *already* accepted in the *Beloved*—*already* we are regarded as one with Christ—and when He returns, we are instantly to be changed, and made manifestly like Him, whilst we are yet beneath the skies; and thus we shall have confidence, even whilst beholding the glory and the terror of that day, when the heavens and the earth shall shake. In this, we shall prove the perfectness of His love in its dealing with us. The being changed in the twinkling of an eye, into Christ's heavenly likeness, will give us confidence in that "Day of Judgment.

tians, will be found in the Antichristian Kingdoms at that hour. Neither those kingdoms, nor heathen countries, are the *first* subjects of the dealing of the Lord's hand. Nevertheless, seeing that the Antichristian Kingdoms and the Land of Israel have been, in past ages, the home of multitudes who have died in the Lord, the graves of such will open, and every sleeping saint will be seen awakened for the glory of the first resurrection. The *whole* earth, therefore (for some believers may have died in, or be living in even heathen lands), will teem with glorified saints, and with angels sent forth to gather them to the Lord. The Lord will be visibly present in the air, whilst these things are transpiring in the earth below.

It is thus that the Day of the Lord commences *in the earth*. It will commence by signs in the created heavens (Luke xxi.); by the withdrawal of all natural sources of light; by the descent of the Lord, accompanied by the holy angels, into the air; by the trumpet being blown; by the dead saints rising from their graves in glory, and by the living saints being changed and glorified whilst yet in the earth; by the instantaneous severance, through the instrumentality of angels, of the changed saints "out of the midst" ($\epsilon\kappa$ $\mu\epsilon\sigma\sigma\nu$) of their professing brethren who remain unchanged (see Matt. xiii.); by the taking up of all the glorified saints into the air, to meet and to come with their Lord. For as soon as His saints have been gathered to Him and have fallen into their appointed place in the train of His glory, and as soon as " the tares," (*i. e.* those who are found to be mere professors of His name), have been borne away by angels to their place of punishment, the Lord will instantly descend to the earth. " His feet shall stand in that day upon the Mount of Olives. * * * Jehovah, my God, shall come, and all the saints with thee." Zech. xiv. His object will be the rescue of Jerusalem, for the time of her forgiveness and glory will have come. Antichrist will have gathered all the strength of the Ten Kingdoms to Armageddon, not knowing, or not believing, that he will gather them there " for the war of the great day of God the Almighty," (εἰς τὸν πόλεμον τῆς ἡμέρας τῆς μεγάλης τοῦ Θεοῦ τοῦ παντοκράτορος). See Rev. xvi. 14. Whilst encamped at Armageddon, he will assail and capture Jerusalem, which will have rebelled against him, will carry half of the people into captivity, (see Zech. xiv. 1) and will destroy the two witnesses of God (Rev. xi. 7) when they shall have finished their sackcloth testimony. But not satisfied with this, he will further seek, in union with Moab, Ammon, and others of the ancient enemies of Israel, to crush Israel utterly, and to blot out their name from the earth. " They have said, Come and let us cut them off from being a nation; that the name of Israel may be no more in remembrance." Ps. lxxxiii. 4. But the Lord will interpose. He will, indeed, scourge Jerusalem and purge out thence the sinners; but He will also forgive and defend it. In that day shall " Jehovah of Hosts

defend Jerusalem." Isaiah xxxi. 5. In the second
and third chapters of Joel we find the description of
that great "day of battle and war." See Job xxxviii.
23. "Assemble yourselves and come, all ye Gentiles,
(כָּל־הַגּוֹיִם) and gather yourselves together round-
about; thither cause thy mighty ones [saints and
angels] to come down, O Jehovah. Let the Gentiles
be wakened, and come up to the valley of Jehoshaphat, for there will I sit to judge all the Gentiles
round about. Put ye in the sickle, for the harvest
is ripe; come, get you down, for the press is full, the
fats overflow; for their wickedness is great. Multitudes, multitudes in the valley of decision; for the
day of Jehovah is near in the valley of decision.
The sun and the moon shall be darkened and the
stars shall withdraw their shining. Jehovah also
shall roar out of Zion, and utter His voice from
Jerusalem, and the heavens and the earth shall shake;
but Jehovah will be the hope of His people, and the
strength of the children of Israel." Joel iii. 11, 16.
The claim which the Lord has upon one city of the
earth as the city "which He hath chosen to put His
name there," becomes the instrumental means of
bringing the armies of earth into immediate conflict with the Hosts of Heaven. The very city which
God hath chosen for Himself that He might make
it the joy and the praise of the whole earth—that
city to which He will say, "Arise, shine, for thy
light is come, and the glory of the Lord is risen
upon thee," is the very city around which men will
gather in fierce fury that they might utterly destroy

it, that they might cut off the remembrance thereof
from under heaven. " Spirits of devils working
miracles," will have gathered the Kings τῆς οἰκου-
μένης ὅλης—of the whole Roman World (Rev. xvi.
14.) for this object. But which shall triumph?
Man leagued with Satan, or Jehovah? " Thus hath
Jehovah said unto me, Like as the lion and the young
lion roaring on his prey, when a multitude of
shepherds is called forth against him, he will not be
afraid of their voice, nor abase himself for the noise
of them; so shall Jehovah of Hosts come down to
fight for Mount Zion and for the hill thereof. As
birds flying, so will Jehovah of Hosts defend Jerusalem; defending it also He will deliver it; passing
over he will preserve it   *   *   *   And
Jehovah shall cause His glorious voice to be heard
and shall shew the lighting down of His arm, with
the indignation of His anger, and with the flame of
a devouring fire, with scattering, and tempest and
hailstones." Isaiah xxxi. 4, and xxxii. 30.

Yet not even the knowledge that the Lord has
come in manifested glory to take Jerusalem under
the shield of His protection, will prevent Antichrist
and those who are with him from continuing their
assault upon it, and so rushing upon the thick
bosses of the buckler of the Almighty. He, and the
Ten Kings of the Roman Kingdoms that are with
him, are distinctly described in the Revelation as
daring to confront the majesty and the glory of
Christ's own presence. " These shall make war
with the Lamb, and the Lamb shall overcome them;

because he is Lord of lords and King of kings; and those that are with Him are called, and chosen, and faithful." Rev. xvii. 14. "And I saw the Beast and the kings of the earth, and their armies gathered together to do battle with Him that sat upon the horse and with His army." Rev. xix. 19. It will not, indeed be the first time that man will have dared to confront and resist the visible presence of the glory of God. Neither the miracle of the divided waters of the Red Sea, nor the presence of the fiery cloudy pillar spreading darkness over the Egyptians, but light over Israel, prevailed to stay the wrath of Pharaoh and to prevent him from rushing into the midst of the divided waters. There also the subject of the contest was the fate of God's earthly people. Pharaoh said, "I will destroy them:" God said, "They are my people." We cannot marvel therefore if like madness of fury should be manifested again; especially when we remember that Antichrist and his armies will be gathered into the land of Israel by the immediate agency of unclean spirits. Those spirits of evil that will just before have dared to struggle against Michael the Archangel and his angels even in the presence of God's own glory in Heaven, (see Rev. xii. 7.) may well be expected to renew the struggle in the earth beneath, inhabiting the bosoms of mortal men, strengthening for the last time their tongues to blaspheme, and their hands to resist the God whom they hate.

The destruction of Antichrist and those who are

associated with him, is distinguished, both as to time and as to circumstances, from the destruction of those who retain the nominal profession of the name of Christ. Nominal Christians as represented in the parables of Matthew by " Tares " sown among the Wheat, and by " bad fishes " mingled with the good in the gospel-net, are not destroyed by judgments poured on them *in* the earth, but are removed by holy angels *from* the earth, that their souls might await in an unseen prison-house and in punishment the final judgment of the great day. On the other hand, all those who shall be gathered under Antichrist, to serve and to worship him, will be visited with visible judgment here. " Their flesh shall consume away while they stand upon their feet, and their eyes shall consume away in their holes, and their tongue shall consume away in their mouth." Zech. xiv. 12. They will be trampled in the winepress of the fury and wrath of God *here* (see Rev. xiv. 19).; their bodies will then be revived, they will be cast into Tophet and their eternal torment will begin. See Rev. xiv. 8. The " Tares " will be gathered by angels ; the Antichristians destroyed by the Lord Himself. The " Tares " will be gathered and removed, whilst the Lord is yet in the air, whither the saints also are to be caught up ; the Antichristians will be destroyed *after* the Lord has descended to the earth. The Antichristians, in revived bodies, will be consigned to their eternal torment at the commencement of the Millennium, whereas all nominal professors will, in a disembodied state, await in punishment the final resurrection and the judgment of the great day.

This is the hour so often referred to in Daniel, when "the stone" shall smite "the Image," and cause it to become as the chaff of the summer threshing-floor—when " the Beast shall be slain, his body destroyed and given to the burning flame "—when " that determined shall be poured upon the Desolator"—when " he shall come to his end and none shall help him "—when " Michael shall stand up," and the remnant of Israel be delivered. That remnant is continually mentioned in the Prophets, but it is sufficient to mention one passage. " And it shall come to pass, that in all the land, saith the Lord, two parts therein shall be cut off and die ; but the third shall be left therein. And I will bring the third part through the fire, and will refine them as silver is refined, and will try them as gold is tried : they shall call on my name, and I will hear them : I will say, It is my people : and they shall say, The Lord is my God." (Zech. xiii. 8, 9.) They are also mentioned as an afflicted and poor remnant, who shall trust in the name of the Lord ; but of whom it is said, that He will make them " a strong nation."

It is no wonder that their hearts should be subdued and broken. They will have witnessed the terrors of the reign of Antichrist—will have seen the plagues of the Revelation poured out upon Israel and the Antichristian nations—will have beheld the heavens darkened—the Lord descend in glory—the graves open—the saints taken—the Day of the Lord come upon Jerusalem—the Heavens and the Earth shaken. They will see, and yet find themselves protected through all these things; delivered—forgiven —and not forgiven only, but accepted in all the preciousness of that Name, which they and their nation had rejected and abhorred. "They will look on Him whom they have pierced," and He will com-comfort them, and will say, with fuller love than Joseph said unto his brethren, "Now therefore be not grieved, nor angry with yourselves, that ye sold me hither : for God did send me before you to preserve life. And God sent me before you to preserve you a posterity in the earth, and to save your lives by a great deliverance. So now it was not you that sent me hither, but God." Not one ray of light that had been sent to break the gloom of man's past history, will be absent in that hour of fulness. Every such joy has been typical or anticipative, and points onward to an hour of accomplished blessing, that will then have come. All these joys will be verified then, either in the Saints above, or in Israel below —different branches of "the one family in heaven and in earth."*

* As an attempt has been made by many to alter the translation of this most important passage, respecting the *one* family in heaven and in earth, I would earnestly request that my remarks on this text may be read in "*Occasional Papers*," vol. i., p. 31.

There will be many others spared besides the remnant of Israel; principally among the heathen. Thus it is said, that God will send those who are spared in Israel, "to the isles

The *spiritual* blessings of each individual Israelite, and of every other Believer who lives during the

afar off, which have not heard His fame, nor seen His glory ; and they shall declare His glory among the Gentiles."

There is no reason to believe that the heathen nations will, when the Lord returns, be in any material respect, other than they now are ; except that some of them, may become more hardened through intercourse with anti-Christian, or with nominally Christian nations. It is not likely that many more heathen nations will, *as nations*, assume the profession of Christianity ; although many individuals among them may bear the name of Christ—some truly—others nominally.

It is, however, the plain duty of believers to preach the Gospel to every creature ; and to visit, if they can, every land. Right prophetic expectation will quicken, not impede, true missionary energy. Nevertheless, we know that every land will not be visited by the Gospel before the Lord comes, else it would not be said, that there would be regions "that had not heard His fame," at the hour of His return. St. Paul says, that in his day "the Gospel had been preached IN all the creation" ($εν$ $πασῃ$ $τῃ$ $κτισει$, Col. i. 23) ; and this was true as soon as it ceased to be confined to Israel, and was preached among men, as men : but Scripture nowhere says that it has been, or will be preached *to* every creature in the present Dispensation. The Church was *commanded* to preach it to every creature ; but what the Church was *commanded* to do, and what it *has* done, are different things.

Although those who are gathered at Armageddon, *i.e.*, the armies of all the Antichristian nations, utterly perish under visible judgment, inflicted immediately by the Lord ; —and although all among those nations who have borne the mark of Antichrist will also perish ; yet some (those doubtless of youthful age) who have not worshipped Antichrist will be spared. Thus we find it said, that every one that is left of all the nations which came against Jerusalem, shall even go up from year to year to worship the King, the Lord of hosts. (Zech. xiv. 16.)

Millennium, will be essentially the same as ours in this present Dispensation :—our distinction being, that we are "first-fruits," (Rom. xi.)—those who have *first* trusted in Christ" (προηλπικοτες). Indeed we may give as the description of our Dispensation, that it forestalls the *spiritual* blessings of Israel in the Millennium—we having those blessings in the midst of tribulation and sorrow, whereas they will have them when all the outward circumstances of life around them will be circumstances of tranquillity, peace, and joy—Satan being bound, and the Prince of Peace reigning. *We* have already been brought under that New Covenant, which will *then* be made with the House of Israel, and with the House of Judah. It is a covenant of grace, primarily designed for them, which they for a season have despised ; but we, through abounding mercy, have already been brought under its provisions. Every blessing that we receive as saints, we owe to the being graffed into *their* olive tree, from which they, for a season, have been broken off. But they are again to be graffed in, to receive in more unhindered power than we, of the freshness of its sap, and of the riches of its fulness. Every vessel of the Tabernacle that typified to them the blessings of redemption, is a type already fulfilled to us. From the Altar to the Mercy-seat, all is ours. But it will be equally theirs. Often therefore, from the language of their future thanksgiving, we borrow the expressions of our present joy.

Israel in the Millennium will still be in bodies of flesh and blood, still having experimentally to prove that in the flesh "dwelleth no good thing." The removal of Satan and his temptations will not change the inherent evil of man's nature : and if, when the stimulus of Satan's temptations is removed, and the external order of human life regulated according to God, the flesh be still found to lust against the Spirit, the inveteracy of its evil will only be the more consciously proved, and the more painfully felt. The nearness of the glory and holiness of Christ, the visible presence of saints and angels, the possession of every outward blessing abundantly poured upon creation and themselves, will make them the more acutely sensible of the presence of an evil principle within themselves, still opposed to holiness, and to God—something that "is not subject to the law of God, neither indeed can be." None therefore, will have more occasion to say, "His blood is drink indeed :" none will more need to think of Him, who will be " the Lord their Righteousness," and whose priesthood will sustain them in the presence of God. They will require, and will receive the grace of that same Spirit—the Spirit of the Father and the Son, who now indwells in the people of God. In them, He will be still the Spirit of *hope*, for they will look forward with joy, to the hour of their resurrection, when they shall be changed into the likeness of Him with whom they will be united in life ; and join the rest of the redeemed in " New Heavens and a New Earth," where fallen flesh will no longer be, but where all shall be perfect in the likeness of Christ.

There are certain truths, dependant on the immutable character of God, and on the nature of evil in man, which no circumstances can alter, no variation of Dispensations change. The great truths of redemption, and the arrangements of God consequent thereon, as made known in the New Testament, must be as true in the Millennium, as now. It is an unchangeable truth, that without shedding of blood is no remission : that if any one be in Christ Jesus, he is a new creature : that he that is in the flesh, cannot please God : that every one, who through faith "receives abundance of grace and of the gift of righteousness," shall finally "reign in life." These and such like blessings pertain necessarily to *all* the redeemed, and by considering them, we gain clear and certain knowledge of the condition of the Millennial saints as to all that affects their essential and eternal relations to God. The Epistles reveal their spiritual—the Prophets their outward blessings. By combining the descriptions of both, their condition is given with a minuteness, that leaves little to be desired.*

---

* It is almost impossible to estimate the amount of evil that has arisen from representing the *spiritual* blessings of Israel in the Millennium, as different from ours. Many have been hindered thereby, from considering millennial doctrines at all ; for they have not unreasonably asked, whether they are expected to believe, that the doctrines of Christianity are mutable, and that saintship in the Millennium, is something essentially different from saintship now. They have consequently refused, and rightly so, to lend any ear to statements which involve such consequences.

There are few parts of Scripture, which believers are

The distinctive spiritual characteristics of Christianity, therefore, will not alter in the Millennium: on the contrary, it will be the sphere in which they will be exhibited more perfectly than they ever have been.

---

accustomed to read with more comfort, than those parts of the Psalms and Prophets, which speak of the *spiritual* blessings of Israel after they are brought under the New Covenant. But those who maintain the system of which I speak, instead of teaching us to distinguish between the *spiritual* and the outward blessings of Israel, and to appropriate to ourselves the former without the latter ; refuse to us the application of millennial Scripture altogether, and represent the Christianity of the Millennium as something *essentially* different, both as to its condition, and as to its final prospects, from Christianity *now*.

Millennial Israel will be sons of God (Hosea i. 10 and Jer. iii. 19)—so are we.

They will be under the Mediatorship, Sacrifice and Priesthood of the New Covenant (Jer. xxxi. 31)—so are we. (Heb. ix.)

They will be circumcised by the circumcision made without hands: *i. e.* by the death and resurrection of Christ (Col. ii.)—so are we.

They will "please God," and therefore, must have been brought into living union with Christ, through the Spirit, even as we, for "they that are in the flesh" (*i.e.* they who are unregenerate) "*cannot* please God." (Rom. viii. 8.)

They say to Him, "The Lord our Righteousness"—so do we.

They will be raised in His likeness, at the *last* resurrection, in virtue of being IN Him—we are similarly raised at the *first* resurrection, in virtue of being IN Him. (See 1 Cor. xv. throughout.)

They will look forward to New Heavens, and a New Earth, (Isaiah lxv.)—so do we. (2 Peter iii.)

In this present Dispensation, the corporate testimony of Christianity early failed. The Church at Jerusalem was scattered—the Gentile Churches retained not their separateness—the corporate testimony of Christianity ceased to bear witness for God—and that of individual Christians has been isolated and feeble in the midst of abounding evil. "Because iniquity shall abound, the love of the greater part (τῶν πολλῶν) shall wax cold." But when the corporate testimony of Christianity has been transferred to Israel, it will never again fail, or be dishonoured. Christ, as the Head of Israel, will discipline and sustain them. They shall have "teachers who shall not be removed into a corner any more"—"their eye shall behold them"—"the Spirit shall be poured out upon them from on high"—they shall hear a voice, that shall say, "this is the way, walk ye in it." Their Church-position is symbolised in the Scripture, by *one* golden candlestick fed perpetually by golden oil —a candlestick never to be removed. (Zech. iv.)

A nation, thus made the depository of Christ's Truth is *the* nation through which, instrumentally, the whole earth is to be ordered. "Out of Zion shall go forth the law, and the word of the Lord from Jerusalem." They are not only to be "a golden candlestick"—they are also to be "a royal diadem in the hand of their God"—a royal, as well as a priestly nation. "Thou shalt also be a crown of glory in the hand of the Lord, and a royal diadem in the hand of thy God." (Isa. lxii.) Christ also, the Head of Israel, is to sit as a Priest upon His

z

Throne. There will be no discrepancy *then*, between the Truth of God and the governmental arrangements of the nations. The Temple is to be sustained by Him who occupies the Throne.

But the Person of Christ is heavenly; His glory heavenly; His home, Heaven; and it will continue to be so, even when He is administering the government of Israel and the earth. When God legislated for Israel of old, He really descended on Sinai; but He did not relinquish the Throne of His glory in the heavens. When Moses and Elias appeared in glory on the Mount of Transfiguration, they actually stood upon an earthly mountain, and were seen by earthly eyes; but their home was in the clouds of glory into which they ascended. And thus in the day of Christ's manifested glory, the saints who are associated under Him. and with Him in it, are distinctly called, "the Saints of the High Places;" and the Kingdom is called, "the Kingdom of Heaven," because it is administered by heavenly hands.

The mention in Ezekiel of the visible glory of the Lord returning to *Jerusalem*—the Psalm which says, "Pray for the peace of Jerusalem," THERE are set the Thrones of the house of David"—the promise to the Apostles that they "shall sit on thrones, judging the twelve Tribes of Israel"—are all evidences, that the seat of Christ's administrative government in the Earth, will be established in Jerusalem, no less truly and visibly, than God was manifested on Sinai. "At that time they shall call

Jerusalem the throne of the Lord; and all the nations shall be gathered unto it, to the name of the Lord, to Jerusalem." (Isa. iii. 17.) "Behold, the days come, saith the Lord, that I will raise unto David a righteous Branch, and a KING shall reign and prosper, and shall execute judgment and justice in the earth. In His days Judah shall be saved, and Israel shall dwell safely: and this is His name whereby He shall be called, THE LORD OUR RIGHTEOUSNESS." (Jer. xxiii. 5, 6.) "Of the increase of His government and peace there shall be no end, *upon the throne of David, and upon his kingdom.* . . . . . The zeal of the Lord of hosts will perform this." (Isaiah ix. 7.) The Temple at Jerusalem is also expressly spoken of in Ezekiel, as one of the places of Divine Glory. "Afterward he brought me to the gate, even the gate that looketh toward the east: and behold, the glory of the God of Israel came from the way of the east: and His voice was like a noise of many waters: and the earth shined with His glory. . . . . And the glory of the Lord came into the house by the way of the gate whose prospect is toward the east . . . . and, behold, the glory of the Lord filled the house. . . . . And He said unto me, Son of man, the place of my Throne, and the place of the soles of my feet, where I will dwell in the midst of the children of Israel for ever." (Ezekiel xliii. 1.) This is the period of which it is said in the Psalms, "Because of thy temple at Jerusalem shall kings bring presents unto thee." (Psalm lxviii. 29.)

But in the prophecies which speak of the future

glory of Jerusalem, Mount Zion is peculiarly spoken of as the hill or mountain of God's glory. Thus the sixty-eighth Psalm, speaking of Zion, says, "The hill of God is as the hill of Bashan; an high hill as the hill of Bashan. Why leap ye, ye high hills? this is the hill which God desireth to dwell in; yea, the Lord will dwell in it for ever."

The two mountains of power brought into connexion with Israel, are Sinai and Zion : Sinai—the place of righteousness according to Law; Zion—of righteousness according to grace. The relation of Israel and Jerusalem to Zion, by and by, will be as real and as visible, as the relation of Israel to Sinai of old. The glory of God was seen on Sinai. The glory of God *will* as truly be seen on Zion. Israel was gathered around Sinai, and thence received care and legislation from God. Israel *will* be gathered around Zion, and receive care and legislation. At Sinai, were the terrors of unsatisfied holiness. At Zion, there will be grace, mercy and peace from God the Father, through the Lord Jesus Christ. There will be found "Jesus the Mediator of the new Covenant, and *the blood of sprinkling*, that speaketh better things than that of Abel." At Sinai, if a beast touched the mountain, it was to be stoned, or thrust through with a dart: but the sides of Zion shall be a vision of peace. The cow and the bear shall feed, their young ones shall lie down together, they shall not hurt nor destroy in all God's holy mountain. "And the Lord will create upon every dwelling-place of Mount Zion, and upon her assemblies, a cloud and smoke by day, and the shining of a flaming fire by night : for upon all the glory shall be a defence. And there shall be a tabernacle for a shadow in the day time from the heat, and for a place of refuge, and for a covert from storm, and from rain." (Isaiah iv. 5.)

Thus the *sides* of Zion will be the scene of peace, glory, and miraculous protection. But " the *height* of Zion," is the place, where that heavenly power is fixed, from which this protection, and these blessings flow. " They shall come, it is said, and sing before the Lord in the height of Zion." The glory of God was in the height of Sinai; whilst the Camp of Israel, the Tabernacle, the cloudy Pillar, and the virtually royal seat of Moses (for he was *King* in Jeshurun) were all at the foot of the mountain below. Zion is twice mentioned in the New Testament—once in the Hebrews, and once in the Revelation, as the place of Divine Glory, and of the glory of risen Saints, in which flesh and blood could not share. On Zion were seen standing, those who were redeemed from the earth—able to learn the song that was sung before the throne above—able also to follow the Lamb *whithersoever* He went. In other words, they were able to do the will of God in earth, AS it is done in heaven. This can only be true of those, in whom mortality is swallowed up of life—and therefore, to such, the government of earth is committed —"Saints of the High Places." " They go from strength to strength, every one of them in Zion appeareth before God." (Psalm lxxxiv. 7.) Zion being the centre of the earth's government, it is the place in which they might be expected to appear.

The great distinctive characteristic however of Zion, will be, not so much in the glory that is *on* it, as in the glory which is *above* it. " Ye shall see," said the Lord Jesus, " heaven opened." The heavens were not opened in peaceful blessing over Sinai. Sinai was the claim of God's unsatisfied holiness— and it ended in the heavens being as brass, and the earth as iron. But Zion will be the witness, that the claim of holiness *has* been satisfied, and that the sweet savour of peace, through the one accepted sacrifice, has ascended into the heavens. The heavenly places therefore, not made with hands, shall be opened towards Zion and the earth, and the Heavenly City of the saints made manifest, in token, that God has by ONE, even by Immanuel, the Son of His bosom, been glorified in the earth, and that He thenceforward designs to give according to the value of that which He hath received. It will be the hour of *descending* blessing.

The truths that pertain to Israel—(for to them belong the promises and the covenants)* have not been inoperative during the time that the nation of Israel has been scorning them. They have reached, quickened, and comforted multitudes, who have found in them, the cause of their sufferings, and the subject-matter of their service through dark and

* "To whom pertaineth the adoption, and the glory, and the covenants, and the giving of the law, and the service of God, and the promises ; whose are the fathers, and of whom, as concerning the flesh, Christ came, who is over all, God blessed for ever. Amen." (Rom. ix. 5.)

troubled hours of conflict and of sorrow. But where will the suffering children of the truth be when the hour of the promised glory comes? They will belong to no earthly city. Their blessings will be in a new creation—in the city of the Living God, the Heavenly Jerusalem. But they are not only to be blessed themselves; they are to be employed, and made a blessing to others. They, and the Heavenly City in which they dwell, will be among the gifts bestowed on those, who will have been made heirs of salvation in the earth below.

After the blessings received in the Person, redemption, and offices of the Son of God, there are probably none at which converted Israel will marvel more than in the provision made for them in the risen saints, and in the heavenly City. The "Sons of Aaron the Priests" were accustomed of old to enter on behalf of Israel into the tabernacle of God. The risen saints will be the antitypical priesthood; but they will minister in no Temple made with hands. The Heavenly City, and Heaven, will answer respectively to the Holy Place, and to the Holy of Holies in Israel's ancient Temple. In both of these, the risen Saints will act for Israel. But they are not a Priesthood only; they are a Royal Priesthood—Priests and Kings, and as such will come forth in kingly power, to teach and to guide those in the earth beneath. Israel, softened by grace, humbled by affliction, and humbled by mercy, will be no longer too proud to receive the guidance of heavenly wisdom. The character of " the Saints of the High Places," who will then watch over Israel, is taught in the symbols by which God has been pleased to indicate the excellency of the Heavenly City in which they dwell. The varied lustre of the precious stones which adorn it—the purity of the pearl gates, on which were written the names of the twelve Tribes of Israel—the transparency of its golden streets, well suited to the feet of those, who are represented as standing on a sea of crystal—are all symbols of a heavenly excellency, which will, by them who possess it, be necessarily communicated in measure to those who are morally fashioned under their care. Accordingly, the earthly Jerusalem will be made, in some degree, to answer to its heavenly pattern. There too, we read of stones of fair colours being found. "Behold, I will lay thy stones with fair colours, and lay thy foundations with sapphires. And I will make thy windows of agates, and thy gates of carbuncles, and all thy borders of pleasant stones. All thy children shall be taught of the Lord; and great shall be the peace of thy children." Such are the effects of the heavenly agency directed towards the Beloved City. It becomes *in measure*, the counterpart of the city that is above, and forms as it were, another court of the same Holy Temple.*

---

* The Courts of the Temple appear to have been the intended type of the millennial arrangements—Heaven itself being the anti-type of the Holy of Holies—the Heavenly Jerusalem answering to the Holy Place.

Both these Courts were covered, and were therefore invisible to the worshippers without. They were called *ναος* in

It is well fitted, therefore, to be the centre of truth, and the centre of governmental influence in the earth; and being sustained in righteousness through grace, it will not fail in its high calling. "In righteousness thou shalt be established." "Their seed shall be known among the Gentiles, and their offspring among the peoples: all that see them shall acknowledge them, that they are the seed whom the Lord has blessed." "The children of Jerusalem shall be made princes in all the earth," and the nations shall at last be regulated according to God. They shall be made glad as with new wine—wine which they had never tasted before—no longer the wine

contradistinction to ἱερον, which last was applied to all the sacred inclosure. The inner courts could only be entered by Aaron and his sons, who typify the Church of the First-born in their millennial relation to Israel. (See Lev. ix.) The veil being rent between these two courts, the heavenly Priesthood have access into both.

The earthly Jerusalem will answer to the external court, where Israel worshipped; and exterior to this was the court of the Gentiles; for the Gentiles also will become worshippers in the Millennium.

In the arrangements for the worship of Israel of old, the offerings of those who were not *personally* permitted to enter the Holy places were brought *by them* no further than the outer court: nevertheless the honour of the gift was regarded as rendered to the Holy Places, and to Him who dwelt there. So will it be in the Millennium. The Kings of the earth will not be able *personally* to enter *into* the heavenly City; (nor indeed any who yet continue in bodies of flesh and blood,) but they will bring their glory and honour *unto* (εἰς) it, mediately through the earthly City, which will be the external court of the One Temple.

of the wrath of the fornication of the daughter of
Babylon. We can well understand, therefore, why
it should be said; "for Zion's sake, will I not hold
my peace, and for Jerusalem's sake, I will not rest,
until the righteousness thereof go forth as brightness, and the salvation thereof as a lamp that burneth
. . . . ye that make mention of the Lord, keep not
silence, and give Him no rest, till He establish, and
till He make Jerusalem a praise in the earth."*

The full and ordered glory of the Millennium, however, is not introduced until some time after the
Day of visitation upon Jerusalem. That Day of
visitation will be only *one* day. "It shall be *one*
day, known unto the Lord." (Zech. xiv.) In it,
Israel will be nationally forgiven; and the remnant
spared in the Land of Israel, will look on Him whom
they have pierced, and mourn. But the greater part
of Israel will be in distant lands—some having been
carried captive during the days of Antichrist, others
scattered by his persecutions, whilst others will be

---

* It is very commonly thought that the Ten Tribes have
been lost since the time of their first captivity : and they are
supposed to be still dwelling in some unknown region. But
there is not the slightest authority in Scripture for saying
that they are lost: on the contrary, "*both* the Houses of
Israel," are declared to have rejected Jesus. "He shall be
for a sanctuary ; but for a stone of stumbling, and for a
rock of offence *to both the houses of Israel.*" Moreover, Paul
says, "to which promise our *twelve* tribes instantly serving
God day and night, hope to come:" and James writes expressly to the converts among the twelve tribes. The Scripture therefore does not regard them as lost.

voluntarily sojourning in the uttermost regions of the earth, worshippers of the wealth and mercantile greatness of Babylon and Tyre. These will not escape the judgments that fall, more or less, upon the whole house of Israel: "As I live, saith the Lord God, surely with a mighty hand and with a stretched-out arm, and with fury poured out, will I rule over you; And I will bring you out from the people, and will gather you out of the countries wherein ye are scattered, with a mighty hand and with a stretched-out arm, and with fury poured out. And I will bring you into the wilderness of the people, and there will I plead with you face to face. Like as I pleaded with your fathers in the wilderness of the land of Egypt, so will I plead with you, saith the Lord God. And I will cause you to pass under the rod, and I will bring you into the bond of the covenant. And I will purge out from among you the rebels, and them that transgress against me: I will bring them forth out of the country where they sojourn, and they shall not enter into the Land of Israel: and ye shall know that I am the Lord." (Ezekiel xx. 33.)

But if the wilderness be the place where this part of Israel is "pleaded with," and purified; it is also the place where they shall find mercy. "Therefore behold, I will allure her, and bring her into the wilderness, and speak comfortably unto her. And I will give her vineyards from thence, and the valley of Achor for a door of hope; and she shall sing there, as in the days of her youth, and as in the day when

she came up out of the Land of Egypt." (Hosea ii.
14.) " According to the days of thy coming out
of the Land of Egypt, will I show unto him marvellous things. The nations shall see and be confounded
at all their might : they shall lick the dust like a serpent, they shall move out of their holes like worms
of the earth : they shall be afraid of the Lord our
God, and shall fear because of thee." (Micah vii.
15.) This is the time of which it is said : " I will
even make a way in the wilderness, and rivers in the
desert. The beast of the field shall honour me, the
dragons and the owls : because I give waters in the
wilderness and rivers in the desert, to give drink to
my people, my chosen." (Isa. xliii. 19.) "The
Lord shall utterly destroy the tongue of the Egyptian
Sea ; * and with His mighty wind shall He shake

* Tongue or " bay " of the Egyptian Sea. This word
" tongue," is rendered " bay," three times in Joshua xv. and
xviii. The bay of the Egyptian Sea is that part of the Red
Sea which Israel formerly crossed. It is a bay about 200
miles long, extending from the promontory of the wilderness of Sinai to Suez. The land of Israel will by and by
include the wilderness of Sinai. (See Ezekiel.) Thus when
the seven streams of the Nile, and the bay of Suez, shall be
dried up, Egypt, Israel, and Assyria will stand in close and
uninterrupted connexion—the closeness of their physical connexion symbolising the intimacy of their moral union. The
millennium abounds with arrangements intended to symbolise higher blessings. It is as it were a system of living
symbols. The union of Egypt, Israel, and Assyria is thus
mentioned in the Scripture. " In that day shall there be a
highway out of Egypt to Assyria, and the Assyrian shall come
into Egypt and the Egyptian into Assyria, and the Egyptians

His hand over the river, and shall smite it in the seven streams, and make men go over dry shod. And there shall be an highway for the remnant of His people which shall be left from Assyria, like as it was to Israel in the day that he came up out of the Land of Egypt." Besides those who are thus immediately gathered by the Lord, we read of others brought by the nations at the commandment of the Lord. "I will say to the north, Give up; and to the south, Keep not back: bring my sons from far, and my daughters from the ends of the earth." (Isa. xliii. 6.) "In that time, shall the present be brought unto the Lord of Hosts, of a people scattered and peeled, and from a people terrible from their beginning hitherto; a nation meted out and trodden under foot, whose land the rivers have spoiled, to the place of the name of the Lord of Hosts, the Mount Zion." (Isa. xviii.)*

shall serve with the Assyrians. In that day shall Israel be the third with Egypt and with Assyria, even a blessing in the midst of the land: whom the Lord of hosts shall bless, saying, Blessed be Egypt my people, and Assyria the work of my hands, and Israel mine inheritance." (Isa. xix. 23—25.)

* Whilst Israel is being gradually assembled, judgments are sent upon many nations, which, although they have escaped Antichrist, have nevertheless been rebellious against the Lord, and persecutors of Israel. It is during this period apparently, that the Gog and Magog nations assail the land of Israel, in the manner narrated in Ezekiel. See ch. xxxviii. The ordered glory of the millennium will not have been introduced (although Israel is forgiven) at the time when they are thus attacked. This invasion must not be mistaken for the rebellion mentioned at the close of the millennium.

Whilst the Lord is thus re-gathering Israel, and at the same time sending many judgments among the spared nations, who are to be broken before they are healed, He will introduce His saints into their heavenly mansions above, according to the promise— " I will come again and receive you unto myself, that where I am, there ye may be also. In my Father's

There appears to be a considerable interval between the appearance of the Lord in destructive glory, and the period when He will be "inaugurated" on Zion, and introduce the peaceful glory of the millennium. There was a considerable interval between the destruction of Pharoah and his hosts at the Red Sea, and the descent of God, as the manifested Legislator of Israel on Mount Sinai : and the conflict of Israel with Amalek intervened. So there will again intervene a period betwixt the destruction of Antichrist and his hosts, and the inauguration of Christ's glory on Zion—in which interval Israel's conflict with Gog and Magog and other enemies, will occur. Christ's glory, when He first appears to take His saints, and to deliver Israel, is symbolised by the Morning Star, which rises before the sun, whilst the earth is yet sunk in the deepest darkness of night. "The stars," as not belonging to our system, are fit emblems of distant and unknown glory. But when the hour comes for the peaceful glory of the millennium to be brought in, then the Lord is represented as the Sun arising with healing on his wings. His glory will then be adapted to the condition of the earth and of men upon it, as when He was seen by human eyes on the Mount of Transfiguration. But when seen in the sphere of His unearthly glory, " even John fell at His feet as dead." Flesh and blood can have no communion with His glory as the bright and morning star : but the changed saints will. "To him that overcometh will I give the morning star; " *i. e.* he shall be brought into the sphere of my own unearthly glory.

house are many mansions." This is the period of which it is said, that He who loved the Church and gave Himself for it, will present it unto Himself "a glorious Church, not having spot, or wrinkle, or any such thing." (Eph. v.) See also Rev. xix.

"And I heard as it were the voice of a great multitude, and as the voice of many waters, and as the voice of mighty thunderings, saying, Alleluia : because the Lord our God the Almighty hath reigned. Let us be glad, and rejoice, and give glory to Him, because the marriage of the Lamb is come, and His Wife hath made herself ready. And it was given to her that she should be arrayed in fine linen bright and pure; for the fine linen is the righteousness of the saints." (Rev. xix., Tregelles' version.) The Church unitedly, and each believer individually, will recognise themselves to be perfect then, and the joy of each will be full. Christ will be known as their redemption, their righteousness and their life.

The value of the Atonement once perfected on the Cross will then be *fully* proved by them. The blood of the Holy One shed in death was at once the witness that the great Surety had fully borne the appointed wrath, and that He had fully perfected and sacrificially presented the appointed obedience. Whilst "made a curse" and bearing the veritable wrath of God in the stead of His believing people, He did at the same time give Himself for them, "an offering and sacrifice to God for a sweet-smelling savour." The sin-offering "burnt up" without the camp, and the burnt offering "burned" on the altar, present us with different aspects of Christ's death, but they are both combined in the one sacrifice. Although the sin-offering was itself "*burnt up*" without the camp, yet its fat was burnt for fragrance on the altar. "Jehovah smelled a sweet savour." Thus the excellency of Christ's obedience in life and in death, and the value of all that He was as the sin-bearing Sufferer, was sacrificially presented for us on the Cross as on an altar, and under the full value of the imputation thereof all believers stand. "By the obedience of One" we are "constituted righteous." *By working out a righteousness for us on earth*, He hath become "the Lord our righteousness;" and the righteousness so provided is the ground of our acceptance and blessedness alike in time and in eternity. We are blessed not on the ground of any personal change wrought in us or on us, but solely on the ground of a righteousness provided for us by the obedience and suffering and death of another, even of Immanuel— God manifest in the flesh. Hence in the offering of the Cross we find "redemption." We are redeemed *from* wrath and redeemed *unto* God. There, too, we find "righteousness," for all the claims of God have been met by the obedience consummated in the one finished oblation of the Cross. Therefore God is able to recognise us as right in relation to the claims of His *judicial* Courts. We are found to be and pronounced to be "*en règle*" in relation to the requirements of those Courts. We find in the Cross "sanctification" also, for Christ having given

Himself for us as an offering and sacrifice to God of a "sweet-smelling savour," the sanctity of that oblation is reckoned to us, so that we draw nigh into the Courts of God's worship — His Temple-Courts, under the imputation of the holiness of the oblation offered on the Cross. Incense fills the sanctuary, and we stand under its fragrance. Therefore we read, "*sanctified* by the offering of the body of Jesus once," "Sanctified by His blood." Christ is made unto us wisdom from God, both "righteousness and *sanctification*, as well as redemption."

But whilst the saints individually and collectively, are thus filled with all fulness in Him; there will also be awarded to each, the individual meed of grace. Each will be placed before the tribunal * of

---

* I have used the word tribunal in preference to judgment-seat, because less liable to misapprehension—the thought commonly connected with judgment-seat being that of arraignment as a criminal.

Indeed the thought of criminal arraignment *ought* to be connected with the "great white Throne," before which the wicked dead raised at the close of the millennium will stand, to be judged out of things written in books according to their works. This is strictly judgment (κρίσις); but it is said that he who believeth shall not come into judgment. (κρίσις.) See John v. 24. All who have believed in Jesus previously to His return, will be raised in the first resurrection, and will reign with Him during the millennium: consequently, they will not stand before the great white Throne at all. Nor will the saints who live during the millennium stand before it to be arraigned, because the Book of Life will be opened, and their names will be found written there. Consequently, they too will not come into judgment

Christ—not to be judged (he that believeth shall not come into judgment κρισις, John v.) but to be re-

(κρισις). The prayer of every saint, in every dispensation must be, "Lord, enter not into judgment with Thy servant; for in Thy sight shall no man living be justified."

But although the saints are not to be brought before this judgment-seat of Christ to be arraigned, they are to stand before the tribunal of Christ to "give account" of their past services and ways, in order that He may discriminate between that which is precious in those ways, and that which is worthless—and, having already forgiven them the evil, may reward them for that which is good. Thus, the victorious General of old, was accustomed, at the close of a campaign, to call his soldiers before his tribunal, not to arraign them, but to enquire into their conduct, and to reward them.

There is one passage in 2 Cor. v. 10, which seems to teach, that believers will stand before the tribunal of Christ, to receive *according to* that which they have done, whether good or bad; in which case, saints would receive *according to* their evil. But the passage, rightly translated, does not teach this. It does not state that the saints are to receive *according to* that which they have done, but *with reference to* (πρός) that which they have done. If a parent, at the close of the day, were to call his children before him, in order to enquire into their conduct, and after pointing out to them those things which they had done amiss, were to say, " These are things which, although I forgive them, I cannot reward; but these other things which are praiseworthy, I will reward "— in such a case, the children would receive *with reference to* what they had done, but they would not receive *according to* that which they had done.

It would appear, from the close of the twenty-fifth of Matthew, that those who are found professing the name of Christ at His return, will instantly be separated by the Angels into two bodies; according to the reality or falseness of their profession. After having been thus divided, they

warded—to receive from Him, recognition of all that He can recognise for praise, in their past services and ways. Then the cup of cold water will be remembered—then it will be seen, that he who has received a Prophet in the name of a Prophet, shall receive a Prophet's reward, and that he who has received a righteous man in the name of a righteous man, shall receive a righteous man's reward. To one it shall be said, Have thou authority over five; to another—over ten cities. This difference of reward is not inconsistent with each indi-

will be placed for a short moment before the Throne of His glory in the air, in order that the evidences of the one being His people, and the other not being His people, might be declared, and the one be rejected, the other received. But although the sentence that consigns the one to misery, and the others to blessedness, is openly pronounced; yet the goats are not then finally judged, nor the sheep definitely rewarded. The first are, at the close of the millennium, to be placed before the Great White Throne, to be judged according to their works—the latter are to stand before the Tribunal of Christ to be rewarded. The separation therefore of the sheep and goats is not strictly a judgment scene. It is merely the public declaration of that principle, which is already every day acted on by the Lord, in consigning some to the place of torment, where their souls are reserved for judgment, and in taking others to Himself in Paradise This is not called judgment, although in a certain sense it is judgment. The ground of His thus acting is to be openly proclaimed by-and-by: but before that hour comes, He teaches us respecting it in this prophetic parable, in order that it may bear influentially on us throughout this dispensation. "Inasmuch as ye have done it to one of the least of these my brethren, ye have done it unto me."

vidual saint being made like unto Christ. The promise is not restricted which says—when He shall appear we shall be like Him, for we shall see Him as He is. All shall "awake up in His likeness and be satisfied."

After these things the Heavenly City, which is one especial sphere of the saints' glory, descends from God out of Heaven. But although descending *from*, and therefore *contrasted with*, Heaven ; yet it does not descend *into* the Millennial Earth. The Adamic Earth is not adapted to its glory. It remains therefore throughout the Millennium, *connected* indeed *with* the Earth, but not *in* the Earth —and it is not until the first Heavens and Earth have passed away and *new* Heavens and a *new* Earth created, that it descends again, and finds in the new Earth a place suitable for the habitation of its glory.

Its relation to Heaven and to the Earth during the Millennium, is analogous to that which the Holy Place occupied in the Temple. It was situate intermediately between the Holy of Holies and the external court where Israel worshipped. The Holy Place was the place of Priestly service, the place of intercession, the place where the golden Candlestick was set—the type of Christ, in that pure, perfect, unchanging heavenly light, wherewith, whether in Earth or Heaven, He hath shone and ever shineth *for His people*. All this, and more, the Heavenly City will be. Thence the regulations of God's government, as well as the instructions of His grace, will reach Israel and the earth. "The nations shall walk by means of the light thereof, and the Kings of the Earth shall bring their glory and honour unto it." There, also, remedial means will be provided for meeting the exigencies of mortal life below. In the vision of the City were seen Trees of Life; and "the leaves of the Trees were for the healing of the nations."

The connexion of the power and glory of the New Creation with the circumstances of a fallen Earth, will thus be the great secret of Millennial blessing. This, indeed, is not a new principle in the works of God. The present condition of His saints affords an analogous example. Without changing their old natures, but allowing their flesh to remain flesh, He has been pleased to connect therewith that which is *new*—"the new man which after God is created in righteousness and true holiness;" which also He sustains by the indwelling power of His own blessed Spirit. Hence, the repression of the evil that would otherwise be dominant in us, and the production of fruits of heavenly origin, where otherwise, all would be earthiness and corruption. But God, in bestowing blessing, is not satisfied with the mere repression of evil. All that is of the first Adam in us, whether in body, soul, or spirit, is *finally* to pass away; and all is to be made new. Everything that is outward and everything inward in us, is to be brought into the likeness of Christ, according to the power of the new creation of God.

Throughout the Millennium, the frame-work of this lower world remains essentially unchanged. Although creation will no longer groan as now in the bondage of corruption, yet corruptibility and death will still remain in plants, and animals, and men. In men there will also be the presence of in-dwelling sin. But there will be a power of life operating from above—from Heaven, and from the Heavenly City, whereby the working of corruption, whether physical or moral, will be restrained, and the Earth be caused to teem with living blessing. This will especially be the case in the Land of Israel, which will then "be the joy of all lands."* "Thou shalt no more be termed forsaken: neither shall thy land any more be termed Desolate: but thou shalt be called Hephzibah, and thy land Beulah: for the Lord delighteth in thee, and thy land shall be married." It would be impossible to quote all the passages, which speak of the fulness of bless-ing manifested, when once Israel and the Earth are regarded by God as taken possession of by the Lord Jesus in the title of redemption. All the Prophets and Psalms abound with descriptions of that hour.

Nor are these descriptions limited to outward blessings. The Psalms describe also, the peace, humility, and inward grace which will characterise Israel then. See, for example, such Psalms as the 131st: "Lord, my heart is not haughty, nor mine eyes lofty: neither do I exercise myself in great

* Extending then from the river of Egypt to the Euphrates.

matters or in things too high for me : . . . . my soul is even as a weaned child." And again, " Behold how good and how pleasant it is for brethren to dwell together in unity; it is . . . . as the dew of Hermon, which descendeth on the mountains of Zion, for there Jehovah hath commanded the blessing, even life for evermore." Then, too, they will say with deeper feeling than we, " Bless the Lord, O my soul, and all that is within me, bless His holy name. Bless the Lord, O my soul, and forget not all His benefits; who forgiveth all thine iniquities; who healeth all thy diseases." (ciii.) And again, " I will extol thee, my God, O King, and I will bless thy name for ever and ever. Every day will I bless thee, and I will praise thy name for ever and ever . . . . My mouth shall speak the praise of the Lord, and let all flesh bless His holy name for ever and ever." (cxlv.)

The imprisonment of Satan and his angels, the presence of the visible glory of Christ and His saints, the investiture of the Son of Man with the sovereignty of earth, the establishment of Jerusalem in a Church-position, as the pillar and ground of truth, its establishment also as the centre of governmental influence throughout the earth, the release of creation from its groan, the outpouring of the Holy Spirit upon all flesh—these and other like things, will give to the millennial age a character, as contrasted with that of the ages that have preceded it, as the works of Christ are contrasted with the works of Satan. Christianity, although still militant, will cease to occupy the place of suffering and reproach. It will be no longer needful to go without the gate, bearing His reproach, because the city itself will be the place of righteousness and truth. The Church of the present Dispensation quits the wilderness, leaning, as one weak and exhausted, on the arm of the Beloved : but she is succeeded in her place of service and of testimony by another, who "looks forth as the morning, fair as the moon, clear as the sun, and terrible as an army with banners." Israel will succeed into our place of testimony ; but it will be a place no longer marked by weakness. Truth will be sustained by power, and surrounded by circumstances worthy of its essential excellency. Nevertheless, the servants of the truth, who yet remain in the flesh, will not be without their dangers. The pride and vain glory of man's nature will still remain in all except those who are glorified in heaven; and past experience teaches us, that hearts that have stood well through hours of adversity, have failed when brought under the sunshine of prosperity and joy. The preservation, therefore, of the saints of the coming dispensation, when surrounded by circumstances of dignity, and rest, and glory, will be another instance of the *manifold* grace of God which is alike able to manifest its protective, preserving power whether they who are its objects be in lowliness, or in exaltation, in tribulation, or in triumph.

But however great the blessings of the millennial age, they still fall very short of the perfection of

God. Sin, death, and occasional transgression, will yet be there, and *repressive* power (something unknown in heaven) will be perpetually needed, in order to prevent manifestations of evil, and sights of sorrow. The spirit therefore of the millennial saints will long for something more perfect yet to come. They will be taught, even as we, to look for New Heavens and a New Earth, wherein dwelleth righteousness.*

The distinctive characteristic of the Millennium therefore, is not to be found in the greatness of its blessings ; for blessings higher and more abundant will be in the New Earth. The great distinctive characteristic of the Millennium is this, that it is the period when Christ assumes and exercises power in order to subjugate every enemy. This is the object avowedly proposed when Christ takes to Himself His millennial power. Its exercise is seen in the destructive judgments whereby the Millennium is commenced—in breaking up the evil systems of every nation throughout the earth—in punishing disobe-

* In Isaiah lxv. 17, the subjects of joy and thanksgiving, presented to Israel at the commencement of their millennial blessing, are *two*—one future ; the other, present. The final intention of God to create New Heavens and a New Earth, is *first* spoken of, and presented to them as an object of *hope :* next is mentioned, that which God will at that time be giving them, as a present joy; for at *that time* He will make Jerusalem and her people a joy.

"Behold, I create new heavens and a new earth," strictly— Behold, I, the Creating One of new heavens, &c. For this *abstract* use of the present participle as not defining time, see " Occasional Papers," No. II. page 96.

dience—in destroying the rebellious nations at the close of the millennial reign—in finally punishing Satan, and destroying Death. The subjugation of enemies is so distinctively the object of the millennial reign, that the power which Christ assumes for this purpose, He lays down as soon as it is accomplished. "Then cometh the end, when He shall have delivered up the kingdom to God, even the Father; when He shall have put down all rule, and all authority, and power. For He must reign, till He hath put all enemies under his feet. The last enemy that shall be destroyed is Death . . . . And when all things shall have been subdued unto Him, then shall the Son also Himself be subject unto Him that put all things under Him, that God may be all in all." (1 Cor. xv.) How wonderful therefore, that a dispensation whose distinctive characteristic is, power exercised for the subjugation of enemies, should be one distinguished also by blessings so transcendant that they seem to irradiate earth with the light and glory and happiness of heaven. Millions too will be saved, who would have been lost for ever, if the history of man in the flesh had been made to terminate at the commencement and not at the close of the millennium.

The millennium, however, does not conclude, without affording another instance of the inveterate evil of the human heart. Unregenerate man can neither be gained by mercy nor subdued by terror. Unawed by the judgments that introduce the millennium, and uninfluenced by the mercies that characterise its course, unwarned by the experience of preceding ages, and heedless of the lessons furnished by their own, the millennial Gentile nations,* as soon as Satan is again allowed to tempt, will instantly fall into the snare, and give themselves to him. They will deliberately assemble, in order to confront the visible glory of Christ, which they will long have known as present in the earth, and filling it with blessing. They know that Jerusalem is "the Beloved City," and Zion "the citadel of the saints," —they know that the glory of Christ is there; and yet none of these things will hinder the mad presumption of their evil. " And they went up on the breadth of the earth, and compassed the citadel of the saints about and the beloved city; and fire came down out of heaven and devoured them." Thus ends the earthly history of unregenerate man. The general judgment follows: the dead are judged, and then He that sitteth on the Throne will say: " Behold, I make all things new."

The glory of "the New Heavens and New Earth," we little apprehend. Even the present creation was made excellent and glorious. "The heavens declare the glory of God, and the firmament showeth His handy work: day unto day uttereth speech, and night unto night showeth knowledge." The sun in the firmament, and the lily of the field, alike declare the wisdom and the power of God. But all this creation, so wonderful and so glorious, was connected

---

* The Gentile nations only will apostatise. Jerusalem and Israel will remain faithful to the Lord.

with one, who was of the earth—earthy : with *him*, the heavens and the earth were created, and with *him* the heavens and the earth pass away.

If, then, a creation so glorious was connected with one who was of the earth—earthy, what will be the glory of that which is to be created in adaptation to Him who is the Second Man, the Lord from Heaven —a creation to be placed under His Headship, and to stand for ever in His blessedness ? If we could estimate the difference between the person of Adam and the person of the Son of God, we might then appreciate the difference between the glory of the first, and the glory of the New Creation.

We are thus led on by Scripture to the first day of the completed blessing of the redeemed—the first day of their new history ; when the Heavenly City, the Bride of the Lamb, descends into the New Earth. She had not descended into the Millennial Earth.* She had been connected with it, and ministered to it ; but she had not descended into it. She had been kept apart, as it were in holy separateness, until nothing should remain beneath, unsuited to her own purity and glory. The Heavenly Bridegroom had, throughout the millennium, been exercising His power in order to subdue every enemy ; and when that had been effected, and all things had

---

* It is very important to observe the difference between individual and corporate symbols. Individually the saints do visit the millennial earth, and act in it—but in their corporate glory, represented by the heavenly city, they do not enter in.

been made new, she is introduced as His Bride into the new inheritance. How different the thoughts with which we contemplate the old, and the new history of man. The Scripture, which had commenced with the first day of his *first* history, concludes with the *first* day of this—his *new* history. We know not all that is beyond; but we know that He who hath made us for ever kings and priests unto God, has not restricted us even to the New Heavens and New Earth, but will give us to behold and to share His own glory above the heavens; and that He who is His Father, and our Father in Him, has promised to show, in the ages to come, the exceeding riches of His grace, in His kindness towards us through Christ Jesus.*

* The contrast between the *new* and the *first* earth; and between the *heavenly* and the earthly Jerusalem is so plainly marked in Scripture, that it seems wonderful that it should have been overlooked by any. For example, it is expressly said, that "the first heavens and the first earth pass away, and no place is found for them," *before* the New Heavens and New Earth are created. In the New Earth, there is to be no sea—in the millennial earth, the sea is continually mentioned. In the new earth, there is no more sickness or death—in the millennial earth, remedial means are used against sickness and death; the last enemy is not destroyed until the close. In the New Earth, there is no sin, nor any liability thereunto —in the millennial earth, sin remains in the flesh of man; Satan can never enter into the new earth, nor into the Heavenly City: but he will re-enter the millennial earth, at the close of the Millennium, and will effect a great apostasy. The contrast between the heavenly and the earthly Jerusalem during the Millennium, is no less marked. In the

heavenly there is to be no Temple—but we read much of
the millennial Temple of Israel. In the heavenly city, there
is to be no succession of day and night. There shall be no
night there. But whilst the first earth remaineth, seed time
and harvest, day and night shall not cease.

Difficulty has been occasioned to some, by not observing
that the ninth verse of Rev. xxi. should be made the commencement of a new chapter. The first *eight* verses of the
twenty-first chapter, describe the relation of the heavenly
city to the *new* earth—whereas, the subsequent part of the
chapter *retraces*, and describes its relation to the *millennial*
earth.

The *twentieth* chapter should commence at the *eleventh*
verse of the *nineteenth* chapter—beginning " I saw heaven
opened," and be continued to the end of the eighth verse of
the *twenty-first* chapter: for the subject of all this passage
is strictly consecutive. It begins by a vision of the glory of
the heavenly Bridegroom, with which He is prepared to meet
His enemies, and subdue the earth—next the destruction of
Antichrist and his armies—then the binding of Satan—then
the millennial reign—the concluding apostasy—the passing
away of the first heavens, and the first earth—the judgment
of the dead—the creation of the New Heavens and the New
Earth, and the descent of the heavenly city into the new
earth. These events are spoken of consecutively as they
will really happen ; and therefore the passage which treats
of them continuously, should of course be read as one
chapter.

That the latter part of the 21st chapter after the 8th
verse, and the commencement of the 22nd chapter refer to
the relation of the heavenly city to the earth *during* the
Millennium, is manifest from this, that means are thence
employed for " the healing of the nations." In the new
earth, there are no nations that need healing. The words,
" and no curse shall any longer be," are of course to be restricted to the subject spoken of—that is, the heavenly city.
They will not be applicable to the earth, until all in the earth
is made like the heavenly city.

APPENDIX.

___

(A.)

I HAVE already referred to the works of several of the early Christian writers, to show how generally it was believed that the fourth or Roman Empire would finally be divided into Ten Kingdoms, according to the prophecy of Daniel; and that a *personal* Antichrist would arise at the end of the age.

It may interest some, to be supplied with further references; but before I make any more quotations, I again explicitly state, that I do not refer to these writers as having any *authority* whatsoever. It may be interesting to know the *opinions* of these early writers, and to trace some of the rays of light, which, through God's mercy, mingled with the deep, deep gloom of the earliest years of post-Apostolic Christianity. But no one who appeals to the Fathers, as guides, can understand, or appreciate the Scriptures: for no two things can be more contrasted, than the Revelation of God in His Holy Scriptures, and the errors and omissions of the Fathers.

Let us take, for example, one of the most important doctrines of our holy faith—the union of the

Believer with Christ as the risen Head of the redeemed. We are not only, from the moment we believe, forgiven all trespasses through the blood of His Cross, but God has also granted unto us union with Him as now glorified in the heavens. As truly as the first Adam, by his transgression, entailed on us the imputation of his guilt, and brought us from Paradise into this sorrowful world, and made us heirs of his fallen condition of being and of his corruption, so truly has Christ, by means of the righteousness which He wrought out for us during the time of His obedience and suffering on earth, entailed on us the imputation of that righteousness; in consequence of which imputation, and as an attestation of its infinite meritoriousness, union with Christ, heirship with Him is granted to us in that new creation of which He has become the risen Head, when finally we are to be made partakers of His holiness and to share His glories. How seldom do we find even an allusion to these truths in the early Fathers.

Nor is the gospel of grace taught there in its simplicity. It is not sufficient to say, that Christ has been offered as a sacrifice for sins. We may own *that*, and yet maintain, that the being brought under the power of that sacrifice, is not, in itself alone, a condition of everlasting salvation; or we may say, that the instrumental means employed to bring sinners into saving connection with that sacrifice, are, the ceremonial ministrations of the Church, and not "the foolishness of preaching." We may, if we please, *reverse* the word of St. Paul, and say, "Christ sent me to baptize, not to preach the gospel:" so we destroy the Gospel.

The Fathers too, appear to have been entirely unconscious of what the Apostle meant, when he said to the *Gentile* olive-branch, that it should be cut off, *unless it continued in God's goodness*. They seem never to have considered what was involved in Gentile Christianity not having continued "in God's goodness;" and were strangers to the prophetic history of our Dispensation.

Some of the Fathers accepted the doctrine of the Millennial reign of Christ: others did not. Jerome, for example, derided it and called it " a fable;" not choosing to distinguish between the speculative and absurd theories which they who maintained Millennial doctrine associated with their statements, and the manner in which that doctrine is taught in Scripture. The early writers, in treating of the Millennium, were not careful to put the Jews in their peculiar and pre-eminent place of blessing; they were anxious to appropriate to themselves that place of rest and supremacy that is reserved for Zion and Jerusalem in the next Dispensation; for they desired to " reign as kings " *now*, and eschewed the suffering and reproach that is the appointed portion of the servants of Christ till the present Dispensation closes. They failed also in apprehending the distinction between the condition of the Millennial earth, which is Adamic, and the condition of the New Earth which will be made (*after* the

Millennium has closed) worthy of the risen glory of the Last Adam, the Son of the living God: and they perceived not the difference between the Jerusalem to which Israel will be gathered on earth—an earthly city inhabited by men yet in the flesh, and the new and heavenly Jerusalem, the city of the risen and glorified saints, into which "flesh and blood" cannot enter. The Fathers also, one and all, utterly failed in recognising that this Dispensation is one of failure throughout. They received not the truths revealed in the eleventh of Romans. They saw not that the Gentile olive-branch—that which symbolizes professing Christianity amongst us Gentiles, is to be "cut-off" under judgment, because like Israel before, it has not continued in God's goodness. They hid from themselves the consequences of their own failure.

It is a melancholy truth, that most of the Christianity of these later days has been as little sensible as the Fathers of the failure of Gentile Christianity, and as blind with respect to its coming doom. The Millennial prospects of Israel are still for the most part ignored; and Gentile Christianity, "wise in its own conceits," continues to appropriate to itself the triumph and the glory reserved for Zion and Jerusalem in the coming Dispensation. Later Christianity has done what the Fathers did *not* do, that is, misrepresent the closing events of this Dispensation as respects the nations. The subjoined extracts will show that many of the concluding events of our Dispensation were pourtrayed by the Fathers scripturally and clearly. They saw the destiny of the Ten Kingdoms of the Roman World. They recognised the coming and reign of THE Antichrist. They taught that the season of unequalled tribulation—"tribulation such as never was"—is yet future, and will conclude this present age. They saw that the Coming of the Lord in glory would terminate this age, and the brief though terrible reign of Antichrist. As to these things their testimony was truthful. They did not, as to this, do what later Christianity has done—ignore the coming judgments, and prophesy peace where there is no peace.

QUOTATIONS FROM THE FATHERS.

First Century.

THE Personality of Antichrist, and the rise of the Ten Kingdoms is distinctly referred to in the Epistle of Barnabas—the companion of St. Paul. It was written between the years A.D. 70 and A.D. 80.

"The consummating period of trial as has been written, and as Daniel says, draws near; for the Lord has cut short the times and the days, in order that His beloved may hasten to His inheritance. Thus saith the prophet, Ten Kingdoms shall reign on the earth, and after them shall arise a very little one (pusillus) who shall subdue three at once . . . . Of this one, Daniel says again, And I saw the fourth Beast, wicked and strong, and fiercer than the other Beasts that came from the sea; and on it there appeared ten horns, and there came up another short horn in the midst of them, and overthrew three of the great horns. Therefore we ought to understand." (Latin version of § iv., Greek original being lost.)

Again in § xv.

"In the six thousand years all things shall be finished. And He rested on the seventh day; this means, when His Son shall come, and shall abolish the time of the Wicked One (τον καιρον Ανομου) and shall judge the ungodly, and shall change the sun and moon and stars; then He shall rest gloriously (καλως) on the seventh day."

Of these quotations it may be observed :—

I. That the expression "consummating period of trial" is a virtual reference to the last verse of the ninth of Daniel—and to other parts of Daniel where "Consummation" or equivalent expressions are applied to the concluding period of the Dispensation.

II. The words, "hath cut short the times," is a virtual quotation of the 24th of Matthew, respecting the unequalled season of tribulation—which season is not connected by Barnabas with the destruction of Jerusalem (which had just taken place) but with the future actings—the little Horn of the fourth Beast.

III. The use of the word ανομος, "Wicked One," is a reference to the second of Thessalonians, and to Isaiah xi.—where that name is given to Antichrist.

Second Century.

Justin Martyr, A.D. 150—thus speaks of Antichrist :—

"He who is about to speak blasphemous and audacious things, against the Most High, being already at the doors—whose continuance Daniel signifies as about to be for a time, times, and half a time." (Trypho, p. 159.)

And again :

"Foolish are they who do not understand, what indeed has been pointed out by all the testimonies of the Prophets, that two Comings of Christ are spoken of ; one in which He is preached as the Sufferer inglorious—dishonoured and crucified—the second, that in which He will come with glory from

Heaven, at the time when the Man of Apostasy, who speaketh great things against the Most High shall be on the earth, and dare wicked things (ανομα) against us Christians."

Justin Martyr allows to Trypho the Jew, that Elijah, the Prophet, will come before the advent of the Lord in glory and fulfil the prophecy of Malachi. He contends, also, that John the Baptist was, *in principle*, Elias, as coming in his spirit and power.

Irenæus.　A.D. 180.

Irenæus, the disciple of Polycarp, who was the companion of the Apostle John, writes more fully on these subjects than any of his predecessors. He speaks of Antichrist as an " impious, unjust, and lawless " monarch, exalting himself as the one only Idol—" an idol which included, in itself, the manifold wickednesses (varium errorem) of all other idols."

Irenæus quotes the greater part of 2 Thess. ii. respecting the Man of Sin, and applies it to Antichrist —says that the Temple in which he will sit, is *the Temple in Jerusalem*—quotes Matthew xxiv. as to the abomination, and unequalled season of tribulation, and applies it to the time of Antichrist's blasphemy in Jerusalem—speaks of his arising as the little Horn after the ten last Kings of the Roman Empire—and quoting the words of Daniel—" time, times, and the dividing of time," explains them of the three years and a half of Antichrist's reign. (Usque ad tempus, tempora et dimidium temporis—hoc est, per triennium et sex menses.)

Irenæus also quotes Dan. viii. respecting "the King of fierce countenance," and interprets it *of Antichrist acting in Jerusalem.* He then quotes Dan. ix., the last verse of which, he applies to Antichrist, and says—

"At the half of the hebdomad, Daniel saith, the sacrifice and libation shall be taken away, and in the Temple shall be the Abomination of desolation—and until the consummation of the time, a consummation shall be appointed upon the desolation, (et usque ad consummationem temporis, consummatio dabitur super desolationem)—but the half of the hebdomad is three years and six months." (Irenæus adver. Her. ch. xxv.)

In the 26th chapter, Irenæus again speaks of the ten kings, and quotes Rev. xvii. and Dan. ii. as referring to them. He speaks of these Kings as destroying Babylon, which he supposes to be *Imperial* Rome, and there concurring to give their power to Antichrist.

In the 30th chapter, he observes further:

"But when Antichrist shall have ravaged all things in this world, reigning three years and six months, and shall have sat in the Temple at Jerusalem, then the Lord shall come from Heaven in clouds in the glory of the Father, to cast him and those who obey him, into the lake of fire. But He will bring in for the righteous, the times of the kingdom, that is to say—rest:—the seventh day sanctified; and will restore to Abraham the promise of the inheritance, in which kingdom, saith the Lord, many shall come from the East and West, and shall sit down with Abraham, Isaac, and Jacob."

Irenæus, like most other of the early Christian

writers, supposes that Antichrist will arise from the tribe of Dan.

Tertullian, A.D. 190—200.

Tertullian expounds 2 Thess. ii. of Antichrist. He observes :

"The breaking up and dispersion of the Roman State among the ten kings, will bring on Antichrist; and then shall be revealed that Wicked One, whom the Lord Jesus shall slay with the Spirit of His Mouth, and shall destroy by His appearance."

" Also in the Apocalypse of John, there is laid down the course of the times, during which the souls of the martyrs beneath the altar, demanding vengeance and judgment, are instructed to wait. First, the earth must drink in its plagues from the vials of the angels ; and that harlot city must suffer merited destruction by the ten Kings, and the Beast Antichrist with his false prophet, make war upon the Church of God ; and then the Devil being banished for a season to the bottomless pit, the privilege of the first resurrection will be adjudged from the Thrones, and afterwards, fire having been sent down, the sentence belonging to the universal resurrection, will be pronounced from the books.

Respecting the Witnesses he observes :

" Enoch and Elias are translated ; their death is not found, being delayed. Yet they are reserved to die, that with their blood they may extinguish Antichrist." (Tertullian, quoted by Mr. Maitland in his Apostles' School of Prophetic Interpretation, p. 165.)

Cent. III. Hippolytus.

For quotations from Hippolytus, who lived in the

very early part of this century, [see "Babylon, its revival and final desolation" as advertised at end]. He is, I believe, the only writer* who intimates, that the admixture of clay and iron in the toes of the Image, had reference to the rise of popular power. He says, speaking of the Image :

"After these come the Romans, being the iron legs of the Image—strong as iron: in order that the *democracies* which are about to arise, might be pointed out, answering respectively to the ten toes of the image, in which there will be iron mingled with clay." *(Mai; Chain on Daniel.)*

He, too, considers Enoch and Elijah to be the two witnesses.

Origen. A.D. 225.

Even Origen, who introduced such a fatal habit of allegorising Scripture, maintained the doctrine of a personal Antichrist. After referring to 2 Thess. ii. he says :

"To explain the whole of this, is not our present business. But there is in Daniel a prophecy about this same Antichrist, which cannot but excite the admiration of any one who will read it with common sense and candour. For there, in words truly divine and prophetic, are described the kingdoms that

---

* Unless the words of Lactantius be considered an exception, when he says, speaking of the fall of the Roman Empire ; "The empire will be subdivided, and the powers of government being frittered away and shared among many, will be undermined. Then will follow civil discords, and there will be no respite from destructive wars, till ten kings arise at once, dividing the world among themselves, to consume, rather than to govern it."

were to come, beginning from the time of Daniel down to the destruction of the world. And this prophecy may be read of all men. Now see if Antichrist is not spoken of there also in these words, In the end of their kingdom when their transgressions are filled up, there shall rise a king impudent of face and understanding problems, &c.

"And that which I have already quoted from the words of Paul, that he shall sit in the Temple of God, showing himself that he is God—even this also is said by Daniel, and in this manner, In the Temple shall be the abomination of desolation; and until the end of the time shall a consummation be given against the desolation." (Origen, as quoted by Maitland, p. 171.)

Thus Origen considered the 2nd of Thess. ii. and the last verse of Dan. ix. respecting the abomination, to belong to Antichrist in Jerusalem.

Victorinus.

Victorinus lived towards the end of the Third Century, and is highly spoken of by Jerome. Speaking of the false Prophet in Rev. xiii. he says that,

"He will cause that a golden Image of Antichrist should be placed in the Temple at Jerusalem; and that an apostate angel (angelus refuga)* should enter thereinto; thence to utter voices and oracles. He will also cause that slaves and free men should receive as a mark on their foreheads or in their right hands, the number of his name, that otherwise no one might buy or sell." (Vict. in locum.)

Victorinus considered Enoch and Jeremiah to be

* For "*refuga*," used in this sense, see Augustine Civit. Dei, lib. xx.

the two witnesses; and explains the " abomination," of the idolatrous worship of Antichrist *in Jerusalem*.

Cent. IV. Lactantius. A.D. 300.

The following is his account of Antichrist. He speaks of him as one who by the assistance of a false prophet, will perform signs and wonders, whereby he will allure men to worship him.

" He will command fire to descend from Heaven, and the sun to stand still in its course, and an Image to speak ; and these things shall be done at his command. By these prodigies the greater number even of wise men, will be enticed by him. Then he will attempt to overthrow the Temple of God, and will persecute the righteous people ; and there shall be pressure and trial, (pressura et contritio) such as never has been from the beginning of the world.

" All who shall believe in, and receive him, shall be marked by him, as so many sheep: but they who shall reject his mark, shall either fly to the mountains, or be seized and put to death with exquisite torments. He shall also roll up righteous men in the books of the prophets, and so burn them. And it shall be given him to desolate the world for forty and two months. This is the period in which righteousness will be cast out, and innocence detested. This is he who is called Antichrist—but he will feign himself to be Christ, and will fight against the true Christ." (Lact. Inst. vii).

Lactantius is vivid in his descriptions, but does not sufficiently limit himself by Scripture. Where, for example, does he learn that Antichrist will stop the sun, or burn the righteous by heaping around them the writings of the Prophets? He seems more guided by the pseudo-Sibyl (whom he continually quotes), than by Scripture in many of his statements. He believes also that there will arise immediately before Antichrist, another king very like him in wickedness; and to this supposed forerunner of Antichrist he applies many descriptions that belong to the true Antichrist. Long after the time of Lactantius, a notion prevailed that the last king of the Franks, after reigning with vast power, would lay down his authority in Jerusalem and be succeeded by Antichrist. (See Hoveden and others.) These notions may have arisen from the circumstance of Antichrist's being invested, during the last 1,260 days, with a totally different character of power from that which he holds previously, while the servant of the woman (Rev. xvii.) *i.e.*, whilst sustaining the Babylonish system. It is exceedingly important to distinguish these two periods in the history of Antichrist.

Before the death of Lactantius, the Roman Empire, under Constantine, assumed the profession of Christianity. On the twentieth anniversary of his conversion, Constantine invited the bishops of the whole empire to dine with him. Eusebius speaking of that banquet, says that it surpassed all power of description. The cuirassiers and spearmen drawn up in a circle, guarded with naked swords the entrance to the palace; and through the midst walked fearlessly the men of God, on their way to the inner chambers. There some reclined beside the emperor, whilst others occupied couches ranged

on either side. The whole seemed to shadow forth
an image of the kingdom of Christ, being more like
a dream than a reality. (Eusebius quoted by Maitland.)

A great change (says Mr. Maitland) for Eusebius,
who had lived in the days when the sword grew
blunt and the lictor weary in the massacre of Christians. For it was not so much as hinted in prophecy
that the Iron Kingdom would become a nursing
father to the Church. It was strange, therefore, to
see Constantine circulating, at the imperial expense,
costly editions of the Scriptures, and stranger still to
see the bishops drinking wine with the representative
of the fourth beast;—now no longer stamping and
blaspheming, but uttering words of piety and praise.
For thus spoke the Autocrat of East and West:
"Now that the Dragon is removed from the administration of affairs, through the providence of the
supreme God, and by my instrumentality, I imagine
that the divine power has been made clear to all
men."

By this Dragon Constantine meant the devil; and
in order to advertise more publicly his religious intentions, he caused an allegorical painting to be set
up before the gate of his palace. In this picture,
executed in wax, in the encaustic manner, Constantine
was the principal figure: above his head shone the
cross, and beneath his feet, skulking in the depths of
the sea, writhed the Dragon, "that adverse and hostile
beast, who, through the tyranny of atheist monarchs,
had aforetime ravaged the Church of God."

To heighten the effect, Constantine was made to hold a dart, the point of which was buried in the body of the Dragon. In illustration, Eusebius quotes from Isaiah xxvii.: "He shall smite the Dragon, that fugitive serpent, and shall slay the Dragon, that is in the sea."* (Septuagint.)

It was no wonder that in the midst of all this evil, the testimonies of Prophecy should be neglected or perverted; "Eusebius," observes Mr. Maitland, "still handled the prophecies, explaining them as much as possible in reference to things past; and when that was impracticable, neglecting them altogether." Arianism succeeded to this, and occupied all in controversy. It may be regarded as a scourge upon the evil that had abounded.

Hilary of Poictiers, A.D. 350.

"Antichrist, being received by the Jews, will occupy the holy Place, in order that, in the very spot where God was wont to be worshipped by the prayers of saints, there he might be venerated and received with divine honours by the unbelievers." (Hilary, on Matthew xxiv.)

After speaking of the mother of James and John, being told that the honor she sought for her children, could only be granted to those for whom it was destined by the Father, Hilary observes,

"Yet truly that honour seems to me in such sense to be reserved, that the Apostles will not be altogether distant

* See Maitland, p. 209.

from it, inasmuch as they will sit on the seat of the twelve Patriarchs, and there judge Israel. And as far as we may be allowed to form a judgment from the Gospels themselves, Moses and Elias will be His (the Lord's) assessors in the kingdom of heaven. For when the Lord had promised, that some of the Apostles, before they tasted death, should see the Son of Man coming in His kingdom, He took Peter, James and John, and appeared in glory; Moses and Elias, being His companions on the Mount."

Hilary proceeds to state his conviction, that Moses and Elias are the two prophets that are to precede the advent of the Lord, and to be slain by Antichrist: and, that although very many have supposed either Enoch or Jeremiah to be one of the witnesses, yet he feels convinced that Moses will be the companion of Elias—partly, because of his having been on the Mount of Transfiguration, and partly, because of the peculiar circumstances connected with his death and burial.

Ambrose.

Ambrose, who lived about the close of the same century, A.D. 380, thus writes of Antichrist.

[When ye shall see Jerusalem compassed with armies.] "Truly Jerusalem has been compassed by an army, and stormed by a Roman general; whence the Jews thought the abomination of desolation was set up when the Romans, mocking the Jewish ceremonial, threw a swine's head into the Temple. With which I am not so mad as to agree—(quod ego nec furens dixerim) for the abomination of desolation is the abominable advent of Antichrist who with ill omened sacrilege (sacrilegiis infaustis) will defile the inner chambers of men's minds, and will moreover sit literally in the Temple, usurping the throne of Divine power * * * * then will come desolation, seeing that most will fall away from true religion, and lapse into error. Then will come the Day of the Lord."

Ambrose then quotes 2 Thess. ii. Like most of the early writers, he supposes that Antichrist will rise from the tribe of Dan. (page 523, vol. I.) He thinks that the Apostle John will be united with Elias and Enoch in their final testimony, misunderstanding, I suppose, the last verse of the 10th chap. of Revelation, his words are:

"For that Beast, Antichrist, ascends from the abyss to contend against Elias, Enoch and John, who will have returned to earth for the sake of the testimony of the Lord Jesus."

Gregory Nazianzen.

Gregory Nazianzen, who was born in A.D. 324, after describing the convulsed and torn condition of Christianity, (over which one might weep like Jeremiah,) thus writes:

"To what will these things grow, and at what point will they stop? I fear lest the things now around us should be the smoke of the expected fire, lest Antichrist should come in upon these things and make our failures and weaknesses the occasion of his own greatness; for he will not, I suppose assault those, who are in sound spiritual health, nor those who are fenced about with love." (Oratio 21. p. 419.)

The following fragment is found in the works of Gregory, but probably wrongly ascribed to him.

"With respect to the abomination of desolation standing

in the holy place, they say that the Temple at Jerusalem will hereafter be built—Antichrist being about to be believed on by the Jews as Christ, and being about to seat himself there, and to appear king of the whole Roman world ($\tau\eta s$ $o\iota\kappa ov\mu\epsilon v\eta s$), but he shall come for the desolation of the world, for he is the abomination of desolation."

Cyril, A.D. 360.

Cyril was Bishop of Jerusalem. He writes as follows :

" These things we teach, not inventing them for ourselves, but learning them from the divine canonical Scriptures, and especially from Daniel (just before quoted). Even as Gabriel the Archangel interpreted, saying, that the fourth Beast should be the fourth Empire on the earth, and should surpass all the Empires that had gone before. I have already said, that ecclesiastical writers have delivered down, that this Empire is the Roman. For after the Assyrian Empire had risen into distinction first—second, that of the Medes and Persians—third, that of the Macedonians—the fourth Empire, which at present exists, is that of the Romans. Gabriel proceeds to explain, that its ten horns are ten kings who shall arise : and after them, shall arise another king, who shall exceed in evil all that have gone before—not only the ten, but all who have preceded ; and he shall subdue three kings. . . . . And who this person is, and from what energy he acts, do thou, O Paul, signify. ' Whose coming,' he says, ' is after the working of Satan, with all power, and signs, and deceiving wonders,' intimating this, that Satan uses this person as an instrument, personally acting in him ($\alpha v\tau o$-$\pi\rho o\sigma\omega\pi\omega s$ $\epsilon v\epsilon\rho\gamma\omega v$.) Again, the Apostle says ; 'Who opposeth and exalteth himself against every thing that is called God, or that is worshipped . . . . so that he seateth himself in the Temple of God.'—What Temple ?—The destroyed Temple of the Jews. God forbid it should be that in which we are.

Why do I say this? I will tell the reason, in order that I may not be thought to be showing favour to ourselves. If he comes to the Jews as Christ, and desires to be worshipped by the Jews, in order that he might the better deceive them, he will be most diligent about the Temple, thus causing it to be thought that he is of the family of David, the one destined to raise the Temple built by Solomon . . . . At first he will assume the appearance of philanthropy—but afterwards, will show himself full of stern severity, especially towards the saints of God; for he says, 'I beheld, and that horn made war with the saints,' &c.—and again, 'There shall be a time of tribulation—tribulation such as hath not been, since the time there was a nation upon earth.' On this account, the Lord knowing the mightiness of the adversary, gives permission to the godly, saying, 'Then let those who are in Judæa, flee,' &c.*—But if any one be conscious in himself of being strong, so as to conflict with Satan, let him stand fast: (for I do not despair of the nerve of the Church) and let him say, 'Who shall separate us from the love of Christ?' Let the cowardly consult for their own safety—but let them who are of a good courage stand fast . . . . but thanks be to God who has circumscribed the greatness of the affliction within the compass of a few days—for he says, that 'for the elect's sake those days shall be shortened.' Antichrist shall reign three and a half years only. I say not this from the Apocryphal writings, but from Daniel; for he says, 'and it shall be given into his hand until a time,' &c.— now a time is one year," &c.—(Cyril, Catech. XV.)

Chrysostom.

Chrysostom, who lived A.D. 390, wrote on the

* It cannot be said that there is a permission granted to the saints to remain either in Judæa or Jerusalem: for the command to depart is most express. What Cyril says may perhaps apply to those who will be in other parts of the Ten Kingdoms.

2 Thess. ii. just as the others who preceded him. Speaking of Antichrist, he says:

"He is called a son of perdition, because he himself will perish. And who is he? Satan? By no means; but a certain man, receiving all the operation of Satan. There shall be revealed, it says, the man who will be extolled above all that is called God, or that is made an object of worship. For he will not incite men to worship idols, but it will be himself an Antitheos. He will put down all gods, and command men to worship him as the very God. And he will sit in the Temple of God; not only that which is in Jerusalem, but in the churches everywhere."

Chrysostom speaks of Elias coming to restore all things. Of John the Baptist he says:

"How then did John come in the spirit and power of Elias? By receiving the same ministry: for as the one was forerunner of the first coming, so will the other be forerunner of the second coming in glory."

Cent. V. Jerome, A.D. 400.

"Therefore let us say, that which all ecclesiastical writers have delivered, that at the end of the world, when the kingdom of the Romans is to be destroyed, there will be ten kings to divide the Roman world amongst themselves, and that there will arise an eleventh, a very little king (regem parvulum) who will overcome three of the ten kings,....... after the destruction of which kings, the seven other king will submit their necks to the conqueror. And behold, he says, there were eyes like the eyes of a man in that horn. Let us not think, according to the opinion of some, that he is either a devil or a demon, but one from among men, in whom the whole of Satan is about to dwell bodily. And a mouth speaking great things: for he is the man of sin, the son of perdition, so as to sit in the Temple of God, showing that he is God.

"'I beheld on account of the great words that the horn spake,' &c. The judgment of God comes to crush pride : therefore the Roman Empire will be blotted out, because that horn spake great things. . . . . . Time signifies a year, times (according to the idiom of the Hebrews, who themselves have a dual number) signify two years—half a time, six months ; during which period, the saints are to be given over to Antichrist, that the Jews might be condemned, who, not believing the truth, have taken up with a lie. Concerning which period also the Saviour speaks in the Gospel, 'Unless those days were shortened there should no flesh be saved.'"

Speaking of the vision in the eighth of Daniel, Jerome says :

"Most of our people (plerique nostrorum) refer it to Antichrist and say, that what was done under Antiochus in type, is to be fulfilled under the other, in reality."

Apollinarius, as quoted by Jerome, speaks of Antichrist as placing, during the last hebdomad, the abomination of desolation, *i. e.* an idol, and the statue of his own god in the temple, and that it would be the last desolation and condemnation of the people of the Jews, who having despised the truth of Christ, have received the lie of Antichrist.

Augustine, A.D. 410.

Augustine quotes at length 2 Thess. ii., and observes :

"No one doubts that the Apostle said these things of Antichrist; and that the day of judgment, which he here calls the Day of the Lord, will not come, unless he, whom he calls an apostate, that is to say, from the Lord God, shall first come. . . . . But in what Temple of God he is about to sit, is uncertain ; whether in that ruined Temple, which was constructed by Solomon, or in the Church: for the Apostle would not call the temple of any idol or dæmon—the Temple of God."

His observations on the 2nd of Thessalonians ii., are chiefly remarkable for a peculiar explanation of the passage respecting the "mystery of iniquity." After saying that he had no opinion of his own to give, he states the following as an interpretation which he had heard from others.

"They consider the words, ' *Ye know what hindereth*,' and ' *the mystery of iniquity worketh*'—to be spoken concerning those evil and false professors who are in the Church, until they arrive to so great a number as to make a vast multitude for Antichrist ; and that this is the mystery of iniquity, because it seems hidden. The Apostle therefore exhorts the faithful to persevere tenaciously in holding fast the faith, saying, ' Let him who holds fast continue to hold fast (*i.e.* the faith) until it (the mystery of iniquity) come out from the midst (donec DE medio fiat)—that is, until the mystery of iniquity which is now hidden, come forth from the midst of the Church. For they consider the words of John in his Epistle to pertain to the self-same mystery—' They went out from us; but they were not of us,' &c. As therefore before the end . . . . there have gone out many heretics from the midst of the Church, whom he calls many Antichrists, so all will by and by go out who belong, not to Christ, but to that last Antichrist, and then he will be revealed."

Augustine considers that the miracles wrought by Antichrist will be, not pretended but real miracles, performed by the agency of Satan. He refers to the instances of Satan's power, in the Book of Job, in confirmation.

Augustine speaks of the four Empires mentioned in Daniel, as being those of Assyria, Persia, Macedon, and Rome; and refers to the commentary of Jerome on Daniel as a book which he highly approved. He adds that it is impossible for any one to read Daniel in the most careless manner, without seeing that the reign of Antichrist, although brief, will be most fierce against the Church. He interprets the time, times, &c., &c., as meaning three years and a half, and speaks of the unequalled season of tribulation as future. (Augustine, De Civitate Dei, Lib. 'xx., Cap. 19 and 23.)

Theodoret, 430.

Theodoret, like those who have preceded, explains the metals of the second chapter, and the beasts of the seventh, as referring to the four successive empires of Assyria, Persia, Greece and Rome. Speaking of the little horn in the seventh chapter, he says that the prophet thereby indicates Antichrist. He supposes that it is called little, because Antichrist will arise from a little tribe of the Jews. He quotes and applies the 2 Thess. ii. in the same way as the writers above quoted. He forcibly describes his violent persecution of the saints, and says that they are to be delivered into his hands for three years and a half, at the end of which time he will be destroyed by the personal appearing of the Lord Jesus.

In his commentary on the eleventh of Daniel, he explains the prophecy respecting the vile person, of Antiochus Epiphanes—considers that those who are described as strong and doing exploits in the 32nd verse, are the Maccabees—and thinks that Antichrist is not mentioned in that chapter until the 36th verse, as " the king who shall do according to his will." After speaking (says Theodoret) of Antiochus Epiphanes, the prophet passes from the likeness to the antitype; for Antichrist is the antitype of Antiochus, and Antiochus the likeness of Antichrist. He then quotes the 2 Thess. ii., and the words of our Lord in Matthew respecting the unequalled tribulation, and applies them to the period of Antichrist.

In his commentary on the 2 Thess. ii., Theodoret thus notices the opinion of some, as to the restraining power :—

"Some have imagined the Roman sovereignty to be the restraining power—others, the grace of the Spirit, for, say they, whilst the grace of the Spirit restrains, Antichrist cannot come   But it is not possible that the grace of the Spirit should altogether cease, for how could those prove superior to Antichrist's wiles, who are deprived of the assistance of the Spirit ? As to the other supposition, there will be no other Empire that will succeed the Roman, for the divine Daniel has represented the Roman Empire by the fourth beast, but it was on this beast that the little horn sprang up that was to make war with the saints. This is the very person concerning whom the Apostle said the things that have just been quoted [i. e. from the Thess.]. I do not believe that the Apostle meant either of these things (i. e. Theodoret did not believe that either the Roman sovereignty or the grace of the Spirit was the restraining power), but I conceive that to be the truth, which has been said by others, namely, that since it is the appointment of Almighty God that he should appear at the time of the end, it is God's decree that now hinders his manifestation."

Theodoret, in his commentary on Daniel xii., speaks very fully of the mission of Elijah, previously to the return of the Lord Jesus.

Andreas.

Andreas, who was Bishop of Cæsarea late in the fifth century, wrote a commentary on the Apocalypse. It appears that some persons at that time supposed the Babylon of the Revelation to be the Euphratean city. On this Andreas remarks :—

"We might indeed wish that it were so, and that on that city should fall the punishment of proudly raging against Christ and His servants. But to that opinion it must be opposed, that the ancient teachers of the Church consider these things to be prophesied against the Babylon of the Romans, because the ten horns belonged to the fourth beast, that is, to the Roman Empire. And out of that beast grew one horn, which is to root up three and subdue the rest, and to become king of the Romans.* And this, under pretence

* It is obvious that there is no more difficulty in Antichrist's reigning over the Ten Kingdoms of the Roman Empire from Babylon, than in Constantine's reigning over the Roman Empire from Constantinople. It is not true that Antichrist destroys the City of Babylon. He destroys a certain governmental system which had been located in Babylon, and which is represented by the Woman of the 17th of Revelation. She is destroyed 1,260 days before the City. The woman is the City *morally*, not the City *physically*.

of fostering their power ; but in truth to overthrow it utterly. Therefore if anyone chooses here to understand a condensed representation of that kingdom which has ruled from the beginning until now, and which has indeed shed the blood of Apostles, prophets, and martyrs, he will not err from the meaning. (Andreas, as quoted by Maitland.)

Cent. VI. Cassiodorus, A.D. 520.

Cassiodorus, who was a Roman senator, again suggests the thought of Babylon in the Revelation, meaning the Chaldean city.

" When John wondered who the Harlot could be, whom he had seen sitting on a Beast which had seven heads, and ten horns, the Angel gave him an interpretation. Some understand the Harlot to represent the city of Rome, situate on seven mountains, and exercising sole dominion over the world. Others say that it is spoken rather of Babylon, sup-

---

(For further remarks on this subject, see " Babylon, its Revival," &c., as advertised at end. See also " Thoughts on the Apocalypse.")

Scarcely any one could read the works of Hippolytus, without the thought being *suggested*, that the Chaldæan Babylon, and the Babylon of the Revelation were identical ; for he quotes Isaiah and the Revelation as referring in their prophecies concerning Babylon to the same event, and who can doubt that Isaiah refers to the Chaldæan Babylon ?

The words which Hippolytus addresses to the Apostle John, viz., " She, O blessed John, was the cause of thy banishment " forbid our positively saying that Hippolytus considered Antichrist's Babylon to be the Euphratean City, but he may have thought that as Babylon had migrated from Chaldæa, through Persia and Greece, to Rome, so it might, in the latter day, return to the Land of Shinar again.

posing what is said of her position to refer, not to mountains, but to arrogancy of power—(prætumidis potestatibus.) He says that the Harlot will be utterly destroyed by those nations whose former mistress she appeared to be. He states also, that ten Kings will have power in the earth, but that one of them, who is called Antichrist, is reserved for the end of the age, and makes war against Christ, but his iniquity succumbs under the conquering hand of the Lord."—(Complex. in Apoc. p. 235.)

Aretas, who is supposed to have lived about 650, again mentions Antichrist in connexion with Babylon. Speaking of the Saracens, he says, that the seat of their sovereignty (το αρχειον αυτων) is at Babylon, and that Antichrist, the King of the Romans, will become their master. Aretas himself seems to doubt whether the term Babylon is to be understood generally as referring to the world and worldliness, or whether it means Constantinople. He considers that Rev. xvi. 19, does refer to Constantinople. "This is no other," he says, "than the city of Constantine, in which righteousness once prevailed, but now murderers." Aretas speaks of the Roman Empire being divided into its final parts, a little before the appearance of Antichrist, and says that Elias and Enoch will oppose his miracles for three years and a half in Jerusalem.

Gregory of Tours, born A.D. 559.

"Concerning the end of the world, I believe what I have learnt from those who have gone before me. Antichrist will assume circumcision, asserting himself to be the Christ. He will then place a statue to be worshipped in the Temple at Jerusalem, as we read that our Lord has said, ' Ye shall see the abomination of desolation standing in the holy place.' "

Gregory was a friend of Gregory the Great, who wrote much in the same way.

After this, the darkness which had been increasing for ages settled into the deep night of Popery. Nevertheless, the expectation of THE Antichrist remained ; although all right knowledge of the Millennial reign, and every connected truth, seems utterly to have been lost ;* and a false Church used its very knowledge of the evil to come as a means of sustaining its own position of sin.

* Thus Alcuin, who lived in the time of Charlemagne, and died in A.D. 804, in the midst of much that is superstitious and erroneous, says : "But if by the Beast we understand Antichrist merely, his ascent from the pit will be his nativity from that part of the Jewish people which is sunk in the deepest impiety — namely the tribe of Dan. . . . . And because the persecution will be most cruel at Jerusalem, therefore the martyrdoms of the saints are spoken of as being *there :* for the Jews will be the principal adherents of Antichrist, until they who are to be saved among them are converted by the preaching of Elias and Enoch."—(Alcuin in Apocalyp.)

About the year 1400, Berengaud, in the midst of much that is worse than worthless, says : "The time of persecution, as appears to me, is limited to three years and a half, in which Antichrist will labour with all his might, both by his own agency and by that of his disciples, and by the display of wondrous signs, to get the worship of mankind concentrated in himself." He applies the last verse of Rev. xiii. to Antichrist.

The opinions of the middle ages on these subjects can be clearly gained from Roger of Hoveden, who lived in the reign of Henry II. of England. It is not necessary to credit his history, nor to receive his narrative respecting Richard the First, in order to gain from him some of the current opinions of the time.

Hoveden states that Richard the First, on his way to Palestine, sent for Joachim, an abbot of a Calabrian convent, to meet him in Sicily, as he was desirous of hearing him speak on prophecy.* Joachim came. Amongst a great many other things that were false, he told Richard that Saladin was the immediate forerunner of Antichrist, who was already born at Rome, and would be raised to the Papal throne. This the King resisted, and said to Joachim, "I thought that Antichrist would be born at Antioch, or at Babylon from the family of Dan, and would reign in the Temple of the Lord at Jerusalem, and would walk in that Land in which Christ walked, and reign in it for three years and a half, and contend against Elias and Enoch, and would kill them, and afterwards himself perish."

Hoveden, after relating this story, whether true or false, goes on to give an account of the generally prevailing doctrines respecting Antichrist. It is very diffuse, and too long to be transcribed here. It may be seen in the Scriptores Anglicani, fol. p. 681. It is chiefly remarkable for the distinct

* Joachim speculated wildly on prophetic subjects. He is considered to be the first inventor of the system of 1260 *years.*

assertion of Antichrist's connexion with Babylon. Hoveden says, " As our Lord and Saviour provided for Himself Bethlehem, that there He might for us deign to assume humanity and be born, so the Devil knows a fit place for that abandoned one, who is named Antichrist, whence that root of all evil ought to spring, namely, the city of Babylon ; for in that city, which was of old the illustrious and glorious city of the Gentiles, and the head of the kingdom of the Persians, Antichrist will be born." . . . . "After having been born in the city of Babylon, he will come to Jerusalem and assume circumcision, saying to the Jews, 'I am the Messiah promised to you, who have come for your deliverance, to gather and defend you who have been scattered.'"

In reviewing these extracts, it is manifest that throughout all these writers a general agreement exists as to the closing hours of this dispensation being hours of darkness and not of light : they did not expect the progress and universal triumph of truth. Moreover, they knew that the Head of the Apostasy would be a secular person, and the Head of the Roman Empire—whether the seat of that Empire were Rome, Constantinople, or Babylon. This was maintained before as well as after the rise of Popery. They remembered also the connexion of the Jews and Jerusalem with the final Apostasy. It is lamentable to think that Protestantism, with the recovered Scripture in its hand, should have extinguished the last remains of prophetic light that glimmered in the midst of fallen Christianity.

If we now desire the truth, we must turn simply and exclusively to the Holy Scriptures as our guide. Peter said, speaking of the darkness of the latter days, " Remember US the Apostles of the Lord and Saviour." He who blindly adopts as his guide the principles of Barnabas or Irenæus — or those of the day of Constantine — or even those of the Reformation in many things, will find himself carried away from the pure streams of the Scriptures of God. It is easy to see how a dread of rising Infidelity and the discovery of the mistakes of Protestant writers on prophetic subjects, may drive many back to the principles of the early ages, and thereby into the current which finally carries into the abyss of Popery. A recognition of the early fall of Christianity (for how early did the Gentile Churches cease to answer to their symbol of golden candlesticks) and ability to distinguish between mere ceremonial Christianity and that which is the result of the pure testimony of truth, are essential to a right understanding of prophetic Scripture. He who does not see that the Gentile olive branch has failed to continue in God's goodness, will be little able to apply any part of the Scriptures aright.

It is very manifest, that the corrupt systems of Christianity, in the East and in the West, have not renounced one of their evil practices. On the contrary, they are rather rivetting their chains of darkness. It is equally plain, that none of these systems are becoming *universally dominant;* though it may be, that some are being strengthened in certain spheres in which they are to be permitted to operate. In the mean while the *secular* systems, profiting by the divisions and jealousies of *religious* systems, are acquiring increasing power over them. Very recently the representative of the secular power of France, surrounded by the ministers of his government, called on Popery to minister subordinately in his presence; and Popery obeyed.* He stood as the King; and the Priest ministered in his presence. The present relation of false religious systems to the secular Powers, is becoming far more analogous to that of the false Prophet to Antichrist, than any thing that is found in the past records of Ecclesiasticism. If the secular Governments are content to press nothing as having exclusive claim to be believed—if they will consent to sustain any system of falsehood, whenever expediency requires, there is little doubt that they will, for a time at least, remove many a difficulty from their path in a world in which Satan rules. Their system will, for a season, prosper more than any system that has preceded. Nor will it be pure Antichristianism. But it will *introduce* Antichristianism. It will be the Harlot; though not the Beast.

Men are not prepared for the hardened infidelity of Voltaire. When, during the first French Revolution, its terrible voice was heard from Paris, the nations trembled. Neither governments nor their subjects desire the restoration of the ancient rule of

* This was written in 1849.

Popery, nor the introduction of Atheistic Infidelity. But when it is said, under the guise of philanthropy and charity and humility, We know not what Truth is; let us discard all regard thereunto in our social and governmental arrangements—men listen. They forsake the Bible, and give their energies to the formation of a system, to which, when it is finished, Antichrist will succeed.

This is the path into which the secular systems have entered; and they are treading it with a proudly resolute step. Nor is it, I believe, possible, for any individual or any system, to avoid assisting them in their course, except by cleaving simply to the Scriptures as our only guide, and separating from every thing that refuses to bow to their authority and submit to their control.

(B.)

Extract from Jewish Chronicle of November 9, 1849.

The following extract, from a letter in the Jewish Chronicle, shows how rapidly the Jews are ripening for the reception of the last great Deceiver. "I am come in my Father's name, and ye receive me not, if another shall come in his own name, him ye will receive." The infidel rejection of what God has *revealed* respecting the eternity of wrath—and the resolution to determine for themselves what does or does not befit His goodness—together with their rejection of Him by whose stripes only they can be healed, place their heightened anticipations of prosperity in their Land in a light in which it is indeed fearful to contemplate them. The same Journal from which I extract this letter contains the following note—"Reason and Faith—God has created two great lights; the greater light to rule man's busy day, that is, Reason; and the lesser light to rule his contemplative night, that is, Faith. But Faith herself shines only so long as she reflects some bright illumination from the brighter orb."

EXTRACT.

"But whilst the contending Nazarenes dispose of Palestine and Mosaism, each in full accordance with the peculiar essence of his effervescent zeal, what says the poor Jew, who is the innocent cause of all this theological strife ?   Ask *him,* 'Will the Jews again be restored to their native Palestine ?' and he will refer you to his greatest authority on earth : 'The Lord thy God will turn thy captivity, and have compassion upon thee ; and will return and gather thee from all nations whither the Lord thy God hath scattered thee.'   This is the golden age in the womb of futurity, which constantly upholds the desponding Israelite under the bitterest tribulation ; this is the goal of his dearest and fondest hopes ; awake or asleep, at the altar or at the mart, in prosperity or misfortune, Jerusalem, dearly, fondly cherished Jerusalem, is engraven in the innermost recesses of his heart, never, never to be erased. Thus whilst the heathen poet looked back to the past for the excellence of a *bygone* golden age, the Israelite, with unfading hopes and undying faith, still beholds in perspective that glorious vision of a golden age *yet to come,* which every generation lives in the hopes of attaining.   'Whoever goes into the grave,' says Leopold Dukes, 'without having lived to see its attainment, can at least take the hope with him, that his successors will be more fortunate than himself.'   And yet, good Heavens ! this fond remembrance, this doating and undying love for the land of his fathers, which forms such a bright feature in the character of the Jew, has been held up before an honourable and enlightened assembly as a just and sufficient cause for his disfranchisement !

*   *   *   *   *

"But whilst all orthodox and patriotic Jews look forward with hopes unfaded and faith unshaken, towards the final fulfilment of that heavenly promise of restoration which for eighteen dark and dreary centuries has been their solace in exile and misery, whilst they look forward to the re-possession of Palestine with as much certainty as we look for the rising of the daily sun, there is yet one point whereon there is much of conjecture and speculation.   *How* will the Jews be restored ?   Will a great and glorious Messiah lay prostrate the nations of the earth, and bid the eagles in the air to bring the scattered Israelites on their expanded wings ?   Will the days of miracles again be revived as of yore, when the God of the Hebrews said, 'Let my people go, that they may serve me ?' Or, will a second Cyrus proclaim, 'Let the house be built ?' Will a *true* Barchocab, with glorious majesty, sparkle in the horizon over 'a people scattered and peeled, whose land the rivers have spoiled ?' Will he close up the breaches thereof, and raise up the ruins, and build it as in the days of old ? Will he, with 'grace poured into his lips,' enrapture the world, and stand triumphant, 'fairer than the children of men ?' or, shall he conquer with meekness, and be 'the despised and rejected of men ?' Will he 'deal prudently,' and be 'exalted, extolled, and very high ?' or must he first be 'bruised for our iniquity,' that the 'chastisement of our peace come upon him, and with his stripes we be healed ?' Must he, like a mighty warrior, 'with dyed garments from Bozra,' wade his way through opposing squadrons ? or shall he, with 'the spirit of wisdom and understanding, smite the earth with the rod of his mouth ?' Will the order of nature be inverted, that we may have signs and wonders ? or, must we expect in him a second Maccabee, who will re-establish the kingdom of David, whose valour will outshine all wonders, whose patriotism will outdo all miracles ?

"But whilst we must leave it to learned divines and theologians to enlighten us on these topics, let us examine the question as mere laymen. Firstly, *How far* is the restoration of the Jews by mere mortal aid practicable ? Secondly, Can we reasonably suppose that the attempt at such a restoration would be repugnant to the will of Providence ?

"1. One of the greatest difficulties which stands most prominently in the way of the restoration of the Jews by mere mortal aid is, the impression which is indelibly fixed in the heart of every religious Jew, that none but a heaven-inspired Messiah can accomplish this important mission. Hence, were the most powerful empire on earth to undertake their restoration, the Jews (unless convinced by ocular demonstration that such was Heaven's will) would themselves have but little confidence in its successful issue. Some would absolutely refuse to emigrate to Palestine; and those who, out of great love and patriotism, might eagerly embrace the opportunity of once more beholding the land 'of their fathers, would feel most bitterly disappointed on finding that even in Jerusalem, with every freedom and encouragement, Mosaism, *without a direct miracle from heaven*, could never again be re-established in its original splendour. Were the temple once more reared on its ancient foundation, were the priests ready at the altar, and nothing else were wanting but the *fire from heaven*, no priest dare proceed with his office, for no *strange fire* must come upon the altar of God. What kind of Jewish restoration then, *is* practicable? and *how far* can we expect it from mortal aid?

"Judge Noah, who is no visionary, has pointed out to us the rapid advancement of the Christian power. He shows us Turkey deprived of Greece, Russia assailing the wandering hordes of the Caucasus; he points to England's contests with the native princes of India, and its war with China; France he beholds carrying its victorious arms through the north of Africa; and Russia he sees, with a steady glance and firm step, approaching Turkey in Europe. 'England,' says he, must possess Egypt, as affording the only secure route to her possessions in India through the Red Sea. Then Palestine, thus placed between the Russian possessions and Egypt, reverts to its legitimate proprietors; and for the safety of the surrounding nations the Jews are placed there, by and with the consent of the Christian powers.' This hypothesis of our highly gifted co-religionist has been good humouredly sneered at by the 'Athenæum' (one of the most respectable periodicals in this land, and one which, for the last thirteen years, to my certain knowledge, has constantly and invariably shown a most friendly disposition towards our race); and yet far more unlikely things have taken place in this wonderful world of ours. When the American printer Franklin visited England, and foresaw the future greatness of his native land, he too was sneered at, but what were the '*Colonies*' then, are now the *United States*. Let but the spirit of democracy make the same rapid progress in the next half century, as it has done in the preceding one, and what is humble Palestine now, will yet rise into *the Republic of Judea*. The European powers will not need to put themselves to the trouble of restoring the Jews individually or collectively. Let them but confer upon Palestine a constitution like that of the United States, where every man, by a three years' residence, acquires the rights of citizenship, and the Jews will restore *themselves*. They would then go cheerfully and willingly, and would there piously bide their time for a heaven-inspired Messiah, who is to restore Mosaism to its original splendour. They would go, and what is now a barren, desolate, and impoverished wilderness, would again become a land flowing with milk and honey, as it was in the days of yore.

* * * *

"Now, the principal and greatest sin our forefathers committed against God was *idolatry*, the wrath of heaven was kindled against them, and the first temple was destroyed. Banished and captives, they were sent to Babylon, and as *a natural result*, the children partook of the punishment of their parents unto the *third and fourth* generation. After seventy years' captivity, a patriotic Jew obtained a great monarch's permission, and the *innocent* descendants were restored to the land of their fathers. Again the Jews sinned, and the second temple fell in ruins before the Roman's merciless torch; the Israelites suffered the penalty of their transgressions. But they are *idolaters* no longer. In this wide world there is not a people or class which is freer from idolatry, bigotry, or immorality. The most civilised and enlightened nation on earth is not freer from *sin* than are the modern Jews. If, then, the glory of God consists in His *goodness;* if He visits not the sins of the parents on the children *beyond the third and fourth generation;* if the present Jews are as free from sin as any nation on earth, *how can* we *reasonably* suppose that our restoration would be *repugnant* to the will of Providence ? If it is not against the will of Providence that other nations should possess kingdoms and governments, why should the Jews, who are not less worthy of His goodness, mercy, and forgiveness, still remain exiles and wanderers ?

"The Jew *must* and *will* aspire to restoration; and 'Heaven helps those who help *themselves.*' Those who maintain that the Jew of the 19th century must suffer for the sins of his fathers committed in the first century, insult the dignity and justice of an all-*merciful* and just Providence. They conceive a god of clay, and mould him after their own form, and after their own image. I remain, Sir, with great respect, yours faithfully,

"HERTZ BEN PINCHAS."

———

(C.)

On Dacian Hungary.

The following extract from a letter written from Temesvar, October 29th, 1849, will be read with interest. It shows that part of Hungary which was included in the Ancient Roman province of Dacia, is altogether in a different condition from that part of Hungary west of the Vallum Romanum, which was not included in the Roman Dacia. Traces of the occupation of this province by the Romans, are still most discernible; and it seems far more susceptible of improvement than the other parts of Hungary which did not come within the Roman Empire. In Roman Hungary, the feudalism of the Magyars, whose principle is, *" that nations must be moulded to governments, not governments to nations,"* is likely to be supplanted by more liberal principles, which the Austrian Government is desirous of introducing among the Daco-Romans. If Dacia is to be considered an integral part of the Roman Empire, such principles are likely to flourish in these eastern parts of Hungary, but not in the central districts west of the Vallum Romanum. The Vallum ran north from the Danube to Temesvar. The Banat (*i. e.* Duchy) of Temesvar was anciently Dacia Ripensis.

"Temesvar, Oct. 29, 1849.

"The Banat of Temesvar is the cornucopia not only of Hungary, but of the whole Austrian Empire; even Lombardy,

highly as it is favoured by nature, must yield precedence to
the Banat of Temesvar, and one must go to the Delta of the
Nile to find a similar soil. This may be easily understood,
when we reflect that the lower part of rivers having large
alluvial deposits, are necessarily the richest, and on referring
to the map, it will be seen that by a very peculiar geographical configuration, the Banat has the best part of the alluvial
washings of the Theiss, the Maros, the Save, and the Danube.
. . . . Intersected by the 45th degree of latitude, and thus
midway between the Equator and the Pole, the Banat is for
all these reasons the granary of the Austrian Empire, and
produces wheat of a quality nowhere else to be found in the
Imperial States. But the eastern part, being hilly, is rather
fitted for wine culture, which is of a very pleasant quality,
its white sorts resembling Moselle and Rhine wines. The
mineral wealth of this part of the Banat is not less remarkable. In the vale of Mehadin * * * * * General Count
Hamilton, re-discovered in 1736, after an interval of more
than a thousand years, those sulphurous springs renowned
through all the Roman Empire for their power and efficacy;
and in the extensive coal mines of Oravieza, near Weiss-
kirchen, the King of Hungary possesses a treasure more
valuable than all the gold of Schemnitz and Kremnitz, if it
become, as proposed, the terminus of the great railway which
in a few years will stretch over Central Hungary to
Temesvar. * * * * The substratum of the population is
Wallachian, to distinguish whom from the inhabitants of
the Ottoman principalities of the Danube, we shall henceforth adopt the designation of Daco-Romans. As far as the
dark obscurity of the history of this country before the
Roman conquest allows us to inquire, the Dacians, the
aborigines, spoke a language resembling the Thracian, but
here, as well as throughout most of Europe, the Roman conquest and colonisation made a *tabula rasa* of the original
element. Ancient Dacia, which, under Decebalus, its native
king, offered so obstinate a resistance to the legions of Trajan, was gradually forgotten, and its three great divisions

received Latin names, corresponding to its physical geography. The Banat was called Dacia Ripensis, from the rivers that so peculiarly define it; Transylvania was called Dacia Transalpina; and Bessarabia and the present principalities adjoining the Black Sea, Dacia Mediterranea. Hence, at this moment, between 7,000,000 and 8,000,000 men inhabiting these provinces speak a dialect that is susceptible of a grace and elegance little, if at all, inferior to that of their fellow Romans on the banks of the Tiber; and notwithstanding a certain admixture of Sclavonic words, dating from the irruptions of the seventh century, the Daco-Roman forms usually approach even nearer to the Latin than the Italian does; but in consequence of their subsequent connexion with the Lower Empire and the Oriental Church, arising from their easterly position, Cyrillian letters are preferred to Roman in writing the language, notwithstanding the efforts that have been made to restore the original character. · Of these populations about 3,000,000 inhabit the Austrian Empire, principally in the Banat and Transylvania; and painful as civil wars are in their operations and results, it is impossible to help feeling satisfaction in the emancipation of a race whose history and language are linked with the classic recollections of our youth, from the galling despotism of a faction that sought to extirpate the very language and nationality of the Daco-Romans. Italy has a self-developed civilisation, and needs no art, science, or literature from Germany; but Austria is certainly fully entitled to the thanks and sympathies of the Daco-Romans of the Danube.

"From 1718 to 1779 the Banat was an integral part of the Austrian Empire, and in that period the aspect of the duchy was completely altered from that of a desolate Turkish Pashalic to that of a flourishing and prosperous European province. Millions were expended by the cabinet of Vienna in cutting the great navigable canal that connects Temesvar with the confluence of the Theiss and the Danube, in draining the marshes, settling German colonies on the reclaimed lands, and in rebuilding Temesvar (the capital) in the truly

pompous style of Louis Quatorze, then the favourite passion
of Charles VI. Owing to this *interregnum* of an improving
European government between 1718 and 1779, or a period of
60 years, the Banat has not the least resemblance to the inte-
rior of Hungary; and if a stranger were to have his eyes
bandaged, he would suppose that he had been carried back
towards the centre of Europe instead of being nearer the
Turkish frontier. The results of this period are seen not
alone in the straight streets, Italian portals, and somewhat
too ornate mouldings of the façades of Temesvar, but are
most striking and palpable in the contrast which the German colonies show to the Asiatic, Sclavonic, and Roman
races around them.   Keresztur is the last Magyar village
I passed through on my way from Szegedin; there the complete backwardness terminates; and at St. Miklos, a town
of 1,700 inhabitants, principally German, and partly Wallachian, the civilisation re-commences. * * * * * But
to return to the Banat, the German colonist, in spite of
his unamiable, litigious spirit, which degenerates to avarice,
and his independence, which amounts to obstinacy, is
morally, physically, and intellectually the superior of the
Roman. This is shown not only in dwellings and persons,
but by other signs; for instance, the wheat of the very
same soil is in the market of Temesvar, worth twenty per
cent. more, if grown on a German than on a Daco-Roman
farm. . . . . . The great cause of the abasement of the
Daco-Roman is the gulf that has hitherto separated him
from his superiors. The Austrian material improvements
in the Banat last century, had little or no effect on his
moral and intellectual culture. The Magyaro—mania, which
adopted the principle that nations must be moulded to
governments, not governments to nations, roused his indignation. The Constitution of the 4th of March, embracing
the opposite principle of giving the Daco-Roman access to
superior education, to tribunals, to the enjoyment of offices
lay and clerical, and trial by jury in the natural channel of
his own language, has been hailed with satisfaction by the

whole nation (some few of whom are large landed proprietors in the Banat), while, if energetically carried out, it opens up a new era for the revival of civilisation among races that excite an imperishable interest in the bosom of every European who remembers that the laws, the letters, and the arts of the more fortunate nations of the West of Europe have their bases in the jurisprudence of the political fabric of the Roman Empire."

CONCLUSION.

REMARKS ON THE FRANCO - PRUSSIAN WAR AND ITS RESULTS.

THE first edition of this work was, as I have already said, prepared in 1848—a period when democratic violence seemed to threaten the stability of almost every Throne in Western Europe. Many changes have since been, and many are still in progress. Nevertheless the anticipations *then* expressed have not been falsified. Monarchic absolutism has not in any portion of the Roman world succeeded in extirpating "*the clay*," nor has democratic violence succeeded in ridding itself of "*the iron.*" There may, possibly, yet be many wars, many convulsions, involving vast national and individual suffering; but the end is not uncertain. Ten democratic monarchies will divide between them the Roman world (την οἰκουμενην), and will, federally united, inaugurate, and, for a season, sustain the reign of latitudinarian Antichristianism, until at last, wearied and harassed by the confusion and strife which Latitudinarianism must necessarily engender, and desiring also a more complete annihilation of the Truth than Latitudinarianism can, in consistency with its principles, effect, the Monarchs of the Ten Kingdoms will give themselves over to an organised system of atheistic infidelity, will avowedly reject both Jehovah and Christ (see Psalm ii.), and, being of one mind, will "give their power and authority to the Beast"— Antichrist. Then, throughout the whole Roman world all whose names are not written in the Lamb's book of life will glorify and worship *him*; for "the Dragon will give him his power, and his throne, and great authority." Rev. xiii. 2. Such will be the end of the boasted liberty of human thought. Just in proportion as men throw off from themselves the restraint of God and of His truth, they become debased, abject servants and slaves of Satan. Whilst imagining themselves to be free, they blindly seek after, serve and worship, whatever Satan proposes to them.

The progress that has been made, during the last twenty-five years, in bringing into closer association with each other most of the countries of the Roman world, and in separating (either legislatively or completely) from the Roman kingdoms countries that do *not* fall within the Roman boundary, has been very marked. The Crimean war brought the eastern part of the Roman world into a much closer association than before with the western Roman nations; and the union then formed does not seem likely to be even temporarily interrupted. Community of interest, especially in a day like the present, is a bond of wondrous tenacity and strength. The

Crimean war too, recovered the greater part of Bess-arabic (for Bessarabia belongs to the Roman world) from the grasp of Russia. Hungary, the centre of which does *not* fall within the Roman boundary, has been legislatively separated from Austria, and fur-ther changes are imminent there, and in all those *non-Roman* countries which Austria has vainly en-deavoured to fuse into political identity with her-self. The seemingly indissoluble bond which kept Austria in close political association with Prussia and the other non-Roman states of northern Ger-many was severed so suddenly and unexpectedly as to electrify Europe. The work of centuries was destroyed in a moment. Yet men needed not to have so marvelled. It was a necessary event; for the Roman nations, being appointed to be the centre of the world's greatness during the closing period of its evil history, must move in a separate circle, and have a peculiar history of their own. Ireland (which is non-Roman) feverishly restless and, by England, victimised to priestcraft, is yearly weaken-ing the ties by which she has been linked to Eng-land. Italy which, twenty years ago, seemed more distant than ever from attaining the objects of her long-cherished hopes, has at last succeeded. Rome is hers, and constitutional or democratic monarchy is established both in Italy and in Austria. Austria once the great pillar of the Papacy, and the enemy and trampler-down of Italy, has changed her course, and become Italy's friend. The temporal sovereignty of the Papacy has ceased: and although the canon law is still, throughout western Europe, struggling with the civil law for supremacy, yet the latter triumphs. The *supremacy* of ecclesiastical power must finally give way to the stronger sceptre of the secular monarch. Becket must yield to Henry. The struggle may be prolonged and disastrous in its consequences, but the issue is not doubtful.

There has been, it is true, one most important event that has seemed to stay or turn back the tide of progress, as respects the territorial development of the Ten Kingdoms. The Franco-German war, instead of giving back to France those portions of Roman territory which Prussia had annexed, has ended in giving more to Prussia, so that Prussia's position on the west bank of the Rhine, instead of being weakened, has been materially strengthened. This may seem to be a retrograde movement; and in one respect it is: but in another and more important point of view, it is not. The Franco-German war will be found in result to have accelerated rather than retarded the expected development.

For many years past, France (though, in some cases, as in her war with Austria, her plans have been marvellously overruled) has been the great obstructer to the development of the Ten Kingdoms. France and the Papacy have been confederates in obstruction. France, had for her darling object, pre-eminence among the nations of Europe. Despising equality, she coveted leadership. Professedly the patroness of liberty, she was, nevertheless, quite willing to keep on other countries (such as Rome and Spain) the most cruel and oppressive yokes, if her own pre-eminence was aided thereby. Accordingly she schemed for a Latin league, of which she was to be the head, and which was in western Europe to extirpate " the clay," and to return to " the iron " alone. What was " Cæsarism " but this? Imperialism was to sustain Ecclesiasticism, and before this two-fold power the modern " clay-iron " governmental theories were to perish. Accordingly, Italy and other neighbouring states were kept down by France, and their native energies crippled. Italy was to be terrified by threats, and Spain debased and enfeebled by priestcraft. Even the development of the East was by France impeded unless the development accorded with her desires. If Egypt advanced, it must be under the tutelage of France, and Tunis was to be a French appanage. A plot formed by the Imperial Government in France, and the Papal Government in Rome against the liberties of western Europe and against Protestant-ism, was doubtless the immediate cause of the war with Prussia. Soldiers supplied by France, and legions of priests supplied and controlled from in-fallible Rome, were to inaugurate and sustain the new regime. It was a dark and deadly plot; but God mercifully interposed and frustrated it. God fought against France, and in one moment dashed to the ground her atrocious schemes. Instantly, the secular power of the Papacy fell. Italy, for the first time became really free, and the iron hand of France was removed (in all probability, finally) from her and from other nations. The establishment of the freedom of Italy, the confirmation of the severance between Austria and Northern Germany, the fall of the temporal power of the Papacy, the determination evinced in Italy and elsewhere to secure the supremacy of the *civil* over the *canon* law are, as respects the progress of the Ten Kingdoms, events of far greater moment than the temporary annexation to Germany of a few provinces of France. It may be that France may not regain her lost territory until the development of the Ten Kingdoms *in federal union;* or they may be regained previously, either by convention or by the sword. The present monarch of Prussia and Germany fears and honours God, and God has prospered him; but his subjects, previously leavened with infidelity and radicalism, have, since their contact with France, received much added moral poison. The horizon of Germany is not devoid of clouds of dark and threatening aspect. The storm may be comparatively distant; but if it come, it will probably come with a violence and fury as yet unparalleled. See Heine's anticipations respecting the future of Germany. An explosion there would strike Europe more terribly than any that has occurred in France; for there is a strength and vigour and manhood in Germany that the childishness and fickleness, and quickly cowed spirit of France knows not. But it is vain to speculate. It is sufficient, as to the present question, to say that the moral changes that are in progress through the late victories of Prussia, are of infinitely greater

moment than the temporary loss of provinces by
France. It should be remembered, too, that territorial changes are not, like moral changes, necessarily
slow. They may be accomplished in a day. England once possessed far more of France than Prussia
now holds; and she held it, apparently, on a far
more secure tenure: for Normandy and other circumstances had brought England into relations to
France far closer than Germany has ever held. Yet
in a moment the energy of a fanatical peasant-girl
scattered the armies of England, and restored whole
provinces to France, and took from England well
nigh every token of her dominion there, save an
empty title which, at a comparatively recent period,
our monarchs have been wise enough to resign.

We must not forget that God has not ceased to
be the Governor of the universe. Although, for
the most part, He hides the operation of His hand,
and often permits men to pursue their godless
schemes successfully, and allows them to defy His
power and to spurn His wisdom and love, yet He,
nevertheless, does sometimes intervene to check the
course of triumphant evil, to award punishment
where punishment is due, and thus to make it manifest, by some marked intervention of His hand, that
He only is supreme, and that He is " a God by whom
actions are weighed."

Is there any nation upon the earth which, since
the period of the Reformation, has more daringly
outraged and defied God than France? Inconstant
in other things, she has been constant in her rejec-

tion of God. At the time of the Reformation she was favoured with much Protestant light. Many a herald of mercy was sent to her, and one of the chief pillars of the Reformation was raised up from amongst her own people. The history of France differs from that of Spain as to this. Spain was not to the same extent, favoured with light. Spain, never had a Calvin. But the trumpet of Truth was loudly sounded in the ears of France, and marked results followed—results that gave to France prolonged opportunities of judging between light and darkness, God and Baal. Deliberately she chose Baal. Was there ever a night in the annals of Christendom more marked with malignant, demoniacal atrocity, than the night of the twenty-fourth of August, 1572. That was one of the answers of France to the mercy of God in sending her that light which, on the night of St. Bartholomew, she quenched in blood. Another answer was given by her when she revoked the edict by which protection had been granted to Protestantism, and so drave it from her borders. That deed, though less ostensibly atrocious than the slaughter of the night of St. Bartholomew, brought sufferings no less deadly in result on many a fugitive martyr who refused to exchange the Bible for Tradition. So Truth was trampled down, and Priestcraft enthroned. It reigned in France until outraged human nature, disgusted by its falsehoods, sickened by its moral depravity, and terrified by its cruelties, made, at the end of the last century, a spasmodic effort, and suddenly burst the hateful and intolerable yoke. The licentiousness which had reigned in the Tuilleries, and the savage cruelties of which the Bastille was the exponent (both being the results of a *priest*-directed despotism) received just retribution, and fell before an outbreak of revolutionary fury, the like to which civilised Europe had never before beheld. Blood compensated for blood : shackles were struck off, and liberty was gained. But it was not holy liberty ; it was not liberty that sought to be directed by Truth. It was the liberty of unsanctified, unregenerate hearts, that wearied and disgusted with sacerdotal fictions, had steeled themselves into infidelity and believed nothing. The wit and sarcasm of Voltaire, seeing that it amused and promised liberty of thought and action, were far more grateful than the mumbled falsehoods of the priest that had so long enthralled them ; and they cared not to distinguish between true Christianity and its counterfeits. Thus, Satan being chosen, not God, a reign of godless, blaspheming infidelity followed the reign of Priestcraft. The name of God was openly rejected ; His holy word avowedly renounced ; liberty was found to be license ; and fraternity soon proved itself to be such fraternity as exists between the tiger and his prey. France clothed herself in garments that reeked with the blood of her own citizens. Terror reigned, and treachery lurked in every dwelling. Such was the retribution from Heaven, which often appoints that evil should punish evil. And when France ceased from civil strife, it was only that she might spread woe and desolation over Europe. The heart of Germany still thrills at the remembrance of the deeds of those, who, like so many fiends, entered her hamlets and her cottages to let loose their brutality, and to gratify their lust. Under the leadership of one who foreshadowed the arrogance, selfishness and cruelty of Antichrist more, perhaps, than any monarch that has yet been, France, through a long series of years, devastated the terrified nations of Europe, and deluged them with blood, giving them no rest, till, at last, exhausted by her efforts to ruin others, herself succumbed, and sank for a season into paralysed decrepitude. Since then, France has had many a vicissitude. Time for reflection has been allowed her; opportunity for becoming acquainted with the Scripture has been afforded, but again every mercy has been despised. It may, I believe, be safely said, that France was never more morally depraved, that she was never more socially and governmentally base, and that her rulers were never bent upon a fouler and more abominable design than when she made her sudden, tiger-like spring at Prussia. France hated Prussia, but Rome hated Protestantism, and Rome was again potent in France, and on Rome the enfeebled government of France leaned. Before the military strength of France, aided by the well-trained priestly hosts that had been located in Germany, it was hoped that Prussia, and with her western Protestantism, would fall. But God had other thoughts. The blow which France intended for others was caused to fall upon herself, and Protestantism—unworthy, worldly, slumbering Protestantism, though for her sins she well deserves to be smitten to the dust—received unmerited protection from the long-suffering mercy of God. It is a lesson given from Heaven. Has France learned from it? Has England taken warning?

England, absorbed in the pursuit of "material" interests, having Mammon for her idol, and lavishing honours and rewards on Intellect, wherever found, if only she thinks that such intellect will consent to serve and worship her Idol — England takes warning from nothing. Her eye is closed, her ear heavy. Syren-sounds, which Satan has gathered around her, have lulled her, and she desires not to awaken. Her responsibilities are greater even than those of France; for a period of light, far brighter and more extended in time than that granted to France, has been vouchsafed to her; and she had opportunity to profit by the lessons that the histories of France, and Spain, and Italy have afforded. She has had full opportunity of considering the difference between nations in which the Bible has been honoured, as the one authoritative record of God's will, and nations in which Ecclesiasticism has reigned. England, on many occasions of danger and need, has had the shield of the Most High God marvellously stretched out over her, because the Bible, and not the so-called Church, was acknowledged as having the authority of God. But now all is changed. Notwithstanding the withering curse that Popery has so manifestly brought on neighbouring nations (witness the present condition of Spain)—notwithstanding the deadly savage infidelity that has sprung up in those nations as a result of the ignorance and moral debasement resulting from Priestcraft, a large and influential section of the highborn and educated in England are rushing back into the darkness and idolatries of Romanism, with an unreflecting, fanatical eagerness that astonishes, while it delights, the well-trained emissaries who have been sent out to decoy. They have little need of their subtlety; little need of their practised skill. The net is scarcely spread, when the willing foot hastens into it.

The cold, stolid, heartless indifference of England to that which the powers of darkness are effecting within her borders, is one of the most appalling spectacles that the history of mankind has yet presented. The Protestant Reformation of the sixteenth century was a work of God, as sure and certain as any which He has ever wrought on earth, in behalf of His truth and people. Consequently they who avowedly set themselves against it must be adversaries of God. They set themselves against God to trample down, and to hinder the effects of, the greatest work, which in these latter days His Spirit has wrought. Men may learn the solemn truth too late; but the last great day will show that they who have, either through indifferentism and ignorance, or through worldliness or antipathy to the Truth, helped in casting down the distinctive truths of Protestantism, have set themselves against the work of the Holy Ghost. "It is a fearful thing to fall into the hands of the living God;" a fearful thing to meet that "fiery indignation which shall devour the adversaries."

Forty years ago, a plan to subvert the doctrines of the Reformation was organised in Oxford. The character of the movement was evident from its very commencement to all those who chose not to hide from themselves the truth. It was a plot, dark and deadly, that ought from the beginning to have been sternly resisted by all those who feared God. The character of the Serpent marked it from the beginning: its methods were tortuous, double-tongued, and subtle. Every position should have been abandoned, every tie broken, every friendship renounced that might even seem to unite to those who were engaged in working this mine of Satan. The complete and finished *legislation* of God is contained in Holy Scripture, and in it alone. To put down the Scripture from this place and to invest with *legislative* authority a body of uninspired, unauthorised, carnal men, was one of the first objects of the Tractarian school. The manner in which the plan was carried out was not less revolting than the object proposed. To write ambiguously and *suggestively*—to say, and yet not to say *definitely*—to mingle with preponderating falsehood some portion of qualifying truth, lest a too naked exhibition of error should alarm; to nullify truth (if some recognition of truth was expedient) by some neutralising statement of error, lest truth too nakedly exhibited should lead into the light; to make subtle distinctions, and to mystify by words; to magnify petty and circumstantial differences, so as to hide *essentiality* of likeness—such methods were, from the very first, not altogether eschewed by the Tractarian teachers. At last the moral sense of those who listened became deadened, and the doctrine of "*non-natural*" interpretation was unhesitatingly avowed. Can we wonder that men of honourable and upright feeling should have been stumbled? Can we be surprised that a mind such as that of Dr. Arnold should have revolted from a system in which he saw the falsehoods of ancient Ecclesiasticism stealthily revived with a subtlety that seemed to throw into the shade the tortuousness of former days? I justify not Dr. Arnold's course. Doubtless, he laid in Oxford the foundations of that Sadducean infidel movement which is now, in this country, struggling with Sacerdotalism, for ascendancy. Alarmed and disgusted by the teaching of Dr. Newman, he became, in an evil hour, acquainted with Bunsen, and was beguiled—not knowing that in Bunsen he had met with one whose system required that the neologian principle of "non-natural" interpretation should be employed to neutralise Holy Scripture just in the same way that Dr. Newman and Dr. Pusey had employed it to nullify obnoxious Protestant Confessions and Articles. I justify not Dr. Arnold; but I say that fearful responsibility rests with those who, instead of leading his unsettled mind to the Scripture, scared him and others from the truth by presenting to them sacerdotal fictions from which, intuitively, their souls revolted. How different might have been the result if, when he and others were enquiring after truth, he had been met by the acknowledgment that, as soon as the Apostles died, declension set in throughout the whole professing Church; that the condition of the visible Church, universally, is a lapsed condition; that the visible Church of this dispensation (symbolised in Scripture by the Gentile olive branch (Romans xi.) has *not* " continued in God's goodness," and is to be " cut off;" that the doctrines, practices and arrangements of Christendom *now*, no more resemble those of the Apostolic period than the condition of Israel in the days of Jeremiah or Malachi resembled Israel's condition in the days of Joshua or David. If the lapse of professing Christianity in this dispensation had been acknowledged as Scripture has pourtrayed it; if Scripture had been appealed to and not tradition, or post-Apostolic usage; if the mistakes, worldliness, and transgressions of Protestants had been acknowledged; if it had been admitted that the foundations of all things were out of course, and that there would be no rectification of the general derangement until the Lord shall take to Him His great power (see Rev. xi. 17, and Dan. vii. 14), and return; if the Scripture had been honoured and appealed to as the alone test, and the alone rule; if there had been true humiliation and confession, and a seeking to the mercies and forbearance of God, how different might have been the result!*

Society in England were not unaware of the efficient efforts made by Dr. Newman, Keble, Dr. Pusey and others, to subvert that work of mercy and grace which, at the time of the Protestant Reformation, the Holy Ghost had wrought. But they looked on with careless eye. They had heard that the Reformation was an act of God's mercy; but

---

* I am sorry that I am not able to put my hand on a passage which I remember to have read in one of Dr. Arnold's published letters, in which, after speaking of his utter dissatisfaction with the past and present condition of Christendom, he asks, whether it be possible that we have been altogether deceived in imagining that there has been since the days of the Apostles progress in good—whether the fact may not be just the reverse—whether, since the Apostles died, Christendom, as a whole, may not have steadily advanced in error. I do not profess to quoté the exact words of Dr. Arnold, but such is the general sentiment of the passage to which I refer. If at this interesting and important era in his life anyone had been near him to cherish and develop this germ of truth and to direct him to Holy Scripture, and he had been taught to wait for these times of "restitution" and rectification which are to be when the Lord shall at last "take to Himself His great power and shall reign" (Rev. xi.), how different might have been Dr. Arnold's course ? But he fell into the toils of Bunsen, who moulded his mind and determined his future path. Bunsen clearly saw the corruption of Christendom, but he turned not to Scripture, but to a Christ within, which virtually amounts to a self-rectifying power possessed by human nature. Hence the theory of the verifying faculty which, in result, makes every man a god to himself.

they were not prepared to pronounce dogmatically about it. There had been many divisions among Protestants. Gallio careth for none of these things. Why should he, if his own material interests are not involved? Indifferentism was ready to welcome any form of compromise, so the work was allowed to advance. It was a system that suited excitable and imaginative minds. It suited those who, having æsthetic tendencies, craved after the gratification of the eye and ear. It suited minds that were silly, weak, and womanish. It suited those who preferred to be thought for rather than to think for themselves. It suited all who refused to enter any path except one in which they could walk " by sight," and who therefore refused to recognise an *unseen* heavenly Temple not made with hands (see Hebrews ix.), and an *unseen* Priest, and an *unseen* Intercession based on an *unseen* (because once-finished) sacrifice, and who insisted on having, instead of this presence of God, a *visible* material Sanctuary, formed by their own hands, and *visible* priests consecrated by themselves, and *visible* sacrifice appointed and offered by themselves, or else would have nothing. Well, they have made their choice; but where does it leave them? It leaves them just where Israel was, when, refusing to wait for the return of Moses—saying, " We wist not what is become of him," they formed a visible object of worship for themselves, and (although still professing to serve Jehovah, see Exodus xxxii. 5) served him by bowing down before an idol which their own hands had made.

The Reformation was not the result of any self-devised scheme for changing or remodelling existing arrangements, either in the Church or in the world. It was the result of deep personal exercise of soul in some, who having learned their danger, had said in bitterness of Spirit, " What must I do to be saved ? " Although the atoning work of Christ had been in word acknowledged, yet it was not acknowledged in the manner in which it is set forth in Scripture. The true doctrines of our holy faith had been exterminated, buried, lost. For what is the distinctive doctrine of the Gospel of God ? It is this, — MERITORIOUSNESS SAVETH. But what Meritoriousness saveth? Our own ? We have none. How could we, when God has said, " He that offendeth in one point is guilty of all." What meritoriousness then saveth ? The meritoriousness of *Another*—Even the meritoriousness provided by God in the vicarious obedience and vicarious suffering of a Divine Substitute. This obedience and this suffering sacrificially presented on the Cross and by God accepted, is something wholly external to ourselves. From beginning to end, it was the work of Another. But how can a work external to ourselves, become *as to its meritoriousness* ours ? There is only one way in which the meritoriousness of Another's work can become ours, viz., by *ascription* or *imputation*. If the meritoriousness of the sacrificial service of Immanuel, God manifest in the flesh, become ours, it can only become ours because God is graciously pleased to ascribe to us the value of that which is not our own. Therefore we enlarge our definition and say, *Meritoriousness made ours by imputation saveth.* He who had before been God *the Creator* became, through the Cross, God *the Redeemer*, to all His believing people. That there is this way—this one only way of being saved, through the imputation of another's merits, is made known by the preached Gospel. God "preacheth peace by Jesus Christ." "By the foolishness of preaching," not by ritual ordinances, "God saveth them that believe." God, in the Gospel, proclaimeth the meritorious work of Christ as that which giveth to all who cast themselves thereon, a sure title to salvation and glory. They, consequently, who credit the Word of God, and who, in accordance therewith, rely on that which God proposeth to them as the appointed object of reliance, have justifying faith. "Faith cometh by the report or message" (*ακοη*), "and the report by the Word of God." Thus faith (*fiducia*, not simply *fides*), wrought in the soul by the Spirit using the written or preached word, is the appointed link that connecteth with that meritoriousness which, when imputed, giveth the sure title to salvation and to glory. "Whom He justified them He also glorified." In the Covenant of Grace—the covenant of redemption, a King, Shepherd, Bishop, Priest, and Advocate is provided, who ever watcheth in all faithfulness over all those who, through faith, are brought under that Covenant— guiding, sustaining, chastening, as necessity may require. "He is able to save to the uttermost them that come unto God by Him, seeing He ever liveth to make intercession for them." Shall we, for preservation, instruction, and guidance, trust in *Him*, or in the services of a pretended Church, and its self-constituted Priests, who have no commission from God? The priests of Ecclesiasticism are unknown in the New Testament. The Apostles of our God and Saviour, through whom, as inspired, the *final* legislation of the Church was given, never dreamed of arrogating to themselves the power, or of exercising the functions, to which the priests of Apostate Christendom aspire. They would have deemed such pretensions blasphemous. Imagine an Apostle, after having written, "THERE REMAINETH NO MORE OFFERING FOR SIN," seeing that Christ hath once and for ever offered—imagine an Apostle, after having written, by the inspiration of the Holy Ghost, such words as these, daring to subvert the statement by declaring that it was necessary still to offer "*propitiatory* sacrifice, both for the living and the dead," and that he was empowered to offer it!* What should we have said of such an one? Should we not have deemed

* The third canon of the 22nd Session of the Council of Trent, says, "If anyone shall say that the sacrifice of the Mass is only one of praise and thanksgiving, or that it is a mere commemoration of the sacrifice accomplished on the Cross, but that it is not *propitiatory*, or that it profits the recipient only, and that it ought not to be offered for the living and the dead for sins, punishments, satisfactions and other necessities, let him be accursed." See also Catechism

him to be a Judas? I give but one example. There are numberless others, whose enormity is not less flagrant.

---

of Council of Trent, p. 249. " We therefore, confess that the sacrifice of the Mass is one and the same sacrifice with that of the Cross : the victim is one and the same, Christ Jesus, who offered Himself, once only, a bloody sacrifice on the altar of the Cross. The bloody and unbloody victim is still one and the same, and the oblation of the Cross is daily renewed in the eucharistic sacrifice, in obedience to the command or our Lord : 'This do, for a commemoration of me.' The Priest is also the same, Christ our Lord ; the ministers who offer this sacrifice consecrate the holy mysteries not in their own, but in the person of Christ. This the words of consecration declare ; the priest does not say, 'This is the body of Christ,' but, 'This is my body ;' and thus invested with the character of Christ, he changes the substance of the bread and wine into the substance of His real body and blood. That the holy sacrifice of the Mass, therefore, is not only a sacrifice of praise and thanksgiving, or a commemoration of the sacrifice of the Cross, but also a sacrifice of propitiation, by which God is appeased and rendered propitious, the pastor will teach as a dogma defined by the unerring authority of a General Council of the Church. If, therefore, with pure hearts and a lively faith, and with a sincere sorrow for past transgressions, we immolate and offer in sacrifice this most holy victim, we shall, no doubt, receive from the Lord " mercy and grace in seasonable aid." So acceptable to God is the sweet odour of this sacrifice, that through its oblation he pardons our sins, bestowing on us the gifts of grace and of repentance. This is the solemn prayer of the Church ; as often as the commemoration of this victim is celebrated, so often is the work of our salvation promoted, and the plenteous fruits of that bloody victim flow in upon us abundantly, through this unbloody sacrifice.

"The pastor will also teach that such is the efficacy of this

The rapidity with which the worst dogmas of Jesuitism and Ultramontane Popery have taken

---

sacrifice, that its benefits extend not only to the celebrant and communicant, but also to all the faithful, whether living or numbered amongst those who have died in the Lord, but whose sins have not yet been fully expiated. According to Apostolic tradition the most authentic, it is not less available when offered for them than when offered in atonement for their sins, in alleviation of the punishments, the satisfactions, the calamities, or for the relief of the necessities, of the living. It is hence easy to perceive that the Mass, whenever and wherever offered, because conducive to the common interests and salvation of all, is to be considered common to all the faithful." Such is the doctrine of Trent.

It will be observed that the expression " unbloody sacrifice" is used in this extract. The general wariness of the Romanists fails them here. They should not have used the word " unbloody," for by it they overthrow their own great doctrine of Transubstantiation. Elsewhere they dwell upon the presence of the actual body and blood.

Besides, if they were to adhere to this word, which an infallible Council ought never to have sanctioned, how could there be remission of sins through an " unbloody" sacrifice ? " Without shedding of blood is no remission." The passage, as a whole, needs no comment. It carries with it its own condemnation to every one really taught by the Spirit of Christ. The Council of Trent were afraid to deny in so many words, the imputation of the righteousness of Christ ; no doubt they had acuteness enough to see that all who deny it must deny also that He gave Himself for us, an offering and a sacrifice to God for a sweet smelling savour. If there be no imputation of His righteousness, there can be no imputation of the value of that which He offered. Accordingly, they do not deny the fact of imputation, but they make the extraordinary statement that we are not justified by the

F F

root in England, is marvellous. It reminds us of those awful words, "God shall send on them strong

---

mere imputation of the righteousness of Christ [*sola imputatione justitiæ Christi*], as if it were possible for the righteousness of Immanuel to be ascribed to any one, and yet that he to whom it was ascribed was not thereby regarded as possessed of perfect righteousness! Is there deficiency in the righteousness of the Holy One?

"By the obedience of THE ONE shall the many be constituted righteous." We must either accept this verse, or cancel it. The truth respecting justification is admirably expressed in the eleventh Article of the English Confession:— "ONLY on account of the merit of our Lord and Saviour Jesus Christ, through faith, not because of our own works and deservings, are we reputed righteous before God." See also the following extract from the "Helvetian Confession:—

"To speak properly, then, it is God alone that justifieth us, and that only for Christ, by not imputing unto us our sins, but imputing Christ's righteousness unto us. Rom. iv. 23—25..... Faith doth apprehend Christ our righteousness, and doth attribute all to the praise of God in Christ; in this respect justification is attributed to faith, chiefly because of Christ whom it receiveth, and not because it is a work of ours; for it is the gift of God. Now, that we do receive Christ by faith, the Lord showeth at large, John vi. 27, 35; 48—58, where he putteth eating for believing, and believing for eating. For, as by eating we receive meat, so, by believing, we are made partakers of Christ. Therefore, we do not part the benefit of justification, giving part to the grace of God, or to Christ, and part to ourselves, our charity, works, or merit; but we do attribute it wholly to the praise of God in Christ, and that through faith. Moreover, our charity and our works cannot please God, if they be done of such as are not just; wherefore, we must first be just, before we can love, or do any just works. We are made just (as we have said) through faith in Christ, by the mere grace of God, who

delusion that they should believe a lie." Nothing that has occurred since the Reformation has more encouraged the hopes of the Romanists than that which has taken place in England. Even the doctrine of "Development" (a doctrine which only apostatising hearts could receive) has been welcomed here. It is a doctrine utterly subversive of all that a Christian heart counts dear, but it is one absolutely needed to sustain the truthless fabric of Romanism. I say "truthless," because Romanism, as to all that *distinctively* brings it into contrast with Protestantism, is truthless. It is not easy to defend a truthless system, so long as that system professes to adhere to truth—truth as revealed in Scripture. The Romanists

---

doth not impute unto us our sins, but imputeth unto us the righteousness of Christ; yea, and our faith in Christ He imputeth for righteousness unto us." § ix.; chap. xv.

In this passage there is much precision of thought and language. It is the only Protestant Confession as far as I am aware, in which the *important* distinction between God imputing to us the righteousness of Christ (Rom. v. 19), and imputing faith FOR (λογιζεσθαι εις Rom. iv.) is mentioned. See this subject further considered in Tract entitled, "*The doctrine of Justification in a risen Christ considered*," as advertised at end : also "*Occasional Papers*," No. I. p. 87. It may be observed also that the expression "made just or righteous," being ambiguous, would be better expressed by the Scripture words, "constituted righteous" (Rom. v.), by which is meant that Christ's obedience, which can only become ours by imputation, places us in a condition in which God is able to recognise us as right in relation to the claims of His holy courts, which admit the principle of the righteousness of a substitute being pleaded.

were not unconscious of this difficulty at Trent, and
they have encountered it many a time subsequently.
Not only Scripture, but even many of the statements
of the Fathers, are thorns in the way of Papal progress. The Papists have found it hard to argue
against plain passages of the Scripture, or plain quotations from the Fathers; and sometimes their own
past traditions or practices have encumbered them.
Jesuitism wants a clear field for its operations where
no inconvenient references to the past may interfere
with its present sovereignty and its title to legislate
afresh. A nullification of the past is needed, and
this the doctrine of "Development" effects. If the
Apostolic period was, doctrinally and practically, a
season of infancy merely—if manhood, strength,
and knowledge were not to be expected *then*—if
maturity in the doctrines of Christ was only to be
reached after centuries of progressive instruction
had passed—if the Holy Ghost, *as given to the inspired
Apostles,* was sent permanently to abide in a chosen
body on earth, and was gradually to lead on that
body to perfectness in the knowledge of Christ, *then,*
doctrines suited to the infancy of Christianity might,
in the days of its maturity, be set aside, and the
Church would cease to be subjected to stereotyped,
unchanging, *written* rules, and would stand under
the present guidance of the voice of the Holy Ghost
speaking in and through the visible Head of the
Church—who, being thus officially infallible, might,
as having the authority of God, enlarge, modify, or
alter past enactments, as change of circumstances

may require. Any one who reads Dr. Manning's "Mission of the Comforter," may see that, according to his system, God, in the person of the Holy Ghost, is as *authoritatively* present in the earth now, as, in the person of the Son, He was present in Immanuel—God manifest in the flesh. It might almost be supposed that Dr. Manning thought that the Church was an incarnation of the Third Person of the Trinity. We cannot wonder, therefore, that it should be held that the voice of God as truly and as authoritatively speaks in and through the visible Head of the Catholic body, when that Head speaks officially, as did the voice of God in Christ Jesus. The doctrine of Infallibility is, of course, absolutely necessary to the maintenance of a doctrine such as this. Wherever, or in whomsoever the Holy Ghost speaks, He must speak infallibly. If the doctrine of the continued authoritative presence of the Holy Ghost be conjoined with the doctrine of "Development," the desired conclusions naturally follow. The instruction of the first Apostles was designed for the Church in its infancy, but we have now instruction, equally Apostolic, designed for the Church in its maturity.* It may certainly appear

---

* "Those who contend most strenuously for antiquity, admit that a change took place in the fourth century, from the Christianity of the Apostles, to that of the Fathers. See 'British Magazine,' Vol. IX. p. 359. 'Three centuries and more were necessary,' says a writer in this journal, 'for the infant church to attain her mature and perfect form and due stature. Athanasius, Basil, and Ambrose, are the fully-

somewhat strange that such a wondrous position of infallible legislative authority as is thus claimed should not, like that of the Apostles, be sustained by miracle: for claims such as these require to be authenticated by something better than the liquefaction of the blood of St. Januarius, or occasional apparitions of the Virgin Mary. It may seem to be a difficulty, too, that the infallible utterances of this new instruction do unquestionably contradict (and that not unfrequently) the written utterances of the Apostles of our God and Saviour—utterances, moreover, which were, by these Apostles, declared to embody unchanging, unalterable truth. There may be a little difficulty as to this, but shall such difficulties (which, after all, are easily surmounted by a little faith) impede the reception of a doctrine so important, so transcendently blessed as that of the authoritative presence of the voice of the Holy Ghost in "the one body?" Myriads of votaries, willing and eager to err (for delusion has come upon them) speak as with one voice and answer "No!" They severally adopt the words of Dr. Pusey, and say: "I believe *explicitly* all which I know God to have revealed to His Church; and *implicitly* (implicitè) any thing, if He has revealed it, which I know not. In simple words, I believe all which the Church

---

instructed doctors of her doctrine, morals, and discipline.' According to this hypothesis, Paul and Peter, and John were infants compared with Ambrose, and we are to receive a new doctrine from the fourth century." *Vigilantius and his times*, by W. S. Gilly, D.D.

believes." (*Pusey's Eirenicon*, p. 7.)   Dr. Pusey also says: "*We* of course believe that God the Hol Ghost, the 'One Spirit,' who animates and informs the 'One Body' of Christ, teaches truth in her in a way different from that in which He, the Author of all Faith and Grace, is present with all Truth, wherever it is taught and accompanies it by His Grace."   These words, though somewhat vague, are evidently designed to be an acceptance of Dr. Manning's dogma of the *authoritative* and *legislative* presence of God, the Holy Ghost, in the "One Body." *

* No true servant of Christ, will, I suppose, deny, that whilst the Holy Ghost, as the giver of grace and the giver of gifts, dwells in each individual believer (" gift " being qualification to serve God in the special sphere assigned, whether it be that of Timothy, or Apollos, or of Phœbe, Gaius, or Dorcas), He is *also* present wherever two or three are *rightly* gathered in the name of Christ, to watch over them for blessing.   None but believers can assemble truly in the name of Christ, and even they cannot assemble *rightly* if they be unable, through ignorance, error, or want of gift, to secure in their meetings right order and " sound speech." To gather in the name of Christ, and to gather rightly, are different things.

Sometimes, the word "presidency," has been used to denote the relation which the Holy Ghost holds to Christ's people when assembled in His name.   In what sense is it used? I can understand the word as used of the relation of the Lord Jesus to His disciples at the Last Supper.   He did there personally *preside*.   Is it supposed that there is any similar presidency attributable to the Holy Ghost?

If it be answered " Yes," how in that case did not His *presidency* put an instant end to the " much disputing," of

Anglicanism, as it is now being exhibited around us, is Jesuitised Romanism—that is to say, Romanism of the most advanced and deadly type. Its guiding principle is implicit, unquestioning, abso-

which we read, when the whole Church were assembled with the Apostles in Jerusalem ? ·Acts xv. 7. There was indeed a direct *interference* of the Holy Ghost, but how ? Through the instrumentality *of the Apostles* Peter and James. He empowered them to speak, and after they had spoken authoritatively by His inspiration, the letter could be written —" It seemeth good to the Holy Ghost and to us," etc.

The system of Rome and of every other body that wishes to legislate and to command authoritatively, requires that they should claim a continuous presence of the Holy Ghost for fresh legislation, and for *authoritative* interpretation of what God has already written in the Scripture. Rome has long doubted whether she would say that this presence cf the Holy Ghost is to be looked for in the Church when gathered in Council, or in the Church's visible head. She has recently decided on saying that this presence is in her Chief Pontiff. Certainly the more such authority can be individualised, and the more it can be made visible and tangible, the sooner will inconvenient questions and discussions be silenced. No doubt, whenever the infallible voice of the Spirit speaks, it must be obeyed, whether it legislate, interpret or direct. But as I have already said, all authoritative legislation—all infallible control has ceased since the Apostles died and the canon of Scripture closed. Blessed be God for an infallible written rule. These men who say they are Apostles, would like to write fresh Scripture for us every day, and to leave us no authoritative unchanging test of falsehood and truth.

We have great reason to remember the words, "thou hast tried them which say they are Apostles, and are not, and hast found them liars." Rev. ii. 2.

lute submission to the voice of God reaching us through our ecclesiastical superior, whom we are unhesitatingly and undoubtingly to obey, even if he command us to perform an act which our conscience tells us to be one of deadly sin. Let any one read the celebrated sermon of Ignatius Loyola, *"De Obedientiâ,"* and say whether I have overstepped the limits of truth in saying what I have said. When the heart and conscience are once withdrawn from the guidance of " the Scriptures of Truth " (that is a name which God Himself hath given to His written word)—when we imagine ourselves to be virtually in the presence of God, manifested either in a body, or in an individual, so that we hear His authoritative voice—when we consent to be deluded into the belief that the concurrent testimony of our understanding, of our conscience, and of Scripture, are to be set aside, if the voice of God in the " *One Body* " so command— when we deliberately adopt a principle such as this, we have no more title to the name of Christian than has one who follows oracular voices such as those which were heard in Delphi of old,—or one who obeys the Apostle of the Mormonites,—or one who deifies his own supposed " verifying faculty," and listens to it as to the voice of God. God speaks in and through the Scriptures ; they are sufficient to make " the man of God *throughly furnished* unto all good works." He, therefore, who withdraws from that voice and directs to other voices, must, whether he be a priestly Pontiff or an excited fanatic, be the adversary of God, and the enemy of Christ. "Every one that leadeth onward (ὁ προάγων) and abideth not in *the doctrine of Christ* hath not seen God." This "doctrine of Christ" we find in the written word, and in that alone.

Is it not obvious—ought it not to be patent to everyone who reflects, whether he be statesman or peasant, that the authority which God has mercifully delegated to the Cæsars of earth that they might maintain order therein, must be taken from them if there be in the earth one who is able to speak infallibly with the voice of God? The distinction implied in the words, "Render unto Cæsar the things that are Cæsar's, and to God the things that are God's"—a distinction absolutely vital to the order prescribed by God during the present dispensation, must be utterly set aside if there be on earth a Throne whose occupant is able to speak infallibly with the voice of God. In that case theocratic power must have supplanted the power of Cæsar; and therefore, in coming to the supreme secular throne we should come, not to the throne of Cæsar, but to that of God. All mere secular authority can have no place in the presence of one who is empowered to speak and to legislate with the infallible voice of God. The system espoused by our modern Beckets involves all this. It is a system which has worked of old, but it is working with greater energy than ever now. Do we smile at its folly? Do we call it madness? Well, it may be madness; but madmen, if unrestrained, are able to spread around them terrible ruin. We are not accustomed to allow to madmen scope for the effectuation of their destructive plans first, and to incarcerate them afterwards. Civil government is an ordinance of God. Are we content that it should be even temporarily superseded by a system which, while contradicting alike the voice of nature and the words of Revelation, pretends to wield over us the infallible authority of God?

And as civil government, *as instituted by God*, must perish if the pretensions of Popery be carried out, so the true order and doctrine of the Church must perish too. What part of the order of the Church, as prescribed in the Scripture, would remain if the ecclesiastical arrangements of Popery were received? Rome aspires to be the guiding centre of all other Churches. She wishes that all other Churches should revolve around her like the planets around the sun. But, if we search the Scripture, we shall find that no such place of central authority was ever granted to any *Gentile* Church. The Churches gathered from among the Gentiles, whether in Ephesus, Smyrna, or elsewhere, are all symbolised by candlesticks of gold, one like unto the other, none being exalted into pre-eminence above the others.* A place of supreme authority, like that aspired to by Rome, was never granted to any Gentile Church. It is reserved for converted Israel in another dispensation. For any body among the Gentiles to pretend to it, is rebellion and sin.

* See this further considered in "Thoughts on the Apocalypse," pp. 17, 18, as advertised at end of this volume.

Again, they boast of Apostolic Succession and the like. Why then was not Paul, the great Apostle to us Gentiles, ordained by those who were Apostles before him? He never even saw any of the other Apostles until after he had exercised his ministry for years. (See Galatians i.) Here, then, the link of succession was broken at its very commencement. God never appointed any such succession. The Apostles, in their distinctive office, have no successors. The distinctive place assigned to the Apostles was that of *legislation*. Through them, or other inspired men closely associated with them, the Church of this dispensation was to receive its *completed* legislation. The greater part of the New Testament was written by the Apostles themselves. Mark was closely associated with the Apostles Peter, Barnabas, and Paul. Luke was the companion of Paul, and in one of the Epistles of Paul, the Gospel of Luke is quoted as " Scripture." (See 1 Timothy v. 18, and Luke x. 7.) None ever succeeded or were intended to succeed the Apostles in their office of legislation. The laws of Christ are not to be altered. They need not, like human laws, to be amended or improved. As soon as the Canon of Scripture closed by the book of Revelation being given, the legislation of the Church was complete. Since the Apostles died the functions of the servants of Christ have not been legislative but *administrative*. Their duty has been to administer the laws which by His Prophets and Apostles, God has written. All therefore, who, since the Apostles died, have assumed to themselves the right of authoritatively legislating for the Church, have, by that very act, constituted themselves rebels against the authority of God. We exceed not the limits of truth in saying, that there is not one point in the ecclesiastical order of Rome that is not right contrary to the order of the Apostolic Churches. Not a fragment of Apostolic order remains.

We might multiply such charges almost indefinitely. No one can hold the doctrine that Rome teaches respecting the glorification of Mary and the saints, without virtually adopting the heresy of Hymenæus and Philetus, and saying, that the resurrection is past already. None of those who have fallen asleep in Jesus, (and Mary and Peter have) *can* rise until the hour of the first resurrection comes, and that cannot be until the Lord returns. The Apostle speaking of the "order" ($\tau\alpha\gamma\mu\alpha$) of the resurrection says, " Christ the first-fruits, afterward they that are Christ's at His coming; then ($\epsilon\iota\tau\alpha$) cometh the end" &c.* These words, unless we reject them,

* The Apostle expressly says that he is speaking of the "order" ($\tau\alpha\gamma\mu\alpha$) of resurrection in respect of *all* those who rise in the resurrection of life. "Christ the first-fruits, afterwards ($\epsilon\pi\epsilon\iota\tau\alpha$) they who are Christ's at His coming, then ($\epsilon\iota\tau\alpha$—not $\tau\sigma\tau\epsilon$) cometh the end." $E\pi\epsilon\iota\tau\alpha$ and $\epsilon\iota\tau\alpha$ are particles of sequence, equivalent in this passage to *secondly* and *thirdly*. Consequently, there cannot be more than *three* periods of resurrection. I. Christ's. II. Those who are Christ's at His coming. III. That of those who are converted during the Millennium and rise at its close; this last being the period at which the wicked dead also are raised.

are decisive. They forbid our saying, that either Mary or any other of the sleeping saints can, either by assumption or otherwise, be glorified, or can quit the grave until "the Church of the firstborn" shall *simultaneously* rise at the return of the Lord in glory. "David," says the Apostle, "is not ascended into the heavens" (see Acts ii. 34), and what ·is true of David is equally true of Mary, and Peter, and Paul. Their spirits, indeed, are with Christ in Heaven, consciously and ineffably blessed, having such com-

---

Some have endeavoured to nullify this conclusion by saying, that the same particles of sequence are used in the commencement of the same chapter, and applied to the order in which different classes of the disciples were permitted to see the Lord after He quitted the grave.

"Afterward he was seen of James, then (εἰτα) of all the apostles," &c. As there were other occasions besides those mentioned on which the Lord was seen by several of His disciples, so, it is urged, there may be several other periods of resurrection besides those mentioned in the passage before us.

This argument may seem plausible, but it utterly fails when examined. If in the commencement of the chapter the apostle had said that he was going to tell us respecting the order in which the Lord had been seen by ALL those to whom He showed Himself, then the cases would have been parallel. But the Apostle does not say that he is speaking of *all* who had seen the Lord. He is speaking only of some. On the other hand, in the passage in which he is speaking of the *order* of resurrection in glory, he expressly says that he is speaking of all who should so rise. As in Adam all die, so in Christ shall ALL be made alive. But EVERY ONE in his own order, Christ the first-fruits. None therefore can rise and be taken to glory except at the two periods mentioned in this passage.

CONCLUSION.   · 447

munications from God as it may please Him to make
to the souls of His people in their disembodied state,
but their *bodies* yet remain in the dishonour of
death.   But even if their bodies had been raised,
and if the integrity of their personal condition in
glory had been attained, even *then* they could
neither hear nor answer prayer.   How could anyone in Heaven hear prayers offered on earth, unless
he were *omniscient* and *omnipresent?*   To suppose that
Mary or the saints can hear or answer prayer is to
invest them with the attributes of Deity, and to
invest any *creature* with the attributes of Deity is
IDOLATRY..   Rome is idolatrous, in that she prays
to Mary* and the saints, as if they were omni-

* In the "Glories of Mary" it is said :
"Mary so loved the world as to give her only-begotten
    Son."—p. 449.
Go to Mary . . . . *Our Salvation is in her hands.*
    . . . . He who is protected by Mary will be saved ;
    he who is not will be lost."—p. 136.
According to the same high authority, MARY is :
"Our ONLY city of refuge."—p. 90.
"The ONLY advocate of sinners."—p. 90.
"The ONLY hope of sinners."—p. 90.
"In Mary finally we shall find life and eternal salvation."—
    p. 124.
"No one is saved but through thee" (Mary).—p. 135.
"O immaculate Virgin, we are under thy protection, and
    therefore *we have recourse to* THEE ALONE ; and we
    beseech thee to prevent thy beloved Son, who is irri-
    tated by our sins, from abandoning us to the power of
    the devil."—p. 233.
"No one comes to me " (Jesus Christ), "unless my mother
    draws him by her prayers."—p. 540.

present and omniscient; she is idolatrous, because she worships "bread," pretending that it is changed into God; she is idolatrous in that she bows down to images, and renders to them a " homage that is due unto God alone." "Hard is it, indeed, and *impossible*, any long time to have images publicly in churches and temples, without idolatry." (*Homily on Peril of Idolatry*, xiv. part 2.) Idolatry is not only contrary to the laws of the Church of Christ, it also violates a natural relation in which man as man stands to God. Consequently, nations that govern-

---

"She is the sinner's ladder; she is my greatest confidence; she is THE WHOLE *ground of my hope.*"—p. 538.

Add to this the authority of an infallible Pope, and of the Breviary itself:

" *Modern heretics* cannot endure that we should salute and call Mary our Hope—'Hail OUR HOPE!' *They say that God alone is our Hope, and that He curses those who put their trust in creatures. This is what the heretics say;* but, IN SPITE OF IT, *the Holy Church obliges* all ecclesiastics and religious *each day to invoke and call* Mary by the sweet name of *Our Hope*—THE HOPE OF ALL."

" The Virgin Mary is our *greatest hope*; yea, THE ENTIRE GROUND *of our Hope.*" Gregory XVI. (the late Pope), August 15th, 1832.

" Thou (Mary) art THE ONLY *Hope of sinners.*" ["Tu es Spes unica peccatorum."] Roman Breviary, 9th September.

The Editor of " The Armoury," whence I have taken these extracts, asks, as well he may,—" Is this then Christianity or a substitute for Christianity? Is it THE Gospel or is it ' *another* Gospel which is not another?' Is it Christ or Antichrist?"

mentally sanction ecclesiastical idolatry have been, and will be, as nations, punished. But what is punishment here, compared with that which shall be when the hour of repentance and of mercy shall have passed? Is it not written that all "idolaters" and all "liars," even "every one that loveth and maketh a lie," shall not only be excluded from God's heavenly City, but "shall have their part in the lake which burneth with fire and brimstone, which is the second death?" See Rev. xxi. 8, and xxii. 15.

A terrible blow has been inflicted on Protestantism in England—a blow from which it will never recover. The reaction will lead to scepticism and neology. Dr. Newman seems to think (and few, I suppose, will dispute the claim) that the triumph over Protestantism in England is chiefly due to the efforts of three men—Keble, Dr. Pusey, and himself. Very awful were the lines that suggested themselves to Dr. Newman when he, Keble, and Pusey met for the last time :—

> " When shall we three meet again ?
> When the hurly burly 's done,
> When the battle 's lost and won."

Well, battles may be lost for God *here*, and triumphs won for Satan. Such triumphs may be rejoiced in *now*, but will they be rejoiced in in the day of Christ? Will not they who have won them wish *then* that they had never been born?* "What

* The action of Keble against Protestantism, although not so ostensible as that of Dr. Newman and Dr. Pusey, was not

G G

is a man profited, if he shall gain the whole world, and lose his own soul? or what shall a man give in exchange for his soul?" (Matt. xvi. 26.)

---

less determined. Indeed, Keble was not unfrequently the adviser of Dr. Newman.

"Dr. Newman was somewhat doubtful about remaining vicar of St. Mary's, when he was conscious of drifting fast to Rome, and so asked the opinions of his friends; among others Mr. Keble, who was in favour of the living being retained. Thereupon Mr. Newman writes to Mr. Keble—'The following considerations have much reconciled my feelings to your conclusions. *I do not think that we have yet made fair trial how much the English Church will bear.* I know it is a hazardous experiment—like proving cannon. Yet we must not take it for granted that the metal will burst in the operation. It has borne at various times, not to say at this time, a great infusion of Catholic truth without damage. As to the result—viz., whether this process will not approximate the whole English Church, as a body, to Rome—that is nothing to us. For what we know, it may be the providential means of uniting the whole Church in one, without fresh schismatising or use of private judgment." (See *Nonconformist*, as quoted in *The Record* of August 15, 1873.) Mr. Keble, therefore, was fully cognisant of Dr. Newman's tendencies and designs, and wished him to remain in the English Church that he might undermine its Protestantism. The stealthy progress of Anglicanism is marked by such incidents as the following. In the early editions of Keble's hymns, that for November 5th contains the following stanza:

"O come to our Communion Feast,
    There present *in the heart*,
Not in the hands, th' Eternal Priest
    Will His true self impart."

This stanza in a later edition, published after Mr. Keble's death, is altered thus:

At the time of the Crusades, the voice of Peter the Hermit was heard as if it had been the call of

> " O come to our Communion Feast,
> There present *in the heart*,
> *As in the hands*, th' Eternal Priest
> Will His true self impart."

Canon Liddon justifies this alteration on the ground that " in Mr. Keble's own judgment and intention the words, 'not in the hands,' did not deny the objective reality of Christ's presence in the Eucharist. According to Canon Liddon " Mr. Keble used to say that the word ' *not* ' in the phrase referred to was employed in the Scriptural sense of ' *rather than*,' instead of in the ordinary sense of a direct negative." Alas ! what shall we say of those who are content to propose or to receive an explanation such as this. The use of such arguments as these is in itself sufficient to show that the Truth of God is not with those who employ them.

Whatever judgment may be formed as to Mr. Keble's opinions when the early editions of "The Christian Year" were published, I suppose few will deny that ultimately he utterly rejected (might I not say, abominated) the doctrine of the Reformers as to the Eucharist. The Bishop of Bath and Wells in his recent charge observes :—" To confound the adoration of our Lord in heaven, which the thankful remembrance of his death must call forth in every devout communicant, with the adoration of the Sacrament itself, as Mr. Keble does in his singularly weak and painful work on Eucharistical Adoration, is the part either of a very confused intellect, or of a very unfair controversialist." (Charge, &c., p. 36.)

Yet Keble is the person in whose honour and for the perpetuation of whose doctrines a College is built in Oxford, whilst the stolid indifferentism of England looks on and smiles ; or if it be for a moment startled by an apprehension of coming danger, it seeks its refuge in "compromise," and so hopes to ward off the day of evil. But God and *right principle* are not in ts thoughts.

God : and now the voice of the prophets and priests of Anglicanism is obeyed by thousands with no less alacrity. The broad way that leadeth to eternal death is trodden with exulting step, and the crowd augments so rapidly, that many a deceived heart is led to imagine that ultimate triumph *must* attend their course, and that the nations of earth will finally gather themselves around the banner of Catholic unity which Anglican devotedness has reared.

But all these imaginations by which Satan is deceiving them are false, even as regards this world. They and their principles will have no final triumph even here. They are not the Zion of God. They are not that Jerusalem to which it shall be said, "Arise, shine, for thy light is come, and the glory of the Lord is risen upon thee." The Ecclesiasticism of God and the Ecclesiasticism of man are two different things. No form of sacerdotal religiousness, whether Jewish, Roman, Greek, Anglican or Mahomedan will ever succeed in raising itself into universal dominancy. If pontifical Rome were, as of old, concerned with a corner of Western Europe merely —if she could confine the strength of earth to Gaul, Spain, Italy, Austria and Britain, and keep other nations in barbarism—if the countries I have named were made willing to subserve her designs, she might then, perhaps, think of dominancy. But the days of such limitation are past. The governmental plans to be adopted now must be such as will subserve the interests and commend themselves to the awakened intelligence of the wide world. Do the counsellors of the Vatican dream that they would succeed (even if Protestantism were extinguished) in forcing into the narrow circle of their "infallible" rule the rising intelligence of Egypt and Greece, European and Asiatic Turkey and Northern Africa, not to speak of Russia, India, China and Japan, and of scattered but influential Israel? The drag-net that is to enclose this multitude of peoples must be somewhat larger than any that ecclesiastic Rome ever has handled or ever will handle. In the early centuries, Ecclesiasticism, when less corrupt than at present, had a prolonged and terrible conflict in Egypt and the East with the Gnosticism, Philonism, Platonism, Judaism and Pantheism that there prevailed; but it succeeded not in extinguishing these systems, nor does it succeed in extinguishing the same elements of vicious thought in Oxford now. Ecclesiasticism and the systems with which it contended in the early centuries did indeed in one thing succeed. Through the influence which they severally exercised, they succeeded in well nigh extinguishing the lamp of truth; they succeeded in awakening the wrath of God and in bringing down on the East the dread inroad of Mahomedanism. And now an hour is drawing nigh when a more terrible personage than Mahomet will appear, and Rome and Athens, Egypt and Assyria, Antioch and Jerusalem, will, with England and the West, enter his mighty "drag-net," and be for a time the servants of his glory. Before him the whole Roman world (πασα ἡ οικουμενη) will bow down and worship. See Rev. xiii. It will be the result of the judicial infliction of God on former iniquities.

I repeat therefore, that there will be no realisation of the present dream of Roman and Anglican Ecclesiasticism. No form of Catholic religiousness will reign supremely. Herod will be chief, not Caiaphas; and Herod must become latitudinarian, or he must cease to reign. Accordingly, in countries such as Egypt, Turkey and Tunis, where Mahomedanism has hitherto been in the ascendant, we are beginning to see its exclusiveness resigned. So also in countries where Popery has dominated, other influences are penetrating. Austria and Italy are examples. In England, where Protestantism once ruled, Popery, availing itself of the aid of that truthless Latitudinarianism which is seeking to introduce equality of creeds, has strengthened itself both within and without the Anglican Establishment; and so the *dominancy* of Protestantism in England falls. At present, a patch-work garment is being prepared. Ultimately, indeed, when the time shall come for Antichrist to be revealed in the full power of his unfettered despotic sway, the hell-woven web will become altogether black. There will be strict unity then—unity in atheistic blasphemy. But the transgressors are not yet "come to the full." At present, the web that Satan is intending to weave is one of divers colours. Even true Christians may, if only they will be sufficiently pliable, find for their systems a place in the midst of the motley construction. Let nothing, no, not even the Bible, be asserted to be *exclusively* and *authoritatively* true. Let liberty be granted to human thought, and let all men please themselves, if only they will submit to such restrictions as governments may see fit, for the sake of civil order, to impose. Men must consent to forego aggressiveness. They must not irritate their neighbours. Compromise must be lawful,—nay, more, it must be a duty, where none know certainly what Truth is. Such will soon be the prevailing cry. Such are the principles on which Latitudinarianism will establish its Throne. Before it, Ecclesiasticism will (perhaps at no very distant period) be made to cease from its vauntings, and will become content to occupy a niche (it may be an humble niche) in the Pantheon of Truthlessness. The true servants of Christ only will refuse to join in the unholy concord. Mordecai-like, they will refuse to bow; but they will have to seal their testimony with their blood. Christianity, if it cease to be aggressive, ceases to be the Christianity of God.

But although Ecclesiasticism will not finally dominate in England, yet it may attain temporarily vast, if not paramount influence in Western Europe. It has succeeded already in destroying the ancient influence of Protestantism in this country, and there may be in the rest of Western Europe a prolonged and disastrous struggle between Jesuitism and Latitudinarianism. Before the latter finally triumphs, Ecclesiasticism may have local and temporary successes that may bring terrible sufferings and terrible chastisements on the countries in which such successes are achieved. The present base abandonment of Protestantism by England *may* bring on England immediate and sore judgments. It is possible, indeed, that the triumphs of Anglican Ecclesiasticism may do no more than assist in so far destroying the authority of the Bible, as to accelerate the advance of Neology and Indifferentism. In that case, the progress toward the end would be smoother and more rapid; and England, prospering with an evil prosperity, would have her eye more closely sealed—sealed judicially, and become the most efficient present instrument in the world for promoting the reign of latitudinarian Antichristianism. But it may be otherwise. The progress of Anglicanism may, for a season, drag England back into such close association with the idolatries and abominations of Popery, as to bring down on our country *immediate* judgment. The surging wave of godless democratic licentiousness is very discernible in England. Jesuitism too is rife amongst us. Jesuitism, if not pandered to and obeyed by those who rule, allies itself to the multitude, and not unfrequently stimulates democracy to its worst excesses.

For many a year, England, reckless as to God's Truth, and cowed by the frowns of Sacerdotalism, has, in Ireland, offered hecatombs to propitiate Rome: and she has now begun to offer them at home. Has she attained her object? Is Rome satisfied? She never will be, unless England will go on yielding till she has nothing more left to yield. Is England prepared to denude herself thus? Not quite. Her "material interests" would be touched if she were to go too far. A time, therefore, of resistance to the claims of theocratic Rome must, sooner or later, come. England, will at last be obliged to say, "I can yield no further." But is England prepared to dare the storm which *may* (might I not say, *will?*) burst upon her head when she has summoned up sufficient courage to give plain unambiguous utterance to those words? What would Ireland be to her then? Has Jesuitism no skill in effecting the disruption of society, especially when such destructive elements are at hand, as are supplied by the radicalism, and socialism, and infidelity that lurks among the masses of England? And suppose (for it is not quite impossible) that Jesuitism should succeed in consolidating the military strength of France, and Spain, and Belgium, and should bring it to bear upon recalcitrant England—is England prepared, with Ireland victimised to sacerdotalism, and with her own people Jesuitised and democratised, her Bible and her God virtually abandoned, her ancient political strong-holds cast down, or else given over to the enemy—is England prepared to meet the storm? I think not. I think she would grow pale and tremble. I think she would temporise, and compromise, and be like King John in the presence of the Pope's Legate. Would that I could think otherwise. Would that I could think that she would humble herself before God, and confess, and seek unto His mercies. But I dare not hope that she would. She would temporise probably, and consent, perhaps, to join in a Latin league, and to sacrifice Italy or anything else, if only she could secure her own material prosperity. But would God allow this? I do not prophesy. I merely make suggestions which may, perhaps, prove altogether vain : but certainly it is not *impossible* that the arm of Germany, aided perhaps by Russia, might again be strengthened to smite the western Latin nations (should they combine in an avowed or virtual Catholic league) with a blow more-terrible than has ever fallen on them since they shared in the desolations that accompanied the fall of Imperial Rome. I do not say that it will be so. It may be quite otherwise. The sources from which calamity may appear likely to spring, are not always those from which it does spring. Possibly, no desolation may *at present* come. But when conscience tells us that chastisement is deserved, and when there is no humiliation or repentance, every cloud that appears on the horizon may well be dreaded as the precursor of a tempest of ruin. It *may* be, however, that no storm will at present break. It may be that the dangers of a Latin league may be escaped. Austria, Prussia * and Italy may be allowed to consolidate

---

* Austria, it must be remembered, is not internally strong, and more territorial changes impend over her than over any other country of the western Roman world. Prussia has to dread internal agitations, and this the Jesuits know. If England was to sustain the joint action of these three powers with all her influence (and that not on the ground of mere

their strength and act in concord, and become for a time the guardians of the tranquillity of Western Europe. In that case, probably, the smooth-tongued but godless Latitudinarianism (which the *political* section of the Nonconformists have done so much to cherish) may quietly and rapidly advance under the fostering hand of England—Rome herself submitting to be borne onward by a tide which she will find herself powerless to resist. In that case, great but godless prosperity (morally more to be dreaded than desolation) may be allowed to lull England into a slumber of death from which she will not awake until, with the other Roman nations, she meets, at Armageddon, "the great and terrible day of the Lord." On the other hand, it *may* be that the Latin nations (of which England is one) may, after an effort to regain a mediæval position, succumb either to external enemies or to internal faction, and fall, so as for the final arrangements of the Roman World to emerge out of a chaos of previous ruin. It is certainly possible (though I will not say probable) that Egypt and the Eastern nations of the Roman world, aided by the intelligence and energy of the Jew and the Greek, may be the actual constructors of the great

---

expediency, but for the sake of the Bible and in the fear of God) there might be stronger reason of hope. But does England ever act now except on the ground of expediency? It is to be hoped that Rome will not bribe England, nor act on her through the idiosyncrasies of her ministers or the religious recklessness of liberalism.

Babylonian system of Latitudinarianism that is to be; and that, by means of it, the Latin nations of the West may be revived after they have been smitten and crushed for a season into decrepitude. Time only will show whether the Eastern countries of the Roman World are from the present moment onward, steadily to advance in civilization and strength under the tutelage of the Latin nations of the West; or whether the West is first to be smitten, and afterward to be revived by influences from the East; or thirdly, whether (through Russia, Prussia, or other agencies) all the Roman nations, Eastern and Western, (πασα ἡ οἰκουμενη) are to be smitten down first, and afterward to be revived by agencies not at the present moment to be discerned. Time will determine these questions, and will, in all probability, soon determine them. Whenever hardened and unbelieving Israel are permitted to re-gather themselves to Jerusalem, and begin there to act as a recognised nation, the end will be nigh, and we shall be able to trace the steps by which that end will be reached with a definiteness and precision that is impossible now: for, as I have elsewhere said, *historic* prophecy (that is, such prophecy as treats of dates, personages, specific localities and the like) is suspended during the time of Israel's national extinction. Scripture is silent as to the history of the nations during the time of Jerusalem's desolation; but when Jerusalem nationally re-appears, the long interrupted course of historic narration will be resumed, and we shall be enabled definitely to trace the steps by which the consummation is to be attained. In the meanwhile let all who fear God endeavour to read aright the signs of this awful hour. Evidently there is no repentance, no humiliation or confession, or calling upon God whose mercies fail not.

But it may be said, "Is Protestantism guiltless?" "Has Protestantism no stains?" In answering that question we have to distinguish between false Protestantism and true. I acknowledge with shame that there are many bearing the name of "Protestant" whose worldliness, godlessness, licentiousness and covetousness, would bring reproach on Mohammedanism or Paganism. If there had not been, within the circle of nominal Protestantism, an apostasy from the principles of true Protestantism, Romanism would not have attained its present triumph in England. I do not vindicate nominal Protestantism: I do not say that even true Protestants are blameless. On the contrary, I acknowledge that our sins have been many and great, needing the deepest humiliation and confession. Nevertheless, the acknowledgment which true Protestantism has ever made of Holy Scripture, as the one sole depository of God's Truth among men, gives to Protestantism a position which never can be held either by Romanism, or any other system that denies the sole and paramount authority of the Word of God. Protestantism may have failed, and has failed, in carrying out the principles of Scripture; but it has not avowedly rejected or neutralised the authority of Scripture. It has not set Tradition on the throne. In a word, it has not avowedly dethroned God and enthroned Man. *

* Let anyone read the following citations (which I copy as given in "The Armoury" of September, 1873), and say whether my language is too strong :—

EXTRACT from the "Confessio Romano-Catholica in Hungariâ Evangelicis publicè præscripta et proposita."

"IV. We confess that whatsoever *new* thing the Pope of Rome *may have instituted (quicquid Papa instituerit novi)*, whether it be in Scripture or out of Scripture, is *true, divine,* and *salvific ;* and therefore ought to be regarded as of *higher* value by lay people than the *precepts of the living God (ideoque a laicis majoris æstimari debere Dei Vivi præceptis).*

    *   *   *   *   *

"XI. We confess that the Pope has the power of *altering Scripture,* or *increasing* and *diminishing* it, according to his will.

    *   *

"XXI. We confess that *Holy Scripture* is imperfect, and a *dead letter,* until it is explained by the Supreme Pontiff, and permitted by him to be read by lay people."

(Libri Symbolici Ecclesiæ [Romano-] Catholicæ, editi a Streitwolf [a Romanist]. Gotting. 1838, Tom. ii. p. 343.)

"The Scriptures are *not* the *foundations* of the Catholic faith." (Cardinal Pallavicini's History of the Council of Trent; vi. cap. 19, n. 7.)

" *Tradition is the foundation* of the Scriptures, and surpasses them." (Card. Baronius : Annal. an. lviii. No. 11.)

"The Scriptures without the traditions are neither absolutely necessary, nor are they sufficient." (Card. Bellarmine, " *De Verbo Dei,*" lib. iv., cap. 4.)

Protestantism, therefore, has in it a germ of life,—a principle of recovery. It has a sound basis on which to build; a lamp to guide the steps of its repentance. But when the one light is quenched, as it is quenched both by Rome and by Neology, what can there be but hopelessness?

Protestantism has greatly failed in tacitly, if not avowedly, accepting some of those perversions of Truth on which Ecclesiasticism, both in the East and in the West, has based its system. For example, Rome pertinaciously maintains that a promise of standing indefectibly, as the corporate witness of Truth unto the end, has been made by God to the visible Church of the present dispensation. This statement Protestantism should have strenuously resisted. No promise of indefectible standing in the earth has been made to the visible Church of this dispensation. On the contrary, the Scripture has explicitly declared that the place of testimony to Christ's truth, professedly held by Gentile Christendom, would through disobedience and sin be *forfeited*. The Gentile olive branch has not "continued in God's goodness," therefore it is to be "broken off." See Rom. xi.

Protestants would not have dallied with or tolerated the doctrine of "development" in any of its forms, if they had given heed to that which Scripture teaches respecting the advance of evil in *this* dispensation. "This know, that in the last days perilous times shall come." The "development" of this dispensation is development of evil, not of good.

Where there is most of augmentation, there will be found most of corruption. In a dispensation that is to be marked by retrogression and departure from the Truth, the way that leadeth to destruction must be broad; the way that leadeth unto life must be narrow. "Fear not, *little* flock." Truth is not now with the many, but with the few. Under such circumstances, "Catholicity" cannot be the mark of those who follow God : it must be the mark of those who follow Satan.*

There is, indeed, to be a dispensation in which Truth will prevail. *After* the Lord shall have returned in glory and smitten the unrepentant evil of earth, and when He shall have bound Satan and converted Israel, and made Jerusalem the centre of light, legislation and government to the whole earth, and when visible glory shall rest on Zion, and when Christ, without quitting the sphere of His glory above the heavens, "shall reign in Mount Zion and in Jerusalem and before his ancients gloriously"— when these things shall have been accomplished,

---

* Christ has indeed promised that He would be with His Apostles "alway even to the end of the age;" and He is not unfaithful to His promise. The Apostles, by their inspired writings contained in Holy Scripture, continue to testify even "to the uttermost parts of the earth," and Christ sanctions and blesses that testimony. In promising to bless the Apostles in their testimonies, the Lord has, by implication, promised to bless all who accept and aid in maintaining those testimonies; but He has not promised to bless any who depart from the Apostles' doctrine and open up strange paths for themselves.

then indeed there shall be Catholicity, and unity, and indefectibility, and the visible Church shall be guided by and be obedient to an infallible Head—that Head being One who "shall sit *as a Priest* upon his throne," for He shall be Melchisedec, a Priest-King, and by His hands all things in earth as well as heaven, shall be controlled. Rome rightly says that there can be nothing in earth so precious as God's Truth, and that consequently, secular power *ought to be* in all things its servant. Rome errs not in saying that the world can never be truly blessed until there be a supreme central authority established by God, before which all nations and kings must bow. Rome errs not in asserting such abstract truths as these; they are mere truisms. Rome's sin consists in her false *application* of these truths. That place of indefectible catholic testimony and of supremacy in the earth which Rome arrogates to herself, is not intended for her, or for any other body in this Dispensation of failure, corruption, and sin. It is reserved for another people in another Dispensation. Rome seeks to clothe her polluted self with those garments of honour that belong to repentant and forgiven Jerusalem—that *holy* City, which shall indeed be the City of the great King. " They shall call thee the city of the Lord, the Zion of the holy One of Israel. . . . . . Violence shall no more be heard in thy land, wasting nor destruction within thy borders; but thou shalt call thy walls Salvation, and thy gates Praise. . . . . . Thy people also shall be all

H H

righteous; they shall inherit the land for ever, the branch of my planting, the work of my hands, that I may be glorified. A little one shall become a thousand, and a small one a strong nation : I the Lord will hasten it in his time." Here, at last, will be seen indefectibility. The banner of truth, entrusted in the next Dispensation to the hands of Israel, will not be dishonoured by them, or betrayed into the hand of the enemy. The place of testimony assigned to Israel will be maintained by them stedfastly unto the end.

Ecclesiasticism has ever struggled to annihilate the future of Israel. One of the first watchwords of the Anglican party in Oxford, was a declaration that Israel had for ever forfeited their promised blessings, and that those blessings were transferred to the present Gentile body—that is to say, to all those who were gathered into the holy unity of Catholicity by the mystic virtue of Apostolic succession. In vain the Scripture, speaking of Israel, says, "To whom pertaineth the adoption, and the glory, and the covenants, and the giving of the law, and the service of God, and the PROMISES." "No, the promises do not pertain to Israel, they pertain to us," say Rome and her votaries. The cankered Gentile olive-branch that is about to be cut off under judgment, boasts itself against that natural branch which is soon to be graffed back into its own olive-tree. Read the Catechism of Pope Pius IV. See how Rome appropriates to herself the promises of Israel there. The false use made of

Millennial Scripture in that Catechism gives to it a plausibility which otherwise it would utterly lack. Pure falsehood is dangerous, but *false applications of truth* are not less dangerous. Men are soon spell-bound by the voice of the flatterer. No instrument of deception is more potent than that. They soon learn to say, " The Temple of the Lord, the Temple of the Lord are WE." *We* are the Zion of God. The Law of the Lord is to go forth from *us*. "Kings are to be our nursing fathers, and their queens our nursing mothers." "To us shall it come, even the first dominion." (Micah iv. 8.) Such is the cry of the would-be mistress of Gentile Christendom, and of those who bow down to her. They willingly forget that it is not appointed to the people of God in this Dispensation to reign at all, much less to reign as Zion. The garb of the true Church now is that of Nazareth. Its right home is Bethany— the house of the poor and afflicted one. Did the Apostles desire to reign as kings? Were they not as "the filth of the world—the offscouring of all things"? To reign now is the token of apostasy, not of blessing. Cæsar held the sceptre of earth, and that by God's appointment; Paul had it not. The "morning without clouds" must rise upon this dark earth before that new Dispensation comes, in which Truth and its servants are to reign. But men whose chief object is their own exaltation, and who say that in exalting themselves they exalt God, care not about thoughts like these. A heart loving to be deceived is quickly satisfied;

it will soon learn to feed on ashes, and declare that it is feeding on the finest of the wheat.

I cannot deny that great guilt attaches even to true Protestantism, in that it has not guarded, as it should have guarded, the future of Israel; and has not distinguished, as it should have distinguished, the present from the coming Dispensation. Protestantism has not (as it should have done) wrested the Millennial promises from the grasp of Rome, and shown their right interpretation. Protestantism has often sanctioned the ascription of Millennial promises to men in the present Dispensation; and not unfrequently, in rejecting false *applications* of truth has, in rejecting the application, rejected also the truth. The character of this Dispensation, both as to its course and as to its close, and the character of the Dispensation that is to be, have often been as much ignored by Protestantism as by Popery; nor even yet has the depth of the error been recognised, or its guilt acknowledged.

Protestantism was not, as the Apostolic Church was, perfect in constitution, government and laws, when it first appeared. The Protestants were men who had, through the help of God, struggled out of depths of darkness in which they had been buried. An eye that has long been accustomed to darkness is slow to bear the effulgence of light. Moreover, in withdrawing from evil, we are far more ready to judge of our progress by estimating our distance from the evil we are retiring from, than by ascertaining the nearness of our approximation to the good that should be attained. Light very gradually dawned on the Reformers. There was much personal weakness, slender unity, many and threatening dangers —dangers before which a stouter heart than that of Melancthon might well have quailed. Under such circumstances to trust *only* in God was very hard. It was very hard practically to recognise in their ecclesiastical arrangements that Christ was He who held the symbolic stars, that is, the ministry of the Churches, in His own right hand, and that He only could give evangelists and pastors and teachers, and that we cannot create them for ourselves. Have we not to acknowledge that Protestantism, finding it hard to wait, whilst the urgency was great, yielded, and began, and that extensively, to supply to itself ministers, and to commission those whom God had not commissioned.

Again, it was hard for the early Protestants, when they found the mighty strength of Popery, then dominant in Western Europe, arrayed against them and ready to devour,— it was hard for them to look only to Him who, having governmentally "the Seven Spirits of God," was able to strengthen them against every danger, and who did, for that very purpose, propose Himself to them as the one and only right object of their confidence. To trust only in God in the practical circumstances of life is not easy, especially when aid from other sources is available. Aid was proffered from other quarters. Secular power in some countries was not unwilling to throw over Protestantism its shield :. but then, Protestantism had to pay a price for the protection, and that price was the acceptance of certain fetters, which, more or less, prevented unrestricted freedom of service being rendered to Christ alone. It is not too much to assert, that if the Protestants had duly meditated on the seventh chapter of Daniel, and had thence formed their estimate of the course and end of secular power in the present Dispensation, they would have discerned the snare prepared for their steps, and refused a protection purchased at such a price.

The great preservative principle of true Protestantism must ever be separation *from* evil, and separation *unto* God—separation *unto* God involving obedience to His written Word, for by that Word He guides those whom He separates. Separation from evil has ever been the great principle of God. God separated Israel from Egypt. A few months passed; Israel apostatised, worshipped the idol which themselves had made, and a second separation was needful. "Moses took the tabernacle, and pitched it without the camp, afar off from the camp, and called it the Tabernacle of the congregation. And it came to pass, that every one which sought the Lord, went out unto the tabernacle of the congregation, which was without the camp," . . . . *and there* "the Lord talked with Moses." (See Exodus xxxiii. 7—9.) An analogous place was assumed, and rightly assumed by Protestantism at the Reformation. By separating from idolatrous Christendom, and going without its camp, Protestantism proclaimed its conviction that they from whom it separated, were in active rebellion against God. Therefore, conscience towards God, and obedience to His Word, compelled Protestantism to assume a new position. Evidently, its prosperity in that new position must depend on the fidelity of its adherence to the Scripture. If it owns only *it*, and seeks so far as circumstances allow, to obey *it*, there will be blessing; if not, confusion and woe.

I say, "so far as circumstances allow," because it is a dangerous delusion to suppose that, the moment we begin to retire from the worldliness and corruptions around us, we shall find ourselves capable of holding the same place as the Church of God once held whilst it retained its unity and its government and its order, and was recognised by God as being "the pillar and ground" of Truth. Lengthened sickness entails decrepitude, and from decrepitude we cannot expect the energies of health. Nor is it expedient that they who have enfeebled themselves by their disobedience should be exempted from proving some of the consequences of their sin. Did Hezekiah, and Haggai, and Nehemiah find strength in the repentant remnants of Israel, which were gathered around their respective leaderships, or did they find weakness? Even Hezekiah, (though the weakness of Israel was not then developed to the same extent as subsequently) even Hezekiah was obliged to say, " The good Lord pardon every one that prepareth his heart to seek God, the Lord God of his fathers, though he be not cleansed according to the purification of the Sanctuary." Blessed words: and they were heard and answered. (See 2 Chron. xxx. 18.) In the book of Nehemiah too, we read that when the remnant who were under his guidance were gathered to hear the long neglected book of God read and expounded in their ears, they "wept;" " all the people wept when they heard the words of the law." (Neh. viii. 9.) Till then they did not know the extent of their departure from the ways of God; nor did they till then become acquainted with their weakness, and the consequent enfeeblement of their ability to obey aright. Therefore they wept. Their tears were not feigned tears; their humiliation and contrition was sincere; therefore they were comforted: " Weep not; let joy in Jehovah be your strength." God can prepare a way for the steps of those who are weak, as well as for the steps of those who are strong; and obedience to Him is in walking, not in some high path that is *not* proposed to us, but in that path that *is* proposed to us by Him as the path specifically suited to our condition. There are circumstances in which the first step in the path of obedience is confession—confession of our past failure and of our present weakness, and our ill-desert and incapacity. The remnant of Israel in the days of Haggai and Nehemiah were not *able* to stand forth in the strength that pertained to their forefathers in the time of Joshua and David. But they were not hypocritical. They did not pretend to a strength which they had not. They took the place of weakness; and they found blessing. Are *we* not weak ? The want of unity that prevails is a sufficient proof of our weakness. Can any of us pretend to the primitive order of the Church of God ? Then let us not be hypocrites. Let us not pretend to be Apostles when we are not ; nor to be Apostolically ordered Churches when we are not. A ship-wrecked few may look back on, and regret the order, and strength, and stateliness of their once well-officered and well-appointed ship : but they cannot recreate that which has ceased to be. If our King should have supplied us with directions suited to a ship-wrecked condition, let us use these instructions ; but let us beware of pretending not to be what we are—shipwrecked.

Ambiguities, says one of the Protestant confessions, are to be avoided in the Church of God. There should be no doubtful sounds *there*. " If the trumpet give an uncertain sound, who shall prepare himself for the battle ?" (1 Cor. xiv. 8.) The Spirit of Christ is the Spirit of unity; and He dwells in every believer, however feeble. We *ought* therefore " to speak the same thing : " we *ought* to be " perfectly joined together in unity of mind and of judgment." This the Scripture requires. (See 1 Cor. i. 10.) But are we this? And why not? Because by insubjection of thought, and insubjection of deed, we have in manifold ways grieved the Spirit of God, and we are chastened. It is an humbling fact to confess, (but it is true,) that if all the servants of Christ now on earth could be gathered together, we should find neither unity of thought, nor unity of testimony. Scarcely ten would intelligently agree together in their explication of the Scriptures of Truth.

Protestantism has had great and distinctive blessings, and through its agency thousands have been saved : for true Protestantism has pointed to Christ, not to the Church, as the Ark : it has not directed to an unreal refuge. Nevertheless, the history even of true Protestantism is not one that can be reflected on without sorrow. During the reign of Elizabeth, and of the Stuarts, and even during the Commonwealth when great liberty was accorded to the action of many true Christians; and also, in more modern days, when Christian Liberalism has been allowed to develop its plans, many a scheme has been formed and many a deed done, which would not bear the test of God's Holy Word. We are not to entice, much less to coërce or force the unconverted world within that holy circle which God has drawn around them that believe, and around them only. We are not to draw the sword even for the defence of Truth. Those who, *for such a reason*, draw the sword, are to perish by it. God will not permit His Truth to be sustained by violence. We may and should, when we have opportunity, reason with, entreat and instruct our Rulers ; but we are not to threaten, nor to revile. We have to remember Paul before Agrippa. We are not so to separate between our official and our individual positions as to imagine that we are justified in doing officially that which we should regard as sin, if done by us individually. We are not to form Jehoshaphat-like alliances with the enemies of God. We are not to confound between that sphere of action which God has appointed to the World, and that which he has appointed to the Church of Christ. The name of "Cæsar" is written over the one sphere : the name of Christ over the other. We are not to act as if the foundations of all things were not "out of course;" or as if they could be righted until Satan shall have been bound and the sovereignty of the world shall have become that of Jehovah and His Christ. Protestantism would have avoided many a pitfall if it had given heed to that steady and abiding light (the light of Prophecy) which God has sent "to shine in a dark place"—a place not only dark, but which is to wax darker and darker, until the "morning without clouds" shall suddenly arise upon it and abolish its darkness for ever. But this light, so precious and so necessary, Satan buried. At the commencement of the present century, Israel's and the earth's prospects, both in the present and in the coming Dispensation, were hidden from the eyes of God's own people. An impenetrable cloud rested upon the future. The operations of Satan, and the operations of God were alike hidden. But God, in undeserved mercy, pitied our condition. Just at the very moment when Sacerdotalism on the one hand, and Neology on the other, were about to gather up their strength for their onslaught on the Word of God, and when, consequently, God's servants required, more than ever, to be "girded about with truth," the long-hidden light of Prophecy was again unveiled. The light thus restored was so clear, and its value was, by many, so distinctly recognised, that a new era of blessing seemed to have come. The Scripture began not only to be searched, but to be understood; its various parts became harmonised; and many a difficulty that had seemed insuperable was solved. The coming glories of Christ and of His people, both in Heaven and in earth, began to be apprehended according to the Scriptures. Harmony of thought, and consequent unity of testimony, seemed to be no longer hopeless. It was a bright and cheering prospect; but the brightness was soon, very soon, dimmed. The ray of heavenly light that had visited us from above, encountered the obstructions of our darkness, and it has now become quenched, or else distorted. According to one system of interpretation extensively accepted in this country, that holy and heavenly vision in the Revelation, where some are seen "standing on a sea of glass mingled with fire, and singing the song of Moses the servant of God, and the song of the Lamb"—a vision that belongs only to the saints in glory, and is too holy to be interpreted of any whilst yet militant on earth—this vision is supposed, by the system to which I refer, to be the expression, on the part of God, of His estimate of the present condition of *England*—careless, latitudinarianised, apostatising England. "If our light be turned into darkness, how great is that darkness!" The history of the manner in which revived prophetic Truth has been treated, during the last forty years, adds another dark page to the history of Christianity. Some have despised and rejected it; others have darkened and perverted it; whilst they who have received, and (to a certain extent) welcomed it, have used it with a Laodicean lukewarmness, or with an unappreciating carelessness that has too clearly shown that we have no real estimate either of its holiness, or of its exceeding great preciousness. " Be ye clean that bear the vessels of the Lord." "Come out from among them, and be ye separate, saith the Lord, and touch not the unclean thing, and I will receive you and be a Father unto you, and ye shall be my sons and daughters, saith the Lord Almighty." There is no truth more holy than prophetic truth, none that requires for its use more personal, practical separation unto God. Have we thus used it? Is there not need of deep humiliation and contrition, and repentance, amongst us all?

A kind of sceptical hopelessness as to the possibility of attaining clear and certain views of revealed Truth, seems to pervade even the true people of God. Doubtfulness, and division of sentiment appear to be accepted as a normal and necessary condition. Unity, if anywhere found, is a mere apparent unity based on compromise; or else, if there be not compromise, it is a unity not in the service of the Truth, but in the service of some patent error. Not a few, recognising these things, say, " The foundations of all things are hopelessly out of course"—and they sit down despairingly, or else seek in philanthropic or evangelistic efforts to avoid the danger of absolute inactivity. It is right to be philanthropic, and right to evangelise; but it is *not* right by such efforts to seek to silence our consciences, and to make amends for our neglect of the Word of God. Yet, sorrowful and discouraging as the aspect is, we must not forget that the arm of the Shepherd of Israel "is not shortened that it cannot save, nor is His ear heavy that it cannot hear." If there were humiliation and an earnest cry unto Him that He would be pleased to send forth the power of His Spirit and give. repentance to His people, and that He would grant them "eye-salve" that they might better know themselves and Him in the ways of His power and of His grace, and become instructed in that which is written in His holy Word, and so be led into unity of faith and knowledge—if believers would pray for these things as earnestly as they pray for other blessings which they regard as more immediately affecting themselves, we should soon see the present aspect of Christianity alter. Teachers would be raised up to unfold what is written in the Scripture, and the trumpet would cease to give an uncertain sound. Mariners may have great energy, and activity, and courage, but what if they have no chart, or compass, or use them not? What if there be one at the helm who thinks that he can steer safely and well, though chart and compass be laid aside? We might recognise the daring of such a man, but should we deem such daring to be true courage, or anticipate for the bark guided by such a pilot anything save disaster and ruin?

If we judge from present appearances, we, in this generation, have, I fear, little to expect save disaster. The tide of Truth seems fast ebbing; its channels are being dried up; and God's people will, sooner or later, find their little barks stranded. They will discover at last, that faithful, efficient service to God cannot be maintained apart from the diligent and prayerful use of revealed Truth. We cannot wonder if they who have attempted to serve without it, should be allowed to prove the futility of the effort, and be caused to find, by bitter experience, that in forsaking the light and guidance of God's Word they have forsaken *His* guidance. "Some of them of understanding shall fall, to try them, and to purge, and to make them white, even to the time of the end: because it is yet for a time appointed." (Dan. xi. 35.)

Blessed will be that day when some among God's people shall discover that they have, *as God's priests* (for all believers are priests), defiled their priestly garments, and walked (although His servants) carelessly and disobediently in many things. When they shall discover this, and shall humble themselves, and shall cry earnestly to God that He would be pleased to do for them what He did for Joshua (see Zech. iii.), will God refuse to hear? Will He not take away their defiled priestly garments, and clothe them with change of raiment, and give to them again a place of honoured and efficient service—honoured in His sight, though by men rejected and despised? God can show riches of grace towards His people, when, after having sinned as His servants, they again turn back unto His mercies. He can meet them in the same fulness of grace in which He received them at the first, when they came to Him clothed in the filthiness of their own natural corruption. He will never "break the bruised reed, or quench the smoking flax." Wherever there is contrition and repentance, He will cause mercy to rejoice against judgment, and He will not upbraid with the past.

Nor is there any action of grace more blessed than that which restores and welcomes back the servants of God, after they have wandered and returned. "If thy people," said Solomon, "sin against thee (for there is no man which sinneth not), and thou be angry with them, and deliver them over before their enemies, and they carry them away captives, unto a land far off or near, yet if they bethink themselves . . . . . and turn and pray unto thee . . . . . saying, We have sinned, we have done amiss and have dealt wickedly . . . . . . then hear thou from the heavens, even from thy dwelling-place, their prayer and their supplications, and maintain their cause, and forgive thy people which have sinned against thee." (2 Chron. vi. 36.) It will be a blessed hour when the true Church, or a remnant amongst them, shall remember these words of Solomon. We have indeed no visible Temple, or Priest, or Sacrifice.

"We walk by faith, not by sight." But we have an unseen Temple, filled for ever with the fragrance of a sacrifice once offered, and we have an unseen Priest who "ever liveth to make intercession for those who come unto God by Him." When the Church, or a remnant in it, shall discern how far they have wandered from the Word of God, and how little they have apprehended its truths, and shall recognise how they have individually as well as corporately failed; and shall, with humbled and chastened hearts, turn to the unseen Temple, and Sacrifice, and Priest, and say, "We have sinned and committed iniquity, and have rebelled even by departing from thy precepts and from thy judgments," we cannot doubt that they will abundantly prove the sweetness and preciousness of restoring grace—that grace which, without upbraiding, brings back to the justly forfeited place of blessing, and wipes away tears that might justly be allowed to flow on for ever. "Who is a God like unto thee, that pardoneth iniquity, and passeth by the transgression of the remnant of His heritage? He retaineth not His anger for ever, because He delighteth in mercy." (Micah vii. 18.)

A full, uncompromising, faithful testimony to God's Truth as revealed in Holy Scripture will most certainly be borne by some (they may, perhaps, be but a few, *converted, for the most part, out of Israel*), before the present Dispensation closes. If not, we should not read in the Revelation such words as these: "Here is the patience of the saints: here are they that keep the commandments of God, and the faith of Jesus." (Rev. xiv. 12.) And again, " They overcame him [Satan] by the blood of the Lamb, and by the word of their testimony ; and they loved not their lives unto the death." (Rev. xii. 11.) These are they of whom Daniel speaks, as " understanding ones," who, after having been chastened through some "fall" (the nature of which is not described) whereby they are to be " tried," and " purged," and "made white" (see Dan. xi. 35), will stand forth as God's honoured servants, just when Antichrist is about to attain the climax of his power, and will give a testimony the like to which has not been since the era of Apostolic Christianity closed. They will have read aright the lessons of the past ; they will understand God's Word, and therefore will see clearly into the future. Their words will be as words of fiery rebuke against the corruptions with which Ecclesiasticism and Latitudinarianism will have overspread the nations ; and men, though they may gnash with their teeth, will in their consciences tremble. The manner in which this testimony is raged against by Satan, on whose head the diadems of the Ten Kingdoms are in the vision seen, and the commendation which by voices in Heaven is bestowed on those who bear that testimony, is a sufficient evidence of its power. When the servants of God are feeble, Satan raises no storm against them, nor does God commend.

The period at which these last servants of Christ will testify, will be a marvellous one. Man as man will have been tried; Israel will have been tried; Christendom will have been tried; and they will all have been found wanting. Lawlessness and transgression will have ripened, and will have well nigh attained the maturity of their appointed growth. The places, the individuals, the principles, and the circumstances which God, through His Apostles and Prophets, has definitely described as the signs of the time of the end, will be fully manifested then. Those servants of Christ of whom I speak as appointed to bear the closing testimony, will view the scene around them with understanding and chastened hearts. They will not deem "the Harlot," or "the Beast" to have run their course, or to have waxed feeble, for they will see both standing before them in the developed plenitude of their God-defying strength. They will not say (as so many now do) that "the day of the Lamb's wrath" came and passed when ancient Paganism mouldered in the days of Constantine. They will not teach that the vials of wrath *have been* poured out, or the trumpets of woe *have been* sounded. On the contrary, they will see all these long-threatened, yet long-delayed plagues, beginning to be accomplished around them in all the dread reality of their terribleness. The dream that they have passed and are gone will be dispelled then; and the equally evil dream that these plagues belong not to *this* Dispensation at all, will be dispelled likewise. They will not say (as multitudes now do) that prophetic instruction respecting things to be accomplished in the earth, forms no part of the lesson intended for the Church of God. They will draw no false distinction between *Judæo-Christian* Truth and *Church*-truth, nor refuse to include under the latter the instructions of the Lord, and of the Pentecostal Apostles, and of the Book of the Revelation. They will not follow the steps of Marcion.* They will not exclude Abraham, and Daniel, and David, from the Church of God *in glory ;* or shut out the millennial saints, or any believer of any Dispensation from being, *finally,* partakers of the inheritance of the saints in light. They will define the Church in glory, as being a body chosen in Christ before the world was, and including *all* who are redeemed by His blood and quickened by His Spirit. They will not say that the Christianity of the next Dispensation is different from that which now¹ is; or teach that there are " two gospels, two ways, and two ends of salvation." Instead of assigning to another and future Dispensation, those parts of the Revelation which speak of the triumphs of the Harlot and the Beast and of the out-pouring of the vials of God's wrath, they will see in those visions the exact description of the very circumstances in which they are themselves serving. They will recognise themselves as being Members, and honoured Members, of that one body which Christ hath " purchased by His own blood," and will know themselves to be sealed by the One Spirit. As they read the visions of glory

* See doctrines of Marcion considered in "Thoughts on Parts of Isaiah," page 187.

with which the Revelation abounds (all which visions give different *aspects* of the glory of the redeemed) they will see in these visions the description of the glories, which at an hour that will have well nigh come, await them; and not them only, but *all* who have hoped in Christ. Their testimonies and their sufferings will be as to kind, place, and all connected circumstances, exactly those which the Revelation describes. Their hearts will burn within them, as they read the description which God's own hand has written of their own peculiar history; and they will give Him thanks and take courage. They will say, *We* are they who are getting "the victory over the Beast, and over his image, and over his mark, and over the number of his name," and soon we shall stand on the sea of glass as conquerors, and sing the song of Moses the servant of God, and the song of the Lamb. (See Rev. xv.) When the day of their conflict begins, they will comfort one another, and say, *We* are they who are noted in God's Word as overcoming "by the blood of the Lamb, and by the word of our testimony, and as not loving our lives unto the death;" and soon God will avenge us on our adversary, and shut him out from accusing us and our brethren in His presence; and, yet a little while longer, and our adversary shall be utterly cut off, and cease from trampling down God's people, and God's truth for ever. Whilst their hearts will be glowing with such thoughts and such expectations, what if any one should tell them that they

erred in imagining that they belonged to the
Church of God, for that the first resurrection had
already taken place,—that the Church was already
complete and glorified ; and consequently that they
could not be numbered among those of whom it is
written, "Christ loved the Church and gave himself for it, that he might present it unto himself a
glorious Church, not having spot, or wrinkle, or
any such thing; but that it should be holy and without blemish ?" What would they think of those who
should tell them that they must not expect any such
relation to Christ as this,—that they must be satisfied with a far lower place, and with more distant
love ?

Such words would be to them idle sounds. The
Holy Ghost within them would have made them
consciously to know their "sonship" and "heirship,"
and to realize the unities of the redeemed—"one
body," "one Spirit," "one hope," "one Lord,"
"one faith," "one baptism," "one God and Father
of all." These unities, secured by the faithfulness
and grace of God, would be too consciously present
to the apprehensions of their souls, for the voice of
any charmer, charm he never so wisely, to prevail
against the certainty of their convictions. The Holy
Ghost will dwell in them, not indeed as a Spirit enabling them to work signs and miracles, but as the
Spirit of truth, and holiness, and power, enabling
them to apprehend their calling, and therefore to
defy the terrors of that hour of the concentrated
power of Satan; and strengthening them to give

such a testimony to the truths of Scripture as has not been heard since the Apostles ceased to labour. The voice of prophecy, rising, as it were, out of the grave, will through them be again heard, and that with close, clear, precise, definite application to the persons, places, principles, and circumstances that men will behold palpably present before their eyes. They will still preach the "Everlasting Gospel," for the day of grace vouchsafed to this Dispensation, will not have ended; but they will also say, "Fear God and give glory to him, for the hour of his judgments is come." They will speak of the hour being close at hand when the axe, long laid at the root of the trees of this world's greatness, will be lifted up to give the long-threatened stroke. The past history of Israel, and of Christendom, and of the world generally, with all its varied lessons, will be vividly present to the apprehensions of their souls; and they will discern and eschew the pitfalls into which even true.* Protestantism has fallen.

* I cannot regard any Protestantism as "true," that does not unequivocally reject the sacerdotal figment of baptismal regeneration, and that does not regard the bread and the wine in the Lord's Supper as simply symbolic. They are symbolic of an absent and *past* event, namely, the once-made *sacrificial oblation* on the cross, of the holy body of Christ whilst yet in the flesh. That hour is past. Though we once knew Christ after the flesh, yet now henceforth know we Him [so] no more. The symbolic bread and wine point exclusively to the body of His flesh, once broken for us, and not to any relation to us of that glorified and spiritual body which He now hath above the Heavens. This alone is sufficient to show that the supposition of *the presence* of His body and

No wonder that Satan's servants should tremble before a testimony like this. The Reformation was local; its early adherents few; yet still it made the ecclesiasticised and idolatrous nations of Western Europe tremble. The voice of one man shook Scotland. Much more will this coming testimony, which will be less divided, less localised (for it will penetrate Israel, and all the kingdoms of the Roman World), arouse and anger the nations. For it to prevail, would be for all that they love to perish. They will loathe it therefore with an intensity of hatred. Acting together with a dread concurrency of action which Satan has never yet been able to bestow, but which he will then be permitted to give to the Ten Kingdoms of the Roman World, they, instigated and guided by him, will put forth their united confederate strength to quench this last testimony to *grace and truth*, and they *will* quench it—that is to say, they will take from the beacon-light which God's mercy had kindled, its concentration, and will scatter the light, and employ themselves in pursuing

---

blood in any sense whatever at the celebration of the Supper is false and indeed heretical. It diverts the soul from that one especial aspect of truth which it is the object of the Lord's Supper to present, namely, the benefits that flow from the past, once-offered and finished SACRIFICE. As to "baptismal regeneration" it is undoubtedly true, as one of the Papist Bishops, that burned our English martyrs, said, that baptismal regeneration and the doctrine of justification by faith cannot stand together. If one be true, the other must be false.

its fragments, and in stamping out, so far as they can, each one of its fugitive sparks. The Harlot of Babylon will drink herself drunk with the blood of the martyrs of Jesus; and when that city of *Latitudinarian* Antichristianism gives place to *despotic* Antichristianism, Antichrist will take up her work, and cause that all who refuse to worship him should be killed. The nations over whom Satan reigns will triumph, and greatly rejoice, as they see the light of God's truth extinguished, and His servants crushed. But there will be other and deeper joy in the hearts of the crushed ones, and their joy will abide for ever. They will have heard with the ear of faith the words that have been spoken respecting them in Heaven—"They overcame him [the Accuser] by the blood of the Lamb, and by the word of their testimony, and they loved not their lives unto the death;" and they will remember the promises that are made in the Psalms and in the Prophets to the "afflicted and crushed ones;" and they will know that the hour of their deliverance is nigh, and they will feel that Christ is glorifying Himself in them—therefore they will rejoice "with joy unspeakable, and full of glory."

Will any say, These things, even if true, are future, how do they concern us? I reply, the Church of God is one, and what concerns it, concerns us. But apart from this; although Babylon is not yet formed, and Antichrist is not yet come, yet are not the principles that will make Babylon and Antichrist what they will be, working latently but

energetically all around us? We may be very sure
of this—that there is not one system upon earth
that men look on as influential and potent, that is
not, more or less, helping on the progress of society
to that hour of darkness and apostasy which the
Revelation describes. Must we wait until we see
everything palpably demonstrated to the eye before
we give heed to the warnings of God in the
Scripture respecting the character of the closing
hour? Are there no such things as embryo principles, having in them all that essentiality of evil,
which development may expand, but does not
increase? Can we see nothing with the eye of
faith? Are the descriptions which the Prophets
have given touching the closing scene useless,
because the hour of exact fulfilment is not yet fully
come? It is not thus that faith reads the Scriptures. It detects the *principles* of Babylon where it
sees no Babylon, and watches, and warns, and testifies accordingly. It sows beforehand the very seeds
and directs to the selfsame paths that will be cultivated and prized by those who shall overcome "by
the blood of the Lamb, and by the word of their
testimony" in that yet future hour when the Enemy
shall come in as a flood. Though we lack their grace,
and faithfulness, and vigour, yet there may be a
certain identification with them in principle, and
feeling, and desire, and such identification is not
without its honour. It is not valueless in God's
sight. On the other hand, if we despise the voice
that comes from Patmos, ratifying and confirming

all that the Prophets had before spoken, what can we expect but darkness? Must we not become like salt that has lost its savour? We have not to be wise above what is written, but we cannot be wise apart from what is written.

CORRIGENDA.

Page 269, line 8, omit inverted commas before "*when.* Insert inverted commas before *their* in next line.

„ 429, „ 6, for "*Spirit*" read "*spirit.*"

„ 442, „ 3, for "*hath not seen God,*" read "*hath not God.*"

„ 469, „ 17, after "*commissioned,*" place note of interrogation.

„ 472, „ 24, for "*and our ill-desert,*" read "*and of our ill-desert.*"

WORKS BY BENJAMIN WILLS NEWTON.

———•◦•———

AIDS TO PROPHETIC ENQUIRY. First Series. Second Edition. Price 3s. 6d.

BABYLON: ITS REVIVAL AND FINAL DESOLATION. Second Series of "AIDS TO PROPHETIC ENQUIRY." Price 3s.

PROSPECTS OF THE TEN KINGDOMS OF THE ROMAN EMPIRE CONSIDERED. Third Series of "AIDS TO PROPHETIC ENQUIRY." Second Edition, revised. Price 7s.

THOUGHTS ON THE APOCALYPSE. Second Edition, revised. Price 8s. 6d.

THOUGHTS ON ISAIAH. Price 3s. 6d.

THOUGHTS ON PARTS OF LEVITICUS. Vol. I. Price 3s. 6d.
Vol. II. Price 2s.

THOUGHTS ON SCRIPTURAL SUBJECTS. Price 4s. 6d.

ROMANS VII. CONSIDERED. Second Edition. Cloth, 1s. 6d.

NOVEL DOCTRINES RESPECTING SINLESSNESS CONSIDERED. Price 6d.

GOSPEL TRUTHS. Second Edition. Price 1s.

NOTES EXPOSITORY OF THE GREEK OF THE FIRST CHAPTER OF THE ROMANS. Price 2s. 6d.

OLD TESTAMENT SAINTS NOT EXCLUDED FROM THE CHURCH OF GOD. Price 1d.

ORDER OF EVENTS CONNECTED WITH THE APPEARING OF CHRIST AND HIS MILLENNIAL REIGN. Second Edition. Price **6***d.*

OCCASIONAL PAPERS ON SCRIPTURAL SUB- JECTS. Vol. I. With Map of the Ten Kingdoms, colored, mounted, and in cloth case, price 10*s.* 6*d.*

Vol. II. Price 4*s.*

REMARKS ON A TRACT ENTITLED "JUSTIFI- CATION IN THE RISEN CHRIST." Price *3d.*

IN A DISPENSATION OF FAILURE, CATHO- LICITY THE SURE TOKEN OF APOSTASY. Price *2d.*

DUTY OF GIVING HEED TO THE PREDIC- TIONS OF SCRIPTURE RESPECTING EVENTS THAT ARE TO PRECEDE THE RETURN OF OUR LORD. Second Edition. Price *2d.*

THE SECOND ADVENT OF OUR LORD NOT SECRET, BUT IN MANIFESTED GLORY. Price *2d.*

THE DAY OF THE LORD. ON ZECHARIAH XIV. Third Edition. Price *2d.*

THE WORLD TO COME. Third Edition. Price 1½*d.*

DOCTRINE OF SCRIPTURE RESPECTING BAP- TISM. Price 1*s.* 6*d.*

JESUS WASHING HIS DISCIPLES' FEET. Price *2d.*

ON THE PROPHECIES RESPECTING THE JEWS AND JERUSALEM. Third Edition. Price *2d.*

14 DAY USE
RETURN TO DESK FROM WHICH BORROWED
LOAN DEPT.

This book is due on the last date stamped below, or
on the date to which renewed.
Renewed books are subject to immediate recall.

FEB 27 1968 6 4

REC'D LD   FEB 21'68 -2 PM

LD 21A–45m-9,'67
(H5067s10)476B

General Library
University of California

Lightning Source UK Ltd.
Milton Keynes UK
11 October 2010

161072UK00005B/22/P